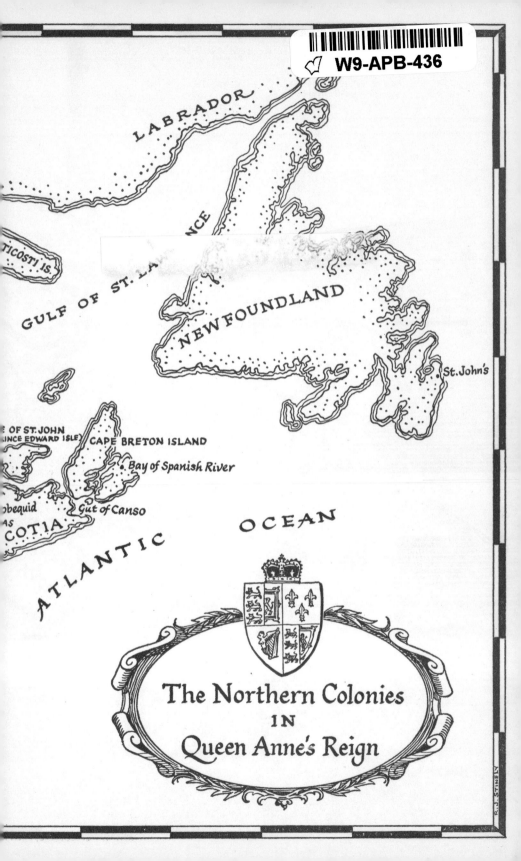

LABRADOR

TICOSTI IS.

GULF OF ST. LAWRENCE

NEWFOUNDLAND

St. John's

E OF ST. JOHN
(PRINCE EDWARD ISLE)

CAPE BRETON ISLAND

Bay of Spanish River

bequid

Gut of Canso

COTIA

ATLANTIC   OCEAN

The Northern Colonies
IN
Queen Anne's Reign

Samuel Vetch

Colonial Enterpriser

The Institute of Early American History and Culture is sponsored jointly by the College of William and Mary and Colonial Williamsburg, Incorporated. Publication of this book has been assisted by a grant from the Lilly Endowment, Inc.

MARGARET LIVINGSTON VETCH

Artist and date unknown. Courtesy of the Museum of
the City of New York

SAMUEL VETCH

Artist and date unknown. Courtesy of the Museum of
the City of New York

Samuel Vetch

Colonial Enterpriser

By

G. M. WALLER

PUBLISHED FOR THE

Institute of Early American History and Culture

AT WILLIAMSBURG, VIRGINIA

BY

The University of North Carolina Press · Chapel Hill

923.273
W15s
39,601
August, 1960

For

Marguerite, Susan,

and Martha

Preface

OR THE BRITISH EMPIRE the central fact of the first half of the eighteenth century was the struggle against France. The preceding century had ended with the conclusion of an uneasy truce after the War of the League of Augsburg. Emerging English imperialism had been set back. The military potential of France cast a shadow over England; her commercial rivalry and political preponderance in European affairs threatened English goals. Louis XIV, championing the cause of England's Catholic Pretender, imperiled the religious and constitutional gains of the Revolution of 1688, and he stood to gain even more advantage if he should join to the House of Bourbon the Spanish lands which seemed about to slip from Hapsburg hands upon the death of ailing Charles II.

British imperialism had also failed in the North American colonies. The counterpart of the European conflict had been King William's War, the first colonial war between French and English settlers in the New World. It had settled none of the issues of territorial and trade rivalry, important alike for the colonists and for the home governments which viewed the colonies as extensions of their political and economic power in Europe. The peace settlement of 1697 had forced New England to give up one of its prizes of the war, Nova Scotia. An attempt to reduce Quebec during the war had aborted. The struggle had exhausted the Indian allies of the English, leaving them vulnerable to French overtures. Its bloodshed had discouraged frontier settlement; its expense had depleted colonial treasuries. The ravages of French privateers had cut heavily into the profits of colonial merchants and shippers.

As the eighteenth century opened, a third imperialism under

the English Crown had recently been thwarted. The Northern Kingdom of the Scots, aspiring to colonial wealth, had attempted to challenge English trading monopolies and establish a settlement in Spanish territory on the Central American isthmus. It, too, had failed.

After these several defeats, the renewal of warfare between England and France in 1702 marked the beginning of better fortune for the emergent empire. The imperial aim of American colonists, Englishmen, and Scots began to coincide. There was a growing realization of common ends and the methods to achieve them: England and Scotland were united finally in 1707; successive Whig and Tory ministries showed a new sympathy toward colonial problems; and the colonies themselves co-operated in the common goal of conquest of New France during the closing years of the war.

Samuel Vetch, a soldier of fortune turned imperialistic enterpriser, lived and thrived in this heady atmosphere of a growing imperial system. He was a native of Scotland, with the same paradoxical cosmopolitanism which makes so many from his small country valued settlers of other regions. He could utilize the ties of blood and loyalty to further his enterprises, and he was equally at home in England or the colonies. Vetch was loyal to no single nation—he was a citizen of the empire. In him worked the uneasy aspiration of the three groups which had struggled separately until now without success: British imperialists, colonial expansionists, and his fellow Scots. Vetch sought to harmonize their divergent interests for the greatness of the empire and for his own glory.

Vetch was of the class termed gentlemen, the son of a prominent minister, but he was little more than an adventurer at the beginning of the conflict with New France. It offered him opportunity, and opportunity coincided with his experience and capacity. By the close of the second colonial war, Vetch had in turn become advocate of imperial conquest, leader in the resulting expeditions against Canada, military governor of Nova Scotia, and, finally, civil governor of that provincial outpost.

He was in all things a practical man, and through his career we may arrive at a more coherent idea of the tangled process by which Americans groped toward colonial maturity. For the course of eighteenth-century history is not alone explained by a knowledge of the British colonial system. Workable in theory, that system was beset by adventitious factors. Vetch's life illustrates the problems which arose in shaping a colonial establishment and a colonial policy amid the distractions of war, politics, and the general ineptitude of eighteenth-century bureaucracy. His experiences may help to reduce the theories and abstractions of history to some semblance of practical life.

Vetch's career gives emphasis to the fact, sometimes overlooked, that colonization was a continuing process. Penn's proprietary had been established only two decades before Vetch's arrival in New York. Georgia was settled the year of his death. Vetch himself took part in the attempt to found a Scottish trading post on the isthmus of Panama. He looked on the area between Maine and the St. Lawrence, including Nova Scotia, as admirably suited to colonization and, like many others, busied himself for years in England trying to obtain a grant in this region. The colonization of North America by the English, far from being finished by the early years of the eighteenth century, was going on throughout the colonial period.

Contrariwise, Vetch's own peregrinations indicate the reality of the "Atlantic community." The ocean was a two-way street. The colonists were not men who had left the Old World for good and all; many of them traveled back and forth, continuing to speak of England as "home" even after years of residence in the New World. Few social or business or religious institutions did not have close affiliations in the old country. Vetch and his pre-Revolutionary descendants never consented to think of the colonies as evolving states. They were integral, if somewhat isolated, parts of a flourishing imperial system.

Vetch himself is a strangely elusive figure. Despite the survival of a large body of his correspondence, his personal life is obscure. We know little of his reactions to the heat of particular events, and frequently his motivations are not clear to us. If we have little knowledge of this man's introspections, however, we are well informed about the outward form of his life. And quite aside from the importance of his accomplishments, Vetch's career was colorful and broad, reflecting details of contemporary problems and social life. His memory deserves well of those on both sides of the ocean whose ancestors were his countrymen, and his life is worth the attention of the historian.

AUTHOR'S NOTE

Except where noted (NS), dates in the text of this work are given in Old Style. I have not followed the form for indicating the year which was commonly used for the period between January 1 and March 25, in which the old and new year were hyphenated. Dates after January 1 are given as of the new year. Spelling and punctuation in quotations have been modernized in many instances, except where they added flavor to the quotation.

Contents

Preface   vii

Chapter

    I. Youth   3

    II. Darien Venture   15

    III. New York Beginnings   30

    IV. Design for Trade   47

    V. Penalties of Trade   69

    VI. Canada Surveyed   94

    VII. Glorious Enterprise   121

    VIII. Enterprise Disappointed   142

    IX. Enterprise Limited   158

    X. Outpost Governor   182

    XI. Tory Design   207

    XII. Inglorious Enterprise   219

    XIII. Trials of a Governor   235

    XIV. End of the Enterpriser   261

Bibliographical Note   287

Acknowledgments   298

Index   301

Lost causes have a way of shrinking in importance in the memory of later generations, and the historian must go back to the days before their overthrow, and view them in the light of their hopes. Time is not always a just winnower; it is partial to success and its verdict too often inclines to the side of the biggest cannon or the noisiest *claque*. The exhuming of buried reputations and the revivifying of dead causes is the familiar business of the historian, in whose eye forgotten men may assume as great significance as others with whom posterity has dealt more generously. Communing with ghosts is not unprofitable to one who listens to their tales.

—Vernon L. Parrington

List of Illustrations

Portrait of Margaret Livingston Vetch   frontispiece

Portrait of Samuel Vetch   frontispiece

The French Fort at Port Royal, 1710   193

Samuel Vetch

Colonial Enterpriser

CHAPTER ONE

Youth

THE SCOTS MERCHANTMAN, *Caledonia*, six hundred tons burden and mounting fifty guns, rolled through the Atlantic swell and came to anchor inside Sandy Hook in New York's lower bay. A late afternoon sun glinted from another sun displayed on the flag flying from the halyard, a sun with golden tongues of flame rising into a red sky from a blue sea, the device of the Company of Scotland Trading to Africa and the Indies.

Early the next day, the ship's pinnace was swung out and launched, and it sailed up the bay, through the Narrows, to the little provincial capital on the end of Manhattan. The small company of men who tumbled out on the dock were the surviving leaders of an ambitious project to plant a Scottish colony on the Isthmus of Darien in Central America. They were more dead than alive. Their once proud ship, which had sailed from the Road of Leith, down the Forth, to the New World over a year before, now lay helpless, without water or provisions, its crew decimated by famine and fever. Onlookers did not need to hear the "tragical narration" of the disastrous attempt at colonization. The distress of the men was written on their faces, where "famine and death was discerned . . . at the first aspect."[1]

It was distress of soul as well as body. The project of found-

---

1. George Moffat to Ormston, N.Y., Aug. 12, 1699, John H. Burton, ed., *The Darien Papers* (Edinburgh, 1849), 143-44 (cited hereafter as *Darien Papers*); George Pratt Insh, ed., *Papers Relating to the Ships and Voyages of the Company of Scotland Trading to Africa and the Indies, 1696-1707* (Publications of the Scottish Historical Society, 3rd ser. [Edinburgh, 1924], VI), 131, 267-70 (cited hereafter as *Shipping Papers*); Francis Russell Hart, *The Disaster of Darien* (Boston, 1929), 54-56; George Pratt Insh, *The Company of Scotland Trading to Africa and the Indies* (London, 1932), 119-20. Frank Cundall, *The Darien Venture* (New York, 1926), 18, has an illustration of the flag of the Company.

ing a settlement on the Isthmus of Darien had enlisted the support of Scots in all walks of life, had become practically a national enterprise, and now all the zeal and hard work, the high hopes and aspirations had come to nothing. The three men who came ashore to beg relief for their fellows left aboard bore a heavy burden of concern for their disastrous venture, augmenting their physical misery. Of the dozen councilors appointed to serve as leaders for the colony, these alone were left to carry the responsibility. They were the captain of the ship, Robert Drummond, his brother Thomas, and Samuel Vetch.

Such was the inauspicious arrival of Samuel Vetch in His Majesty's Northern Colonies on Friday, August 4, in the summer of 1699. Landing at the small provincial port through necessity rather than choice, he was a man whose presence on the colonial scene would shape some of the important developments to come. He had already compressed into thirty years experiences which would last most men a lifetime. The excitement of his earliest years, however, had been mainly vicarious, deriving from the hectic existence of his father William Veitch (the son always omitted the *i* from his name), a leading member of the Scottish Covenanting clergy who endured persistent persecution under the reign of Charles II.[2]

William's ancestors were evidently men of substance, for he referred to "their considerable estate" which they held "for a hundred years together" in and about the town of Dalkeith; the last of it was disposed of by William's eldest brother. William was the youngest child of John Veitch, who served as minister at Roberton, in the shire of Clydesdale, for forty-five years. His mother was the daughter of a Glasgow merchant named Johnston and was, according to her son, "a pious and frugal woman, very dexterous in housekeeping and educating of children."

2. Thomas McCrie, ed., *Memoirs of Mr. William Veitch and George Brysson written by themselves with other narratives illustrative of the History of Scotland from the Restoration to the Revolution* (Edinburgh, 1825), (cited hereafter as *Veitch Memoirs*) ; *Memoirs of Mrs. William Veitch, Mr. Thomas Hog of Kiltearn, Mr. Henry Erskine and Mr. John Carstairs,* Issued by the Committee of the General Assembly of the Free Church of Scotland for the publication of the works of Scottish Reformers and Divines (Edinburgh, 1846), (cited hereafter as *Mrs. Veitch Memoirs*). For Samuel Vetch and his own family, I have followed the spelling "Vetch" favored by him. In speaking of his father and other connections of the family I use "Veitch" as they did.

William was a good student, achieving honors at the college of Glasgow and attracting the notice of the Reverend John Livingston, one of the Scots "worthies," by whom Veitch was persuaded to abandon the study of "physic" for the ministry. Originally, he had been drawn to medicine because so many of his brothers were already in the ministry; now he followed in their footsteps. But this was the beginning of the "cloudy season" of the church. Veitch lost his first position, as chaplain with the family of Sir Hugh Campbell of Calder, and went to stay with his father, who had likewise been ousted from his church at Roberton and had moved to nearby Lanark. It was there, in the fall of 1664, that William Veitch met and married "a young virgin in that town called Marion Fairly."[3]

Samuel's mother was a "wife of eminent piety," according to the testimony of her husband. Her family was from the region of Edinburgh, where it was old and respected. The editor of her memoirs has characterized her as one "most deservedly esteemed and honored by the pious and distinguished of her own day." From her own account, she "endured an amount of domestic affliction and vexatious persecution . . . more trying than martyrdom itself." Samuel grew up in a household in which the immediacy of God's actions and will was deeply felt. But all too often God was left as the only father for the numerous young Veitches while William was pursuing trouble wherever it might be found in the form of political or religious opposition to Scottish tenets.[4]

The young couple had scarcely settled on a farm in the Westhills of Dunsyre near Lanark when William Veitch was called to take part in the uprising against the King at Pentland Hills in the fall of 1666. After some days of very nonclerical exertions, during which he rode at the head of a cavalry force, entered Edinburgh as a spy, and had sundry narrow escapes, he found the King's men in the ascendency and himself sentenced to death and his property to forfeiture. He had no recourse but to escape to England, where he took his mother's maiden name and joined other fugitives from the persecution.

His first son, William, was born in the spring of 1667. Mrs.

3. *Veitch Memoirs*, 3, 19-20, 22.
4. *Mrs. Veitch Memoirs*, ii.

Veitch had taken refuge with her brother-in-law John and had then returned to the farm near Lanark to be near her own family. There her husband visited her secretly from time to time, when he was not preaching up and down England, at Newcastle, in Lancashire, at Leeds, Nottingham, or London. The authorities in Scotland were perfectly aware that Veitch was occasionally in Lanark. The household was continually molested by parties of troopers descending on it in the dead of night, offering to break down the doors if Mrs. Veitch did not allow them to search for her husband. With another child on the way, she was advised by her husband to sell the farm and move into Edinburgh to avoid further annoyance.

In Edinburgh, on Wednesday, December 9, 1668, Samuel was born. He was baptized the following Sunday by John Blackadar, a leading member of the Covenanting clergy, and the witnesses included William Livingston, a son of the famous minister at Ancrum and the brother of Robert Livingston, the baby's future father-in-law.[5]

William Veitch heartily disliked his wandering existence. In 1671, he was prevailed upon by the people along the border in Northumberland, where he had been preaching, to take his family out of Scotland and settle down as minister to those who were opposed to the English dispensation. "In creels" Mrs. Veitch brought her two small sons from Edinburgh to their new home in the village of Fallowlees, Rodberry parish, Northumberland. Even this "moorish, retired place" did not free the father from interference by neighboring adherents of the Established Church, so shortly afterward the Veitches moved five miles farther into the country to Harnamhall, a farm and house suitable for holding meetings. Here Veitch's meeting found a large attendance and many conversions, accompanied by sundry "savoury" confessions.

For Samuel, the constant presence of his father's friends and followers must have meant an early acquaintance with the sociability of a minister's household. It also meant an awareness of God and the stern precepts of the Presbyterian creed which had been borne in upon him from his first consciousness. Never far absent from the family's thoughts, too, were the threats of un-

5. *Veitch Memoirs*, 26-48, 49-58, 258, 259.

friendly neighbors of the Anglican persuasion and the jealous opposition of the regular ministers. They had always to remember
that they were fugitives from Scottish justice and that William
Veitch was under sentence of death; this necessitated the continued use of the surname Johnston and prevented the family
from enjoying pleasant associations with relatives and friends in
Scotland. Nevertheless, Mrs. Veitch was to remember with
gratitude the seventeen years of "kind entertainment" in England.[6]

As Samuel grew up at Harnam, other children were added to
the family at frequent intervals: a brother James, who died when
he was a year old; another brother John; a sister Elizabeth; and
a third brother Ebenezer. When Samuel was nearly nine years
old, a new owner of Harnamhall forced the Veitches to move to
Stantonhall.

Almost at once, the Anglican minister of the parish began a
persecution of Veitch. This minister, Thomas Bell, was, surprisingly enough, a Scot himself and had been helped through
college by Veitch's brother. With the assistance of the local
justices, Bell forced Veitch into hiding. Vexed at being unable
to capture him, Bell told the Duke of Lauderdale, then the King's
Commissioner for Scotland, of the dangers inherent in allowing
"vagrant Scotch preachers" to spread infection against the Establishment south of the border—it "was like to pass Tyne Bridge,
and approach the very noble parts of the nation if not timeously
prevented."

The authorities struck swiftly. Several troops of horse and
dragoons were sent to the Northumberland borders to crush the
meetings of Covenanters and arrest the abettors. An informer
who knew that Veitch had returned home one night guided the
troops to Stantonhall and before dawn on a cold January morning
soldiers smashed in the windows and seized the unlucky minister before he could escape. William Veitch was hurried off to jail, then
transferred to Scotland on order of the King to be tried for non-
conformity and for his part in the Pentland Hills uprising. The
year was 1679, and excitement over the Popish Plot was at its
height; no one could tell to what excesses the King and court
might be forced.

6. *Ibid.*, 59-62; *Mrs. Veitch Memoirs*, 3, 29.

It was a bitter blow to Mrs. Veitch and her six small children. To finance her husband's defense, she sold off the stock on the farm. The minister, Bell, boasted that Veitch would be hanged promptly and would "trouble them and the countryside no more." It was but small comfort that a few days later the designing Bell, while returning home drunk late at night, fell into a river and froze to death.[7]

Veitch's friends took his case to Shaftesbury, the Whig leader, and to the Protestant champion, the Duke of Monmouth. The Duke personally pleaded for Veitch with his father, but Charles II only observed that if the information he had was true Veitch deserved more deaths than one. "I have written with my own hand to execute him," said the King, "and what I have written I have written." But the jealousy of Lauderdale, the King's Commissioner for Scotland, helped save Veitch. Reluctant to allow the Whigs intercession with the King, Lauderdale and others of his Council agreed to a sentence of banishment, which hurriedly was presented to the King before Monmouth could take further action. As the powerful Lord Stairs said, "This will be to our credit, and stop the mouths of all in Scotland who reflect on our severity," rather than letting Monmouth arrange things so that "the dirt will lie upon us."[8]

Despite Veitch's release, the family was not freed from adversity. Without the farm stock it was impossible to harvest the summer's crops. Frequent moves had depleted the family reserves, and the years at Stantonhall had been difficult because of the poverty of the Northumberland parishioners. Now whatever property Veitch had been able to retain in Scotland was declared forfeit. And when Veitch returned to Stantonhall in the late summer of 1679, his adversaries in the neighborhood resolved to re-arrest him. While this was not legal, the times, Veitch knew, would provide him "little access to redress such irregularities as they might commit." Since he would not refrain from preaching—the only course of action which would have pacified the authorities—he went into hiding and again carried on a fugitive

7. *Veitch Memoirs,* 260-61, 66-77, 84-88; *Mrs. Veitch Memoirs,* 3-4.
8. *Veitch Memoirs,* 91-100, 107-16; *Mrs. Veitch Memoirs,* 5-6.

ministry along the western border of England and Scotland, visiting his family as he could, surreptitiously.

Arbitrary government under Charles, and the likelihood of worse under James, was fast alienating all parties and classes, and in Scotland the regime lost the support of many who had been loyal previously. Divided as Scottish Protestants were, they were united against Rome. James, Duke of York, who had replaced Lauderdale in the government of Scotland, imprisoned the prominent Earl of Argyll for refusing to subscribe to a test act which seemed to point in the direction of Catholicism. Argyll escaped in December 1681 and went directly to the Veitches at Stantonhall. The doughty minister promptly decided to escort the nobleman to London, despite the price on Argyll's head. Mrs. Veitch, no less staunch in the Covenanting cause, concurred in her husband's resolution, even though she had seven children to care for and another about to be born.[9]

After covertly making their dangerous way to London, Lord Argyll as "Mr. Hope" and Veitch as "Captain Forbes" lurked in the suburbs, keeping abreast of the plots the Whigs were laying for an attack on the Crown. By September 1682, Argyll thought it best to escape to Holland, and in the spring of 1683 Veitch returned to Stantonhall, just before the disclosure of the Rye House plot brought down the Crown's vengeance on the plotters who remained in London and sent Monmouth to join those malcontents foresighted enough to get away to the Netherlands. Veitch had been a leader in the Scottish side of the plot and therefore remained in hiding. Wearied of aliases and realizing the very real danger to which his presence subjected his family, he finally had "to steal over to Holland" himself. His brother and sister-in-law went with him, and shortly afterward Mrs. Veitch sent the eldest boys, William and Samuel, to join him.

It must have been hard for Mrs. Veitch to see her fifteen- and sixteen-year-old lads depart. But they were reaching the age when the authorities might consider them sharers in their father's guilt, and, at any rate, the Veitches, who were risking their very lives for the cause of religion and self-government, had dedicated their sons to carry on the cause. William and Samuel were destined for the

9. *Veitch Memoirs*, 117-20, 131-32; *Mrs. Veitch Memoirs*, 6.

ministry; in the safety of Holland they could imbibe the Calvinism which was proscribed at home. They began studies in their new home to prepare themselves for one of the Dutch universities.

That Mrs. Veitch remained steadfast in her faith at this time testifies to her spirit and moral inheritance. Her landlord ordered her to move—the action was symptomatic of the intensified oppressions that accompanied Charles II's attainment of uncontrolled power. It would do a man no good to be renting to such notorious Covenanters. But if she were to move, how could she be sure that her husband's letters would reach her? To add to her grief and distraction, her twelve-year-old son John was dying. Then news came that a storm had arisen during her older sons' voyage and many people had been lost.

The boys arrived safely in Holland, however, and found their father in the center of affairs in the colony of Scottish refugees. In pursuance of the Rye House plan, the scheme of Monmouth's invasion of England, to be accompanied by Argyll's landing in Scotland, was underway. It went swiftly forward after the death of Charles II and the accession of James early in 1685. Although it brought him under additional penalty, Veitch, an indefatigable campaigner, returned to his old haunts along the Scottish border in Northumberland. In the midst of such exciting events, it is little wonder that Mrs. Veitch heard from Holland that "her sons didn't mind their books as they should."[10]

After the failure of Monmouth and Argyll, the elder Veitch was hunted relentlessly, but he survived both "Kirke's Lambes" and the "Bloody Assizes," and after things quieted down he ventured into Newcastle, where his wife had found sanctuary. There, in the dead of night, he was able to see his family and friends, who had been trying to find out what had become of him. Even then, when "our night was dark, and all things looked with a black face," Mrs. Veitch "was persuaded that she would see presbytery established, and her husband a settled minister, in the church of Scotland, ere she died."[11]

And so it happened. To free his fellow Catholics from persecution, James II had to acquiesce in liberty for dissenters as well.

10. *Veitch Memoirs*, 133-46, 154, 221; *Mrs. Veitch Memoirs*, 8-9.
11. *Mrs. Veitch Memoirs*, 18; *Veitch Memoirs*, 148-50.

Veitch, who as "Mr. Robinson" had taken up preaching again when "Monmouth was not as yet well cold in his grave," was able to come into the open. With toleration for Scotland granted, he received a call in 1688 from parishes in his native land. His wife was anxious to return, to see the fulfillment of that "which she had promised herself formerly in her duties and wrestlings with God, and had expressed her assurance thereof."

At first he had to tread warily, lest his old sentence of banishment be invoked or someone inform against him. After the Glorious Revolution, however, he was able to take an active place in the councils of the church, as minister of various parishes and as a member of the general assembly from 1694 to 1705. But he remained always a kind of stormy petrel in the church, where even after the Revolutionary settlement many loyal Presbyterians could not agree with all the measures of the church authorities. Nevertheless, Veitch, esteemed by his Presbyterian brethren, found himself in easy circumstances in his old age and was able to see his sons provided for and his daughters married into "genteel and wealthy families." He and his wife died within a day of each other, in 1722, and were buried together in the church-yard of their last parish, Dumfries.[12]

When their father embarked for England to do Argyll's business, William and Samuel remained at their studies in Utrecht. But they had little stomach for the ministry. If they were destined to follow their father's footsteps, they looked to the army instead of the church. The elder Veitch had certainly shown a predilection for action, and the times were such that they could serve the crusade against absolutism and against the Roman Catholic Church better as soldiers than as ministers. At Utrecht they were attracted to William of Orange, the Dutch Stadholder, leader of the League of Augsburg against Louis XIV, who was the embodiment of royal power and Catholicism. William was the strongest contender for the throne of England, if it should fall vacant through James' overthrow. He was also champion of the English and Scottish Protestants now that Monmouth had died. To enlist themselves in William's cause must have seemed a more effective course of action to the boys than seeking ordination as ministers.

12. *Veitch Memoirs*, 168-69.

Their father might well have agreed, although Mrs. Veitch did not. "My sons," she wrote, "were both for being soldiers, which troubled my spirit much," but, she added with resignation, "If He had any service for them in that station, I would submit."[13]

When William of Orange sailed on the "Protestant breeze" to Torbay on November 1, 1688, both William and Samuel embarked with his troops. It was a stirring time; great changes impended. In the three years of James' reign, England had been transformed from a kingdom loyal, prosperous, and unified to one disloyal, divided, and stubbornly opposed to its ruler's zeal for the twin evils of absolutism and Catholicism. Letters from home must have told the two young Scots of their native land's suffering under the dragoons. In the cosmopolitan air of Utrecht, they would have been aware, too, of the larger implications of the imminent crisis in England and the international policies which lay in the balance. It is not surprising that, as Samuel Vetch wrote in later years, "I left my studies at Utrecht to attend his Majesty over in that glorious undertaking."[14]

Several English and Scottish regiments had served the Dutch for many years, and it is probable that the Veitches enlisted in one of these. During the invasion, William found such regiments especially useful for duties where his Dutch troops might have offended English patriotism. With a little urging from William of Orange, James II had fled England by February 1689. The Dutch leader and his wife became joint sovereigns, and the power of England was joined to William's League of Augsburg in the "Great Design," continental war against the aggression of Louis XIV.

Immediately, the need arose for English troops on the Continent. Among the regiments ordered back to Holland was the newly formed Royal Regiment of Dragoons of Scotland, which had been added to the regularly established army as the Second Regiment of Cavalry of the Line, known to history as the famous Scots Greys. "Though very young," Samuel Vetch was promoted to commissioned rank as a cornet in this first organization of what

13. *Ibid.*, 169-72, 181-92, 193-219; *Mrs. Veitch Memoirs*, 38-40, 49.
14. Vetch to Blathwayt, N.Y., May 25, 1702 (Henry E. Huntington Library).

was to become a distinguished military group. He was barely twenty years old.[15]

At the same time, Samuel's brother obtained a lieutenancy in the Twenty-Sixth Infantry under the youthful Earl of Angus, who was only eighteen years old. This force, better known as the Cameronians, was recruited from a group of Covenanters to suppress a rebellion against King William which had been raised in Scotland by the Highlanders under John Graham of Claverhouse, the Earl of Dundee. "Bloody Claver'se" had earned the undying hatred of the Covenanters who had been harried for years by his dragoons. It is possible that Samuel, as well as William, had enlisted in the struggle in Scotland and fought at Killiecrankie, before his regiment returned to the Netherlands.[16]

From 1688 until the Treaty of Ryswick in 1697, both men fought in the Netherlands against the French, taking part in the furious battle of Steinkirk and in the rout of Neerwinden. William was wounded slightly at Steinkirk, and his brave colonel, Angus, was killed. Before the end of the war, Samuel was promoted to captain.[17] At home, Mrs. Veitch suffered the terrors of all mothers whose sons are away at war. After the battle of Landen, she wrote, "When I heard that there were so many killed, I was in great fear," but "near five weeks after, they sent a letter, telling that they were both living."[18]

This period was the training ground for the English army which was to serve so gloriously under Marlborough; it was a school of bitter experience, but it proved useful for later campaigns on the Continent as well as for the undertakings of Samuel Vetch and many others in the American colonies. Even with the end

15. J. W. Fortescue, *A History of the British Army* (London, 1935), I, 335, 296-309.

16. *Ibid.*, 353, 325; Vetch to Blathwayt, N.Y., May 25, 1702 (Huntington Lib.).

17. Fortescue, *History of British Army*, I, 340-42; *Mrs. Veitch Memoirs*, 42. The lists and registers of the British army which were omitted from Clifford Elliott Walton's *History of the British Standing Army, 1660-1700* (London, 1894), are available at the Royal United Service Institution, Whitehall Yard, London, but have not been consulted. Nothing in Walton or in Fortescue's appendices yields further specific data on the Vetches' military career in the Netherlands.

18. *Mrs. Veitch Memoirs*, 36-42; Fortescue, *History of British Army*, 353-82; Vetch to Blathwayt, N.Y., May 25, 1705 (Huntington Lib.).

of the war, the danger was not over. William, sailing for home, was shipwrecked and barely escaped with his life. Samuel remained in Holland, dangerously ill. "He wrote that he was fallen sick," Mrs. Veitch later recalled, "and that the doctor said he was in consumption." But it was not that serious. More likely it was one of the fevers of the time brought on by some exposure to the elements and the unsanitary conditions of seventeenth-century army life. He was soon safely home at Dumfries with his family.[19]

19. *Mrs. Veitch Memoirs,* 46-47.

CHAPTER TWO

Darien Venture

O N HIS RETURN the young Vetch found Scotland astir, eager and excited over the prospective plans of the Company of Scotland to colonize Darien. Here was ready-made employment for soldiers whose regiments had been disbanded at the end of the war. His father's distinguished position in the church and the many people of influence who held the Veitches in esteem ensured Samuel a place in the expedition. His military rank and experience gained him a commission as captain in the land forces.

It was an attractive venture, whether regarded from the personal point of view of making a fortune or from the desire to promote the country's prosperity and honor. And for many it must have had the added attraction, as it did for Mrs. Veitch, of being an instrument by which the power of Spain and its church over the American natives was to be overthrown, the means to "turn away some from serving idols, to serve the living God."[1]

The colonists were chosen from a large number of eager applicants. Vetch possessed ideal qualifications: he was young, zealous, and of good family, and he had military experience. The Darien expedition became his school for learning the intricacies of colonization, administration, and trade, just as earlier schools had imbued him with Scots piety and common sense.

The Company of Scotland, established by the Scottish Parliament in 1695, was clearly an attempt to bring Scotland into lawful competition with established English monopolies such as the East India Company. It might also allow alert but as yet unfavored London merchants, acting through the Scottish Company, a chance

1. *Veitch Memoirs*, 22, 223; Fortescue, *History of British Army*, I, 383-95; *Mrs. Veitch Memoirs*, 52.

to break into the existing monopolies. But it had not been King
William's intent to allow the fractious Jacobites and Covenanters
of the northern kingdom advantages over his loyal English supporters. He considered himself "ill-served" by his commissioner,
who had allowed the bill establishing the Company. Vehement
opposition was soon reflected in the English Parliament, and
English investors were forced to withdraw. The Company's
project had become entirely a Scottish national effort.

The nature of the Company's enterprise was determined by
William Paterson, the energetic Scotsman who had been active
in the formation of the Bank of England. He had long held the
dream of a great world trading center located on the Darien
isthmus, strategically astride one of the natural highways of
trade. Taking the lead, he swept the Company forward toward
the fulfillment of his vision.[2]

The Company was rewarded with an unprecedented display of
national enthusiasm; fired with thoughts of colonial possessions
and lucrative trade, the Scots pledged material support to the
enterprise. Peers and periwig makers alike hastened to enroll
themselves on the books of the Company, subscribing in sums
from the minimum one hundred pounds to the maximum three
thousand a total of four hundred thousand pounds, an amount
which has been variously estimated to be at least half of, or possibly more than, the total amount of investment capital actually
available at the time in the whole of Scotland.[3]

Evidence that the colony could count on continued support
from Scotland was indicated by the outpouring of the citizenry
of Edinburgh when the ships sailed, "amidst the tears and prayers
and praises of relations and friends, and of their countrymen."
At last, Scotsmen seemed about to realize the hopes set forth in
a memorial of 1681 for "a Scotts plantation" to which those of
their countrymen who had settled elsewhere in the New World

2. Journals of the House of Lords, XV, 615-16, cited in Insh, *Company of
Scotland*, 57; see also 27-60 *passim*, 82-104, 109-11; *Shipping Papers*, 3-54;
Cundall, *Darien Venture*, 7-8, 15-16.
3. For a list of subscribers, see *Darien Papers*, 371-417. The list includes
one "Robert Veitch, merchant, in Edinburgh, £100" (*ibid.*, 386), who may
have been Vetch's uncle. See also Hart, *Disaster of Darien*, 36-42.

would now "be glad to remove themselves and their families." The highest expectations of the country rode with the three great vessels and two smaller craft when they set out from the Firth of Forth in the summer of 1698. The responsibility for success rested heavily on the shoulders of the councilors appointed to govern the intended colony.[4]

With this colony, as with every one planted by the English in America, the motive of the backers was profit. The instructions made it clear that the council's main duty was to make this new "Caledonia" a paying venture for the Company's stockholders, which meant, of course, the larger number of people living from the Highland Line to the English border. The governing council, appointed by the Company's directors from those actually proposing to go to the colony, included Captain William Veitch, Samuel's older brother. For an unknown reason, William was unable to sail with the colonists. Although Samuel was considered too inexperienced to take the vacant place on the council, he was relied upon to watch the family interests. The position of councilor went to William Paterson, who ended a brief period of disfavor with the directors.[5]

From the beginning, the colonists were beset with serious problems. The Darien area was squarely within the jurisdiction of the existing Spanish political organization. It had been a Spanish possession for almost two centuries and had been the scene of actual settlement. At the time of the Scottish attempt, it was uninhabited by Spaniards, but Carthagena and Portobello, thriving Spanish settlements, flanked it to the east and west, respectively, within several hundred miles, and the Spanish were active just

4. Sir John Dalrymple, *Memoirs of Great Britain and Ireland* (Edinburgh and London, 1771-88), II, 96-97; Insh, *Company of Scotland*, 25, 72, 78; *Darien Papers*, 49-56. No full, connected account of the Darien venture is available. Historians generally have concluded that the project was foreordained to failure. See, for instance, the opinion of Hart, *Disaster of Darien*, chap. IX; Insh, *Company of Scotland*, 71-78; Thomas Babington Macaulay, *The History of England from the Accession of James II* (New York, n.d.), V, 422-35; G. N. Clark, *The Later Stuarts* (Oxford, 1934), 273; Wallace Notestein, *The Scot in History* (New Haven, 1946), 185. But these authorities differ in their judgments of the reasons for failure. It seems to this writer that a careful study of the Scottish effort and the causes for its collapse would indicate that it need not have failed.

5. *Darien Papers*, 49, 178 ff.; *Veitch Memoirs*, 222-23; Insh, *Company of Scotland*, 80-81.

across the isthmus to the southeast.[6] The military nature of the Darien expedition made it clear that the Scots expected opposition from the Spanish. Many of the settlers had been chosen for their military experience, and they sailed in three well-armed ships and two auxiliaries. In his first letter, Vetch proudly boasted of being a good sailor as well as a good soldier; he "had never been sick the whole way." But Mrs. Veitch soon had word that "they were fallen in blood with the Spaniards, and they were like to be in strait for want of help from Scotland, and that ere it were long, it was like it would either prove a grave or a fortune." Vetch wrote that he was not pleased with the conduct of his fellows. A "mixed lot" had gone out on the expedition, young men recommended for the venture only by birth and influence, who were unskilled and too arrogant to take direction. Others were Highlanders, Jacobite in sympathy, who had gone only to escape an unsatisfactory situation at home.[7]

The Scots' landing was unopposed, and they quickly fortified the place selected for their settlement. An agent of the English government, ostensibly looking for profitable wrecks to plunder but in reality keeping an eye on the undertaking, reported that the Scots had twelve hundred men ashore, "as proper as I ever saw." "They are healthy," he wrote, "and in such a crabbed hold that it will be difficult to beat them out of it."[8]

Although the Spanish governor at Carthagena tried to get the Windward fleet to sail against Caledonia, the commander demurred, questioning Spain's right to Darien since it had no settled ports there. By the time the fleet sailed to Panama to confer with the president of the Audiencia, the ships had developed leaks and were judged unseaworthy. Another fleet at Vera Cruz delayed, pleading illnesses and lack of orders, but finally started out against Caledonia after the Scots had abandoned it. A scouting force from Panama had a sharp skirmish with the Caledonians and retired, and a more formidable force which toiled through

6. Hart, *Disaster of Darien*, 146-51, Appendices XIII, XIV, XVI; Insh, *Company of Scotland*, 147-55.
7. *Mrs. Veitch Memoirs*, 52-54.
8. Report of Lawrence Drummond and William Murray to the Directors, *Shipping Papers*, 110-11. In the *Darien Papers*, see Captain Pennicuik's Journal, 83; Mr. Hugh Rose's Journal, 76-77; Paterson's Report to the Directors, Edinburgh, Dec. 1699, 180 ff.; and the letter of Captain Long from Jamaica, 83.

the jungle to attack the settlement gave up and returned to Panama in the face of heavy rains, illness, and lack of provisions.[9]

More serious was the position in which the establishment of Caledonia placed King William. Earlier in the century, the rule had been "no peace beyond the line." Colonial rivalries, disputed territorial claims, and privateering attacks which were little less than outright piracy could continue even when peace reigned in Europe. Now it was becoming increasingly apparent that war in the New World would be likely to involve the mother countries.[10] England could not afford to take that risk, for she was making a strenuous attempt to prevent Spain from falling to the House of Bourbon with the death of the ailing and childless Spanish monarch, Charles II. If French Bourbons or Austrian Hapsburgs gained the Spanish holdings, the balance of power would be upset. By a series of treaties, the English tried to prevent either power from falling heir to all the Spanish holdings. The Spanish were resentful enough at a partition proposed by the English, preferring to "deliver themselves up to the French or the devil, so they may go all together, rather than be dismembered."[11] William therefore wished to avoid further grievances which might cause them to balk at adherence to these important agreements. He promptly disavowed the Scottish enterprise, ordered the respective governors of the English colonies in America and the West Indies to hold no correspondence with the Scots, and forbade trading with them or offering them any assistance whatsoever. The English government instructed its minister at Madrid to make it clear that his government was doing all that the Spanish could have desired to prevent success of the settlement of Darien.[12]

9. Insh, *Company of Scotland,* 153-60; Hart, *Disaster of Darien,* 85-86 and chap. VII.

10. Arthur Percival Newton, *The European Nations in the West Indies 1493-1688* (London, 1933), 335-38. The area of the western hemisphere, beyond the Line of Demarcation of 1494, was considered open for privateering and other armed clashes between colonial rivals even though the nations might be at peace in Europe.

11. Alexander Stanhope, minister to Spain, quoted in Insh, *Company of Scotland,* 147.

12. Letter from Vernon to Stanhope, Mar. 17, 1699, Insh, *Company of Scotland,* 148; Council of Indies to His Majesty, May 16, 1699, communicating message from Stanhope, Hart, *Disaster of Darien,* Appendix XVIII.

The King's command that no assistance should be given the Caledonians was also based on considerations other than maintaining good relations with Spain. Not only were English trading interests jealous of the Company of Scotland, nearby English colonies, such as Jamaica, feared the inroads the Darien colony might make on their profitable trade and the strength of their settlements. Even more distant colonies expressed anxiety that Caledonia would become prejudicial to the English trade. To Governor Basse of New Jersey, the Scotch colony seemed "by nature and situation to pretend in time to be the emporium of trade and riches of America." But whether European diplomacy or commercial jealousy accounted for the English opposition to the settlement and called forth the strict embargo on trade with the Scots, this was not the main reason for the colony's failure. That lay in the actions of the Company and the colonists themselves.[13]

From the outset, the lack of executive power vested in a responsible administrator of the colony proved highly disadvantageous. Government by council left decisions to be argued out among the leaders. The council appointed a different councilor as president each week, an obviously absurd attempt to solve its problems. William Paterson had proposed to govern the colony in its first stages by a president of the council chosen from among the "land councilors" each month for the first four months. By observing the work of these four successive leaders, their abilities for a longer term of office might be judged. But Paterson had been overruled, and the system became, as he put it, "a mere May

13. Basse to Board of Trade, Hart, *Disaster of Darien*, 158-60. Governor Beeston of Jamaica informed the Board of Trade in Dec. 1698, "The Scotch fleet are arrived at Darien. . . . yet if they fix there and are healthy the noise of gold (of which there is a great plenty in those parts) will carry away all our servants, debtors, and ordinary people in hopes of mending their fortunes and thereby will very much weaken that small strength we have"; J. W. Fortescue, ed., *Calendar of State Papers, Colonial Series, America and the West Indies, 1697-98* (London, 1905), no. 1028 (cited hereafter as *Cal. State Papers*). See also the comments in *Darien Papers*, 84 and 149; and Secretary Vernon's remark to Stanhope that England's measures were taken because otherwise the consequence of the Scottish settlement would be "the draining of all our colonies of the young and vigorous men by whom the plantations should be improved and secured"; quoted in Insh, *Company of Scotland*, 148. See also the remarks of Daniel Defoe cited in Hart, *Disaster of Darien*, 161.

game of the government," reducing all things "to uncertainty and contradictions."

Almost at once, jealousies and disagreements sprang up, especially among the sea captains who had "tempers and dispositions as boisterous and turbulent as the elements they are used to struggle with." Some of the councilors, by reason of their position as ship commanders, had a disproportionate amount of authority and a stubborn sense of rightness. It is a familiar complaint in colonial annals. Speaking for the landsmen, Paterson later bitterly criticized those "Marine chancellors" who "took upon them to know everything better than we," even regarding the land settlement.

As a result of the differences, a gradual change in the personnel of the colony's leaders came about. By December 1698, when the leaders prepared to send dispatches back to the Company, disagreement broke out openly. Paterson's recommendation that additional councilors be chosen was refused by the council. The other leaders also insisted that one of the more experienced colonists, Alexander Hamilton, bear the reports back to Scotland, but Paterson argued that Hamilton should not leave; he was the only fit person to manage the trading cargo and was, in fact, the person entrusted by the Company to handle the colony's accounts. Paterson preferred to send Captain Vetch on the trip home; he had apparently formed a good opinion of the young adventurer and considered him "capable enough for that errand." But Paterson was overruled.

To make matters worse, Major James Cunningham of the council "was become so uneasie and possest (as we thought) by so unaccountable conceits and notions, that he gave us no small trouble, and att last would needs forsake not only his post, but also the Colony." It seemed prudent to let Cunningham go in peace, lest he foment trouble on his return to Scotland. Hamilton was instructed to keep an eye on him and forestall any attempt he might make to prejudice the directors against the colonists.[14]

During this time two more of the councilors, Mackay and

14. Paterson's Report to the Directors, *Darien Papers*, 178-83. Major Cunningham of Eckett was a man of influence in Scotland, so it was important to avoid incurring his enmity.

Pennicuik, quarreled. Paterson again attempted to enlarge the council, hoping thereby to resolve the differences, but again he failed. Food was running short. Someone found that Pennicuik was concealing supplies for the use of his own ship, and Paterson accused him of mistreating visiting traders as well; the captain and his compatriots had been virtually guilty of piracy, Paterson charged, in seizing two Spanish traders who had found their way to Caledonia aboard a sloop from Jamaica. Two more councilors resigned—one of them was Jolly, who had opposed any additions— and Samuel Vetch, Charles Forbes, and Thomas Drummond, brother of the *Caledonia*'s captain, were elected to the council.

Much of the disagreement between the councilors arose over the insufficiency of provisions and the inappropriateness of the commodities loaded for trade. The Company had accumulated equipment and stores for two years and had spent the six months before the ships sailed in loading them. Since this was the first large-scale Scots venture into the plantation trade in the tropics, it is not surprising that there were blunders. But the directors must bear the blame for the initial mistakes. The cargo consisted largely of woolen items, the products of expanding Scottish industry, for which there was little demand in the warm Caribbean. And they were priced too high.[15]

Paterson had warned the captain of the *St. Andrew* to check his cargo before they sailed; but the doughty Pennicuik, offended, had refused. By the time the ships reached Madeira, it was evident that insufficient quantities of food had been loaded, and short rations were ordered. Instead of stocking up at that island, the council sent a dispatch to Scotland urging the prompt forwarding of further supplies. Even this message probably failed to make clear the seriousness of their situation, for the councilors feared to write of their needs too completely lest enemies hear of their plight. The councilors spent what funds they had on a generous supply of wine. Not only was the wine a help in warding off the chills and damps of the voyage and the fevers of the coastal jungles, but it was necessary to avoid the customary ducking from the yard-arm, the fate meted out to those who had not previously crossed

15. *Ibid.*, 186-88, 127, 180; Insh, *Company of Scotland*, 115.

the Tropic of Cancer if they could not pay their "tropick bottle."[16]

The directors in Scotland had every intention of sending additional supplies and colonists to Caledonia. In March of 1699, when Hamilton brought the first news of the successful arrival at Darien, the directors hastened to assure the colony: "The honor and interest of this Kingdom being now so firmly and inseparably linked with that of your colony, you may depend upon our supplying you with ships, stores, men, arms, provisions, and other necessaries, to the utmost of our power, and that with all imaginable dispatch."

They had not waited for word from Caledonia to act—a month earlier a brigantine had sailed. Unfortunately, it ran aground soon after leaving the Clyde, and in this wreck on the Western Isles of Scotland foundered the only chance the directors had of getting supplies and a sustaining word to the colony in time to strengthen the adventurers' resolution. Two other ships, sailing in May, did not arrive until after the colony had been deserted.[17]

In the news which Hamilton brought to the directors nothing had been said of the lack of provisions. The council had not wanted to alarm the country with any indication that the venture was in danger of failing; nor did it want to expose its own dereliction in not making good shortages when it had the chance. The reports from Caledonia instead spoke of its "commodious bay," "its pleasant and healthful climate . . . frequently fanned with moderate gales of sea and land breezes," the belief that its soil "promises increase of anything planted . . . plenty of fish, fowl, wild pigs or hogs, even venison." But in a private letter from a colonist to one of the directors was a hint: "I very heartily wish that a mistaken notion of such a prospect may not occasion the old mother to obliviate her new born babe before it be fit for weaning and in a condition of doing for itself."

It was with understandable exasperation that the directors later inquired why, if the colony had been in as good a condition as was reported, it had failed for want of provisions. But it is unlikely

16. *Darien Papers*, 179-80; Hart, *Disaster of Darien*, 57-58; Insh, *Company of Scotland*, 120-22; "A Journal kept from Scotland by one of the Company who sailed on board the 'Endeavor' pink," *Shipping Papers*, 72; Captain Pennicuik's Journal, 78, and Mr. Hugh Rose's Journal, *Darien Papers*, 60-78.

17. *Darien Papers*, 129, 122-25.

that the directors in Scotland were as unaware of the colony's difficulties as they seemed. From the frequent letters which Samuel Vetch sent to his parents it may be inferred that others wrote often. The directors were extremely unwise if they ignored these sources of news. Some things, they must have known, could not be written in official letters which had to pass the approval of dissenting as well as loyal members of the council.[18]

The first news of Caledonia's difficulties came officially only with the council's dispatches of April 1699, which reached the directors in August, after the colony had been abandoned. Four ships were even then preparing to sail for the isthmus, following the two which had gone out earlier. The bonfires and ringing of bells which celebrated the first news of the settlement had been succeeded by disquieting rumors during the summer that all was not well, that the merchandise was faulty, and that misunderstandings had arisen between the seamen and landsmen. Next came news of the loss of the colony's auxiliary vessel, *Dolphin*, and then the council learned that all the English colonies had published proclamations against helping the Caledonians.

The directors could only hope that their colonists would surmount these disadvantages, piously but ineffectually suggesting that their difficulties might be overcome if they would "lead virtuous and religious lives, to secure God's protection and success." More practically, believing as good, shrewd Presbyterians that God helps those who help themselves, they recommended that the settlers should claim the land on the south side of the isthmus, negotiate treaties of purchase with the friendly Indians of the region, and in general utilize their ships and goods to advantage. The directors were of the opinion that the colony's difficulties came from "your people being penned up in a corner close together, in a state of lazy idleness, as we are informed."

These were only words, and they never reached the ones to whom they were directed. The colony had even worse failures of communication than usually afflicted mother countries and their colonies. Probably the "Scots in Barbados, Antegoa, Jamaica, and

18. Directors to Council, Oct. 10, 1699, Paterson's Report to the Directors, Hector MacKenzie to John Haldane of Gleneagles, Dec. 21, 1698, *ibid.*, 165, 178-83, 79-81; *Shipping Papers*, 107-8; *Mrs. Veitch Memoirs*, 52-54.

New England," through whom the directors were mailing dispatches, simply found few ships by which to forward mail after the proclamations against the Scots went out in April.[19]

But the directors did not confine themselves to words. They launched efforts to get England to withdraw its opposition to the colony, they prepared a second fleet to sustain the settlement, and they attempted to arrange credits so that the colonists could draw bills on neighboring English colonies. "We thought you might be better, cheaper, and easier supplied with provisions from the English plantations," they wrote. Provisions were "scarce and dear" in Scotland at the time, the first supply ship had been wrecked, and this method seemed the best way to speed aid to the colony without difficult and tedious transportation. It was a sound move, and the council at Caledonia had already come to the same conclusion. But the directors had acted too late.[20]

As it was, the colonists were fast losing heart as the spring of 1699 wore on. Paterson, whose wife had died on the passage to America, was himself seriously ill and unable to offer much leadership. As one largely responsible for the expedition, he may have represented for his fellow councilors the source of their troubles. Only the staunch Thomas Drummond supported his attempts to encourage the councilors to remain. As the days passed with no sign of the promised relief ships, the colonists began to fear that the English government had bullied the Company into abandoning the enterprise. Even the sovereign remedy was running low, despite the adequate stocks of wine taken on at Madeira. A lack of the accustomed foods and an unaccustomed climate were causing the colonists to take sick and die at an increasing rate. Yams were no substitute for hearty Scottish fare.[21]

Early in June, all the councilors save Paterson moved aboard the ships: Pennicuik and Campbell on the *St. Andrew*, Forbes on the *Unicorn*, Vetch and Thomas Drummond on Captain Robert

19. *Darien Papers*, 126-29, 161-65, 133-40, 130.
20. Directors to Council, Aug. 17, 1699, *ibid.*, 132-33; Moffat to Ormston, Aug. 12, Cleghorn to Blackwood, Aug. 14, Borland to Mackay, Sept. 7, and Samuel Vetch to William Veitch, Sept. 20, 1699, *ibid.*, 143-57.
21. Paterson's Report to the Directors, MacKenzie to Haldane, Borland to Mackay, Sept. 7, 1699, quoting Captain Drummond, *ibid.*, 192-93, 80, 152-53; Insh, *Company of Scotland*, 164; Cundall, *Darien Venture*, 88.

Drummond's *Caledonia*. By mid-month, they had resolved to try to make New England, where the sizable number of Scots in Boston might help them "have provision to get home to Scotland." Orders to that effect were drawn up by the council. Paterson, too ill to resist, was carried aboard the *Unicorn*, and his signature was obtained on the sailing directions. On June 22, the *Caledonia* and the *Endeavour* cleared the harbor, followed the next day by the *St. Andrew* and *Unicorn*.

For most of the colonists this was the inglorious end of a venture fraught with high promise. For many others it was the end of their lives. The *Unicorn*, which struggled into New York ten days after the *Caledonia*, was dismasted in a squall and came in jury-rigged, her sails and rigging shattered, only 100 survivors left out of 250 who had crowded aboard at Darien. The *St. Andrew* lost her troublesome Captain Pennicuik, along with 130 others, after abandoning the *Unicorn* in distress and being chased by the Spanish. She finally put in at Jamaica, where she was abandoned; the survivors were warmly welcomed as colonists by Governor Beeston. He had no objection to adding their strength to his settlement, however he had felt about them as rivals. The little *Endeavour* sank, and her survivors made New York aboard the *Caledonia*, whose losses ran over one hundred.[22]

The indomitable Paterson reached New York more dead than alive and survived to return to England. There he became the storm center of pamphlet warfare lasting for over a dozen years, as he tried to obtain payment of his claims against the Company. In the course of his legal battles, the causes of the colony's failure received a thorough airing.[23]

The leaders of the colony who reached New York had little but praise for Paterson. George Moffat, supercargo on a Scots ship then in New York, attributed the colony's failure to those

22. Campbell to the Directors, Pt. Royal, Jamaica, Aug. 18, 1699, Paterson's Report to the Directors, Moffat to Ormston, *Darien Papers*, 150-51, 193-96, 143; *Shipping Papers*, 113-15, and Nanfan to Bellomont, Aug. 7, 1699, *ibid.*, 116-17; Insh, *Company of Scotland*, 83; Cundall, *Darien Venture*, 103.

23. See pamphlets listed in John Scott, ed., *Bibliography of Printed Documents and Books Relating to the Darien Company*, revised by George P. Johnston (Edinburgh, 1904). A good collection is in the John Carter Brown Library of Brown University. Whether or not the truth emerged from this airing is for the readers of the record to determine for themselves.

councilors who had caused so much trouble in the first months of the settlement. He held "frequent convers" with Vetch and the Drummonds and concluded from them that their predecessors on the council had been personally ambitious and were "both young and not qualified for so great an affair"; but these three reported favorably on Paterson, who "hath been both diligent and true to the end. He has been and is mightily concerned at this sad disaster so that he looks now more like a skeleton than a man." Of Vetch and his two colleagues, too, Moffat gained a good impression. They were so worried about "this disaster that they are now sick—if anything should befall them the whole interest will suffer thereby."

Adam Cleghorn, a Scottish merchant in New York who was preparing to send provisions to Darien on behalf of the directors, wrote in a similar vein to Bailie Robert Blackwood, a prominent Scottish merchant and one of the originators of the idea of a Scottish trading company. Indeed, Moffat and Cleghorn wrote letters so similar in wording that they were probably echoing the views of the remaining councilors. Vetch and the Drummonds may have been so distraught when they arrived that they asked these men to communicate with the Company and told them what to say, rather than trying to write immediately themselves. The Company later censured them for failing to do so.[24]

But even admitting Moffat's and Cleghorn's probable bias, nothing in the record indicates that the councilors who reached New York were at fault in the evacuation of Caledonia. The unfitness of many of the first leaders had reduced the colony to dire straits. Vetch and the others chosen to replace them could finally do nothing but abandon the settlement. Paterson was apparently well disposed toward Vetch, although there were occasional differences between the two men. Thomas Drummond, who early gained the good opinion of Paterson for his work in fortifying the colony despite lack of co-operation from some of the sea captains, was close to Vetch, as was his brother, the captain. Vetch described their relationship in a letter naming Thomas

24. *Darien Papers*, 143-47, 161-65. Actually Captain Drummond did write to Montgomerie from New York under date of Aug. 11 and mentioned an even earlier letter to MacKenzie, secretary of the Company; *Shipping Papers*, 114-15.

Drummond as his "entire comrade . . . a person with whom and with his brother, the Captain of the Caledonia, I have had a particular intimacy ever since we left Scotland and to both of whom I owe as much as to a brother; and must acknowledge to both their praises that the better I am acquainted with them the more I discover the honesty of their intentions and their particular qualifications in their different stations to serve this interest."[25]

Although Vetch wrote his brother from New York that "we have been circumstantiat with Paterson's knavery or folly or both," it seems likely that he referred to Paterson's actions after he had landed from the *Unicorn.* Paterson was reported then "in a crasie condition"; illness and grief "has broke Mr. Paterson's heart and brain, and now hees a child"; he has "lost his sences and does not meddle in anything." Or perhaps Vetch finally concluded that Paterson had been unwise in his whole conception of the colonization scheme.[26]

Notwithstanding these opinions, the surviving leaders were already beginning to reap the fruits of distrust, recrimination, and obloquy which sprang from the failure of the colony. John Borland, a Scottish merchant in Boston with no personal knowledge of the facts, one with whom Vetch was to have close and cordial relations later, at first repeated views similar to those of Moffat and Cleghorn in letters home to Scotland. Within a month, however, extravagant statements crept into a letter he wrote with two other Scots merchants. Grief at the failure of their countrymen's national enterprise engendered their vehement indignation. They labeled councilors and colonists indiscriminately as "Jacobites, Papists, and atheists" and charged that a cabal existed to turn pirate and sell the Company's cargo. The northern colonies were in the midst of the furor over piracy, and the Scots in Boston concluded cryptically, "What will the world say but that the rest of his nation and Captain Kidd, never a barrel the better herrings."[27]

Already the story was becoming confused and the personnel

25. Paterson's Report to the Directors, Vetch to William Veitch, *Darien Papers*, 180, 156-57. See also Byres to the Directors, Feb. 1701, *ibid.*, 222-25.

26. Borland to Mackay, *ibid.*, 156-57, 146, 152-55; Borland, Campbell, and Maxwell to Fraser, *ibid.*, 159.

27. *Darien Papers*, 152-55, 157-59. The aphorism meant, essentially, "one is as bad as another." Kidd, too, was a Scot, and his alleged piracy was the talk of the times.

with it. Still, for Samuel Vetch, the dismal end of such a promising venture was to become the beginning of an even more enterprising career in the colonies. After such an exciting youth and young manhood, many men would have been content to marry and settle down in the quiet of a home, pursuing such trade as they were fitted for. But not Vetch. Participating in great events had whetted his ambition. Perhaps he had something of his father's proclivity for mixing in public affairs. After his army career and his brief experience in the political affairs of colonization, he seemed incapable of returning to the obscurity of ordinary life. Impatient with the commonplace, he sought a career— military, political, or commercial—which would advance his interests and influence. Despite the failure of the Darien venture, he had already played some part in great undertakings. He could not now be content with less.

CHAPTER THREE

New York Beginnings

ITH THEIR ARRIVAL in New York, the Scottish leaders'
first concern was the purchase of provisions for the officers
and crew left aboard the *Caledonia*, who were, literally,
starving to death. As their pinnace pulled alongside the
wharf at the Great Dock, across the East River from Long Island,
the appearance of the well-built, neat, provincial town must have
contrasted strangely with their jungle outpost at Darien. The
houses of multicolored brick, "very stately and high" with their
red and black tile roofs, gable ends toward the street, gave the
settlement at the tip of Manhattan a prosperous look. Vetch and
the Drummonds found an immediate welcome from the handful
of Scottish residents there, and news of their arrival and their
desperate straits must have soon sped through the village.[1]

But without money, with only goods to barter, the problem of
obtaining relief was a touchy one. Lord Bellomont, the governor,
was not in New York. He had gone three months before to
Massachusetts Bay, of which he was also the governor. John
Nanfan, his lieutenant governor, was unwilling to assume any
great amount of responsibility. The Acts of Trade and Navigation were very specific in forbidding trade with foreign vessels,
and Scotland was not considered part of England—it was ex-

1. Moffat to Adam Cockburn of Ormiston, Aug. 12, Cleghorn to Blackwood,
Aug. 14, 1699, *Darien Papers*, 143-47; Petition of Samuel Vetch and Robert
and Thomas Drummond to Nanfan, Public Record Office, Colonial Office 5,
vol. 1043, f. 2 (XI) (Library of Congress Transcripts); "The Burgis View"
of 1716-18, I. N. Phelps Stokes, *The Iconography of Manhattan Island* (New
York, 1915), I, plate 25; description dated Dec. 1704, in *The Journal of
Madam* [Sarah Kemble] *Knight* (Boston, 1920), 52; Robert Livingston
Papers (Livingston-Redmond Collection, Franklin D. Roosevelt Memorial Library, Hyde Park, N.Y.; cited hereafter as Livingston Papers), accounts for
Aug. 5, 1699, and following, Group 1a (all references to Livingston Papers are
in Group 1a, unless otherwise indicated).

cluded from its trade like any other foreign power. The goods aboard the *Caledonia*, which were all that the luckless Darien colonists had to offer in return for food, were Scottish goods, the importation of which was forbidden to New Yorkers. Moreover, Bellomont had received royal commands against helping the Caledonians, and his proclamation to that effect had issued from the press of William Bradford, the official printer, before the governor left the province.[2]

Supported by their local compatriots, however, Vetch and the two Drummonds drew up a memorial to the lieutenant governor asking for the liberty to dispose of as much of their goods as would purchase provisions to get them back to Scotland. This they laid before Nanfan and the Council at Fort William Henry on Saturday morning, the day after their arrival. Legality struggled with compassion, and a compromise resulted. Until the pleasure of the governor could be known, the Scots were allowed to purchase provisions on credit.

Nanfan hurried off a letter to Bellomont advising him of the arrival of the Scottish ship and the plight of those on board and raising the issue of how far the law would allow the barter of stores the Scots possessed. For Nanfan, the obviously miserable condition of the newcomers warranted feeding the Caledonians, and the abandonment of the Darien settlement seemed to have removed the necessity for observing the King's orders against them. Even before this letter could be sent, the *Unicorn* had arrived in worse condition than her companion ship.[3] Bellomont was inclined to agree with Nanfan's summary of the situation. "You know how strict my orders are against furnishing the Caledonians with provisions," he wrote; "yet if you can be thoroughly well assured these ships will go directly for Scotland you may

2. Bellomont to Board of Trade, May 16, 1699, *Cal. State Papers, 1699*, no. 317; Bellomont to Board of Trade, Aug. 24, 1699, E. B. O'Callaghan, ed., *Documents Relative to the Colonial History of the State of New-York* . . . (15 vols.; Albany, 1853-87), IV, 549 (cited hereafter as *N.Y. Col. Docs.*); photostat copy of proclamation, May 15, 1699, P.R.O., C.O. 5, vol. 1042, f. 30 (X) (Lib. Cong. Transcripts).

3. Aug. 5, 1699, New York Council Minutes, VIII, 124 (Mss. in New York State Library, Albany); Nanfan to Bellomont, Aug. 7, 1699, P.R.O., C.O. 5, vol. 1043, f. 2 (XI, XII) (Lib. Cong. Transcripts); Nanfan to Bellomont, Aug. 7, 14, 1699, *Cal. State Papers, 1699*, no. 476, enclosure 12; *Darien Papers*, 143.

furnish them with just provisions enough for their voyage." The
crew of an enemy ship thrown on their shores would not be
permitted to starve. Bellomont said nothing about allowing the
Scots to trade.[4]

George Moffat, the Scottish supercargo, was sharply critical
of the New Yorkers' slavish adherence to the Acts of Trade.
Moffat was the agent of Adam Cockburn of Ormiston, one of the
directors of the Company of Scotland, and in a letter to his em-
ployer and the other directors, Moffat pointed out that since the
Company had established no credit in New York, it would have
been better for the government there to let the Scots use the
trade goods they had aboard. Of course, he noted, the Company
should have established factors and credit for the use of the colony
in places like New York. Moffat guessed that merchants would
not have been lacking to deal with Darien, notwithstanding the
proclamations against it, if this had been done.[5]

But Bellomont was far less worried about the Scots' credit
than he was about avoiding any criticism of condoning illegal
trade. His whole administration was at that moment devoted to
putting down abuses of the English trading regulations. He was
discerning enough to realize that the Scots in the northern colonies
were sufficiently interested in the welfare of the Scottish colonization scheme to act as sureties for advances made to the ships, if
that were necessary. Furthermore, as he pointed out in his letters
to the Board of Trade in England, New York had little choice
in the matter. The Scots "were in a capacity with those ships of
force to insult New York or any other plantation," he wrote.
Nanfan had tried to get the ships to move up under the guns of
the fort, but the Scots had refused and lay five or six miles out
in the harbor. Their excuse, that they did not have enough able-
bodied men aboard to get the anchors up, belied their threat to
the town. It was clear that the Scots were playing all the angles
of the situation to extort the maximum concessions from their
reluctant hosts.

Bellomont's decision to adhere to legal forms and to report

---

4. Bellomont to Nanfan, Aug. 21, *Cal. State Papers, 1699*, no. 477. See
also Bellomont to Board of Trade, Oct. 20, 1698, *N.Y. Col. Docs.*, IV, 591-92.
5. *Darien Papers*, 144-45.

all of his government's transactions with the Caledonians to his superiors in England was the correct one under the circumstances, and he was never called to account for what happened subsequently. As it turned out, the Company was quick to respond to the criticism of their failure to provide credit in the northern colonies. As soon as news of the difficulty was received, credit of £2,000 sterling was forwarded to New York, along with a sharp rebuke to Vetch and the Drummonds to take this chance to "regain some reputation in the world and not forever to be registered with us as your country's betrayers."[6]

Bellomont was worried far more about the Caledonians' intentions. News had reached New England that an expedition of five ships had repossessed the Darien settlement. Upon this "news of the recruits sent them from Scotland of men, arms, and all other provisions," Bellomont feared the *Caledonia* might sail back to the Caribbean. He repeatedly cautioned Nanfan not to let the leaders buy more provisions than would serve to carry them to Scotland, and he reported to the Board of Trade that if Nanfan suffered them to exceed that amount, the lieutenant governor would have to bear the blame.

The governor's suspicions were not without foundation. Captain Drummond did indeed desire to take his ship back to Darien. But Nanfan, able to see the plight of the two ships, was less apprehensive. Despite their provisions, the situation of the Caledonians was not much improved. Some aboard were now "destroying themselves" from plenty, going from one extreme to another. A Dr. Johnson from the Jerseys, who attended the sick, reported that all would recover if properly cared for; but the officers found that proper care was not easy aboard ship. Passengers daily petitioned the New York Council to be allowed to come ashore, and outright desertions mounted until Drummond became concerned that he might be unable to muster enough hands to get his ship back to the Company. The *Unicorn* was so disabled that she could be refitted only at great expense. It was finally

6. *Cal. State Papers, 1699,* nos. 878, 470-75; Bellomont to Board of Trade, Oct. 30, 1699, and Board of Trade to Bellomont, Apr. 11, 1700, *N.Y. Col. Docs.,* IV, 595, 630; *Darien Papers,* 146.

decided to leave her at Perth Amboy and combine her manpower with that of the *Caledonia* for the voyage home.[7]

In spite of these difficulties, Thomas Drummond slipped out of New York with a sloop loaded with men and supplies bound back to Caledonia. This testified to the good faith of the remaining leaders toward the isthmian enterprise, but it came as a rude shock to Nanfan. His cryptic note to Bellomont, "the Caledonians, with the advice and assistance of their countrymen, have played us not fair," greatly agitated the already suspicious governor. He clamored for fuller information about what happened in New York, and confirmation of his worst fears was not long in coming. A letter from Paroculus Parmyter, the naval officer in New York, reported that from their "starving condition" the Scots had now, indeed, grown "very insolent."[8]

The return to Caledonia owed much to Samuel Vetch, who had discovered a way to buy a sloop and furnish it for the voyage while staying within the law. He had become acquainted with Stephen Delancey and Thomas Wenham, two wealthy New York merchants, members of the clique which had enjoyed the favor of the former governor, Fletcher. They had been very active in venturing their money on piratical voyages to Madagascar and had reaped vast profits, in which, it was rumored, Fletcher had shared. Now they gathered in "constant cabals and clubs" to protest the vigor with which Bellomont was attacking illegal trade and piracy, a policy which had resulted in eliminating a source of profit for the colony and in driving away the adventurers who had supplied New York outfitters with sorely needed coin and exotic merchandise. Vetch found Delancey and Wenham willing to fit out a sloop for the Scots in return for a large part of the trade goods of the *Caledonia* and *Unicorn*, which were put ashore as security in his custody.

Vetch would dispose of these as he was able, in satisfaction of

7. Bellomont to Board of Trade, Oct. 20, 1699, *N.Y. Col. Docs.*, IV, 592; *Darien Papers*, 143, 155; N.Y. Council Minutes, Aug. 15, 23 and 29 (N.Y. State Lib., Albany); *Cal. State Papers, 1699*, no. 878, encl. 34-35.

8. *Darien Papers*, 155; Borland to Mackay, Boston, Sept. 19, Nanfan to Bellomont, Oct. 9, Bellomont to Nanfan, Oct. 16 and 23, Parmyter to Bellomont, Sept. 25, Bellomont to Board of Trade, Oct. 20, 1699, *Cal. State Papers, 1699*, no. 878; also in *N.Y. Col. Docs.*, IV, 592.

the New Yorkers' investment. As long as the goods remained merely as security, whatever the future intent concerning their disposition, it would be difficult for the Crown officials in New York to establish a case against the Scots for illegal trade. Nor could it be proved that Delancey or Wenham had actually given aid to the settlement at Caledonia, since Drummond's destination was officially unknown. The only clearly illegal act was Drummond's sailing without proper clearance. And he was safe and away, out of the clutches of authority.[9]

Vetch resolved not to accompany Drummond on his return to Darien. Paterson reported shortly before he left for England, "Mr. Samuel Vetch acquainted me that he designed to stay there this winter and that in the mean time he would look after the effects put ashore to satisfy Messrs. Wenham and Delancey and that by that means he would be in readiness to go back to the colony when he should receive the Company's orders." Finding him determined to stay, Paterson did not argue.[10] This decision did not imply a lack of political courage or resolution. He had heard that another large body of settlers, headed by a new group of councilors, was returning to the colony. His own brother William was one of the leaders. He reasoned that his presence there would be of little help, and he knew that in New York he might be of considerable assistance. He had entrusted Drummond with a letter to his brother, recommending his friend highly and recording his own decision to stay on at New York, where he "could do more service . . . than at home." As a fund for the purchase of future supplies for Caledonia, he asked for a bill of exchange of £2,000 drawn on Delancey and Wenham, "for it is from hence we must be supported."[11]

The councilors had long since agreed that credit in the northern colonies would allow the settlement to be supplied more effectively than from Scotland. Vetch may have thought, too, that such a

9. Paterson's Report to the Directors, and Vetch to William Veitch, Sept. 20, 1699, *Darien Papers*, 197, 156-57; Bellomont to Board of Trade, May 8, 1698, *N.Y. Col. Docs.*, IV, 303. For Bellomont's repeated accounts of the opposition to his measures on the part of the anti-Leislerian party, see Bellomont's letters, *N.Y. Col. Docs.*, IV, 303-538.

10. *Darien Papers*, 197.

11. *Darien Papers*, 156-57.

credit would allow him to compensate Delancey and Wenham for their assistance in the event that it proved difficult for him to dispose of the goods he had on hand.

It was unlikely that Vetch would lack a market. Under the prevailing administration of the customs office, it was not difficult to get goods into the channels of trade without the approval of His Majesty's officers. After the excitement over Drummond's departure died down, the underwriters could quietly assume possession of the Scottish linens, woolens, and hardware and, if necessary, ship them away to trade elsewhere. The port's officials could not be everywhere at once, and it was manifestly impossible for them to keep such a store under constant surveillance. There was too much shore line, there were too many ships, and there were too few officials. If discovered, it could be claimed that the goods were merely being returned to the Company of Scotland or traded on the Company's account with the people of "any country not at war with the English King." Scotland's trading position under the Navigation Act of 1695 put that country in an anomalous but easily exploitable position, as merchants in England had been quick to see and complain of at the time.

Vetch's management of the affair disproved the fears of his countrymen in Boston. Borland and other Scots merchants there had not appreciated the loyalty and effort which Vetch and the Drummonds were expending in New York in the interest of the national enterprise. They reported rumors that the Caledonians were in a "cabal to turn pirates, sell the stuff, and divide the spoils," and they feared the Scots would neither return the ships to Scotland nor go back to Darien. But none of these fears materialized, and nothing indicated they were ever based on fact.[12]

Vetch's own words in the letter to his brother attested to his good intentions. His grueling experience had reinforced his belief that "piety is the best policy and sincere honesty the surest way to honor." A depth of feeling was reflected in his final words, where, in syntax reminiscent of a Presbyterian benediction, he bestowed good wishes on the brother who had been close to him in former adversity: "God himself direct, counsel, and prosper

12. Borland, Campbell, and Maxwell to Hugh Fraser, Boston, Sept. 23, 1699, *ibid.*, 157-59.

you in all your undertakings and send us a good account of you, and a blythe meeting." It was Vetch's last letter to William. The second settlement, like the first, was plagued by dissent among the leaders, and at last it fell to an assault by the Spaniards. William Veitch died aboard ship in the Caribbean while returning home from the defeated colony.[13]

For Bellomont, the escape of Drummond was a serious matter which might be held against his administration. The wrathful governor swore to Nanfan that he wished the lieutenant governor had not "burned your fingers with them." But in submitting to England a full record of the Scots' ungrateful behavior, Bellomont was at pains to absolve himself and Nanfan from any blame. It had proved impossible, he asserted, for the lieutenant governor to check the insolence of his visitors. They had stayed out of his reach and within the bounds of strict legality. Acting under their own authority as councilors of the Caledonia colony, Vetch, Paterson, and the Drummonds had dispatched the sloop and signed the letter of marque and reprisal against the Spaniards which Thomas Drummond carried away with him. The action of Delancey and Wenham had been but one more example of the readiness of New York merchants to advance their fortunes without regard to English laws and duly-constituted authority.

Authorities in England, with a full picture of events from Bellomont's lengthy reports, knew very well the situation with the factious New York leaders and had reason to be well satisfied, in general, with the governor's campaign to bring the province under obedience to royal commands. Nor could anyone who was realistic expect the Scots to have been any less zealous in prosecuting their national enterprise.[14]

Thomas Drummond's departure was not the only "insolence" offered Nanfan by the refugees. While a Scottish merchant ship, the *Adventure*, was proceeding to her anchorage in New York harbor, Captain Drummond sent men with "drawn cutlasses" to invite her master aboard the *Caledonia*. Peter Wessels, the Dutch harbor master, was ordered to bring the vessel to anchor under

13. *Ibid.*, 156-57, 229, and 222-66 *passim; Mrs. Veitch Memoirs*, 55.
14. Bellomont to Nanfan, Oct. 16-23, Bellomont to Board of Trade, and Parmyter to Bellomont, Sept. 25, 1699, *Cal. State Papers, 1699*, no. 878. See also *N.Y. Col. Docs.*, IV, 595.

the guns of the *Caledonia*. The refugees probably hoped to entice the master, Howell, to sail for Darien, but Howell, as Vetch reported it, was too drunk to be reasoned with. It is likely that they kept him that way to prevent him from testifying to his own side of the story; when called to account by the Council, Vetch claimed that they were only delaying the *Adventure* to give advice to the master. Nanfan wanted to remove Drummond from his vessel and make an example of him, if he had had the force, but, as he ruefully wrote the governor, "I had it not and could get no advice from the Attorney."[15]

Lacking the loyal support of subordinate officials and the means to enforce his rulings, the lieutenant governor was in no position to maintain the laws he was instructed to uphold. The governor's Council and the colonial Assembly were made up of, or dominated by, the principal men of the province. These merchants and landowners were unsympathetic with the English problems of trade and revenue. When the colonial leaders in New York sided with the royal prerogative, it was to uphold their own position against the encroachment of their social and economic inferiors, not because they had England's mercantile strength at heart. Governors sought in vain for less provincial-minded councilors, but even men raised from the lower ranks of society soon perceived that their new position gave them, in turn, a chance to promote their own affairs.

The colonial governor could station ships in the ports and call up the militia, but these tenuous agents of his authority were more apt to side with the great men of the colony than with the governor. When their orders seemed contrary to the interests of the colonists, the military moved sluggishly and ineffectively. Captains of English men-of-war in the ports were likely to take the view that it was not their business to fight the governor's domestic battles for him.[16]

In the face of opposition from the entrenched aristocrats, it was impossible to oppose the effrontery of the Caledonians. Important

15. Minutes of Council, Aug. 18-23 and Sept. 12-13, Nanfan to Bellomont, Oct. 30, 1699, *Cal. State Papers, 1699*, no. 878.

16. Bellomont to Board of Trade, Aug. 24, 1699, *N.Y. Col. Docs.*, IV, 550 ff.; Bellomont to Board of Trade, Oct. 24, 1699, *Cal. State Papers, 1699*, no. 890. See also other letters of Bellomont to Board of Trade in this period.

men in the province had no interest in harassing the Scots; some preferred to help them. Indeed, their antagonism to the governor was so great that they welcomed the affair as a means of embarrassing him: they could hit back at his zealous suppression of their trade by giving aid to the Scots. Unable to take action, Nanfan must have sighed with relief when Robert Drummond finally hoisted anchor and sailed away for Scotland early in October.

The refugees sailed without Vetch, whose decision to remain in America was not without foundation. His father had been interested in a scheme of Sir John Cochran's to establish a colony in the Carolinas. At the time, the plan was construed to be a cover for the conspiracy against Charles II. That the project was a reality is indicated by the fact that the elder Veitch had gone so far as to advise his wife to make ready for the trip. Even Mrs. Veitch, though ill-prepared so late in life to make a new start in America and heartsick at the thought of leaving "these covenanted lands," had expressed herself content if God "had more service for me and mine in another land." So the idea was no novelty to Samuel. He had joined the expedition to Darien to seek broader opportunities than his homeland offered. With the final collapse of the Caledonian enterprise, a return to Darien was ruled out. It was only natural that he should stay on in the northern colonies.[17]

But his decision made an unfavorable impression on the directors of the Company of Scotland. It had not taken Paterson long, after he reached Edinburgh, to clear the remaining councilors of blame for the failure of the first expedition. Although unhappy about the abandonment of Caledonia, the Company was persuaded by Paterson that the fault lay with "those moles of Councilors who had not foresight enough to provide for the danger before it came upon them." Paterson had regained his health and his mind; he remained remarkably calm and dispassionate amid the tumult of accusation and recrimination which engaged the backers of the enterprise in Scotland. He was finally able to report that "the Company are exceedingly hearty and sensible and do seem to make amends for any former neglect or defect." The verdict of Scotland was that of Paterson: "In short, our

17. *Mrs. Veitch Memoirs*, 7-8; *Veitch Memoirs*, 147-48, ed. note.

Tarpolian Councilors, and raw heads, and undigested thoughts ruined us. . . . There was not one of the old Councilors fit for government; and things were gone too far before the new took place."[18]

This statement cleared Vetch of any onus attached to the abandonment of the colony. But Paterson was unable to explain to the directors' satisfaction why Vetch had remained in New York or what he was doing with the cargo the *Caledonia* had left there. Nor could Captain Robert Drummond enlighten them any further, for Vetch alone had managed the transactions with Delancey and Wenham. What the Company wanted was an accounting. At Paterson's suggestion, a letter was sent to Thomas Drummond, now safely arrived at Caledonia, asking if he could account for the cargo, "Captain Samuel Vetch having thought fit to stay behind at New York, and giving us but shuffling accounts of those matters."[19]

In a letter to Vetch, the directors used sharp language but were obviously unsure of their ground. Vetch and the goods were clearly beyond their control; it was hard to know how best to proceed, whether to threaten or cajole. They hesitated to accuse Vetch of peculation, unable to decide whether to take a strong stand or to give him the benefit of the doubt in the hope that he was remaining faithful to his trust. And they displayed a defensive awareness that their own shortcomings had contributed to developments. In answer to earlier letters criticizing the choice of goods sent on the expedition, they argued that experienced traders had selected the cargo. "You profess yourself wholly ignorant in those matters," they wrote; therefore, "be more sparing of such censures for the future at least till you learn to be more skillful in merchandizing." As for his remaining in New York, "You tell us it was thought convenient you should stay behind at New York, we never as yet learn by whom it was thought convenient but by yourself."[20]

18. *Darien Papers*, 258-60. "Tarpolian Councilors" or "Tarpaulin Councilors" refers to the sea captains.

19. Directors to Council on the *Rising Sun*, Edinburgh, Feb. 10, 1700, *ibid.*, 266.

20. Directors to a party unknown [Vetch], in New York, Edinburgh, Mar. 1700, *ibid.*, 287-88.

No one knows what happened to the cargo entrusted to Vetch. Without knowledge of the value of the goods or of the prices charged by Delancey and Wenham in supplying Thomas Drummond, it is difficult to know whether Vetch was left with anything he might put to his own use or whether he compounded with the New York merchants for a share in their profits on the venture. But there is nothing to indicate that Vetch had any intention other than to remain in New York as a servant of the colony and its directors.

It is possible, of course, that when news came of the final collapse of the Darien project in the early spring of 1700, Vetch annexed any Company assets remaining in his hands. Paterson and Drummond certainly gave the directors the impression that assets existed for which Vetch was accountable. Moreover, Vetch very shortly set himself up in private trading ventures, although it is true that he did not lack for underwriters and need not have possessed any capital or goods to begin with. His character and the sincerity of his protestations answered the accusations. But if he did convert the goods of the Company to his own use, he was abiding by the morality of his time, which tended to condone any action which went unnoticed by the law. The Scots have a word for it—Vetch was nothing if not "canny."

Vetch also remained in New York for another and compelling reason. He was in love with Margaret Livingston, and the match he had in mind was a promising one. It would have been impossible for Vetch not to have encountered New York's most prominent Scot, Robert Livingston, lord of the Manor of Livingston, an extensive tract on the east bank of the Hudson River. Livingston was the son of John Livingston of Ancrum, the famous divine, whose other son, William, had been one of the witnesses at Vetch's baptism and was Vetch's uncle by marriage. The family connection was recognized from the first; Robert Livingston and Vetch addressed each other as "kinsman" and "cousin."

Several of Livingston's nephews had served on the expedition to Caledonia, and one languished in Carthagena's prison after the capture of the *Dolphin's* crew. Livingston and his eldest son, John, a carefree man about town in New York, had been back to England and Scotland within the last five years and therefore had intimate knowledge of the national project for colonization; they had received frequent urging from the family to assist the colony. Livingston knew the eminent place held by Vetch's father in Scotland's general assembly and knew his powerful connections.[21]

As soon as the New York Council had extended credit to the Scots to buy provisions, Robert Livingston had taken over the supplying of the ships. A close bond of friendship developed between Samuel Vetch and John Livingston. Vetch was welcomed into his cousin's society on visits up the river to the Manor. Here he met Margaret, and cousinly affection blossomed at once into love. She was almost eighteen, within four days of being just thirteen years younger than Samuel Vetch. An agreeable looking but hardly beautiful girl, Margaret was plain featured and had inherited her father's sharp nose. Her portrait indicates a woman of intelligence and strength of character.[22]

Vetch could scarcely have made a more influential connection. Robert Livingston's support provided Vetch immunity from molestation by the governor or lieutenant governor. Livingston had received the good opinion of Bellomont in England during his visit in 1695 when he had apprised the future governor of the New York political situation, which was embroiled with the residual feuds of Leisler's rebellion. Livingston had been as opposed to Leisler as anyone, more opposed than most. But he had been treated badly by Governor Fletcher, Bellomont's predecessor, and had temporarily swung over to a middle position, seeking to oust the anti-Leislerian faction from control in New York. Later, in his efforts to undo the political favoritism of Fletcher, who made excessive land grants and connived at illegal trade, Bellomont, too, found himself in opposition to the anti-Leislerians.[23]

21. Florence Van Rensselaer, *The Livingston Family in America and its Scottish Origins*, arranged by William Laimbeer (New York, 1949); Edwin Brockholst Livingston, *The Livingstons of Livingston Manor* (New York, 1910); *Veitch Memoirs*, 259; Vetch to Livingston, Sept. 11, 1699, William and James Livingston to Robert Livingston, Edinburgh, Jan. 4, 1700, and "Journal," Jan. 11, 1695, Livingston Papers.

22. Vetch to Robert Livingston, Sept. 11, 1699, John Livingston to Vetch, Albany, Sept. 1700, and "Baker's Account," Aug. 5–Sept. 18, 1699, Livingston Papers; Van Rensselaer, *Livingston Family*, 81-82. The portrait, artist unknown, is in the Museum of the City of New York. See frontispiece.

23. "Journal," Jan. 11, 1695, Livingston Papers.

It was Robert Livingston who had introduced Bellomont to Captain William Kidd and had taken an active part in backing Kidd's luckless voyage against the buccaneers. If Livingston had reason to be uneasy about the way that voyage had turned out, he could take comfort in the fact that Bellomont was involved as deeply as he was. Kidd had allegedly turned pirate himself and was now in jail in Boston. Bellomont hoped that by pressing Kidd's prosecution he could rescue his own reputation. If the Kidd affair caused him to cool slightly toward Livingston and seek to dissociate himself from the Scot, it was nonetheless true that he still knew Livingston was essential to the government for his financial prowess and for his experience in handling Indian affairs.[24]

Livingston was a member of the New York Council and within a year was to be reappointed to his important Albany posts: collector of the excise, receiver of quitrents, town clerk, and clerk of local courts. He had long been secretary of the highly important Indian commission, the head of which was Peter Schuyler, sometime Albany mayor, fellow member of the Council, and Livingston's brother-in-law. Livingston was also connected by marriage and business associations with many of the other leading families in the province, among them the Van Cortlandts, Van Rensselaers, Delanceys, and Phillipses. These families were on the anti-Leislerian side and were opposed to Bellomont and his faction. So amid the deep divisions of New York politics, Robert Livingston and, through him, Vetch maintained a foot in each camp.[25] Vetch's connections with Livingston were of inestimable advantage.

24. Bellomont to Board of Trade, June 28, 1698, *N.Y. Col. Docs.*, IV, 331. Bellomont was aware, too, that Livingston was one of those holders of excessive land grants against whom Bellomont constantly inveighed; see *Cal. State Papers, 1699*, nos. 740, 402-7, and Bellomont to Board of Trade, Aug. 24, 1699, *ibid.* The Kidd affair may be traced in the same volume. See also *N.Y. Col. Docs.*, IV, 759-65.

25. Board of Trade Report on Province of New York, Bellomont to Board of Trade, Oct. 2, Order in Council, Oct. 25, Instructions to Bellomont, Nov. 10, 1698, N.Y. Council Minutes, VIII, 165 (N.Y. State Lib., Albany); Sept. 13, 1700, *N.Y. Col. Docs.*, IV, 396, 399, 411, 424. Robert Livingston's wife was Alida Schuyler, sister of Peter Schuyler, and the widow of Nicholas Van Rensselaer. Livingston's brother-in-law was Stephen Van Cortlandt. See letters on trade between Livingston and prominent New York merchants in the Livingston Papers *passim.*

Although identified with Livingston, Vetch was a late-comer and found it easier to keep himself free of party turmoil and to rise above it on important occasions, since his residence in the colony began well after the period of Leislerian excesses.

The courtship of Samuel and Margaret was no whirlwind affair, perhaps because Vetch may have been uncertain at first whether he was going to stay in New York, perhaps because Margaret was slow to make up her mind about accepting him. At any rate, he had to liquidate his responsibilities in the Caledonian venture and establish himself in the colonies. His affairs in New York precluded frequent visits with the Livingstons during the winter of 1699-1700, but many letters passed up and down the Hudson, carried by Margaret's brother John. With the coming of summer, Robert Livingston, busy in New York with the sessions of the legislature, could give little thought to arrangements for a wedding.[26] Letters from Scotland also threatened to wreck the romance. Robert's brother William had heard that Vetch "was making love to your daughter, Margaret," and he added that "if any such thing be concluded with you, I wish them much joy." But otherwise, this brother, who was so close to the Veitch family by marriage and who had witnessed the baptism of the baby Samuel, felt himself obliged to offer "my positive advice that you do what you can to oppose it, and never to suffer it until he clear himself of what the Company had here . . . to lay to his charge." He concluded by saying, however, that if this advice came too late, nothing should be said about it at all.[27]

An even more antagonistic letter from Scotland was written by Livingston's niece, Janet Miller:

Truly out of love to my cousin I thought it my duty to advertise her something of what character that person is under here—yea I should be ashamed to let any here know that your daughter should entertain such a man who is hated by all his country and that for his evil deed; therefore I should beg of you . . . that you

26. Vetch to Robert Livingston, Sept. 11, 1699, Vetch to Livingston, May 11, 1700, Livingston Papers, Group 1a, box 1; John Livingston to Vetch, Sept. 1700, *ibid.*, Group 7a-o, box 1. Livingston's baby daughter Catherine died in Dec. 1699, which may also have acted to postpone wedding plans.

27. James Livingston to Robert Livingston, Jan. 4, and William Livingston to Robert Livingston, Mar. 30, 1700, Livingston Papers.

may not in any means countenance such a match for by his near relations I hear they care not though they never hear any more of any of the brethren William or Samuel. . . . my love to my cousins, especially Margaret. I hope she'll not take it ill that I am too plain, but if I can do anything that may prevent her ruin I have gained my end.

However this opinion may have reflected feeling in Scotland, it did not arrive in time to influence the event. On the very day Janet penned these vehement lines, December 20, 1700, Samuel and Margaret received a license from Governor Bellomont for their marriage at the Manor house on the Hudson.[28]

Because Robert Livingston had not received full payment on his long-standing claims against the government for victualling His Majesty's soldiery during the recent war with the French and was again fully extended in providing advancements for the government, he was unable to furnish Margaret with the dowry he considered appropriate. But he credited £300 to Vetch in 1706 with the notation, "which your wife would have had at her marriage if the Public had paid me what they owed." And the couple did receive a house and lot in New York, estimated to be worth a thousand pounds, in which to begin their life together. Fronting on Pearl Street, this house was one of the most impressive of the dwellings lining the New York waterfront. A "palatial residence with . . . high roof and two stacks of chimneys," it is easily picked out in the "Burgis View" of the town made in 1716.[29]

28. Janet Miller to Robert Livingston, Edinburgh, Dec. 20, 1700, received June 1701, *ibid.; Year Book of the Holland Society of New York, 1905* (New York, 1905), 1. A letter of Margaret's signed with her married name, Nov. 24, 1700, is in the Livingston Papers, which would indicate that Bellomont's license merely formalized a ceremony which had taken place sometime the previous month.

29. Account with Samuel Vetch to 1726, Account Book of Robert Livingston, Livingston Papers, Group 1a, box 5; will of Margaret Vetch, New York Historical Society, *Collections,* Publication fund series, 29 (1897), 244; will of Robert Livingston, 1728, and ed. note by William S. Pelletreau, N.Y. Hist. Soc., *Collections,* Pub. fund ser., 27 (1893), 347; Duncan Campbell to Robert Livingston, N.Y., July 16, 1701, Livingston Papers. For the "Burgis View," see Stokes, *Iconography of Manhattan Island,* I, 247, and plate 25. Livingston bought the house in the 1690's from the then respected merchant and sea captain William Kidd and his wife and brother-in-law. They had received it on the death of Mrs. Kidd's former husband, William Cox, to whom the city had granted it in 1687.

Any house, and particularly such a fine one, was an asset of first importance for Vetch, in view of the congestion in the town and the shortage of housing accommodations. The connection with the Livingstons and this proud home gave Vetch a substantial position from which to begin his career in the colonies. He was not long in finding an outlet for his abilities.

CHAPTER FOUR

Design for Trade

IN SEEKING TO ESTABLISH himself financially, it was natural that Vetch should turn to commerce. The merchants of New York were largely interested in ventures at sea; the principal industries of the town were shipbuilding, outfitting of ships, cooperage, and milling of flour, all auxiliary to the export trade. The great men of the province dealt in the export of furs, whale oil, flour, and other provisions; they also imported a variety of goods, principally from England, the West Indies, and the tobacco colonies.

Vetch had reason to feel well satisfied with the turn of events which had cast him ashore in this thriving business community among people congenial to his tastes. In his own words,

The strange providences which I have been witness to, and in some measure partaken of, . . . and which have concurred to my coming hither, have made me often say with the Psalmist, that his wayes are in the deep water and his paths past finding out, . . . yet I am forced to acknowledge that his mercy is above all his works and his loving kindness past expression to me-wards.[1]

Vetch may have had the capital or goods saved from the wreck of the Darien venture; certainly he could borrow a stake from other merchants. The project of the Company of Scotland had been primarily a trading enterprise. With such experience to offer, along with his own ability, Vetch would find no lack of

1. Vetch to William Veitch, N.Y., Sept. 20, 1699, *Darien Papers*, 156. The quotation from the Book of Psalms was one of Vetch's favorites. It is apparently from Psalm 77, verse 19, although the meaning derived from it is not the meaning attributed to it by Biblical scholars. The habit of taking this Biblical quotation out of context was not limited to Vetch; William Cowper, many years later, apparently drew on this verse for his well-known hymn, "God moves in a mysterious way, His wonders to perform."

partners to furnish capital. As early as the *Caledonia*'s return to
Scotland, he had shipped off a cargo of beaver, otter, and bearskins
obtained from Livingston, for which he paid Brant Schuyler, his
future father-in-law's agent in New York.[2] Vetch was plunging
into trade, the arena of public controversy then convulsing the
province. By some unerring instinct he had again found his way
into the midst of momentous affairs.

When Bellomont had arrived in New York to take up his
governorship, he had found a vastly complicated political situation. It was no simple projection of the animosities aroused by
the Leislerian struggle ten years before and perpetuated by the
excesses in quelling the rebellion.[3] Bellomont's commissions had
established him as governor of New York, Massachusetts Bay, and
New Hampshire. As captain general, he was given command in
time of war of the militia and any Regulars not only in his own
colonies but also in the Jerseys, Connecticut, and Rhode Island.
This return to a semblance of the old Dominion of New England
arose primarily from the threat of the French on the northern
borders of the colonies. The realization of this threat had been
heightened during King William's War.[4]

Unfortunately, in New York the ruling aristocracy, which
might have been counted on to second Bellomont's efforts toward
consolidation and increased royal control, was instead rapidly
alienated by his zeal for a subsidiary matter. For Bellomont had
been set another task. The great East India Company had been
complaining about the depredations on its trade made by pirates.
Evidence coming from the colonies indicated that plunder from
the Indian Ocean was finding its way to America, while American
merchants shipped off rum, wines, guns, and ammunition to supply the marauders. Parliament and the Board of Trade had

2. Vetch to Robert Livingston, N.Y., Sept. 11, 1699, Livingston Papers.

3. Shifting combinations of interests, not principles, accounted for party
standards. Herbert L. Osgood, *The American Colonies in the Eighteenth
Century* (New York, 1924), I, chap. VII; Charles W. Spencer, *Phases of Royal
Government in New York, 1691-1719* (Columbus, Ohio, 1905); Alexander C.
Flick, ed., *History of the State of New York* (New York, 1933-37), II, 155 ff.;
Beverly McAnear, "Politics in Provincial New York 1689-1761" (unpublished
Ph.D. dissertation, Stanford University, 1935). See also the list of Council of
Colony of New York in "Calendar of Council Minutes, 1668-1783," N.Y. State
Lib., *Report*, Bulletin No. 58, 2 (1902), 7-8.

4. *N.Y. Col. Docs.*, IV, 262-73.

recognized this problem and included in Bellomont's instructions orders to crack down on the illegal trade and seize any pirates venturing into the colonies.[5]

It was fatal chance for Bellomont that the war ended before he reached his new governments. Energies which might have been directed to consolidating and strengthening the northern colonies under the pressure of war were instead dissipated in an endeavor to solve the subordinate problem of the regulation of trade. Faced with serving the divergent viewpoints of his royal master and his colonial subjects, the governor was put at an initial disadvantage.

Bellomont was shocked to find that New York, the stronghold of royal prerogative, was also a thriving center of illegal trade. Although Randolph's reports had left no doubt that encouragement to pirates and irregularities in commerce flourished from Virginia to the Piscataqua, there was nothing in Governor Fletcher's reports to prepare Bellomont for the discovery that "piracy and unlawful trade" were "the beloved twins of the merchants of this place."[6]

When Bellomont's new appointees in the collectorship and their subordinate searchers and tidewaiters attempted to carry out their duties, merchants put pressure on them to resign their posts. Violence flared during one attempted seizure. The "generality of the merchants" were so incensed at the attempt that they "corrupted" most of the evidence and terrified those witnesses who were to appear against them. Bellomont reported that "the merchants do daily curse and threaten those few persons that have assisted me in His Majesty's service."[7]

5. Nelson's Memorial, Sept. 24, 1696, Board of Trade to King, Feb. 26, 1697, letters of Jacob Leisler, Abraham Gouverneur, Peter De la Noy, *ibid.*, 206-11, 159-60, 212-24; Fletcher to Blathwayt, N.Y., Nov. 9, Council of New York to Board of Trade, Nov. 23, 1696, Board of Trade to King, Feb. 25, 1697, Board of Trade to Lords Justices, Sept. 30, 1696, *ibid.*, 243, 245, 259-60, 227-28; Bellomont's Instructions, Board of Trade to Bellomont, Mar. 21, 1698, *ibid.*, 284 ff., 299-300. See also narrative of William Willock, Randolph to Board of Trade, Aug. 25, 1698, Randolph and Quary reports, *Cal. State Papers, 1697-98*, nos. 723, 769, 786, 794; Robert N. Toppan, ed., *Edward Randolph* (Boston: The Prince Society, 1899), V, 39-43, 129, 169, 186-87; Leo Francis Stock, ed., *Proceedings and Debates of the British Parliaments respecting North America, 1542-1754* (Washington, 1924-41), II, 314-15, 386, 409.

6. Bellomont to Board of Trade, Dec. 14, 1698, *N.Y. Col. Docs.*, IV, 438. See also May 8, 1698, *ibid.*, 302 ff.

7. Bellomont to Board of Trade, June 1698, *ibid.*, 323-24.

The pirate ships were fitted out mainly in New York and Rhode Island. Merchants such as the Phillipses, father and son, Delancey, Wenham, and Heathcote had an interest in their voyages and sent ships of their own to Madagascar to carry arms, ammunition, and casks of rum and wines to the raiders in the Indian Ocean. Their returns were huge quantities of silver and gold, precious stones, and bales of "East India goods"—calicoes, muslin, silks, tea, and sugar. The same merchants were accustomed to exporting tobacco to Scotland, bringing back Scottish textiles and manufactured articles. They imported wine from the Canaries, cloth from Holland, and French wines and brandy from Newfoundland, all outside the Acts of Trade and Navigation. It was Delancey and Wenham who proved willing to negotiate with Vetch in outfitting the sloop for the return to Darien. Their connection with the notorious pirate Giles Shelly was known to Bellomont, as was Delancey's interest in the *Fortune,* the first of Bellomont's seizures.[8]

Actually, there was much to be said for this trade from the colonial point of view. It brought large quantities of "Arab gold" into the province, pieces of eight and other currencies vastly important to a trading group continually short of circulating media. It allowed the magnates to furnish their homes and dress their women in finery obtainable through legitimate channels only at prohibitive costs. The merchants were always uneasy over the need for returns to England to pay for imports, because, as Bellomont admitted, "their import of English goods do so overbalance their exports of the commodities of these countries that it makes them almost desperate." The illegal trade reduced the imports of English goods and gave the colonists a balance to pay for the remaining goods. Bellomont stated that if he had not discouraged piracy, "they would have brought in £100,000 in gold and silver."

8. Bellomont to Board of Trade, May 18, Randolph to Board of Trade, May 16, Bellomont to Board of Trade, May 25, Bellomont to Commissioners of the Customs, May 27, Bellomont to Board of Trade, June 22, 1698, Board of Trade to Bellomont, referring to Randolph's list of vessels trading from New York to Curacao and Madagascar, Jan. 5, 1699, Bellomont to Board of Trade, July 22, 1699, and Nov. 14, 1698, Board of Trade to Lords Justices, Aug. 10, 1699, *ibid.*, 306-10, 311, 317, 319, 323, 454, 531-38, 542. Also see narrative of William Willock, Randolph to Board of Trade, Aug. 25, 1698, Randolph and Quary reports, *Cal. State Papers, 1697-98*, nos. 723, 769, 786, 794.

It was no wonder that he found "this inrages them to the last degree, that they have missed all of this treasure and rich pennyworths of East India goods." A few years later, as certain pirates were turned off the gallows, Governor Dudley of Massachusetts wryly observed that it seemed a new and harsh thing to hang people that brought gold into the province.[9]

Furthermore, the colonists argued with the facts on their side; if the Acts of Trade were enforced in New York, the illegal cargoes would be landed elsewhere. The trade and population of the royal province would be diverted to the neighboring proprietary and charter governments where royal authority could not exert itself. It seemed to the colonists that Bellomont should have been working toward a unified system of colonies with uniform law enforcement which would not place the royal provinces at a disadvantage. Instead he was subjecting the New Yorkers to laws which were regularly evaded elsewhere.[10]

To give him credit, Bellomont realized the need for a solution to the problem of an unequal trade balance and sought tenaciously to build up new industries—naval stores, salt, potash, and even vineyards—which would furnish the colonies with legitimate exports which England needed.[11] He recognized the justice in the New Yorkers' complaint about the laxity of law enforcement in neighboring provinces, characterizing Governor Cranston of Rhode Island "an original for insolence and nonsense." He subjected the Board of Trade to a constant barrage of demands for trained and loyal officials for the administration of justice, noting "that which is the very soul of government, goes upon crutches in this Province." He realized that the colonies lacked trained lawyers who could determine what the legal structure would allow, counsel the merchants accordingly, and prosecute those

9. Bellomont to Board of Trade, Nov. 14, 1698, Bellomont to Board of Trade, Nov. 28, 1700, *N.Y. Col. Docs.*, IV, 538, 789-97; Curtis Putnam Nettels, *The Money Supply of the American Colonies before 1720*, University of Wisconsin Studies in the Social Sciences and History, XX (Madison, 1934), 244, 280; *Cal. State Papers, 1704-5*, no. 216.

10. Randolph to Popple, Apr. 25, 1698, Toppan, ed., *Edward Randolph*, V, 169; James Graham to Blathwayt, Sept. 19, 1698, Bellomont to Board of Trade, Apr. 27, 1699, *N.Y. Col. Docs.*, IV, 374-76, 507.

11. Bellomont to Board of Trade, Nov. 28, 1700, *N.Y. Col. Docs.*, IV, 789-97.

who evaded the laws. Chief Justice William Smith was a very worthy man, but no lawyer. Bellomont claimed that his naval officer, Paroculus Parmyter, and his collector of customs, Ducy Hungerford, knew more law than Attorney General James Graham. Of those practicing law in the colonies, "so far from being barristers, one of them was a Dancing Master, another a glover by trade, a third . . . condemned to be hanged in Scotland for burning the Bible and for blasphemy." All were ignorant of the law and violent enemies to the government as well. The courts were corrupted to the extent that one New York suitor expressed surprise to find that the way to justice was not, as he suspected, "like the way to Hell, smooth and broad."[12]

The merchants were perfectly willing to accept the benefits of the English colonial system, but they could hardly be expected not to exploit loopholes in the Acts of Trade or their enforcement, when the result was so rewarding. The laws were admittedly vague and uncertain; it was often beyond the capacity of authorities in England to decide disputed cases arising out of seizures by American officials. Under such circumstances, as Vetch discovered, it was tempting to customs collectors and even governors to "compound" with supposed violators rather than press charges. But Bellomont was a man of integrity, morally righteous and uncompromising, and although he saw the difficulties he would not permit any deviations from the letter of the law, if he could help it.[13]

At once, members of his Council, most of whom were merchants, were "ready to mutiny." The customs collector refused to carry out the laws and was suspended from his place on the Council. The suspension of almost all the Council followed, and the leading men of the province gathered to protest the disturbance of their trade.[14] Anger at Bellomont's interference rapidly solidified into

12. Bellomont to Popple, Sept. 15, 1699, Bellomont to Board of Trade, Dec. 15, 1698, Board of Trade to King, Dec. 14, 1699, Bellomont to Commissioners of Customs, Jan. 5 and Nov. 26, 1700, *ibid.*, 586, 441, 598-99, 602-3; New York Colonial Manuscripts, XLVII, 7 (N.Y. State Lib., Albany).

13. Toppan, ed., *Edward Randolph*, V, 118; Charles M. Andrews, *The Colonial Period of American History* (New Haven, 1938), IV, chap. VI *passim*. Randolph said that defects in the Acts of Trade rendered them "obscure and useless in the Plantations"; Penn criticized them as "darkly and inconsistently worded," and Quary agreed.

14. *N.Y. Col. Docs.*, IV, 302-3.

implacable political opposition. Fletcher and his Council had controlled an assembly elected in their interests and through their influence. Bellomont dissolved it, and in the subsequent elections "fighting and broken heads" testified to the party feeling he had aroused. His instructions had called upon him to take care in choosing his officials that "they be men of estate and ability, and not necessitous people or much in debt," as well as persons well affected to the government. But his zeal for His Majesty's laws had alienated the closely knit oligarchy of men with estates and ability who compelled, through their extensive landholdings and business operations, the obedience (if not the loyalty) of much of the population.[15]

Vetch's arrival in New York took place in the midst of these distractions. Although the governor was visiting Boston, Vetch would have found his presence no bar to his first essay at trading. Shipping furs to Scotland was distinctly illegal, but Bellomont would have been no more likely to discover the venture than Nanfan was.

Which party Vetch would side with in the province's rupture was never in question. As a Scot, he was no friend of English Acts of Trade and Navigation. As a member of the Company of Scotland, he had stood for free trade, willing to deal with all visitors to the strategically placed Darien colony—Spaniard, Indian, Englishman, or American colonist. As a friend of Delancey and Wenham, he unquestionably sympathized with the merchants whose petitions against the governor were going to England as he arrived. Moreover, by nature Vetch was not inclined to the "republican and independent principles" with which the Leislerian faction was thought to be imbued.[16]

But through his connection with Robert Livingston and two other Scots, Duncan Campbell of Boston and Attorney General James Graham, Vetch gained a degree of advantage with the

15. *Ibid.*, 285, 377-82, 507-10. The Board of Trade, in Bellomont's Instructions, had specifically pointed this out.

16. The phrase is Cadwallader Colden's, applied to the prejudices of William Smith, the historian, who, Colden believed, failed to grasp the unrealistic nature of the Leislerians' aspirations. Later conservatives have not improved on Colden's frank distrust of the "common man" or his respect for duly constituted authority. See Colden's letter to his son, N.Y. Hist. Soc., *Collections*, Pub. fund ser., 1 (1868), 206, 219, 234.

governor, however short-lived. For reasons of personal interest these men at first had nominally sided with Bellomont, although Livingston and Campbell were at the moment suspect because Bellomont had evidence that they had tried to get part of Kidd's booty. Bellomont too became increasingly dissatisfied with Graham's attitude, and Livingston was one of those great land-owners against whom Bellomont inveighed. But the governor found both Livingston and Graham indispensable and was perforce obliged to keep them in favor. And Bellomont owed an obligation to Campbell; he had lived in the Scot's house during his stay in Boston and had employed him to help capture Captain Kidd.[17]

Although these associations gave Vetch some advantage with the governor, they did not militate in the least against his connections with the opposition. Livingston gave Vetch access to the Schuylers and Van Cortlandts, and through complicated intermarriages and business ties he came to know Nicholas Bayard and William Nicholl, all leaders of the merchant group. David Jamison, another prominent anti-Leislerian, was a fellow countryman. Through these men Vetch certainly came in contact with others prominently in opposition to Bellomont: Colonel Thomas Willet, Robert Lurting, and other churchwardens of Trinity Church, who with the business group were also petitioning the Crown against the governor; Rip Van Dam; Philip French, lately speaker of the Assembly under Fletcher; and the Phillipses, father and son, whom Vetch must have known also in their capacity as "greatest traders to Albany." The elder, Frederick Phillipse, had the reputation of being both the richest and the dullest man in New York.[18]

The young man established business connections slowly, shrewdly evaluating the situation and perhaps negotiating for a ship and cargo. When Bellomont returned from Boston in the

17. *N.Y. Col. Docs.*, IV, 331-32, 315, 584, 598-99, 719, 811-13. Campbell was put forward as a candidate for sheriff of Suffolk County (Boston) by Bellomont as a man "zealous to serve that country to the best of his capacity," but he was not elected and followed the governor back to New York to seek some preferment there. Massachusetts Historical Society, *Collections*, 6th ser., 5 (1892), 73-74.

18. Mass. Hist. Soc., *Collections*, 6th ser., 3 (1889), 497n; *N.Y. Col. Docs.*, IV, 311, 527-28; Lansdowne Mss., no. 849, 1-15 (Lib. Cong. Transcripts). The Robert Livingston papers include exchanges of letters between Livingston and Graham, Jamison, Campbell, and Van Cortlandt.

spring of 1700, Vetch watched political developments with a keen eye for his own opportunities. He and Duncan Campbell accompanied the governor to Albany in August, to observe Bellomont's conference with the Indians. Upon their return, Vetch had a chance to meet survivors of the second Darien expedition, whose ship, the *Rising Sun,* had been wrecked in a storm off Carolina. The same month, October, William Penn and Francis Nicholson, then lieutenant governor of Virginia, visited New York and attempted to reconcile Bellomont with his leading citizens. It was a fruitless effort, but it probably provided Vetch with the opportunity of meeting Nicholson, the man who was to play such an important role in his future.[19]

Vetch's family background, continental education, and erstwhile military rank easily gained him acceptance in the highest levels of colonial society. The eighteenth century, heedful of status, esteemed him a gentleman. He was at ease with the political and business leaders in whose circles he moved, and there was no question of his eligibility for a place in their counsels.

During this time Vetch traveled into New England. There, through the Livingstons, he became acquainted with Fitzjohn Winthrop, governor of Connecticut. Many years before, when he was appointed by Leisler to lead the colonial troops against Canada, Winthrop had come to know the Albany leaders. The friendship between the Livingstons and Winthrops had been a lasting one; young John Livingston had been sent to New England for over a year of schooling under Winthrop's supervision in 1691,[20] and shortly after Vetch married Margaret Livingston, John wed Governor Winthrop's daughter Mary. Winthrop had a high regard for the elder Livingston—John's good qualities had "greatly endeared him to me"—and he had always thought highly of "fayre Mistress Margaret."

It was an immensely useful connection for Vetch. Winthrop was greatly loved and honored by the people of Connecticut as a man of good sense and wide outlook. The role of his family in New England had been an important one; his own position was commanding, and his brother Wait Winthrop was one of the

19. *Cal. State Papers, 1700,* no. 845v; *N.Y. Col. Docs.,* IV, 711, 725.
20. Mass. Hist. Soc., *Collections,* 6th ser., 3 (1889), 511.

leaders of the Massachusetts Bay Colony. In these men Vetch had associates with a breadth of view and cosmopolitan outlook important for his later attempts to solve colonial and imperial problems of defense and administration. More immediately, as it turned out, he had in them friends where he needed friends.[21]

It is likely that Vetch visited Boston, where a sizable group of Scottish merchants resided. One of the most prominent, John Borland, was a brother of the clergyman who had gone on the second expedition to Darien. He was engaged in the lucrative trade between Boston and Newfoundland, Quebec, and Nova Scotia. This trade furnished the French with cloth from England and Scotland, tobacco from the southern colonies, beer, rum, and provisions from New England, and English guns, ammunition, and hardware. In return, furs, French wines and brandy, and assorted European goods were brought to New England.

Bellomont had reported that "a certain merchant," probably Borland, had offered him a partnership in the trade, "which he said would be very beneficial." But of course the governor had refused. It was illegal, for the importation of European goods, except through England, was prohibited by the Act of 1663. But as Bellomont observed, "If the merchants of Boston be minded to run their goods, there's nothing to hinder them." The customs collector Jahleel Brenton had been in England for two years; his deputy was a merchant himself; and the tidewaiters were busy running public houses. Bellomont had his troubles with the merchants of New York, but he could not even begin to reduce illegal trade in New England, where the coastline, the independent political organization "under so loose a management," and the Boston port regulations all conspired to make Massachusetts Bay merchants the most conspicuous example of illegal trading in America.

It was probably in Boston that Vetch found the inspiration for his next trading ventures. At any rate, Borland became his close associate in subsequent commercial transactions.[22] Early in the

21. Fitzjohn Winthrop to Robert Livingston, Dec. 9, John Livingston to his father, Dec. 10, 1700, Livingston Papers. This letter indicates that John was married in Dec. 1700, but printed records usually date it as the following Apr. Mass. Hist. Soc., *Collections*, 6th ser., 3 (1889), 512.
22. John Borland to Robert Livingston, Dec. 1699, Livingston Papers; Top-

year 1701, John Livingston came into possession of a sloop suitable for coastwise trading ventures. This vessel, the *Mary*, named for John's wife, may have been a portion of the dowry received from the Winthrops. In her short career the ship achieved lasting notoriety, and the journal of her voyage has become noteworthy in colonial annals.[23]

While John Livingston devised schemes for utilizing his new instrument of commerce, he brought his bride to New York. Joining the Vetches, they proceeded to the Manor near Albany, accepted the compliments of their kinsfolk, and introduced Mary Livingston to the society of the upper Hudson.

Robert Livingston remained in New York, too busy to accompany them. Bellomont had died unexpectedly while Lieutenant Governor Nanfan was in Barbados on personal business, and the Council and Assembly quarreled over political power. DePeyster, Staats, Walters, and Thomas Weaver, Leislerian sympathizers on the Council, refused to admit the right of Colonel William Smith, eldest member of the Council and its president, to assume interim governing power. Livingston and Schuyler supported Smith against the other councilors and the Assembly, who maintained that the governing power devolved on the entire Council, not on any single member, and refused to admit Smith's veto power or authority to prorogue or dissolve the Assembly. The government was indeed, as Livingston said, "much out of

pan, ed., *Edward Randolph*, V, 39-42; *N.Y. Col. Docs.*, IV, 776, 778-79, 789-97; George Larkin to Board of Trade, Newfoundland, Aug. 20, Bellomont to Board of Trade, Nov. 23, 1700, *Cal. State Papers, 1700*, nos. 756, 953.

23. Robert Livingston to Fitzhugh Winthrop, Apr. 14, 1701, Mass. Hist. Soc., *Collections*, 6th ser., 3 (1889), 66-67; Duncan Campbell to Robert Livingston, Dec. 2, 1700, Livingston Papers. Winthrop planned to will his estate to his daughter and "to put in a stock in money equal with what you shall do for your son to begin a trade." Shortly before his death Governor Bellomont wrote to inquire of the Board whether "Scotchmen are qualified to be owners and masters of ships." It was a matter "of great consequence to the trade of this place," according to the governor; Feb. 21, 1701, *N.Y. Col. Docs.*, IV, 845. One wonders whether he had in mind the possible trespasses against the navigation acts which the *Mary* might commit. Sir Thomas Trevor and Sir John Hawles, respectively attorney general and solicitor general, concurred in the opinion that every Scotchman, being a natural born subject of the king under common law, was accounted an Englishman so far as the Act of Navigation of 1660 was concerned, as explained by the Statute of Frauds of 1662; *Cal. State Papers, 1701*, nos. 188, 390, 507. See also Andrews, *Colonial Period*, IV, 65, 73, 124.

fame, our parties being more divided, I think, than eleven years ago, so little has my Lord's [Bellomont's] administration contributed to our union. The Council, Assembly, and indeed the whole province [are] divided and in a foment."[24]

Political turmoil so embroiled the community that business came to a standstill and little freight was available for cargoes to the usual markets in the West Indies. As an alternative, Livingston and Vetch, partners in the prospective voyages of the *Mary*, considered a venture to Newfoundland. The elder Livingston was dubious; in addition to its illegality, the voyage was hazardous. The Treaty of Ryswick had failed to dispel ever-darkening war clouds, and renewal of the clash between England and France was expected daily. It would go hard with any English vessel caught in French shipping lanes, should war break out. Moreover, the partners had no intention of confining their trade to English ports in the north. If their ship should be apprehended after a war had started, they would face the additional charge in their own colony of trading with the enemy.[25]

Vetch and Livingston, however, determined on the Newfoundland venture. Bellomont had virtually closed down the Madagascar trade; lack of flour and other exports slowed the West Indies trade. The Boston merchants trading to the north reaped attractive profits, and there was no shortage of goods suitable for that trade. Bellomont's death and the distraction of his officialdom seemed to offer commercial opportunities.[26]

Vetch left his wife at the Manor and with the John Livingstons proceeded to New London, where Mary was deposited with her parents. The men sailed on the thirteenth of June for Fishers Island, which, conveniently, was owned by the Winthrop family, and from there they put to sea. The attitude of the Winthrops was similar to that of Robert Livingston. They seemed troubled less by the illegality of the voyage than by uncertainty as to whether the young partners could carry it off successfully. Wait Winthrop wrote from Boston that the voyage "will no doubt

24. Livingston to Winthrop, Apr. 14, 1701, Mass. Hist. Soc., *Collections*, 6th ser., 3 (1889), 66-67; Smith, Livingston, and Schuyler to Board of Trade, Apr. 30 and May 5, 1701, *N.Y. Col. Docs.*, IV, 816, 857-63, 865-67.

25. Mass. Hist. Soc., *Collections*, 6th ser., 3 (1889), 66-67.

26. *N.Y. Col. Docs.*, IV, 789-97.

yield profit if they can go and return safe," and Governor Winthrop confessed to John's father, "I know not what to think of their design but hope you did well understand it beforehand."[27]

Light winds forced the *Mary* into Martha's Vineyard, delaying the voyage a few days. But it gave an opportunity for Livingston to send his father an accounting of his share in the venture, "in fear that it should please God to take me out of the world." Vetch and a third partner, John Saffin, a Boston merchant, were interested in the *Mary* and her cargo of woolens and rum. Livingston was anxious that his wife would get her fair share of the profits if anything should happen to him.[28]

All the fears proved unfounded. The voyage took almost exactly the two months expected; by the last week in August, Vetch and Livingston had returned with a valuable cargo of brandy, claret, and wines.[29] Vetch landed about half the cargo at Boston. He came in openly, depending on Massachusetts' reputation for indulgence of the northern trade. Both Massachusetts and New York had been without a governor since Lieutenant Governor Stoughton's death in July, and if any questions were raised, Wait Winthrop was judge of the Vice-Admiralty Court in Boston. But it appeared that Vetch had tempted fate too far. Within a week of Vetch's arrival, William Payne, the port's deputy collector, seized his cargo of £320 of brandy and wines.

Livingston hastily sailed off with the remaining cargo and put it ashore in the custody of one Captain Merritt at Morrisania, taking care not to risk a landing at New York. That port was not likely to prove safer than Boston for smuggled goods, especially since the town was still politically turbulent. Nanfan had come back to assume the government, the Leislerian party was in full control, and William Atwood had finally arrived to fill the posts of chief justice and judge of the Vice-Admiralty Court, in long-delayed answer to Bellomont's repeated requests for trained

27. Wait Winthrop to Fitzjohn Winthrop, June 16, 1701, Mass. Hist. Soc., *Collections*, 6th ser., 3 (1889), 85; Fitzjohn Winthrop to Livingston, July 16, 1701, Livingston Papers.

28. June 17, 1701, Livingston Papers.

29. John Livingston to Robert Livingston, Morrisania, Aug. 24, and John Livingston to his mother, N.Y., Aug. 28, 1701, *ibid.*

and loyal British officials to administer justice in the colony. It was no time to depend on the venality of port officials.[30]

Vetch's faith in the Winthrop connection was not misplaced, however; nor had he too far misjudged the nature of Boston's port authorities. His friend Borland had the cargo appraised, compounded with Payne for one-third of the nominal value of the goods, and Judge Wait Winthrop held a session of the Vice-Admiralty Court to regularize the transaction. Far from feeling his official responsibilities, Winthrop sympathized with the defendants, expressing his sorrow "for the mishap their being over public has brought them into."[31]

But this activity did not end the matter. Two months later, Judge Atwood published his commission supplanting Winthrop in the Court of Vice-Admiralty. Atwood reopened the case and charged Payne with embezzling the goods seized. It was too late; Vetch had recovered the better part of his illicit lading and "disposed of [it] into hands unknown." Payne refused to plead, and two of his assistants testified only with reluctance. The deputy collector was committed for contempt but appealed his case to the Superior Court of Massachusetts. The court supported him and issued a restraining order against execution of the sentence of the Vice-Admiralty Court.

Atwood was furious. He contended that the Massachusetts court was assuming unwarranted jurisdiction in entertaining an appeal from the Vice-Admiralty Court: it was an affront to His Majesty's court and an obstruction to the exercise of his commission. He pointed out that such power over the decisions of admiralty courts was not even pretended by King's Bench in England—which indicated how little the colonials knew of the law. His efforts were unavailing. Atwood returned to New York unsatisfied, condemning the province's management which encouraged "men to venture upon the like violations of the Laws of England, . . . that there had been too great connivance at this practice." Whether Winthrop joined his fellow justices in the verdict is

30. *Cal. State Papers, 1701*, no. 632, July 10, announcing the death of Stoughton; also see nos. 681 and 344 and *ibid., 1700*, no. 1086. Winthrop was also chief justice in the colony; Mass. Hist. Soc., *Collections*, 6th ser., 5 (1892), 95.

31. Wait Winthrop to Fitzjohn Winthrop, Sept. 1, 1701, Mass. Hist. Soc., *Collections*, 6th ser., 5 (1892), 99.

uncertain. He was nursing a dog-bite, incurred on a visit to a sick friend.[32]

As for Vetch, he was already off to repeat his success. The partners had made a profit and immediately set about loading their vessel for another trip. Governor Winthrop had rejoiced at their safe return, which made amends "for all our fears for them," and considered their next proceeding "well laid." Livingston had endured enough seafaring and planned to remain at home this time, but he busied himself getting beer and apples for the cargo. The other partners had been entrusted with disposing of the wines in Boston, and Livingston counted on them to defray the expenses of re-outfitting. Vetch returned to New London in mid-September, boarded the vessel, and slipped out quietly without the formalities of proper clearance. He had learned by experience that his destination was better not announced, despite its being common knowledge around town.[33]

Vetch wrote Robert Livingston shortly before he sailed, begging him to "give my wife all the encouragement and diversion you can, for I know she is too much given to melancholy." Mrs. Vetch was expecting a child shortly, and Vetch was concerned over the lonely hours she must spend in the big house on New York's waterfront during the two months he expected to be away. Another letter to his mother-in-law covered a shipment of wines for the mistress of Livingston Manor, some "small efforts of our voyage."[34]

The *Mary's* second voyage started off quietly enough, but its conclusion threw Vetch into the midst of New York's frenzied

32. *Cal. State Papers, 1701*, nos. 707-16; Wait Winthrop to Fitzjohn Winthrop, Boston, Nov. 3, 1701, Mass. Hist. Soc., *Collections*, 6th ser., 5 (1892), 101-2. See also *The Case of William Atwood, Esq.* (London, 1703), reprinted in N.Y. Hist. Soc., *Collections*, Pub. fund ser., 13 (1880), 259 ff.

33. Fitzjohn Winthrop to John Livingston, New London, Sept. 3, John Livingston to Robert Livingston, New London, Sept. 3 and 16, 1701, Livingston Papers.

34. Vetch to Robert Livingston, New London, Sept. 16, 1701, *ibid*. Vetch wrote to his mother-in-law on Sept. 8 that "neither distance nor length of time shall make me forget my duty and respect to you." It is probable that he wrote Margaret as well, but the letter has not survived. Letters in the Livingston Papers, Group 2, from Margaret Livingston to her mother, Oct. 13, and from Robert Watts and Duncan Campbell to Robert Livingston, Nov. 26 and 27, 1701, indicate that Mrs. Vetch remained in New York rather than at the Manor during this voyage.

politics. He reached Quebec early in October, the sloop laden with flour, beer, cheese, tobacco, limes, "apple mustard," earthenware, and ammunition. By mid-October he had loaded the vessel with a return cargo of furs, wines, linen, canvas, and an assortment of other textiles. Weighing anchor at Quebec on October 22, he ran out the St. Lawrence, along the north shore of St. John's (Prince Edward's Island), through the Gut of Canso, between Nova Scotia and Cape Breton Island, and south to Cape Ann. The weather was wild, a portent of the storm the voyage was to raise at home. The *Mary* ran under bare poles through great seas, snow, and rain. She anchored off Cape Ann on the twenty-fifth, moved into sight of Salem harbor November 13, and anchored off Martha's Vineyard on the sixteenth.[35]

During an easterly gale on the night of Saturday, November 22, Vetch asked the sloop's master, John Cox, to anchor in the lee of Block Island. According to Vetch's later testimony, the *Mary* went aground in heavy seas, and all aboard took to the ship's boat. They left the *Mary* with furled sails and lashed helm, put out the anchor to hold the ship in the event the wind drove her free, launched the boat, "emptied her of water as well as they could and with great toil and difficulty got all of them (by good providence of Almighty God) safe on shore on Block Island . . . where they continued the remaining part of the said night without finding any dwelling house or other edifice to shelter in, having saved none of the goods nor of their apparel other than what was on their bodies."[36] The next day the *Mary* was gone. Unfortunately for Vetch, she had not sunk but had blown free and dragged anchor, fetching up on Montauk Point at the end of Long Island.

Vetch's version of what happened seems substantially correct. A friend wrote Robert Livingston that some evidence existed that a storm had interrupted an attempt to unload the cargo at Block Island. The ship was found with hatches open, some furs hanging in a sling. But whether it happened as Vetch reported or whether an attempt to smuggle the goods ashore had been inter-

35. E. B. O'Callaghan, ed., *Journal of the Voyage of the Sloop Mary from Quebec, together with an Account of Her Wreck off Montauk Point, Long Island, Anno 1701* (Albany, 1866). The *Journal* was found in a chest belonging to the ship's mate and presumably had been kept by him.

36. Pleas of Captain Samuel Vetch and Mr. John Saffin, merchants, Dec. 12, 1701, Rawlinson Mss., ser. A, vol. 272, f. 24 (Lib. Cong. Transcripts).

rupted by bad weather did not matter. The *Mary* was found on Sunday morning, intact with her attractive and illicit cargo. By Tuesday night word had been sent posthaste to Manhattan. Mrs. Vetch and most of New York heard that islanders had unloaded and stored the cargo, under the direction of one Hobart, justice of the peace, and William Smith, member of the Council. It was known that the sloop belonged to John Livingston and Samuel Vetch, and the damaging journal of the voyage and Vetch's letters had been found aboard. Mrs. Vetch was beside herself with sorrow and grief. It seemed certain that her husband had been cast away and drowned. She and her friends hurried off letters about the catastrophe to her father, their anxiety heightened by the obvious fact that Leislerians now in power would not overlook the opportunity to embarrass their old enemy Robert Livingston by bringing action against his son and son-in-law for this manifest violation of the Acts of Trade.[37]

Governor Nanfan acted quickly, dispatching Lieutenant Charles Oliver to take charge of the *Mary*'s cargo. By mid-December it was reposing in His Majesty's customhouse in New York under the watchful eyes of Collector Weaver. Before the month was out, Chief Justice Atwood had convened a Vice-Admiralty Court and condemned sloop and cargo. The government's prize came to the value of £2,000, New York money, divided a third to the King, a third to Nanfan, and a third to Collector Weaver, who claimed the customary share due the "informer."[38]

For John Livingston, it appeared a case of God giving and God taking away. Even Mrs. Vetch, relieved to discover her husband alive, concluded that God always provided. Wait Winthrop, with magnificent disregard for the principles he was pledged to uphold, wrote that he was "sorry for the disasters that have happened in those parts," but "glad it is not worse."[39] But Vetch,

37. David Jamison to Robert Livingston, Nov. 25, Robert Watts to Livingston, Nov. 26, Duncan Campbell to Livingston, Nov. 27, 1701, Livingston Papers, Group 2, box 1a; Mrs. Vetch to Alida Livingston, Dec. 1701, *ibid.;* O'Callaghan, ed., *Journal of the Sloop Mary*, 33.

38. N.Y. Council Minutes, Dec. 8 and 26, 1701 (N.Y. State Lib., Albany), appeal of case to British Admiralty, Rawlinson Mss., ser. A, vol. 272, f. 24 (Lib. Cong. Transcripts).

39. John to Alida Livingston, Dec. 22, Margaret Vetch to her mother, Dec. 1701, Livingston Papers, Group 2.

safe ashore, resolved to fight the case out and engaged lawyers at once. His plea, as ingenious as it was unlikely, admitted that the sloop had sailed from Quebec but maintained that it was bound for St. Christopher Island in the West Indies. It had come into Long Island Sound merely to put the owners ashore. Since it had been unloaded by Indians and islanders, the goods were manifestly not "imported" contrary to English law.[40]

Atwood and Weaver were unimpressed and maintained violation of the laws on two counts: first, that goods shipped from one port of England to another without customs clearance should be forfeited according to the Act for Preventing Frauds and Regulating Abuses in His Majesty's Customs; and second, that according to the Act for the Encouragement of Trade, no product of Europe could be imported without being shipped by way of England. When Vetch and his partner Saffin persisted in their case and appealed to the Admiralty Court in England, both Weaver and Atwood were furious. Chagrined over Vetch's previous success in frustrating the law in Boston, Atwood was especially angry. The *Mary* had on board some tobacco raised in the colonies, which had not cleared customs, as well as European wines and textiles, which had not come through England. Even if the sloop had been driven in by stress of weather, as Vetch asserted, in Atwood's eyes the plea was "so very defective, not traversing a great part of the charge, that it could never help him if the matter were otherwise pleadable."[41]

Furthermore, the appeal to England smacked of the dilatory and obstructive tactics with which colonial merchants so often tried to evade the laws of trade. "The merchants here," Atwood pointed out, "not liking prosecutions upon breaches of the Acts of Trade, hope to weary the prosecutions by appeals to England." He urgently hoped Vetch's move would not be countenanced.[42]

40. Wait Winthrop to Fitzjohn Winthrop, Dec. 9, 1701, Mass. Hist. Soc., *Collections*, 6th ser., 5 (1892), 104-5; Vetch's appeal, Rawlinson Mss., ser. A, vol. 272, f. 24 (Lib. Cong. Transcripts).

41. 14 Charles 2, c. 11, and 15 Charles 2, c. 7, respectively, cited in Rawlinson Mss., ser. A, vol. 272, f. 24 (Lib. Cong. Transcripts); William Atwood to Sir Charles Hedges, Secretary of State, Dec. 29, 1701, P.R.O., C.O. 5, vol, 1047, f. 29 (*ibid.*); also in *N.Y. Col. Docs.*, IV, 930.

42. See Rawlinson Mss., ser. A, vol. 272, f. 139, 151 (Lib. Cong. Transcripts), for the Leislerians' choice of Champante to represent them in England

Vetch, however, had reason to believe that he might succeed. His resolve to appeal his case to the English Admiralty put him in the forefront of the fight which the leading New Yorkers were waging against the Leislerian faction to protect what they conceived to be their "rights, liberties, and properties." Although a new governor was on his way to replace Nanfan, who had lost control of the situation, the Leislerians resorted to extreme measures.[43]

Just as Vetch's case was being tried in December, a large number of the "principal inhabitants" of New York signed addresses to the King, Parliament, and Lord Cornbury, who had been named as the next governor, setting forth their grievance against the governing regime. The governor and Council promptly threw the ringleaders into prison for sedition. Vetch had been one of the signers, but the accused men would not produce the documents, and he escaped identification. John Hutchins and Nicholas Bayard were held in custody; Nicholas Bayard was charged with high treason; Rip Van Dam, Wenham, and Philip French, who had admitted possession of the addresses, stood in jeopardy of imprisonment.

Ironically, Nanfan, Atwood, and the Leislerians had resurrected the "Act of 1691, For Settling the Recent Disorders," designed to quiet the original Leislerian faction, maintaining the addresses constituted "scandalous libels" and incited the people to disown the prevailing government. They charged that many soldiers had been induced to sign the addresses after being treated to free drinks, without knowing what they were signing. According to the Council, even "Frenchmen, Aliens, and several strangers, persons who had lately come from England and the adjacent Provinces" had signed, but "chiefly . . . the most ignorant of the people, and almost generally without knowing the contents thereof."[44]

The addresses condemned Nanfan's administration for ac-

---

against Vetch's appeal. Champante was their choice as New York agent to England.

43. *Cal. State Papers, 1702,* nos. 343xi, 237; Wenham and French to Charles Lodwick and others, Jan. 28, 1702, *ibid.,* nos. 343v, 231; Jan. 1702, N.Y. Council Minutes (N.Y. State Lib., Albany).

44. Jan. 16, 17, and 19, 1702, N.Y. Council Minutes, *Cal. State Papers, 1702,* nos. 35, 41; Warrant of Governor and Council, Jan. 21, 1702, *ibid.,* no. 343iii.

cepting bribes from the Assembly and either putting "the scum of the people" in office or retaining them from Bellomont's regime. They complained of "insupportable oppressions" and the insatiable malice of the Leislerians, and they prayed for the relief of their grievances. That the signers were solely or chiefly ignorant people, unaware of what they were signing, was clearly a partisan plea without basis in fact. Whether Nanfan and his faction wanted to recognize it or not, the petition bore the signatures of all the prominent and wealthy merchants and landowners who made up the anti-Leislerian party, the "greatest and richest part of His Majesty's subjects" in the colony.[45]

The New York government did its best to maintain that Cornbury was not on his way with a commission as governor. Attorney General Samuel Shelton Broughton, however, refused to co-operate with his colleague Atwood in prosecuting Bayard, and Weaver had to be created "Solicitor-General" to carry on the trial. Actually, Cornbury embarked from England as these events occurred, and the news of his coming was confirmed by a ship which arrived late in January. This only partially tempered proceedings. Bayard and Hutchins were tried and sentenced to death as traitors, but they were reprieved pending appeal to England. Livingston was suspended from the Council, and Nanfan even imprisoned a little boy who appended the words "and hang John Nanfan" to a posted proclamation. During the spring, prominent merchants fled to adjoining provinces to escape the measures of the government. Packed and intimidated juries were forced to follow the dictates of Atwood, and the Assembly, on the eve of Cornbury's arrival in May, sat night and day to enact laws securing the position of the Leislerians.[46]

45. *Ibid.*, no. 41; Petition of the Protestants of New York to King William III, Dec. 30, 1701, *N.Y. Col. Docs.*, IV, 933-42. In addition to those already noted (*Cal. State Papers, 1702*, no. 343v), it included Thomas, William and Richard Willet, Caleb Heathcote, William Smith, and Delancey, Van Cortlandt, Lurting, Saffin, and Beekman. The Albany leaders included Livingston and Schuyler, Robert Watts, Fanueil, Codrington, etc. Many of those who signed were, of course, correctly characterized by their opponents, and even of those substantial signers it was true that some were not freemen of the city or were new arrivals or even transients. But it seems unlikely that transients were without interest in the state of the province. For Atwood's side of the controversies, see *The Case of William Atwood*.

46. *Cal. State Papers, 1702*, nos. 337, 343i-vii, 91, 387, 412, 782vi, 1206;

Again, as in 1689, heats and animosities had led to excesses. A movement to shift power in political, social, and economic life from the aristocracy to aspiring leaders of the middle class was marred by factional extravagance and crushed by opposition of vested interests in the colonies and the mother country. The attempt did not gain the support of those awakening classes even lower on the social scale, who supported the revolutions of the late eighteenth century. Moreover, the paramount interests and capabilities of the aristocracy still demanded that leadership remain in the hands of the men of place and privilege. The movement was simply another swing of the pendulum of selfish party politics, the continuing three-cornered fight for political control and social and economic advantage between the representatives of royal control and the two political factions in New York. It was no attempt at a democratic revolution.

Cornbury's arrival brought the relief which the anti-Leislerians expected. Even before he left England, Cornbury's position was clear. He had employed as secretary Daniel Honan, erstwhile rascally accomplice of Fletcher. When the Board of Trade called the man in question, Cornbury protested blandly that he had no idea of Honan's past connection with the discredited former governor and assured the Board that he would immediately dismiss the man. But Honan remained in the position. The English representatives of the New York magnates had won Cornbury to their side, and his task of overturning the regime in New York was simplified by the indefensible position of the lieutenant governor, royal officials, Council, and Assembly. Ironically, the government in England had to censure loyal officials who had simply sought to uphold the laws, because base motives, combined with excessive zeal, had led them to overstep the bounds of their authority.[47]

Cornbury dissolved the Assembly, removed the Leislerian members of the Council, along with Atwood and Weaver, who fled the province, and arrested Nanfan for failure to account for New York's finances. The acts passed feverishly before his ar-

---

N.Y. Col. Docs., IV, 926; New York Colonial Manuscripts, XLV, 118 (N.Y. State Lib., Albany).

47. *N.Y. Col. Docs.*, IV, 925-27.

rival were disallowed. Cornbury was of course welcomed by the anti-Leislerian faction and easily persuaded of the legitimacy of their grievances and the errors of their opponents. Few could foresee that Cornbury, through his own excesses, was to prove unsatisfactory to both factions in New York.[48]

After waiting out the months of discord patiently and cautiously, Vetch benefited from the arrival of a governor identified with his group. In the case of the sloop *Mary*, Cornbury early indicated his willingness to line his own pockets at the expense of the province and in total disregard of the laws he was expected to uphold. On the very day that the forfeited *Mary* was to be sold, "His Lordship upon terms agreed on with the Captain [Vetch] returned him the Ship; whereby he was enabled to carry on his illegal trade with the French at Quebec."[49]

Atwood had been correct in his proceedings against Vetch, and Vetch clearly had been guilty of illegal trade. But New York merchants had long been accustomed to having their way in trade; the case of the *Mary* was another instance. Bellomont's policies were no more successful in the hands of his successors than they had been in his own.

Meanwhile, at the time of the confiscation of his vessel, Vetch had gained a new responsibility. He was now the head of a family. The month that Atwood proceeded against him, his wife had given birth to their first child, Alida, born on Christmas Day, 1701.[50]

48. Cornbury to Board of Trade, May 3, June 16, and Nov. 30, Atwood to Board of Trade, July 14, Nanfan to Board of Trade, Oct. 5, 1702, *Cal. State Papers, 1702,* nos. 408, 601, 1206, 750, 1021; June 9, 1702, *Journal of the Legislative Council of the Colony of New York . . .* (Albany, 1861), IX, 36.

49. N.Y. Hist. Soc., *Collections,* Pub. fund ser., 13 (1880), 295.

50. Van Rensselaer, *Livingston Family,* 81-82. It is interesting to note that the compiler has found no record of Vetch's other children.

CHAPTER FIVE

Penalties of Trade

THE RETURN OF THE *Mary* did not result in Vetch's resuming his trading with New France, as Atwood had feared. The outbreak of war put that out of the question. When the King of Spain died, the problem of succession, which had perplexed the best diplomats of Europe for years, became crucial. News that King William was forming a large army in Holland had reached New York in the fall of 1701, along with the report that Cornbury was coming to replace Nanfan.[1] Although William died shortly, Queen Anne inherited the struggle against France, and the second phase of the century-long conflict between France and England, open war, resulted when Louis XIV recognized his grandson as the new ruler of Spain and commenced military movements designed to counter opposition from England and its allies.

This was the end of an uneasy truce between the rival claimants of the American continent. Issues raised by the first colonial war had become steadily more obvious and pressing. Trade, the fisheries, hegemony over the Indians, the land itself—all were at stake. The enmity of the mother countries only made it more unlikely that a solution might be found short of total victory, either for England's northern colonies or for New France. In this war, or the next, or the one after that, Englishmen would finally command North America, or else New France, having encircled them, would push their colonies into the sea. At stake, too, was the future of the American continent as an English-speaking region enjoying self-government, individual rights, and religious liberty, though these issues, except for the religious one,

1. William Sharpe to Robert Livingston, N.Y., Nov. 24, 1701, Livingston Papers; *N.Y. Col. Docs.*, IV, 948.

were hardly of interest to early eighteenth-century leaders. Most of them would have abhorred the thought that they were fighting for a future democratic state.

What colonial leaders on both sides did know was that they had entered on a prolonged duel for empire. Vetch and men like him were to see to it that England understood this before the second stage of the contest was over. Vetch was, after all, a soldier by training. With fighting imminent, he sought to capitalize on that experience. In May 1702, he wrote to William Blathwayt, ubiquitous bureaucrat and then secretary at war, asking for a commission as captain of one of the four companies of Regulars maintained by the Crown at New York. Major Ingoldesby, commander of the Regulars at Albany, had long been absent in England, and it was at Cornbury's suggestion that Vetch applied for his post.

But Ingoldesby had made good use of his sojourn in England. He had been prominently identified with the anti-Leislerians for his role in displacing Leisler. Now that the Leislerians were safely disposed of, Ingoldesby returned with a commission as lieutenant governor, retaining the command of the detachment at Albany as well. So Vetch did not get the job he wanted, despite promising Blathwayt "to be grateful to you as far as my capacity will allow me" and ordering a factor in England to make tangible evidence of his gratitude.[2]

Not only was Vetch unable to find military employment, but he was also overwhelmed by a legacy of litigation from his trading ventures. Saffin, one of his former partners, petitioned before the Council against Vetch soon after the sloop *Mary* had been returned. Several more cases involving Vetch appear in court minutes of the following year. The enterprise had plainly ended in a thorough legal snarl; in November 1702, Vetch sold the sloop to the government for use, ironically, in the revenue service.[3]

2. Vetch to Blathwayt, May 25, 1702 (Huntington Lib.); *N.Y. Col. Docs.*, IV, 760-61, 816.

3. June 29, Oct. 29, and Nov. 6, 7, 10, 14, and 19, 1702, N.Y. Council Minutes (N.Y. State Lib., Albany); Peartree vs. Vetch (Oct. 3, 1703), Lurting vs. Vetch (Oct. 3, 1703), Dom Regina vs. Vetch (Oct. 8, 1703), Dom Regina vs. Vetch (Oct. 9, 1703), Vetch vs. Merritt (Oct. 3, 1703), Minutes of the Supreme Court of Judicature of the Province of New York, N.Y. Hist. Soc., *Collections*, DePeyster pub. fund ser., 45 (1913). The N.Y. Colonial Manuscripts once

For a time he remained in New York. His father-in-law Robert Livingston was engaged, as usual, in attempting to get payment of the sums owed him by the colony for supplies advanced to the Regulars. In the summer of 1702, Livingston, Vetch, Robert Lurting, and Thomas Noell, the mayor of New York, served as a committee to present the accounts of the four Regular companies, but Cornbury refused to accept them. Although the governor was quite willing to see Livingston paid, the accounts involved the attempt to embarrass Nanfan, and as long as partisan politics was involved, Livingston's interests had to wait.[4]

The summer of 1702 in New York was hectic. Smallpox was prevalent, and the city was swept by a "malignant distemper," which was as disconcerting as the government's proceedings against the Leislerians. Vetch's father-in-law concluded that Cornbury's administration was no better than those before. The governor's favoritism was directed toward his own enrichment, and he was inevitably embroiled with the Assembly over control of colonial expenditures. Robert Livingston was wise enough to see that the struggle would be long and not likely to help him personally. In the spring of 1703, he sailed for England to try again to recoup the money he had advanced for public use.[5]

At about the same time, the Vetches moved out of their house in New York. Vetch did not condone Cornbury's dishonesty and extravagance, but neither did he care to be a witness to the obstructive legislative tactics of an Assembly bent on asserting revolutionary views concerning its power of self-government. Trade was at a low ebb because of the war, and an acute shortage of coin following the suppression of piracy and the attempt to enforce coinage regulations was an additional handicap. These conditions,

---

held a record of the case between Saffin and Vetch but the Albany fire of 1911 left only one charred fragment of this record, XLV, 157. Also see John Livingston to Robert Livingston, Morrisania, Aug. 24, 1701, Livingston Papers; N.Y. Colonial Manuscripts, XLII, 123-24 (N.Y. State Lib., Albany).

4. P.R.O., C.O. 5, vol. 1048, A, 31 (Lib. Cong. Transcripts); Livingston's report on New York to the English government, *N.Y. Col. Docs.*, IV, 1067; Nov. 12, 1702, N.Y. Council Minutes (N.Y. State Lib., Albany; also in Livingston Papers).

5. Aug. 27 and Sept. 17, 1702, N.Y. Council Minutes (N.Y. State Lib., Albany); *Cal. State Papers, 1702*, no. 1206xlvii-xlix; Livingston to Winthrop, Dec. 1702, Mass. Hist. Soc., *Collections*, 6th ser., 3 (1889), 115-17.

in addition to his lawsuits and his failure to find military preferment, probably induced Vetch's decision to leave the provincial
capital before another unhealthy summer. It may be surmised
that the Vetches went to Livingston Manor temporarily, where
Vetch could fill in for the absent master and escape the seething
currents of New York politics, from which he now stood to gain
little.[6]

Vetch was for the moment at loose ends. But the war, of far
more importance than the internecine political struggles, promised
ultimate opportunity. Its outbreak brought to the fore the problem of Indian relations, with which Vetch was conversant through
his Albany connections. When Cornbury journeyed to Albany
to confer with the leaders of the Five Nations during the summer
of 1702, Vetch had accompanied him.[7] At Albany, Cornbury
had been acquainted with the key role played by the Iroquois in
relations between England's northern colonies and New France.
Canada's economy was based on the fur trade, not alone for the
wealth it brought but for the political advantage. Numerically inferior to the English, the French bought Indian alliances with the
trade. Without such alliances, Canada could not hope to stand
against the English. Also, territorial expansion and the extension of
Roman Catholic Christianity, twin goals of Louis XIV and his
ministers, depended on this trade. Since the peltry resources of
any given areas were quickly exhausted, the French zeal for territory was intensified. Canada needed free range and indefinite
space; it did not dare to remain stationary. The stumbling
block to this expansion was the existence of the well-organized
Five Nations, the one tribe that did not depend on the French for
manufactures but had the English.[8]

6. Quary to Board of Trade, June, Cornbury to Board of Trade, June 1703,
Cornbury to Board of Trade, Feb. 1705, *N.Y. Col. Docs.*, IV, 1049, 1058, 1132.
See also Nettels, *Money Supply of the American Colonies*, 205. Livingston's
Account Book, 1726 (Livingston Papers), indicates that the Vetches moved
in May 1703; the house was rented first to Wenham, May 1703 to May 1710,
and then to David Jamison, May 1711 to 1720. Robert Livingston the younger,
an attorney, rented it until 1722, after which the house was conveyed to Vetch
and rent was paid directly to him. Before that, Livingston had simply credited
Vetch with rent received.

7. June 18, 1702, N.Y. Council Minutes (N.Y. State Lib., Albany). For
the record of the Indian conference, see *N.Y. Col. Docs.*, IV, 987 ff.

8. Edouard Richard, ed., *Supplement to Dr. Brymner's Report on the Canadian Archives, 1899* (Ottawa, 1901), ser. B, XXIX, 214; XXXIV, 456. La

In the course of the seventeenth century, the Iroquois had driven the Hurons, allies of the French and middlemen in the French trade with Indians further west, out of the area between the St. Lawrence and the Susquehanna. Aspiring to be the middlemen themselves between the western Indians and the Dutch, later the English, the Five Nations dominated the region of the Mohawk Valley, tied closely to the English by the cheapness and desirability of English manufactured goods.[9]

The competition, then, between New York and New France, political in nature, was often expressed in terms of Indian relations and Indian trade. New York posed an immediate threat to the French by its close support of the Five Nations. In return, Canada directly menaced the English by attempts to vex, terrify, or seduce the Iroquois, who were not merely a source of valuable trade for New York but also an essential bulwark for the security of all the English settlements. On the alliance with the Iroquois depended the defense against French encroachment, whether it came along the Kennebec or the Hudson, in Acadia or the Connecticut Valley, or offshore where French privateers sailed from maritime ports to harass the colonists' commerce.[10]

At the end of the first colonial war in 1697, the problem of Indian relations became acute. It was obvious to the Iroquois

---

Chesnaye, one of the influential French traders, stated, "If once we lose them [the Indians] we lose them forever. Thus will be lost not only the fur trade, but the colony"; *Collection de Manuscrits contenant lettres, mémoires, et autres documents historiques relatifs à la Nouvelle France* (Quebec, 1883-85), I, 255. See also Lawrence Henry Gipson, *The British Empire Before the American Revolution*, V, *Zones of International Friction, the Great Lakes Frontier, Canada, the West Indies, India, 1748-1754* (New York, 1942), 42.

9. George T. Hunt, *The Wars of the Iroquois* (Madison, 1940), is a recent analysis of the nature of the Five Nations; see especially pp. 6, 9, 18, 21. Bernard DeVoto, *The Course of Empire* (Boston, 1952), accepts Hunt's conclusions up to a point, but he cautions against overemphasis on the commercial character of the Iroquois wars; pp. 96-98, 147-48, 571n, 575n. See accounts of negotiations in *N.Y. Col. Docs.*, IV, 564, 572, 893, 902-3, 905, 920, 987; V, 248, 275, 386-87; Peter Wraxall's *An Abridgement of Indian Affairs . . . in the Colony of New York . . . 1678-1751*, ed. Charles H. McIlwain, *Harvard Historical Studies*, XXI (Cambridge, 1915), xlii, 92, 195; "Continuation" of Colden's *History of the Five Nations*, N.Y. Hist. Soc., *Collections*, DePeyster pub. fund ser., 68 (1935), 359-434, especially 411. For a comparison of prices at Albany and Montreal in 1689, see *N.Y. Col. Docs.*, IX, 408-9.

10. *N.Y. Col. Docs.*, IX, 369, 406; III, 190, 278. Richard, ed., *Canadian Archives Supplement*, ser. B, XI, 268; XIII, 282, provides early expressions which illustrate the realization of the nature of the situation.

that the English were a weak reed. The English attempt at unified direction of the war effort had aroused only jealousy and dogged opposition; it had proved nearly impossible to get other colonies to help New York with men and money. The establishment in New York of four companies of Regulars was an exception to the usual English policy of letting the colonies provide their own defense, but the Regulars were too few, too hungry, and too poorly officered to be effective. Neglected by the home government, they had to be victualed on credit by Livingston, Schuyler, and others, who found themselves out of pocket to a large amount. The subsequent discontent of the Albany leaders, the "most popular with our Five Nations and the principal men in managing them and keeping them firm to our interest," as Bellomont admitted, was unfortunate at a time when the Iroquois alliance needed its most careful tending. In a situation "where all things both for the belly and the back are very near treble the rates they are in England," the troops were in rags, their pay due in Irish debentures which would hardly help feed and clothe them, and their forts falling down. They were not a force likely to inspire the Indians with confidence in their allies.[11]

By 1700, after several years of negotiation, the weary Iroquois, fearful of French strength and disillusioned by English failures, had agreed to terms of peace. The result was not, however, as serious as the New Yorkers feared, for the Five Nations knew that a complete change of allegiance would be as disastrous to themselves as it would be to the English. Their trade with the English could not be supplanted by trade with the French. And they well knew the importance of their affiliation; a complete shift in their alliance would be enough, in the words of one of the great Onondaga orators, "to overturn a whole land"—"this point must be handled tenderly." The Iroquois instinctively realized what their own

11. Report of the Board of Trade to the King, Feb. 25, 1697, *N.Y. Col. Docs.*, IV, 259-60. Bellomont's difficulties along this line have already been noted; see *ibid.*, 624. Massachusetts was unwilling to go along with his plans for New York frontier defense, and the governor wrote that he "would as soon undertake to reconcile 'em to the Mass" as to get the Puritans to contribute; *ibid.*, 671. The Livingston Papers have the accounts of Livingston and Schuyler with the troops, 1691-99, dated July 5, 1704. See also *N.Y. Col. Docs.*, IV, 377, and Stanley McCrory Pargellis, "The Four Independent Companies of New York," in *Essays in Colonial History Presented to Charles McLean Andrews by his Students* (New Haven, 1931), 96-123.

plight would be if either France or England should become clearly the masters of the continent. The policy they now adopted was one of playing the two powers off against each other.[12]

Although the English government recognized the military weakness of the colonies, it was unwilling to help. The Board of Trade reported:

His Majesty has subjects enough in those parts of America, not only to defend themselves against all the attacks they may apprehend from the French in Canada and the Indians joined with them, but even to drive them out from thence, but they are so crumbled into little governments and so disunited in those distinct interests that they have hitherto afforded but little assistance to each other and seem as they now are, to be but in an ill posture, and a much worse disposition to do it for the future.

This was an excellent analysis of the situation, but at that time England was unwilling to remedy the lack of co-operation by lending more effective assistance and leadership. With England itself at war, it was not to be imagined "that so great a number of English there should think it much to employ their own hand and purses in the defense of their own estates, lives, and families, but should expect to be wholly supported from England."[13]

Here the situation rested when Cornbury and his entourage arrived in Albany in the summer of 1702 to meet with Schuyler's Indian commission and representatives of the Five Nations. Cornbury could choose from several courses. The English might urge the Five Nations to break their agreement with Canada and re-enlist on the side of their old allies. This would mean full-scale war before either white men or red had recovered from the last conflict; and after several years of political turmoil, New York was scarcely in shape for further struggle, foreign or domestic. Or Cornbury could accept the arrangement between the Iroquois and the French, relying on Canada's unwillingness to hazard its neutrality with the Iroquois by attacking the English allies. This would leave New York secure until it was ready to mount an at-

12. *N.Y. Col. Docs.*, IV, 570, 893, 902-3.
13. *Ibid.*, 227, 545. The only action taken was recognition of the fact that the four companies had dwindled to half their number; by changing the establishment to correspond to the reduction, each company was to number fifty men instead of the former one hundred.

tack. But it would not protect neighboring Massachusetts Bay. The French governor considered himself obliged to keep the Indians in eastern Canada embroiled with the New England colonists for fear that the Indians there might otherwise conclude a settlement with the English and turn against the French. French and Indian moves against the frontiers of northern New England were already underway, and privateers operating from Canada's maritime ports were threatening New England's commerce.

Still another course was open to the New Yorkers. Hard pressed in Europe, France was not anxious to spare troops and equipment for Canada. The Bourbons were convinced that without Iroquois support the English could take no serious step against Canada. The French minister Pontchartrain believed the English colonies were probably aware that war was contrary to their own interests, as well as to Canada's. If an official neutrality could be arranged, it would be highly desirable. A royal memorial of March 1701 urged the governor of Newfoundland to try to make a treaty of friendly intercourse with the English in the event of European war, and similar instructions went to Canada. It was evident that Canada was ready to withdraw, at least temporarily, from its aggressive policy.[14]

This startling suggestion in the form of an overt and more or less official proposal for neutrality between New York and Canada had been communicated to Nanfan and the New York Council upon the return of an Albany trading party from Canada in May 1701. Nanfan's reply has not been preserved, but he wrote the Board of Trade, "I will never hear of such a thing, believing it to be directly contrary to his Majesty's interest." He probably postponed the matter until the arrival of the new governor.[15]

Cornbury chose the middle ground, between outright war and official peace, reflecting the judgment of the Indian commission. Schuyler and Livingston, heading the commission, seized on the

14. *Ibid.*, IX, 743, 755; Richard, ed., *Canadian Archives Supplement*, ser. B, XXII, 350, 354.

15. Joel Munsell, *The Annals of Albany* (Albany, 1850), IV, 129-30; N.Y. Colonial Manuscripts, XLIV, 119 (N.Y. State Lib., Albany) (badly burned; see E. B. O'Callaghan, ed., *Calendar of Historical Manuscripts in the Office of the Secretary of State, Albany, New York* [Albany, 1866], Part II); *N.Y. Col. Docs.*, IV, 916.

proposal from Canada with alacrity. As the new French governor Vaudreuil heard, "According to news of Indians brought from Orange, speeches of Dekanissore [an eminent Onondaga sachem] and private advices in my possession, I doubt not but the Dutch of . . . Albany will employ every means and will demand a species of neutrality between the government of Montreal and themselves, and that they will even submit some proposals to me."[16]

But it was destined to remain merely "a species of neutrality." Cornbury would not go so far as to negotiate an official neutrality directly with the French. Nor could he accept the mediation offered by the Five Nations without raising again the problem of sovereignty over them. On the other hand, tacit acceptance of the agreement already reached between the French and the Iroquois left New York protected but free to act as future developments might demand—a situation highly advantageous to New York, as the French were quick to point out. It was a compromise, for the Indian commission would have preferred a formal arrangement assuring peace to the fur-trading frontier. But the Albany leaders, with their strong influence on the Five Nations and their inside information on Canada, were probably satisfied with the arrangement.

Cornbury, backed by the government in England, suspected that if the French really intended to maintain peace, they did so because peace was in their interest; therefore they should be opposed by the English.[17] As early as 1699, the English ministry had expressed the opinion that no neutrality treaty was to the advantage of the English. The French were likely to break it and surprise the colonists, who "relying on the faith of such a treaty may be wholly unguarded and unprovided for such attempts." In the

16. *N.Y. Col. Docs.*, IX, 745.
17. *Campbell News Letter*, Boston, Oct. 1703, as reprinted in Lyman Horace Weeks and Edwin M. Bacon, eds., *An Historical Digest of the Provincial Press, Massachusetts Series*, I, 1689-1707 (Boston, 1911) 52. A report "From New York, the 12th current [July 1702] acquainted that the Indians proposed to his Excellency the Lord Cornbury to make peace with the French of Canada, which his Lordship would not admit of, and its believed they are on both sides and receive presents from both. . ."; Richard, ed., *Canadian Archives Supplement*, ser. B, XXVII, 381, 388, 706; XXIX, 414. See also *N.Y. Col. Docs.*, IX, 813; IV, 982.

long run, French and English policies were inevitably opposed. But Cornbury, faced by the current state of his province and with little likelihood of aid from the mother country, was in no position to advocate an immediate call to arms. He was forced to accept the situation as he found it.[18]

Cornbury's policy naturally reflected the thinking of the group of wealthy merchants and landholders whose interests were touched by intercolonial affairs and who, alone among the aspirants to power in New York, had a clearly defined viewpoint on the complex and related subjects of Indian trade, French rivalry, and government conduct. But it was also in line with the past experience of the province's governors, irrespective of partisanship. From the time of Governor Dongan down through the successive regimes of Leisler, Sloughter, Fletcher, and Bellomont, each head of government had recognized the French threat, noted the importance of the beaver trade, both financially and politically, and sought to follow an aggressive policy whereby colonists and Iroquois would unite to drive the French out of North America. And each had come to the conclusion that such a policy was unwise. All attempts to implement it had failed because of jealousy and faction within the province, lack of intercolonial co-operation, inadequate leadership, and ineffective aid from the mother country. A prudent peace was better than the expensive pinpricks which achieved nothing of the objective. Until the European nations settled the affair for the colonists or England provided the organization for a combined force to deal the French a final blow, New York had best avoid the struggle for empire.

It was a conclusion concurred in by the majority of Albany traders, willing or unwilling participants in the policies of past governors; they had learned the same lessons. Until they saw evidence of a campaign with better prospects than those they had experienced, they preferred to continue their trade with the Indians and even with the French. The Five Nations, too, whether at the suggestion of the Albany Indian commission or on their own initiative, had often voiced impatience with past projects and had decided to remain neutral, depending on neither English nor

18. *N.Y. Col. Docs.*, IV, 487, 983 ff.

French, until the English offered the overwhelming strength which would make a renewal of the close alliance safe.[19]

Vetch was acquainted with the frontier situation, but he did not necessarily concur in the present solution. Later events suggest that Vetch accepted the arrangement between the French, the Five Nations, and New York as a temporary expedient at best. The conference, underscoring the lack of leadership and co-operation which past years had disclosed, gave Vetch an idea for the future. The scope of his viewpoint was wider than New York. Even though the Iroquois arrangement protected that province for the time being, colonial leaders would eventually have to recognize, as Vetch did, that it did nothing to secure New England. It was not enough to neutralize the Five Nations while the Indians of northern New England, under French leadership, were left to ravage the frontier and French privateers drove English shipping into port. French aggression posed a common danger which the English colonies could not meet successfully piecemeal. Mere defense was not enough. Limited warfare was costly and ineffective. The present arrangement provided only an uneasy security for one colony and intensified the attacks on its neighbors. United action was the obvious answer.

For a time after the onset of war and his departure from Manhattan, Vetch seems to have done nothing worthy of public notice. But in 1705, leaving Mrs. Vetch at the Manor, he removed to Boston, ready again to engage in coastwise trading between Boston and Canada. His first trading venture in Boston had been such a pleasant contrast to his New York reception that he decided to resume operations from Massachusetts Bay, even though war was now being waged and the trade was illegal. Vetch enjoyed good business relations with John Borland and other Scottish merchants at Boston, whereas his former partners among the New York merchants had entangled him in litigation.

Moreover, the negotiations for prisoner exchange offered a convenient cover for trade with Canada. The desultory raids carried out in the opening years of the war had filled the Boston jail and created a sizable community of New England expatriates in Quebec. In the summer of 1705, the Massachusetts legislature

19. *Ibid.*, 20-23, 176, 235-38, 240.

urged Dudley to arrange an exchange of prisoners.[20] Many of
the captives held by the French had been taken in the attack on
Deerfield in February 1704. John Livingston, who was serving
in western Massachusetts with the Connecticut forces, found his
sympathies aroused by the suffering frontiersmen. When Dudley,
after some exchange of letters with Governor Vaudreuil in Quebec,
authorized a delegation from Deerfield to visit Canada and seek
the return of the prisoners, Livingston volunteered to lead the
group overland from Albany to Quebec along the traders' route.
He returned early in June 1705 with several of the captives and
an emissary of the French government, the Sieur de Courtemanche,
who came to arrange for a general exchange. During these preliminaries, Vetch was in Boston watching his opportunity.[21]

After some discussion, Courtemanche was furnished with terms
approved by the Massachusetts government. The Frenchman,
who spoke highly of the treatment he received in Boston, became
a great favorite of Dudley's. The governor arranged Courtemanche's return by sea, accompanied by his younger son William
Dudley and his "particular friend" Vetch, hoping that the close
personal relationship established would facilitate the negotiations.
He asked Governor Vaudreuil to treat Massachusetts' agents as
well as Courtemanche had been treated.[22]

Vetch and Borland had uncollected debts in Canada from
their previous trade before the outbreak of war. Vetch agreed
to provide the vessel at his own expense and carry on further
negotiations in Canada if he were allowed at the same time to
collect what was owed to him. The trip was made, and the English emissaries succeeded in eliciting from Vaudreuil a proposal
for a general cessation of hostilities and the establishment of an

20. Chaps. 13 and 51, 1705-6, *The Acts and Resolves, Public and Private, of
the Province of the Massachusetts Bay, 1703-7* (Boston, 1895), VIII, 120, 134.
Evidence of Margaret Vetch's presence in Albany in 1705, 1707, and 1709 is
found in *Year Book of the Holland Society, 1905*, 37, 45, 52. Also see Douglas
C. McMurtrie, *Massachusetts Broadsides, 1699-1711* (Chicago, 1939).

21. Mass. Hist. Soc., *Collections*, 6th ser., 3 (1889), 241, 253, 294-97;
chap. 36, 1705-6, *Mass. Acts and Resolves, 1703-7*, VIII, 129-30.

22. Chap. 15, 1705-6, *Mass. Acts and Resolves, 1703-7*, VIII, 121; Parkman
Mss., XXX, 451 ff. (Mass. Hist. Soc.); Nov. 21, 1705, *Diary of Samuel Sewall*,
II, Mass. Hist. Soc., *Collections*, 5th ser., 6 (1879), 142. The first volume of
Sewall's Diary is *ibid.*, 5 (1878), and the third volume in 7 (1882); all will be
cited hereafter as *Diary of Samuel Sewall*.

official neutrality. Vaudreuil was having misgivings about his strategy of keeping the Indians of northern New England on the warpath. The French had directed this group of tribes, the Abenakis, along with the Iroquois converts from Caughnawaga, known as the "Praying Indians," against the English for fear they might otherwise come under the influence of the New Englanders. The Iroquois, at the instigation of the Albany leaders, protested to the French against the raids, fearing that New England might eventually force New York to enter the conflict and thus end the advantageous neutrality and trade enjoyed by the New York Indians and traders. The French governor did not want to risk anything that might embroil the Five Nations.[23]

By 1705 the French ministry, which had been only lukewarm about Vaudreuil's original strategy of inciting the Abenakis, was convinced that such tactics endangered peace with the Iroquois. Pontchartrain wrote that special efforts must be made to preserve that peace and repeatedly recommended "a strict neutrality between the English and French in America." Only if it were found that this policy would mean irrevocable loss of the Abenaki allegiance should Vaudreuil consider keeping the eastern Indians stirred up.[24]

The peace proposal which Vaudreuil sent back to Boston with William Dudley and Vetch was, however, rejected by the Massachusetts legislature. The French governor advanced claims threatening the traditional fishing rights of the New Englanders off the coast of Acadia. His plan also required the agreement of all the English colonies. It appeared that Vaudreuil was trying to bring New York into an official agreement to safeguard further his peace with the Iroquois. If so, he failed to count on the fierce provincial pride which would make such an arrangement anathema to both provinces. Cornbury was apparently never even informed

23. *Journal of the Commissioners for Trade and Plantations, April 1704–February 1709* (London, 1920), 326 (cited hereafter as *Board of Trade Journal*); Petition and Case of Samuel Vetch submitted to Privy Council and Board of Trade, Feb. 1707, *Cal. State Papers, 1706-8*, no. 773; Richard, ed., *Canadian Archives Supplement*, ser. B, XXIX, 401, and Pontchartrain to De Ramesay, June 30, 1707, *ibid.*, XXII, 370; *N.Y. Col. Docs.*, IX, 770-72, 779, 996.

24. *N.Y. Col. Docs.*, IX, 755; Richard, ed., *Canadian Archives Supplement*, ser. B, XXVII, 375, 381, 388, 706.

of the French proposal. The Massachusetts General Court rejected it, and the Queen later upheld the decision.[25]

Nor had Vetch been successful in collecting his debts; the French government opposed the illicit trading of furs to the English and prevented him from shipping any beaver from Quebec. If he were to trade with Canada, he would have to operate away from the capital. His opportunity came when arrangements were made for the exchange of prisoners after the rejection of the neutrality proposal. The transactions took place at Port Royal, in Acadia. Dudley was fully aware that trading was the concomitant of the interchange of prisoners, despite the governor's official proclamation against trading with the enemy and the Queen's Act published in March 1705.[26]

Vaudreuil had suspected from the first that the exchange of prisoners was only a pretext for Vetch's visit. He believed that the Bostonians were engaged in illegal trading and in spying on Canada's fortifications. Pontchartrain also suspected the motives of the English, and he cautioned Vaudreuil against Vetch. Although illegal trade benefited Canada in weapons and manufactured articles, any relations with the English such as these or the similar trade carried on at Albany by the "Praying Indians" endangered the French hold on their tribes. In the summer of 1706, Vaudreuil angrily wrote Dudley: "Sir, you need not wonder, neither can you blame me, about the repeated murders committed upon your people by the Indians, when your own vessels come privately and trade instruments of war with the savages. It is impossible

25. Massachusetts Archives, II, 595, 604 (State House, Boston); chaps. 83 and 85, 1705-6, *Mass. Acts and Resolves, 1703-7*, VIII, 149-50. The General Court approved a draft of a letter to Cornbury on Vaudreuil's proposition, but no copy has been found and it was probably never sent, as Cornbury never made mention of it; see Osgood, *Eighteenth Century*, I, 419; Thomas Hutchinson, *The History of the Colony and Province of Massachusetts-Bay*, ed. Lawrence S. Mayo (Cambridge, 1936), II, 122-23. Also see Hedges to Dudley, Aug. 1, 1706, *Cal. State Papers, 1706-8*, no. 456. The Massachusetts House gave only general reasons for its action—that the terms were not in the interest of the province and contravened Her Majesty's just rights.

26. Vaudreuil and others to Pontchartrain, 1705, noted that Vetch was demanding payment of 1,000 ecus lent by him to De Ramesay at Boston; Richard, ed., *Canadian Archives Supplement*, ser. C, III, 211. Chap. 51, 1705-6, and chap. 54, 1706-7, *Mass. Acts and Resolves, 1703-7*, VIII, 134, 185; *Board of Trade Journal, 1704-9*, 326; *Cal. State Papers, 1706-8*, no. 773; Dudley's Proclamation, Aug. 13, 1703, in McMurtrie, *Mass. Broadsides*; Mass. Archives, XX, 99 (State House, Boston).

for me to keep them in, when you whet their swords yourselves."[27]

Vaudreuil could have saved himself the trouble of pointing out what was going on. Influential elements in Massachusetts had already made an effective protest about the operations carried on by Vetch and others. Once again, the Scotsman found himself a pivot around which the major issues of a colony revolved.

In March 1706, with Dudley's knowledge and permission, Vetch had sailed to the Acadian harbor of Canso in the sloop *Flying Horse*. He intended to meet his debtors there and collect what was due him. Borland had a two-thirds interest in the sloop, which was loaded with "sundry goods and merchandise" for trade. Failing to make connections as planned, Vetch proceeded to trade his cargo at various points on the Acadian coast. After an absence of three months, "nobody knew where," the sloop returned and attempted to land its cargo surreptitiously at Plymouth where a fellow Scot named Murdoch lived.[28]

Suspecting a trade which "put knives into the hands of those barbarous infidels to cut the throats of our wives and children," the deputies of the General Court called for an accounting from Vetch and Archibald Ferguson, the master of the sloop. On the testimony of Ferguson, the House sent a member with a warrant from the governor to seize the *Flying Horse*. Again the luckless Vetch was confronted with a complete set of incriminating documents found aboard his vessel which clearly proved his guilt. "Here is a horrid combustion in town about it," wrote John Winthrop. The legislature was with difficulty restrained from putting Vetch "in a stone cage." Borland, whose complicity was known, had to put up a bond for £1,000.[29]

As the excitement grew, the legislature asked the governor to issue a proclamation to uncover further evidence of illegal trading. The province galley under Captain Cyprian Southack, along with the *Flying Horse* itself, was sent to apprehend others, and even

---

27. Vaudreuil to Pontchartrain, Oct. 19, 1705, Parkman Mss., XXX, 456 ff. (Mass. Hist. Soc.); *N.Y. Col. Docs.*, IX, 779; Richard, ed., *Canadian Archives Supplement*, ser. B, XXVII, 389.

28. John Winthrop to Fitzjohn Winthrop, June 1706, Mass. Hist. Soc., *Collections*, 6th ser., 3 (1889), 333-36; *Board of Trade Journal, 1704-9*, 326; *Massachusetts Acts and Resolves, Private Acts, 1692-1780* (Boston, 1896), VI, 62-63; *Cal. State Papers, 1706-8*, no. 773.

29. Mass. Hist. Soc., *Collections*, 6th ser., 3 (1889), 333-36.

Her Majesty's ship *Deptford*, on station at Boston, was ordered out. By mid-July the legislature had imprisoned Vetch and Borland, as well as four others implicated: William Rouse, Roger Lawson, John Phillips, Jr., and Ebenezar Coffin. They were charged with high misdemeanors, denied bail, and ordered held for the next session of the legislature.[30]

An attempt to appeal to the court for bail soon after Vetch was imprisoned was turned down by Judge Samuel Sewall on the grounds that the matter had been taken out of his hands. Although notified by the speaker of the House that Vetch had been impeached for high misdemeanor and was to be committed to the Boston jail to await trial, Sewall had not been furnished with a copy of the act. He considered himself powerless, although he was frank to state his opposition to the method in which the case was being conducted.[31]

It was a highly unusual proceeding. The regular courts were bypassed on the grounds that the acts had been committed outside of their jurisdiction. The legislature cited its power, derived from the charter, to impose fines and imprisonment, and it obtained the consent of the accused to such a proceeding. According to Sewall, even members of the House were doubtful "whether they have not proceeded too hastily in calling that a misdemeanor which the law calls treason." But Dudley had acted hastily to have the Council vote reassurance to the House that their proposed action was allowable, thereby heading off any suggestion that treason was the proper charge. Sewall and seven others had voted in the

30. Chaps. 11, 14-17, 20, and 38, 1706-7, *Mass. Acts and Resolves, 1703-7,* VIII, 168-72, 178. Wait Winthrop reported, "The great cry here is at present about the Indian traders." He was no longer in a position to assist his friends. "I am sorry for Captain Vetch and the rest, but know not how to help it"; Winthrop to Fitzjohn Winthrop, June 24, 1706, Mass. Hist. Soc., *Collections,* 6th ser., 5 (1892), 142. See *Mass. Acts and Resolves, Private Acts, 1692-1780,* VI, 61, for act passed July 13, 1706. See also Addington to the High Sheriff of Suffolk County, July 13, 1706, Miscellaneous Bound Manuscripts, VII (Mass. Hist. Soc.).

31. Aug. 7, 1706, *Diary of Samuel Sewall,* II, 164. The fines amounted to: Vetch, 200 pounds; Borland, 1,100 pounds; Lawson, 300 pounds; Rouse, 1,200 pounds; Phillips, 100 pounds; and Coffin, 50 pounds; *Mass. Acts and Resolves, Private Acts, 1692-1780,* VI, 62-68. Also see chaps. 68, 73, 79, 80, and 82, 1706-7, *Mass. Acts and Resolves, 1703-7,* VIII, 189, 191, 193-95; Mass. Archives, LXIII, 38 (State House, Boston); July 15 and Sept. 28, 1706, Pincheon Papers, originals in Misc. Bound Mss., VII (Mass. Hist. Soc.); Mass. Hist. Soc., *Collections,* 2nd ser., 8 (1826), 240-42.

negative, but the Council approval passed by the margin of one vote. Dudley advised the prisoners privately to submit, assuring them that he would use his interest in England to see that the acts against them were repealed. Such arbitrary proceedings stood little chance of being upheld on appeal to England. It was all part of the governor's plan for rescuing his friends from their predicament.[32]

Vetch reaped more than he had sown. An outsider, he was logically linked with the Albany traders, whose traffic with the French Indians had aroused the protests of Massachusetts Bay as early as King Philip's War. In the autumn of 1704, Massachusetts and Connecticut had sent delegations to Albany to meet with the Five Nations in an effort to enlist their help. The Iroquois, how-ever, had steadfastly refused to move, pretending that they could do nothing without Cornbury's order. The New York governor had raised no objection to the mission, but neither had he co-operated in urging action on the Indians. New York well knew that New England would like peace with the French, too; Mass-achusetts was hardly in a position to criticize New York's in-activity. The people of New York clearly saw that New England wished to relocate the "seat of the Indian war" in New York.[33]

The men of Albany themselves sympathized with the New Englanders and did all in their power to persuade the Indians to stop raiding or, failing that, to get warnings to the Connecticut Valley of impending attacks. But Colonel Partridge, stout settler of western Massachusetts, while admitting that the Schuylers had been kind in their information and that it was an advantage to have it, nevertheless complained: "Yet they crowd the dart of the enemy on our governments and themselves sleep quietly and do nothing;

32. Chap. 45, 1706-7, *Mass. Acts and Resolves, 1703-7*, VIII, 181; Memo-randum of the Board of Trade, Webster Papers (New Brunswick Museum); *Cal. State Papers, 1706-8*, no. 773. Northey, attorney general in England, had advised in 1704 that trading with the enemy was only a high misdemeanor if no stores of war were exported, but 3 and 4 Anne, c. 14, had thereupon been enacted which made trading with the enemy high treason; Newton, *European Nations in the West Indies*, 419-20.

33. Edward Randolph to Board of Trade, Oct. 12, 1696, *N.Y. Col. Docs.*, III, 241-42. Cornbury had been critical of the conduct of the delegation, which included John Livingston, Vetch's brother-in-law; Mass. Hist. Soc., *Collections*, 6th ser., 3 (1889), 261-64, 267-68, 270-71. Also see Colden's "Continuation," N.Y. Hist. Soc., *Collections*, DePeyster pub. fund ser., 68 (1935), 396.

nor will agree in anything against the enemy, but rather to harbor them." It became an obsession with the settlers of western Massachusetts that New York not only failed to support its neighbors but that the Albany traders were furnishing the French and Indians with the implements of war, often taking in trade the very plunder seized by the Indians in their descents on the Connecticut Valley.[34]

It was Vetch's bad luck that the elections of the spring of 1706 had brought to the Massachusetts legislature many new men from the stricken areas, some of whom had served in the militia during the past two years of crisis. This "parcel of resolute rustics," with friends and relations slain by "those heathen," were in no mood to condone a trade with Canada similar to that carried on at Albany, especially when it had been in the hands of a man who was himself closely related to the Albany magnates.[35]

Vetch had a weak case, but his offense was exaggerated. The governor had sanctioned both voyages, and whatever activity was carried on, Vetch had made only two voyages. The circumstances derived from mixed motives, public and private, and were quite in accord with practices of the day. According to Vetch, too, waiver of the regulation against trading with the enemy had been considered advantageous on the grounds that it would remove some effects of English subjects out of the enemies' hands and produce customs for the Crown. This position was reasonable for Dudley to take, although it was not an adequate explanation for Vetch's attempt to smuggle the goods ashore. Vetch blamed stormy weather for forcing him into Acadian ports and argued that a refusal to trade would have endangered his small crew and his lightly armed vessel. His claim that the trade was insubstantial may have been correct, but as long as the Massachusetts legislature

34. Mass. Hist. Soc., *Collections*, 6th ser., 3 (1889), 222-31, 269, 299, 300, 344; N.Y. Colonial Manuscripts, LII, 45 (3) (4) (5), LIII, 57 (N.Y. State Lib., Albany); *Boston News-Letter*, May 15, June 19, and Dec. 4, 1704, and Jan. 1, 1705, warnings of attack sent from Albany; Hutchinson, *History of Massachusetts Bay*, II, 104-6; and see the protest written in Boston, May 31, 1708, *N.Y. Col. Docs.*, V, 42.

35. List of representatives, 1706-7, *Mass. Acts and Resolves*, 1703-7, VIII, 162. Compare with list of representatives in 1705-6, *ibid.*, 114. The terms were those of John Winthrop; Mass. Hist. Soc., *Collections*, 6th ser., 3 (1889), 333-37.

chose to adhere to the principle involved, that argument was beside the point. Besides, since he did not dissociate himself from the activity of Rouse in the sloop *Anne* and from Rouse's confederates, Phillips in the *Mayflower* and Coffin in the *Hope*, it was likely that the whole group of them was out to make as much of their opportunity as they could.

Vetch maintained that the Indians with whom he had traded lived a thousand miles from New England and were not involved in the frontier raids, and he was supported by two witnesses well acquainted with Acadia: the Boston merchants John Nelson and John Alden. As Vetch suggested, the failure of the Massachusetts legislature to agree to the Canadian neutrality proposal was more to blame for the renewed outbreak of frontier atrocities in the spring of 1706 than was any English trading. But whatever the cause of the raids, they inflamed the passions of the populace, and Vetch, wittingly or unwittingly, had put himself in a vulnerable position. According to his later account, the legislature accepted his first frank statement of his activities. Borland and Lawson, too, had testified and had been thanked for their explanation of the situation. Vetch attributed his later arrest and the proceedings against him to "the mob," who "terrified with great threats" the awed legislature.[36]

The significance of the governor's action in having the case tried by the legislature, instead of in the regular courts, lies in the indication it gives of another issue, hinted at in the very beginning, but one which became clear only a year later—the case had been seized upon by Dudley's opponents in order to attack him politically. Vetch was, at least in part, a victim of political animosities with which he had little connection. If it had not been for the desire of some to implicate the governor, Vetch might have carried on his trade quietly, without protest from the Bay Colony. In this, the Massachusetts affair was similar to the case of the sloop *Mary*, which was indirectly an attack on Livingston.

Despite his New England origins, Dudley had acted the genuine royal executive. In Massachusetts, as in New York, a struggle for independent power on the part of the colonial representa-

---

36. Osgood, *Eighteenth Century*, I, 420; *Cal. State Papers, 1706-8*, nos. 773, 832iii; *Mass. Acts and Resolves, Private Acts, 1692-1780*, VI, 63-68.

tives ran head on into the claims of royal authority. Dudley's policy was England's—the maintenance of a colony which would strengthen the mother country in its struggle against France—and it took the accustomed form of appeals for a regular fixed salary, the production of goods, such as naval stores, which England needed, and adequate provisions for defense. Unlike New York, the Massachusetts legislature could never charge Dudley with misapplication of the revenue. He was recognized for the able, efficient ruler that he was, and he had the grudging respect of his enemies. But the Mathers and their ally in England, Sir Henry Ashurst, the Connecticut agent, represented the moral and political system of the old Puritanism. They led a considerable faction determined to prevent what they considered a threat to the colony's charter and its traditional privileges.[37]

Beneath the clamor of the mob ran these political undercurrents, which were reflected in Vetch's testimony offered to the Board of Trade early in 1707. The outcry, he said, had been "instigated by a party, enemies to the government"; the governor was frightened into approving the acts against the traders "by the threats of the mob to pull down his house, accusing him as a party concerned." When the Assembly first examined Vetch and the others, rumors had forced the body to vote that it was not true they were asking the accused whether the governor was concerned in the trade. Someone obviously desired to establish that charge.[38]

Finally, a year after the trial, the politics involved came into the open. A petition asking for Dudley's removal was presented to the Queen, signed by discontented colonists of Massachusetts and New Hampshire. It was rapidly followed by a pamphlet printed in London in 1707, "A Memorial of the Present Deplorable State of New England," embodying Cotton Mather's attack on the

---

37. Everett Kimball, *The Public Life of Joseph Dudley, Harvard Historical Studies,* XV (Cambridge, 1911) *passim;* Osgood, *Eighteenth Century,* II, chap. XX. Mather had put it frankly, not to say bluntly, to Dudley when the governor first arrived. "By no means let any people have cause to say that you take all your measures from the two Mathers. By the same rule I may say without offense, by no means let any people say that you go by no measures in your conduct but Mr. Byfield's and Mr. Leverett's"; Mass. Hist. Soc., *Collections,* 1st ser., 3 (1794), 137.

38. *Cal. State Papers, 1706-8,* no. 773; Kimball, *Dudley,* 184.

governor. Dudley was charged with complicity in the trade, manipulation of the trial, bribery, and corruption. Nor did the Mathers hesitate to make their charges directly to Dudley. In separate letters, early in 1708, the two ministers accused the governor of a long list of misdeeds which included engineering the proceedings to protect himself.[39]

From the evidence presented, the Board of Trade concluded that Dudley was "highly suspected to be concerned in this illegal trade and (as tis said) he artfully complyed with the Assembly's desire of trying these people. Knowing that several in the Assembly suspected him, he had friends enough in that House to prevent the asking such questions as might touch him; which he could not have done had the prisoners been tried in the ordinary courts where he had not so much influence." In order to bring all the facts to light, the Board recommended a retrial, this time in the courts and for treason rather than misdemeanor. "If they find themselves in danger, tis probable all may come out," the Board concluded; "they will speak plain rather than suffer."[40]

That Dudley managed the trial procedure is beyond doubt. But this fact begs the question of whether he did so because of complicity in the illegal trade or to protect himself from the charges of his political enemies. Dudley's own defense was calm and assured. It took the form of letters to England and the publication there of a pamphlet in rebuttal to that of the Mathers.[41]

39. Kimball, *Dudley*, 182; Mass. Hist. Soc., *Collections*, 1st ser., 3 (1794), 126, 128, 135; *ibid.*, 5th ser., 6 (1879), 32 ff. The Mathers' attacks took the form of admonitions delivered from spiritual overseers, as they considered themselves to be. The governor, in a masterly reply, charged them with forgetting their station and his and with bitterness, prejudice, rumor-mongering, and rehearsing ancient events because of recent disappointments; *ibid.*, 1st ser., 3 (1794), 135. Cotton Mather's side is found in his Diary, *ibid.*, 7th ser., 7 (1911), 581, and 8 (1912), 8.

40. Memorandum of the Board of Trade, Sept. 1707, Webster Papers (New Brunswick Museum).

41. Kimball's study of Dudley, accurate, scholarly, and extremely useful, errs in its interpretation of Dudley's role here, it seems to me. Kimball intimates that Dudley was not behind the method of the trial, calling it only a "supposition" that Dudley promised the prisoners his protection (p. 119). He also stresses unduly, in the face of the evidence, Dudley's "innocence" (pp. 187-88). Evidence found in Dudley's letter, Vetch's Petition, the Memorandum of the Board of Trade, Mather's pamphlets, and the reports of Usher and Quary all seem to point to a different interpretation. Dudley's "A Modest Enquiry into the Grounds and Occasion of a Late Pamphlet, etc.," which was published in

When the Mather pamphlet first reached Boston, the governor's immediate reaction had been less dispassionate. He went before the Council with ill-concealed anger and demanded a vote to clear him. The Council did his bidding the same day, the first of November, agreeing unanimously that the pamphlet was a "scandalous and wicked accusation," contrary to what had always been apparent to the people of Massachusetts. Dudley was credited with keeping the other officers of the government informed of all steps in his negotiations with Canada, and the Council was "sensible of his indefatigable care and pains in a vigorous and successful pursuit of the enemy and protection of Her Majesty's good subjects."

The House, with a sizable faction opposed to the governor, proved less tractable. The Mathers had been outraged by the recent elevation of John Leverett, the governor's friend, to the presidency of Harvard College, a position which the Mathers considered a family preserve. It took several messages from Dudley to bring the deputies to pass the desired vote, and they did so only after being assured that the Council had voted unanimously to vindicate him.[42]

While the deputies were considering whether to burn or back the Mathers' attack, Sewall had sober second thoughts. He sought out Borland, who told him that the governor had been aware of Vetch's trade with the Acadians. From this information Sewall deduced that the testimony of the witnesses cited by Mather was true, "that the governor did connive at their trading with the French, which has opened a tragical scene that I know not when we shall see the close of it." Sewall's son was married to Dudley's daughter, and the two men always maintained friendly personal relations despite their political differences. But Sewall refused

---

London in 1707, may be found in Mass. Hist. Soc., *Collections*, 5th ser., 6 (1879), 65.

42. Mass. Archives, XX, 109 (State House, Boston); Kimball, *Dudley*, 185-86. Kimball assumes that the vote was finally passed because the House could find no evidence against the governor. The Mathers, in a second pamphlet printed in 1708, charged Dudley with intimidation and bribery in procuring the vote. Dudley's record would indicate merely that he knew how to manage his legislatures and carried the House because of its respect for him and the realization that his policy was a sound one. Kimball is unwilling to credit Dudley with so much influence (p. 187).

to compromise his principles. He saw clearly that the governor had allowed "Mr. Borland and Captain Vetch their trading voyage to her Majesty's enemies." He was quite ready to admit that by this the governor had not "designed to hurt the province, but to gratify grateful merchants," and he had no judgment to make on the advisability of Dudley's actions. What annoyed him was the governor's steam-roller tactics in rushing the vote through the legislature instead of setting aside his personal interest in favor of mature deliberation at the Council's discretion.

Sewall told the governor flatly, "This skrewing the strings of your lute to that height has broken one of them," and he insisted upon withdrawing his vote. The governor begged him to keep his action private, but Sewall refused. Townsend, a prominent member of the General Court, seconded Dudley's request. He "ask'd me to withdraw my paper and put it in my pocket, pleasantly," records Sewall; "I answered pleasantly, I could as easily put him in my pocket."[43]

Sewall persisted in his attempt to get at the truth. As a friend of Nathaniel Higginson, who was one of the signers of the petition against Dudley, Sewall wished to see justice done all around, which could only come about if all the facts were ascertained. Another meeting with Borland made it clear that Dudley had never received any pecuniary benefit from the activity of the traders. It was a question of clarifying the distinction between Dudley's acquiescence in Vetch's voyage and actual participation in the trade or its profits. Afterwards, Sewall wrote that he had Borland's affidavit that Dudley had no pecuniary interest in the affair, and that this was not the issue in the withdrawal of his vote—he wished merely to indicate that he no longer believed the governor was ignorant of the trade.

Although Sewall had printed his withdrawal and the reasons for it, he had distributed few copies, "being advised by some friends not to add oil to our flame." Borland, nevertheless, was much exercised at the use Sewall had made of the information which he had been given. "He talked of making a flame" and adamantly refused to show Sewall a copy of the petition which Vetch had pre-

43. Nov. 1707, *Diary of Samuel Sewall*, II, 200, 201, 202-4; Mass. Archives, XX, 111 (State House, Boston).

sented to the English government and which gave Vetch's version of the whole affair. This refusal to "clear the truth of a controverted matter of fact, tho the petition be publicly lying before the Queen . . . and anyone may have a copy for their money," was a source of annoyance to the persistent judge.[44]

Knowledge of Vetch's petition would only have confirmed what Borland had already told Sewall. The judge had already arrived at a sensible view of the matter, one which was obviously in accordance with the facts as they were finally brought out. Usher, Dudley's lieutenant governor for New Hampshire, hinted to the Board of Trade in his aggravatingly vague manner that the records of the trial would show "great villany" and that "several great persons" would be found concerned. Likewise, Colonel Quary, the Board's agent in the colonies, had said that some "topping men" of the Massachusetts government were involved. If these allusions imply anything more than the knavery of the governor, they are sufficiently explained by Vetch's connections with the Winthrops and the Livingstons.[45]

Despite the use which the Mathers made of Sewall's recantation in their second pamphlet, their effusions were too intemperate to carry influence in England; and the pamphlet came too late to influence the Privy Council, which had already acted. Dudley's friends in England were able to maintain him in power against the machinations of the old guard in New England.[46]

Dudley had long since made a persuasive case for his actions in his own letter to the Board of Trade just after the conviction and fining of the traders. Justifying the method followed, he had supported the General Court, arguing that the men of Massachusetts were unversed in English law, hard pressed by the enemy, and aggravated especially with the traders. That Dudley approved of the proceedings is apparent from his unwillingness to foist all the blame for it on the court, despite the fact that he was "sensible that the persons . . . will reflect upon some methods in

44. Dec. 12, 1707, and Feb. 5, 1708, *Diary of Samuel Sewall*, II, 206, 215; Mar. 10, 1708, Mass. Hist. Soc., *Collections*, 6th ser., 1 (1886), 362.

45. *Cal. State Papers, 1706-8*, no. 536; Memorandum of the Board of Trade, Sept. 1707, Webster Papers (New Brunswick Museum); *N.Y. Col. Docs.*, V, 30; Kimball, *Dudley*, 184-85.

46. Kimball, *Dudley*, 180-81.

the proceedings." His own reasons were fear that "an outrage" would be perpetrated on the "delinquents" otherwise and a conviction that the General Court was better suited to resolving the affair and quieting the outraged feelings of the colonists than courts of law. He wanted moderate action and a quick settlement of the case. He admitted friendship with the defendants and sympathy for those "who had suffered to the last degree, if I had not with all skill I have labored to quiet the people." He stressed the fact that he had approved the fines levied only pending "Her Majesty her royal prerogative referring to the fines," pointing out that "the fines are beyond the power of some of them . . . to pay" and urging that they be moderated. Dudley's analysis is probably closest to the facts in the matter. He had handled the affair as he did to prevent his opponents from making effective political capital against him.[47]

In the meantime, while this political storm raged around the Massachusetts governor in New England and old, Vetch had paid his fine, left the colonies, and gone to England. As evidence that his conviction had been a matter of political pressures rather than presumption of his criminality, Vetch observed that the Assembly, "before they passed the Acts," had proposed to send him as their agent to Canada again; after the acts had been passed, it was "proposed in both Houses to send him [as] their agent into this Kingdom to endeavor . . . to procure a body of Scots to settle in Nova Scotia."[48] So bald a statement could hardly have gone unchallenged had it been untrue. Already Vetch was at work on the grand design which was to shape his future and that of the northern colonies in the next few years, the project which he hoped would win him fame and would change the lineaments of North America for the eighteenth century and perhaps longer.

47. *Cal. State Papers, 1706-8,* no. 525.
48. *Ibid.,* no. 773.

CHAPTER SIX

Canada Surveyed

VETCH LEFT MASSACHUSETTS BAY late in 1706. His active nature would not allow him to bide quietly in the colonies while his appeal made its slow way through the offices of the English bureaucracy. His first objective upon his return to England was to press his own case personally. Once cleared, he would take up with the proper authorities the larger business upon which he had been sent, the conquest of Canada.

The success which attended him in both endeavors was attributable in part to the fact that his way had already been smoothed. Robert Livingston had been in England during the past several years; he had returned to the colonies just before Vetch departed. Livingston's affairs were never without their difficulties. On his way over to England, the French had seized him and had taken everything he had to support himself. Once in England, he had spent long days dancing attendance on great men and their underlings before he had obtained a hearing about the money due him. Just before he was to sail for home, he had been clapped into jail in connection with his financial stake in Captain Kidd's voyage. Despite his difficulties, however, he had enjoyed ample opportunity to preach the needs of the colonists for organization and material aid in their struggle against Canada—indeed, he made his own predicament a case in point. If the English government did not pay debts such as those owing him, "no man there will ever disburse money for the public service in the great exigencies."[1]

Livingston had finally collected a good part of his account,

1. Sept. 1706, Livingston Papers.

invested it in large shipments of goods consigned to his wife at the Manor, and amply insured them against loss. He returned more affluent than ever, sporting a new sealskin wig and other marks of increased estate, such as a new desk and a chamber pot. Certainly he was able to help Vetch pay his fine, if that was necessary.[2]

Dudley's outspoken sympathy for the convicted traders and his recommendation of "Her Majesty's favour to any or all of them" added weight to the petitions presented by Vetch on behalf of himself and his fellow defendants. Vetch, in turn, was ready to swear that Dudley was not a partner in the illegal trade, and he did so the following year when the attack on Dudley took place. Moreover, Vetch found staunch friends of Dudley ready to help him. John Chamberlayne, a prominent leader in the Society for the Promotion of the Gospel, had long served as Dudley's representative among the great men of the government and had already done Vetch some service. Through Chamberlayne, Vetch could count on the support of the Bishop of London, who had been inclined toward Dudley's regime by "judicious letters" from the governor written at Chamberlayne's urging. Flattery and presents had won Nottingham and others of the great lords. William Blathwayt, always influential in the Board of Trade and the Privy Council, had been and remained Dudley's sponsor and patron in England. Another was Lord Cutts. The Massachusetts agent Constantine Phips also adhered to Dudley's party and helped Vetch present his case.[3] But Vetch did not count on Dudley's friends alone. A memorandum of the Board of Trade ruefully and ambiguously noted that "Vetch *has made* a certain gentleman, as he himself termed it. I suppose not for nothing." His successes in the following two years were to show that Vetch could

2. Livingston to Lord Treasurer Godolphin, Oct. 12, 1704, *ibid.;* see also invoices totalling thousands of pounds. One shipment was captured by the French in New York harbor, according to Livingston, who professed to be disconsolate. Since it was insured, this would appear to be an example of Livingston's proclivity for calamity howling.

3. Dudley to Board of Trade, Oct. 8, 1706, Vetch's petitions, read Feb. 25, Dudley's defense, to the Queen, Nov. 10, 1707, *Cal. State Papers, 1706-8,* nos. 525, 773-74, 1186ii; Kimball, *Dudley,* 180-81, 188-89; Mass. Hist. Soc., *Collections,* 6th ser., 3 (1889), 532, 540, 542, 544; *ibid.,* 5 (1892), 215; *Board of Trade Journal, 1704-9,* 9. Nottingham, a moderate Tory, and Compton, Bishop of London, were close to the Queen.

muster a redoubtable group of backers to add to those already allied with Dudley.[4]

On the other hand, Dudley's opponents in England were numerous. Sir Henry Ashurst, employed by the Mathers, was ceaseless in his opposition. Ashurst, as agent for Connecticut, worked in conjunction with William Wharton, the Rhode Island agent, to thwart Dudley's attempts to vacate the charters of those two independent colonies. In pressing for action on Vetch's case, they hoped to embarrass the governor and bring about a retrial for treason. Nathaniel Higginson, a Massachusetts merchant in the employ of the East India Company, who was Sewall's friend and a signer of the petition against Dudley in the summer of 1707, joined with the discontented New Hampshire interests and the Mather faction in the effort to implicate Dudley in the illicit trade and bring about his removal.[5]

Fortunately for Vetch, both sides were working toward the same objective, annulment of the acts of the Massachusetts legislature. Dudley's opponents hoped thereby to stamp the Massachusetts action as an assumption of powers outside the purview of the General Court. Since Dudley had sanctioned the proceedings, he would be put in the peculiar position of having connived at an infringement of the royal prerogative and the rights of Englishmen to trial by jury in duly-established courts. Dudley's enemies further hoped that the threat of a retrial, this time on the serious charge of treason, would force the traders to disclose Dudley's role in the illegal trade.

However Dudley might fare, Vetch had little to fear from such a development. He was secure in England and nothing could compel him to return to America to stand trial again. Besides, as those on the Board of Trade admitted, "It will always be in Her Majesty's power to pardon them as she shall see fit."[6]

4. Memorandum of the Board of Trade, Sept. 1707, Webster Papers (New Brunswick Museum), italics in the original. The author is not known. It was not, of course, Blathwayt. Other members of the Board were Sir Philip Meadows, Lord Dartmouth, Pollexfen, Matthew Prior, Mr. Cecil, Lord Herbert of Cherbury, and Pulteney.

5. Kimball, *Dudley*, 176, 182-93; Feb. 27, 1707, *Board of Trade Journal, 1704-9*, 326.

6. Memorandum of the Board of Trade, Sept. 1707, Webster Papers (New Brunswick Museum).

Vetch handed in his petition to the Privy Council in February 1707, and it was promptly referred to the Board of Trade. At the end of the month, the Board reviewed the evidence in the case: the acts passed by the Massachusetts legislature, the accusations, affidavits, and proceedings, as well as the letters from Usher, Dudley, and Wharton. Vetch spoke in his own behalf and for others who had been fined.

The Board of Trade then referred the legal questions involved to the attorney general for his decision. These, in summary, were whether the Massachusetts General Court had the power under the colony's charter to try and punish offenders by legislative acts without jury trial; whether fines levied under such circumstances could be unlimited and therefore confiscatory, as had been alleged in the case of Rouse; whether such action by the Massachusetts government was a precedent adversely affecting the power of the Crown in the colonies; and, finally, whether, if the acts were vacated, the alleged offenders might be tried over again in the ordinary course of the law and, if so, by what method.[7]

A month later, the reply was ready. Northey, the attorney general, held that the colonial legislature had power to make laws but not to execute them. The colony had exceeded its power under its charter; the acts could not be confirmed without establishing a precedent dangerous in its consequences both to the Crown and her subjects. He recommended rejection of the acts and gave it as his opinion that the offenders might be tried in the courts in the regular manner. He disposed of the question of excessive fines by noting that a man's financial position should play no part in the matter, lest poor men be exempted from fines entirely.

The Board of Trade met and agreed to accept Northey's opinion. Vetch, who was present, asked for remission of the fines which had been levied and also argued cogently against a retrial, pointing out that he and his fellow pleaders had already suffered imprisonment and the confiscation of their ships and goods. He submitted two papers containing his views for the Board to consider and forward to the Privy Council.

7. Feb. 20-25, Feb. 25-27, and Feb. 27, 1707, *Cal. State Papers, 1706-8,* nos. 773, 782, 786, 787; Feb. 25-27, 1707, *Board of Trade Journal, 1704-9,* 326-27.

Late in April, the case went back to the Earl of Sunderland for final decision by the Council. In its memorandum for the Council, the Board remained noncommittal beyond endorsing the attorney general's report, although it was suggested that Northey had not considered the nature of the crime. If it were treason rather than misdemeanor and if it were found desirable to expose persons in higher positions, namely Dudley, by bringing the offenders to trial for the more serious offense, then that should be done. On the other hand, it was noted that it was within the Queen's power to pardon the accused. The Board was clearly split, with at least some members anxious to see fit punishment meted out for guilt in no less a crime than "trading and corresponding with Her Majesty's declared enemies."[8]

A long delay followed while the matter was pending before the Privy Council. For nearly half a year Vetch waited for the verdict. Finally, in September 1707, the Board of Trade received an Order in Council repealing the six acts of the Massachusetts government and ordering the accused to stand a new trial. Vetch, in England, was outside of Dudley's jurisdiction, but as soon as the governor received the order, the following spring, he discharged the other defendants, restored their fines, and took surety for them to stand trial at the next meeting of the colony's superior court.[9]

The result was as Vetch had probably anticipated. The case against Dudley had faded in the face of the governor's strong defense. Dudley had defied anyone to prove under oath that he had been financially concerned in any trade on sea or land. Nor was it likely that Bay Colony jurists would press a case against a group of their fellow citizens to uphold the royal prerogative which had struck down the acts of their legislature. Actually, the fact that Dudley had ridden out the storm and was more firmly ensconced in his position than ever was probably assurance enough that the traders in whose case he had become involved would not

8. Mar. 28, read Apr. 17, 1707, *Cal. State Papers, 1706-8,* no. 832, and see nos. 873, 787; *Board of Trade Journal, 1704-9,* 341-42, 345; Memorandum of the Board of Trade, Sept. 1707, Webster Papers (New Brunswick Museum).

9. *Cal. State Papers, 1706-8,* nos. 1121, 1122, 1504; *Board of Trade Journal, 1704-9,* 411; Order in Council, Kensington, Sept. 24, 1707, Webster Papers (New Brunswick Museum).

suffer further penalty. The men came to trial, but the cases were ultimately dismissed in 1708. When Vetch subsequently returned to Massachusetts, the disposition of the other cases dictated the return of his fine and the closing of the case against him.[10]

The two years which Vetch spent in England must have been difficult ones for his family. He had been forced to leave his wife and young children while he followed where his enterprises led him. Sometime before he left Massachusetts, a son William had been born, named for the brother who had shared Samuel Vetch's fortunes until claimed by death after the second Darien expedition.[11]

During his years in England, Vetch visited his parents in Scotland. His father, nearing seventy, was still vigorous with several more years of active service in the ministry before him. His mother had already reached the alloted three score years and ten and was as indomitable as ever. Of the ten children, Samuel and two sisters were the only ones left.[12] Since memories of the Darien disaster still rankled above the border—many continued to hold the leaders in the expedition at fault—it is likely that Vetch waited until after he had reinstated himself at court before making his visit. At any rate, while he was in Scotland, Mrs. Veitch learned that he was now bound on an expedition against "Jamaica."[13]

10. Dudley to the Queen, Nov. 10, 1707, *Cal. State Papers, 1706-8*, no. 1186ii; Dudley to Board of Trade, Mar. 1, 1709, and list of causes tried in Massachusetts Bay, 1703-9, *ibid., 1708-9*, no. 391; Osgood, *Eighteenth Century*, I, 423; Hutchinson, *History of Massachusetts Bay*, II, 117-18; House of Representatives, June 2, 1709, Mass. Archives, LXXI, 520 (State House, Boston).

11. No record of William Vetch's birth or death has been found and genealogists do not list him. Correspondence in the Livingston Papers mentions him, however, and suggests that he was probably born in this period. New York records indicate that Margaret Vetch remained at the Manor while her husband was in England; Holland Soc. of N.Y., *Year Book, 1905*, 37, 45, 52.

12. *Veitch Memoirs*, 216-17, 219.

13. *Mrs. Veitch Memoirs*, 59. Possibly some attempt to keep secret the destination of English troops bound for Canada may have accounted for Mrs. Veitch's confusion. She records Samuel's visit as coming after nine years' absence, which would make it in 1706, as soon as Vetch reached England, but it is questionable that he could have been sure of his future plans so soon. Mrs. Veitch may have confused an early visit with a later one, or with information received later, since she notes that the expedition was a failure. That knowledge and the knowledge that Vetch was to have the governorship could only have come in 1709, or later.

She later found out, perhaps during a second visit from her son, that he was to become governor of Canada when that place had been taken from the French. This project was the ostensible reason for Vetch's trip to England at the end of 1706. Now, after more than a year of concern over his own fate, he was ready to move in the larger business which he had at heart. During the opening months of 1708, he began to build the case which he would present to the government, the scheme of a "Glorious Enterprise" to conquer Canada from the French.

Plans for the conquest of Canada were not original with Vetch; they can be traced back to the first signs of French expansion in the New World. New York, after its accession from the Dutch, became the target of French encroachment almost at once. With its close association with the Iroquois, its important trade in furs, and a frontier providing easy access to and from Canada, that province furnished the chief challenge to France's advancing empire, and New York leaders were first to recognize the French threat and to devise a way to meet it.

From the time of Governor Lovelace in 1670, successive New York governors reported remarkably similar observations and conclusions. Dongan, before he went out of office in 1688, had formulated a position which was adhered to by most of his successors until New France finally fell over half a century later. Minor skirmishes and defensive measures, he believed, would not effectively protect the English from constant harassment. What was needed was a concerted effort, combining English and colonial forces with the Iroquois, to deal the French a blow which would end their aggression once and for all. Leisler had favored such an offensive, had tried it without help from England and had failed. Governor Sloughter favored a similar scheme. His successor, Fletcher, failed to achieve co-operation from the other colonies for a real effort against Canada, even though the English government added its voice—but not its active assistance—in urging combined colonial action. Bellomont advocated the conquest of Canada and sought to use the period of truce between the first and second colonial wars to marshal the resources of the colonies against the threat from Canada, but he too was unsuccessful.[14]

The strategy for the attack on Canada had evolved along with recognition of the need. Not only did it call for a combined operation utilizing English forces as well as colonials and Indians, but it also spelled out the plan of campaign: a two-pronged advance, by land from Albany against Montreal and by sea from New York or Boston against Quebec. The Indians repeatedly inquired about the "considerable force to go with great guns by sea," which indicated that they had absorbed the current thinking on the problem and believed it was the only real solution. It may also indicate that Peter Schuyler, in whom they had such great confidence, was the one who originally worked out the strategy.[15]

Whatever the origins of this strategy, by the time of Queen Anne's War past failures had convinced most leaders in the struggle against New France that the concept was sound. The lack of unifying force of English leadership, inadequate assistance from England, and the absence of English forces convinced the colonists that they could not undertake the requisite task without co-ordinated planning and co-operation. The failure of attacks by New Englanders against the French outposts in Nova Scotia during the early years of the second war underscored these conclusions. Vetch absorbed the prevailing strategic concept directly from his close relationship with Schuyler and Livingston, from his observance of the scene in New York and in Massachusetts Bay, and from his dealings with the Canadian government. He now set out to enlist

14. Lovelace to Williamson, *N.Y. Col. Docs.*, III, 190, and also see 784-86; Bellomont to Board of Trade, Apr. 17, 1699, *ibid.*, IV, 505; *Cal. State Papers, 1685-88*, no. 1479; *ibid., 1689-92*, nos. 169, 717-19. For Sloughter's scheme, see Osgood, *Eighteenth Century*, I, 231. Nicholas Bayard, who had fled to Albany to escape Leisler's clutches, recommended an attack on Canada aided by English forces; Bayard to Francis Nicholson, Aug. 5, 1689, *N.Y. Col. Docs.*, III, 611-12. See also Nicholson, *Cal. State Papers, 1702-3*, nos. 567-68; *N.Y. Col. Docs.*, IV, 224, 210; Historical Manuscripts Commission, *Report on the Manuscripts of His Grace the Duke of Buccleuch and Queensbury* (London, 1903), II, 792; and *Cal. State Papers, 1696-97*, nos. 138-40.

15. *N.Y. Col. Docs.*, IV, 20-23, 176, 235-38, 240. W. D. Schuyler-Lighthall, "The 'Glorious Enterprise': The Plan of Campaign for the Conquest of New France; Its Origin, History, and Connection with the Invasion of Canada," *Canadian Antiquarian and Numismatic Journal*, ser. 3, 4 (1902). Robert Livingston, Schuyler's brother-in-law, was insisting on this strategy on the eve of Leisler's attempt; "Memorandum. . . ," Apr. 22, 1690, Livingston Papers.

British help to bring together the forces necessary to accomplish the grand design of defeating France in the New World.

The Massachusetts men who had convicted Vetch for his trade with the Canadians did not know that even as he plied the waters of the St. Lawrence and coasted along the Maritimes he had dreamed of taking Canada. Early in 1706, he "mightily importuned" John Chamberlayne, Dudley's staunch supporter in London, with the prototype of the plan he was now ready to present in finished form. Chamberlayne faithfully presented this version of Vetch's plan to the Whig junto, commenting that it was the work of "an old Buccaneer, tho a young man."[16]

Even this early proposal was amazingly detailed and persuasive as a report on the needs of the English colonists and the potentialities of Canada for the empire. Vetch suggested using Scots to conquer and settle the country. The Darien failure and the needs of the northern kingdom for colonial and commercial expansion helped shape his thinking, for he pointed out that Canada would be "a healthful place and more agreeable to a people bred in cold countries than the West Indies, which proves a grave to [an] abundance of [the] people that go there." The proposal outlined the potentialities of the country for wheat, peas, grain, timber, fish, and furs. It described Canada's geography and the state of its fortifications, observing that it might be "easily taken by resolved men, well equipped."

In this intercolonial struggle, Vetch observed, all the English colonies were subject to "insult" from the French. The barbarities and murders by the French and their Indians, the plight of English captives in French hands, the massacre at Deerfield, and the enlargement of French dominion along the "back side of Virginia, Maryland, Pennsylvania and New York" threatened all those colonies with Indian attack as soon as France should win over control of the tribes in those areas. Particular attention was given to Acadia, which, in French hands, was "to plantations here, as Dunkirk to England, from whence they fit out privateers and infest our coast." The comparison with Dunkirk was an apt one,

16. John Chamberlayne to Lord ——, Feb. 27, 1706, Egerton Mss., no. 929, f. 90-92 (Lib. Cong. Transcripts).

and it found echoes in the later writing of Jeremy Dummer and Higginson.[17]

Nor did Vetch neglect the advantages which would accrue to the mother country from a victory in Canada. A settlement at Nova Scotia, which once had belonged to England, would provide England's navy "in a little time" with "large stores from thence upon reasonable terms," sparing the expenditure of specie to foreigners and securing fishing rights as well. Good harbors, sea coal, produce—all made this area a valuable acquisition.

Finally, Vetch attempted to offset the current arguments of the English mercantilists who viewed the New England colonies as trade rivals and counted the West Indies as England's real jewels of empire. He noted that New England consumed English manufactured goods, that it imported more from the mother country than it exported to her, and that its exports of provisions had been and still were essential to many of the other colonies in the New World. Actually, New England offered England a favorable balance of trade; the deficiency on the colonial side was made up by her many exports to England's other colonies, by exports of fish to Europe, and, in the final tally, by exports of specie to England. Nor should England forget the necessity it was under to obtain naval stores from New England, which could furnish them in abundance, freeing the Crown from dependence on Sweden. These were arguments which were adopted and given effective presentation much later by Joshua Gee and Jeremy Dummer, who were associated with Vetch in his final years. With all these advantages in favor of preserving New England, England's duty, Vetch continued, was clear. New England "cannot be secured till the French are dispossessed of Nova Scotia, Acadia, and Canada, either by force or by treaty of peace."

Vetch's plan, coming as it did before the completion of the union between England and Scotland, was not likely to be adopted. But with the passage of little more than a year, England might be more receptive to such a plan for utilizing the zeal of its newly acquired compatriots. At least, its proposal and management by

17. Charles L. Sanford, "The Days of Jeremy Dummer, Colonial Agent" (unpublished Ph.D. dissertation, Harvard University, 1952), 128; *Cal. State Papers, 1709*, no. 609.

a Scot would be more acceptable. Then, too, the Whigs were steadily gaining power in the government and would be in a position to do more in 1708 than they were in 1706.

The thinking behind Vetch's argument was clearly not his alone. Others prominent in Massachusetts Bay, as well as many of the New York leaders, were agreed on the problem and the proposed solution. Dudley, as well as Vetch, might have cleared himself with his unthinking frontier opponents if he had not considered disclosure of the scheme premature since England had not yet been won over to it. Dudley certainly knew, as did the French, that Vetch's voyages to Canada had as some of their objectives careful reconnaissance of the St. Lawrence, observation of French fortifications in Quebec, Montreal, and Port Royal, and assessment of Canada's armed strength. The French minister, Pontchartrain, told the Canadian governor of Vetch's boast that "he knows as much about the affairs of Canada as the old residents." As early as 1704, Dudley had written to England urging a single blow to oust the French as the cheapest policy in the long run. It became a regular refrain in his letters to the home government.[18]

Even the Mathers supported the plan of conquest, although they sought to use it as a political weapon to oust Dudley. They maintained that New England would back an attack against Canada or Nova Scotia only under a new governor who could be trusted more than the present incumbent. Their candidate, Sir Charles Hobby, had been recommended to Whitehall as early as 1703 in a letter from Cotton Mather which was preciously phrased and flowing over with Mather's egotism. Cognizant that he was not the only one who aspired to be the "American Marlborough," Vetch wrote to Sewall and the Mathers "that I should be ready to do them all the service [which] lies in my power here, and am sure, without vanity, can do them much more than Sir Charles." Sewall, who had already been won over to Vetch's aims, had

18. Nov. 27, 1704, *Cal. State Papers, 1704-5,* no. 680; Feb. 1, Oct. 2, Oct. 8, 1706, Nov. 10, 1707, and Feb. 16, 1708, *ibid., 1706-8,* nos. 69, 511, 526, 1186i; *N.Y. Col. Docs.,* IX, 779. Also see Richard, ed., *Canadian Archives Supplement,* ser. B, XXVII, 389 (June 9, 1706) and ser. C, III, 211. The attempt to conquer Canada through tactics similar to those advocated by Vetch had been made in 1690 by Sir William Phips, who sailed from Boston in conjunction with an overland attack by New York and Connecticut forces led by Fitzjohn Winthrop. The plan failed.

written earlier to Nathaniel Higginson referring to the conquest as the idea of "many intelligent persons" and asking Higginson to support it in England, even though he opposed Dudley.[19]

Now Vetch asked Sewall to assure his former opponents that he bore no grudges; he asked only that the Bay Colony unite in an address to the Queen asking for British help. If it would do so, he would undertake to get the government to comply. He pointed out the precarious position of the colony not only because of French enmity but also because in the eyes of the English government it had so often taken an independent course. He quoted Sunderland, the Secretary of State and a leading Whig, as saying that the New Englanders were "a people that hated to do anything regularly." If they would back his plan, they could have their victory cheaply and without fear of domination by British Regulars, since his scheme envisaged use of Scots who would both capture Canada and then turn planters and settle it. For the Massachusetts colonists, it would be "the effectual way of securing their country, reducing Port Royal, and settling the Eastward." Thus, while he prepared to present his enterprise to the British government, Vetch did not neglect the task of winning unified backing from the warring factions in Massachusetts Bay.[20]

That he was not entirely successful in New England is not strange in view of the heats of the hour. But the Mathers had little recourse except to support Vetch's plan after discovering that Hobby had gone over to Dudley's camp. Jeremy Dummer, newly arrived in London, where he was later appointed Massachusetts agent, soon joined with Vetch in assuring the government that "we are in very great necessity of present help from Her Majesty, although our General Assembly were not so happy as to agree in forming their Address for it."[21]

19. "Deplorable State of New England," Mass. Hist. Soc., *Collections,* 5th ser., 6 (1879), 41, 78; Sewall Letter Book, I, *ibid.,* 6th ser., 1 (1886), 340, 367-68; Sanford, "Jeremy Dummer," 119; Cotton Mather to Lord Hatton, Nov. 26, and Increase Mather to Hatton, Dec. 8, 1703, British Additional Mss., 29549, f. 109, 11 (Lib. Cong. Transcripts).

20. Vetch to Sewall, via Borland, Apr. 26, 1708, Sewall Letter Book, I, Mass. Hist. Soc., *Collections,* 6th ser., 1 (1886), 367-68.

21. May 31, 1708, *Cal. State Papers, 1706-8,* no. 1511. On Hobby's switch of allegiance, see Sir Henry Ashurst to Wait Winthrop and to Increase Mather, Feb. 1710, Mass. Hist. Soc., *Collections,* 6th ser., 5 (1892), 213, 215.

Vetch's plan also won colonial support from other quarters. After a survey of all the colonies, Quary, the agent of the British government in the colonies, wrote from Philadelphia that the likelihood of the colonists' solving their own problems was slight, and yet, he added, "if some effectual means be not used [in] this war to remove the French, it will be too late afterwards." This unanimity among so many colonial leaders had all but convinced the British government of the need for action against the French in Canada. It remained for Vetch to capitalize on growing sentiment and to induce the British to act.[22]

Late in July 1708, the Board of Trade received Vetch's lengthy paper, "Canada Surveyed," which summed up cogently all the arguments in favor of his scheme, adding some that had not been advanced before and incorporating a definite plan of action based on his own intimate political, economic, and topographical knowledge of Canada.[23] It was a document worthy of the notice it immediately received. It was an unusually lucid presentation of an important problem by a man who was acquainted at first hand with the subject and whose private interests were not at variance with those of the colonies or the mother country. This was a combination of circumstances not always found in reports submitted to the Board of Trade. Subtitled "The French Dominions upon the Continent of America Briefly Considered in their situation, strength, trade and numbers, more particularly how vastly prejudicial they are to the British interest, and a method proposed of easily removing them," the paper dealt with its subject under six main headings.

At the outset, Vetch drew attention to the strategy which the situation demanded. He noted the patent absurdity of allowing a handful of widely dispersed French colonists to hem in the populous British colonies, obstructing trade and harassing the people. For the cost of half a year's losses, Britain's powerful forces could

22. Jan. 10, 1708, received and read June 28, 1708, *Cal. State Papers, 1706-8*, no. 1273; Nov. 6, 1704, *ibid., 1704-5*, no. 643; June 30, 1703, *N.Y. Col. Docs.*, IV, 1061, and see 978.

23. "Canada Surveyed" is reprinted in part in *Cal. State Papers, 1708-9*, no. 60 (and additional material submitted later, in no. 196). It is found in full in the Letter Book of Samuel Vetch, 1709-12 (Museum of the City of New York), and P.R.O., C.O. 324, vol. 9, 221-46 (Lib. Cong. Transcripts).

eliminate the danger pressing on its valuable colonies and win an area four times the size of Great Britain. It was a concept which foreshadowed Pitt's later policy of employing Britain's superior maritime strength in a theater where it would prove conclusive, rather than struggling inconclusively with France on the Continent.

Next, Vetch offered an accurate and detailed description of New France. Port Royal, in Nova Scotia, had been the object of repeated attack by New England as a French privateering base. Unless it was taken, Vetch feared reprisals against New England endangering the sources of naval stores important to England. Vetch pictured the towns and settlements up the St. Lawrence and described the course of the river, the fortifications at Quebec and Montreal, the population, the governing personnel, and the numbers of French troops stationed at each strong point.

The advantages to Britain of the conquest of Canada were detailed from two viewpoints. First, Vetch described the riches of the country which would fall to the empire. Included among the prizes would be enough fish and furs to glut Europe. Despite a short growing season, Canada's fertile soil would furnish wheat and peas in abundance. Timber for shipbuilding and naval stores was another resource of the country. Possession of Canada would give Britain control of the Indians, whom the French now directed against the colonies. Moreover, for Scotland, now a part of the British state and eager for colonial outlets, Canada offered a climate similar to that north of Britain.

But "more pungent and powerful arguments" could be offered concerning the advantages of taking Canada, "which must prevail on every true Briton who hath any regard to the honor, interest, or safety of his country." These were self-interest and self-preservation. Here, as in the plan presented to Chamberlayne, Vetch pointed out the connection, too often missed by English mercantilists, between the colonies in North America and the valuable West Indies plantations. The West Indies, he asserted, were dependent on continental America for necessities such as horses and cattle, for the lumber to build their houses, for the staves which made the casks in which they shipped sugar and molasses, for much of their shipping—for their very subsistence.

The disturbance of trade in the northern colonies hit at the West Indies as well. The French attacks had ruined the fur trade, raised the price of provisions, and interrupted the fishery. Outlying farms had been abandoned. Impressment of men into the militia had created a labor shortage and had raised the cost of goods. Shipping was hard hit by French privateering. The American colonies were languishing under the expense of waging war and maintaining defenses. The energy of the colonists, a vital commodity in new lands, was being drained.

Vetch calculated the losses of each colony for each year of struggle and saw them rising with every year the war was prolonged until the French would succeed in driving the English out of the continent altogether. Compared with the staggering cost of continuing the futile policy of half measures, the remedy was so obvious and the expense so little that "posterity would blame us" if that were not done now which could be undertaken so readily.

Vetch proceeded to outline a carefully devised plan for carrying his scheme into effect. As one who "pretends to know that country as well as any subject of the Crown, and who made it his business to know, with that design of being capable to serve his country," Vetch asked for two battalions of Regulars and six men-of-war to accompany 1,000 colonials from New England. This force would sail against Quebec in May or June, while 1,500 men from Connecticut, New York, and the Jerseys would march from Albany against Montreal at the same time, accompanied by the Indians of the Five Nations.

As a final point, Vetch made his scheme easy of acceptance by the English government, modestly asserting that he was certain only lack of information had prevented the government from seeing the necessity of such an expedition before this time.

A few days after the Board of Trade read Vetch's paper, it met again to consider what action it would take. Vetch was present, eager to learn how his scheme would be received. He was anxious to return to New York and his family, which he proposed to do unless the Board thought it necessary for him to remain. If he were not detained, Vetch intended to sail with Lord Lovelace, who had been commissioned to replace Cornbury as governor of New York.

The Board indicated its interest in Vetch's remarkable document and labeled it a proposal "of great benefit to this Kingdom in relation to trade and to the security of the Plantations." According to practice, however, the Board would consider such a weighty project only if formally directed to investigate and render an opinion. It therefore requested Secretary Boyle to determine Her Majesty's pleasure.[24] Boyle shortly ordered the Board to make a formal recommendation to the Queen on the merits of the proposal in order that the government might decide whether it was "of such use as to deserve encouragement." With this assurance, the Board promised to proceed as fast as the "nature and weight of such matter" would allow and recommended that Vetch stay in England. Vetch was given an allowance of ten shillings a day to help meet the expense of his continued attendance in the mother country.[25]

For a time the matter rested, but Vetch's proposal soon received corroboration. Dudley wrote the Board urging the expedition against Canada and was assured that the entire matter was being seriously considered. During the summer of 1708, George Vaughan, agent for New Hampshire, arrived in England and added his voice to the chorus of colonial pleas for action against the French in Canada. He, too, assured the Board of Trade that this was the only sure way to procure peace for the English colonies and that such an attempt would find hearty co-operation on the part of the Queen's American subjects.[26]

Early in November, the Board talked over the project with Vetch and asked him to prepare a supplementary statement elaborating the details of the expedition against Canada. Vetch promptly suggested that a packet boat should be sent to New England with notification of the project; the colonists should

24. July 27, Aug. 3, 1708, *Board of Trade Journal, 1704-9,* 530, 531, 532; *Cal. State Papers, 1708-9,* vii, no. 71; P.R.O., C.O. 324, vol. 9, 250, and C.O. 5, vol. 1084, 37 (Lib. Cong. Transcripts). Sunderland, the Secretary of State, would normally have dealt with problems of this kind, but he was abroad.

25. Board of Trade to Boyle, Aug. 16, and Boyle to Board of Trade, Aug. 11, 1708, P.R.O., C.O. 5, vol. 1084, 38, and C.O. 324, vol. 9, 253-54 (Lib. Cong. Transcripts); Aug. 13-16, 1708, *Board of Trade Journal, 1704-9,* 534-35; Joseph Redington, ed., *Calendar of Treasury Papers, 1708-1714* (London, 1879), CVII, 30; *Cal. State Papers, 1708-9,* no. 89.

26. Board of Trade to Dudley, July 23, Vaughn to Board of Trade, July 6, 1708, *Cal. State Papers, 1708-9,* nos. 58, 19.

be asked to enlist a force of 1,000 men and provide them with three months' provisions and flat-bottomed landing boats. These colonial troops would rendezvous with the British force at Newfoundland.

At the same time, the colonies to the south of Massachusetts Bay should be ordered to assemble 1,500 men at Albany prepared to march against Montreal. He suggested quotas: 550 men from New York, together with the 300 Regulars quartered in that colony; 350 men from Connecticut; 200 from the Jerseys; and 100 from Pennsylvania. Each colony should supply provisions for its militia, but Vetch suggested that the colonial governments could most conveniently victual their troops by contract with provisioners at Albany. Vetch was not above throwing a little business to his father-in-law, the usual agent for the New York Regulars on the frontier.

The Indian commissioners at Albany were to be given the task of enlisting the Five Nations in the enterprise. The Indians were also to be asked to build the requisite number of canoes to transport the colonial force over the rivers and lakes to Montreal. The troops gathered at Albany were to be armed from the magazine at New York and commanded by Major Ingoldesby, the lieutenant governor of that province, with the doughty Peter Schuyler second in command.

The problem of command, Vetch pointed out, was a serious one which might determine the success or failure of the whole expedition. The over-all commander should be the commander of the forces from England. Regulars and militia should each be commanded by their own officers to prevent bad feeling. From experience at Darien, Vetch knew the trouble which could arise from the clash of authority between land officers and seagoing commanders in a joint operation involving military and naval forces. In this scheme, the mixing of Regulars and militia levies added another complication.

Vetch also outlined a plan to garrison Canada against an almost certain attempt at recapture by the French. He estimated that sixteen hundred men stationed at Quebec, Trois Rivières, Montreal, Port Royal, and in Newfoundland would render the prize secure if some of the more unruly French were deported to the West

Indies. The wisdom of this deportation scheme was to be confirmed by later experience in the Maritimes. Summing up these additional details, Vetch pointed out that his plan called for no greater forces from most of the colonies than they were accustomed to keeping under arms against the French threat. New Jersey and Pennsylvania were exceptions, but they had not been enlisted before, and it was time that they contributed to the common cause.[27]

With this additional information, the Board of Trade proceeded to draw up its recommendations to the Privy Council. Vetch was in constant attendance, along with Francis Nicholson, the former governor of Virginia. Nicholson had returned to England in 1705 and had been frequently consulted in colonial matters by the Board of Trade. As lieutenant governor in New York under Andros during the short-lived Dominion of New England, Nicholson knew the situation in the northern colonies. He had done what he could to help Bellomont attain his ends in New York and had probably become acquainted with Vetch at that time. The enterprise under consideration offered an opportunity for Nicholson; he volunteered to serve in the expedition and bent his energies to furthering its acceptance.[28]

In a final hearing on November 29, Vetch gave the Board the best information he had on the strength of the Canadian forces. He was "almost morally sure" they did not exceed five thousand, a figure on which he had found missionaries, merchants, and Indian traders in Canada agreed. Even the intendant, "who I found designed rather to magnify than lessen their numbers," had claimed only a total of five thousand, of whom some were women (not too many, of course, since Canadian men were rewarded for marrying Indian women).

As for Indian allies, Vetch pointed out that not all those who traded with the French joined them in war. Many tribes, "quite to the Mississippi," never came within hundreds of miles of Montreal or Quebec, although they were in the orbit of French

27. Nov. 8, 15, and 17, 1708, *Board of Trade Journal, 1704-9,* 547, 553, 554; Supplement to "Canada Surveyed," *Cal. State Papers, 1708-9,* no. 196 and also in P.R.O., C.O. 324, vol. 9, 256 (Lib. Cong. Transcripts) and Vetch Letter Book (Museum of the City of New York).

28. Nov. 17 and 29, *Board of Trade Journal, 1704-9,* 554, 557; see also above, note 14.

trade. He knew of only five "little forts" of Indians ordinarily engaged in the French interest—one near Quebec, another near Trois Rivières, two near Montreal, and another upriver. Their total numbers, derived from the reports of the Five Nations and the opinions of the Albany Indian commissioners, ran to about nine hundred, "near double" the number of Indians allied with the English, "yet not able to encounter them because not so warlike" and "so dispersed it would take them above a month's time to bring them all in a body to one place."[29]

With this last session, the Board agreed to give its approval to the enterprise against Canada. The draft of the scheme was completed and ordered transcribed for transmittal to Sunderland and the Privy Council. On the first of December it was ready to be forwarded.

Stressing the importance of the northern colonies for maintaining the West Indies, the representation of the Board to the Queen listed all the supplies furnished by the mainland to the island colonies: bread, drink, fish, flesh, cattle, horses, lumber, staves, rum, and molasses. As an "inducement to Your Majesty's engaging in a vigorous attempt on the French," the Board rehearsed the damages sustained by the English colonies, as Vetch had recounted them. The fur trade had fallen off, the Five Nations were wavering in their allegiance, troops and fortifications had cost great sums of money, and New England, especially, had lost heavily in interrupted trade and ravaged frontiers. The "Eastern country" (Maine) had been abandoned, and the French had settled as far down as the Kennebec, causing the loss of valuable timberland to the Crown. French privateering had cut into trade to the extent that the mother country had been forced to send relief to the West Indies. French aggression was encompassing and hemming in the English settlements.

The conclusion was clear: It would be "to the ease and security of your subjects there and to the increase of the trade so beneficial to Great Britain that the French be driven out of the Northern Continent." Vetch's plan for the expedition was annexed to the report, but the Board preferred to leave military matters up to

29. *Board of Trade Journal*, 1704-9, 556-57; P.R.O., C.O. 324, vol. 9, 266-67 (Lib. Cong. Transcripts).

military men and declined to judge whether Vetch's "manner of doing it be proper and effectual."[30]

At this strategic moment, the Board received further information to send to the Queen and her ministers. From New York, Governor Cornbury had written a letter "wherein many things are contained showing the advantage and facility of expelling the French out of Canada, which being of like nature to Vetch's proposals, we pass along to lay before her Majesty." Cornbury's timely letter re-emphasized the governor's earlier suggestion that Canada be taken. He had written it just after a return from Albany, where a meeting with the Indian commission and representatives of the Five Nations had renewed his conviction that the French might easily "be beaten out of Canada." His estimate of French forces was almost exactly that of Vetch, something less than five thousand. He added the information that Quebec's fortifications were not yet finished.[31]

Along with other recommendations sent to the Privy Council was an interesting suggestion outlining a method by which British Regulars could be furnished for the Canada expedition without decreasing the number of regiments in Marlborough's command or incurring the expense of levy money by enlisting new troops in England. To raise two new regiments, the proposal recommended the simple expedient of taking six men from each of the thirteen companies in each of the twenty regiments in the British service. It was a more practical device, no doubt, than attempting to form a small army of Scots as Vetch had originally suggested.

At about this time, too, the Board of Trade presented to the Queen and her ministers an elaborate paper outlining the territorial claims of Britain in America. Drawn up to help the peace negotiators who were carrying out a desultory and ultimately fruitless exploration of terms with Louis XIV, this document was useful as well in making clear the extent of French encroachment on lands claimed by the English in North America.[32]

Several factors accounted for Vetch's success in committing

30. Nov. 29, Dec. 1, 1708, *Board of Trade Journal, 1704-9*, 557, 559; Board of Trade to Sunderland, Dec. 1, 1708, *Cal. State Papers, 1708-9*, no. 221. Also see P.R.O., C.O. 324, vol. 9, 269 (Lib. Cong. Transcripts).

31. Aug. 20, 1708, *Cal. State Papers, 1708-9*, no. 107.

32. P.R.O., C.O. 324, vol. 9, 288, 296-345 (Lib. Cong. Transcripts).

the Board of Trade to support of his scheme. He had come well
recommended. In his forceful presentation, an attractive personality and consummate tact had played their roles. The Board
had undoubtfully been impressed with his lucid and cogent arguments and by the detailed knowledge he possessed. His military experience helped qualify him to speak about a project en-
tailing military exertion. And adding impetus to his arguments
were the persistent voices from the colonies over many years urging
the attack against Canada, culminating in a swelling chorus in that
year of decision. These were the factors which helped Vetch start
the viscid gears of government turning in an undertaking which
was not to reach its successful consummation for half a century.

Even if nothing more were accomplished, this project was
a significant attainment at a time when the zones of intercolonial
responsibility were still without clear definition. Relatively few
men in America had vision enough to see the true outlines of the
struggle with New France in their full import and almost no one
in Britain, enmeshed as she was in European war. All had been
accomplished, too, in just over four months, a short time as the
machinery of the empire moved.

Despite this comparative speed, it seemed virtually impossible
to hope that the plan would be accepted and the expedition
mounted by the following spring. The enterprise had yet to be
weighed by those with authority to act. The Queen and her
ministers were likely to be guided by considerations at once more
far-reaching and more capricious than those which had governed
the Board of Trade.

Vetch's success in winning its final approval in the short space
of the next three months was a remarkable achievement. The
same elements which had helped him gain his end with the Board
of Trade worked in his favor. In addition, considerations which
had not counted before were influential; he was able to marshal
support among men in high places and to take advantage of the
political situation during Queen Anne's reign. The Duke of
Queensbury and the powerful Duke of Hamilton, Scottish nobles
with whom Vetch found common ties of nationality, were very
close to Anne. These men could be of help. Queensbury was the
recognized political leader and manipulator of Scotland. As one

of the commissioners to negotiate the union between Scotland and England, he had been pre-eminently responsible for bringing that affair to a successful conclusion in 1707. Hamilton had proved himself essential to the Whigs in bringing Scottish support in the crucial elections of 1708. Through his father, who was still high in the councils of the Scottish church, Vetch had influence with these leaders. Nor could they fail to be attracted by Vetch's hopes for a resurrected Scottish colony in Nova Scotia. He could confidently term Queensbury his "patron and protector" and place his "entire dependence" on him. Another Scottish leader, Lord Stairs, was not close to Vetch, but his forebears had pledged themselves to favor Vetch's father with their patronage. Other prominent Scots were William Paterson, James Ogilvy, First Earl of Seafield, and William Carstares, well known to Vetch as movers in the old Darien scheme and in favor with the government for their aid in effecting the union.[33]

More immediately in a position to further Vetch's cause was Charles Spencer, the second Earl of Sunderland. Someone in the Board of Trade had earlier noted that "Vetch *has made* a certain gentleman, as he himself termed it. I suppose not for nothing." That this was either Sunderland or his secretary Pringle was evidenced by the fact that Vetch had at the outset delivered a copy of "Canada Surveyed" directly to Sunderland and corresponded frequently with both men during the following year. Approval of his plan by the Board of Trade had followed swiftly on Sunderland's return from the Continent in December. No better supporter could have been found, for Sunderland was the Principal Secretary of State. Colonial affairs were in his jurisdiction. He was a member of the powerful Whig junto which had been fastening its hold on the government with increasing success. Marlborough was his father-in-law, and Marlborough's Duchess still held a semblance of her influence with the Queen. The Lord Treasurer Godolphin was a part of this circle of influence not only because he was at the head of the ministry in which Sunderland served but because his son had married another of Marlborough's

33. Vetch to Queensbury, June 29, Nov. 16, Vetch to Stairs, Nov. 18, 1709, Vetch Letter Book (Museum of the City of New York).

daughters. It was from Sunderland that Vetch received the Queen's orders, to Sunderland that he reported on the course of subsequent events most often and in most detail, and it was Sunderland whose promise Vetch relied on for his reward.[34]

Besides Queensbury and Sunderland, whom he acknowledged as his patrons and protectors, Vetch cultivated Somers, one of the most prominent of the Whig junto, Godolphin, Boyle, the other Secretary of State, and important though less highly placed individuals like Pringle, Sunderland's secretary, and Popple, the secretary of the Board of Trade. In his later letters from America, he acknowledged that he lay under obligation to each of them. Nor did Vetch neglect the careful politics and the judicious bribing of doorkeepers and lesser functionaries without whom no business took place in the England of that day.[35]

Vetch was careful to play upon the patriotism, ambition, and even avarice of the Queen and her ministers. He pointed out that his project would advance the glory of Her Majesty's arms, enlarge her empire, and augment the trade and happiness of her subjects. It would immortalize the Queen's memory and stand as an everlasting monument to the unparalleled virtue of "the present, matchless ministry."[36]

The political situation was extremely favorable to the acceptance of Vetch's enterprise. In London, the Whigs had been steadily strengthening their position in the government. To their success in the elections of 1705 had been added their triumph in negotiating the union with Scotland, which earned them the favor of their grateful Queen. Anne became the somewhat unwilling head of a ministry increasingly dominated by the Whig junto,

34. *Cal. State Papers, 1708-9*, no. 71; P.R.O., State Papers, Domestic Series, Anne S.P. 34/10, no. 11, and Vetch to Sunderland, June 15, 1708, Blenheim Mss., C.I. 41, cited in Richmond P. Bond, *Queen Anne's American Kings* (Oxford, 1952), 22, 109; Vetch to Sunderland, two letters, June 29, 1709, *passim* Vetch Letter Book (Museum of the City of New York).

35. Bribery of underlings is indicated in Vetch's letter to Pringle, Nov. 18, 1709, referring Pringle to Vetch's agent Douglas for expenses "found necessary" in advancing Vetch's interests and promising Pringle that in case of success he would "gratefully acknowledge your friendship and favor." Vetch Letter Book (Museum of the City of New York). See also the following letter to Mason.

36. See especially Vetch to General McCartney, Mar. 10, and to Popple, Mar. 11, 1709, in which Vetch predicted that the expedition would render the Lords of Trade famous to posterity as true patriots; *ibid.*

allied for the moment with Robert Harley, leader of the moderate Tories.[37]

The election of 1708 confirmed and strengthened the Whig position. Harley, never sympathetic with the junto's ambition, was forced to leave the ministry but continued for a time in the close relationship with Godolphin and Marlborough which had helped to build up the strength of their erstwhile coalition government. Sunderland was at work to break up this triumvirate and expose Harley to the junto; at the same time Harley was working secretly to preserve the Tory support for the Queen, which the Whigs seemed bent on destroying in the interests of their own power. Already Harley and his cousin Abigail Masham were supplanting the Duchess of Marlborough in the Queen's affections. Harley's maneuvering would not affect Vetch, however. Harley was not yet in a position where he would openly oppose the measures of the ministry, and Vetch's scheme was not the kind of project which Harley might advantageously oppose, even in private. Nor was Harley apt to find fault with Vetch personally. Harley was the son of a Whig, who was a moderate and a Presbyterian.

On the other hand, the undertaking offered Sunderland and the junto certain political advantages. The Whigs had not been blind to the strength they might command in Scotland. Sunderland had procured the release of the Duke of Hamilton from prison in order that Hamilton might work for the party in the election of 1708. Support of Vetch's scheme was another way of enhancing Whig prestige in the north of Britain. The union with Scotland in 1707 had made it possible for energetic Scots to appear onstage as principals in the drama of British imperialism. Their activities up to this time had not been less important; but they were now officially recognized as representatives of the Crown. Vetch's scheme, at the outset connected with the dream of a Scottish colony, formed a significant symbol of the union and furnished a means by which it might be made more palatable to those in the north who nourished lingering opposition.

Another consideration was the foreign situation as it affected

37. For an analysis of British politics at this juncture, William Thomas Morgan, *English Political Parties and Leaders in the Reign of Queen Anne 1702-1710* (New Haven, 1920), has been relied upon.

domestic politics. The war in Europe had been slowing up. Despite the earlier victories of Marlborough at Blenheim and Ramillies and the more recent success at Oudenarde, the French King was not willing to offer peace on terms which the Whigs thought they could accept. The Tories were clamoring for an end to the war and would undoubtedly sweep into power on a wave of reaction in the event of a compromise peace.

Unless the Whigs could extract a full and glorious victory over France, which would put Britain deeply in their debt, it would be better to keep the war going. The situation in Spain, where the British forces were bogged down, precluded an overwhelming victory, even though Louis XIV might be brought to offer it. The Whigs therefore used Spain as an excuse not to conclude peace. But the growing unpopularity of the war made it necessary to find some way to break the deadlock developing in Europe and win more credit for the Whig conduct of the war.

A successful campaign in Canada might force terms which would give the Grand Alliance the kind of peace which the Whigs could accept without endangering their hold on the government. Failing that, it would at least give a much needed fillip to the war. Furthermore, it would help Sunderland offset Harley's growing influence with the Queen. It would even serve to counter Marlborough's popularity. Sunderland did not see eye to eye with his father-in-law and would not look askance at a scheme which might turn attention away from Marlborough's theater of war and further undermine the triumvirate, favoring full Whig control of the government as against the fast disintegrating coalition.

Sunderland's support just at this time meant more than it would have at almost any other. A year later, he was on his way out of office. Now, with the Whigs at the apogee of their position during Anne's reign, he was in a dominant position. Godolphin, the nominal head of the ministry, was slipping rapidly from favor. Grieving over the death of her husband, the Queen had practically withdrawn from politics, leaving the Whigs to run the country.

Fortunately, too, for Vetch, his predilections were similar to the chief tenets of the Whigs. Parliamentary supremacy was a principle which implied no lack of patriotism. Since the Glorious Revolution, it was more popular in England than the Tory reverence for monarchy. As a lowland Scot, Vetch was disposed to favor the principle despite his recognition of the place of royal authority in the colonial governments. The Whigs were the party of Dissenters, and Vetch was a Dissenter. They encompassed the bulk of the mercantile middle class, favoring commercial expansion. This was the group most interested in colonies and colonial trade. These, and the prominent nobles who led the party, were the men to whom Vetch would naturally be drawn. The Bank of England backed the Whigs. Vetch's old associate Paterson had been instrumental in establishing that institution. The Whigs' stand for civil liberties was a consistent part of their position, and civil liberties were dear to the man who had so recently claimed an illegal trial to have his sentence invalidated. As for the other side, Vetch would find little to attract him to the Tory camp, dominated as it was by High Churchmen, Jacobites, and the landed aristocracy. In 1709, and in years to come, Vetch was to find his successes when the Whigs were in power.

So it was that Vetch emerged at the end of February 1709 with signed and sealed orders for the expedition, instructions which appointed him to the task of directing colonial preparations for the undertaking, a commission as colonel, with the post of adjutant general to the British field officer who would be in chief command, and the promise of the governorship of Canada after it was taken.[38]

Success in full measure had attended his efforts to engage the government in the Glorious Enterprise. It was a scheme which a lesser man might have thought far too visionary to press upon a bureaucracy busy with full-scale continental war. Vetch, energetic and sanguine, had synthesized the ideas of his contemporaries and applied them to the current situation, fortunately just at the time when conditions were propitious for their consideration. A rare type in the colonies, Vetch thought of the English colonial scene in America as a whole.[39] His scheme drew together the usually

38. Queen Anne's Instructions to Vetch, Feb. 28, 1709 (Museum of the City of New York) ; Public Archives of Nova Scotia (Dalhousie University, Halifax), V, no. 16, and also *Cal. State Papers, 1708-9*, no. 387; P.R.O., S.P. Domestic, Anne, S.P. 44/178, p. 77, cited in Bond, *Queen Anne's American Kings*, 110n. For the promise of the governorship, see Vetch to Sunderland, June 29, 1709 (second letter), Vetch Letter Book (Museum of the City of New York).

39. Many of Vetch's contemporaries both in the colonies and in England were provincial in their views. Few perceived that the power of the English

divergent interests of the colonies and the mother country in a plan which could command the support of both. His was the credit for initiating the first important move toward overcoming the French expansion in America, by means of a well-planned and co-ordinated attack on New France, one in which British naval and military strength would be combined with colonial forces co-operating together, for once, instead of indulging in their usual jealous pulling and hauling. Now the way lay open for Vetch to prove his abilities and the capacity of the colonies. He faced forward to a season of unrelenting exertion.

---

colonies lay in their union or recognized the essential role which the mother country would have to play in bringing it about. The failure of the various plans of union later in the century indicated that provincialism was far from dead. This is not to say that others besides Vetch did not hold the wider view. Some of the abler governors, a few agents of the Board of Trade, and some of the colonial agents in London, as well as individuals like Nelson, Heathcote, and Cockerill, had ideas similar to those of Vetch.

CHAPTER SEVEN

Glorious Enterprise

T HE QUEEN'S INSTRUCTIONS called on Vetch to take ship immediately for America to organize the colonists for their part in the expedition. He lost no time. Within a week he was at Portsmouth. Her Majesty's ship *Dragon* had been designated to carry him and the officers under his command to New York, along with arms and ammunition. Vetch had wisely anticipated that colonial magazines, usually empty, would not be adequate to equip the colonial forces. While the stores of war were being loaded on board, he enlisted a group of artillerymen, gunners, and matrosses for the attacking force.[1]

Prominent among the group of English officers and colonists temporarily in England, who now received billets in the coming expedition, was Colonel Francis Nicholson. His offer to go as a volunteer had been accepted. Vetch's instructions enjoined him to take Nicholson into his counsels out of the Queen's regard for the experienced colonial governor's "known abilities and zeal." The two of them, with the governors of the colonies involved, were empowered to make any decisions which the instructions "by reason of distance of time and place" could not foresee and provide for.

Nicholson's assignment was eminently satisfactory to Vetch, who had formed an immediate friendship with the veteran colonial administrator. Nicholson was a Tory sympathizer and a High Churchman whose inclusion in the undertaking might help assure the backing of those elements in the English government. No

1. Queen Anne's Instructions to Vetch, Feb. 28, 1709 (Museum of the City of New York; also in *Cal. State Papers, 1708-9*, no. 387); Vetch to various correspondents, Portsmouth, England, Mar. 7-11, and Order to enlist and pay matrosses, signed by William Bridges and Thomas Erle, Mar. 8, 1709, Vetch Letter Book (Museum of the City of New York). Matrosses were assistants to the gunners in the artillery train.

one knew just when the complexion of the ministry might change. Vetch was attracted by Nicholson's "extraordinary zeal" for the expedition. The two found themselves in perfect agreement in everything, a state of affairs which Vetch welcomed as a portent of success.

Sunderland directed letters from the Queen to the governors of all the colonies from Pennsylvania north, acquainting them with the expedition and commanding their assistance. They were to consider those parts of Vetch's instructions which related to each of them "as if they were positive commands directed to yourself" and to act "in the manner that . . . Colonel Vetch shall in our name propose to you." In Vetch's instructions each colony was allotted a quota, and the enlistment and organization of the colonial force were set forth in detail.[2]

By March 10, all was in readiness to sail. Last-minute replacements were accepted from among a large number of volunteers for those officers who failed to appear or whose characters were found wanting. Vetch named an agent, James Douglas, to handle his affairs in England, settled final problems of pay and supply, and issued orders that everyone should be aboard early the next morning.[3]

Awaiting a fair wind, Vetch and Nicholson made the most of their remaining time writing letters to the ministry. Enthusiasm ran high for the design, and Vetch intended to keep it that way. He reminded the members of the Board of Trade that the expedition would bring them fame with posterity as "true patriots." He acknowledged his obligations to his supporters and asked Sunderland to remember to issue instructions to the commanding general that Vetch was to be left in command in Canada, "when it shall please God to make us masters of that place." Here Vetch

2. Vetch to General McCartney, Mar. 11, 1709, Vetch Letter Book (Museum of the City of New York); see also *Cal. State Papers, 1708-9*, no. 388, and Clarendon Mss., CII, 201 (Lib. Cong. Transcripts).

3. Vetch and Nicholson to Sunderland, June 29, 1709. This letter is really a journal covering events between March 11 to June 28, 1709. The original is in N.Y. Hist. Soc., and a copy is in Vetch Letter Book; it is printed in *Cal. State Papers, 1708-9*, no. 604 (hereafter cited as Vetch Journal, 1709). See also Vetch's letters, Mar. 10-11, 1709, Vetch Letter Book (Museum of the City of New York).

promised to "make my capacity of serving my Sovereign and my country appear to your lordship and the Ministry."

Only in a letter to General George McCartney, one of Marlborough's brigadiers who was then slated to be commander-in-chief of the expedition, did Vetch's native Scottish caution assert itself and something like prescience make itself apparent. "Nothing can impede our good success," he wrote, "if you do but hurry after us with the designed force." Was it hard to believe that it would all work out as planned? Here Vetch voiced the qualification which was to run like a refrain through his thoughts of the ensuing summer.[4]

The *Dragon* got underway early in the afternoon of March 11. It was a blustery day as the ship moved past Spithead and out of the channel. At sunset strong cross winds struck the vessel. For five weeks she struggled against these unfavorable gales until she found herself driven far north of her proper course. Vetch, impatient to get to New York, chafed at the delay. The ship was shattered by the prolonged buffeting, her main yard was disabled, and water was running short.

Finally, on the evening of April 13, thirty-four days out of Portsmouth, Captain Martin presented Vetch and Nicholson with a written statement of the ship's condition. He was willing to shape his course as they directed, but he suggested that a course for Boston, instead of New York, would find the wind more favorable and would put them closer to their landfall.

It was an important decision. Much depended on the attitude New York would take toward the expedition, and that province was notably jealous of its position as pre-eminent representative of the royal prerogative in America. Would the vessel's arrival in Boston, rather than New York, prejudice the success of the expedition which depended so much on colonial co-operation? Vetch and Nicholson decided that it would not. It had been a tedious passage, and both were glad to authorize the change of course.

After seven weeks at sea, the *Dragon* anchored in Boston har-

4. Vetch to Sunderland, Mar. 11, 1709, Webster Papers (New Brunswick Museum); Vetch to McCartney, Mar. 10, to Popple, Mar. 11, 1709, Vetch Letter Book (Museum of the City of New York).

bor at sunset on April 28. Vetch and Nicholson hastened ashore to wait upon Governor Dudley with news of their enterprise and to arrange expresses to deliver the Queen's letters to the governors of the other colonies concerned.[5] Vetch's instructions, to which the colonies were ordered to adhere, were very much what he had suggested. The forces of Connecticut, New York, New Jersey, and Pennsylvania would attack Montreal overland from Albany while a British army of 4,000, joined by 1,200 men from Massachusetts Bay, New Hampshire, and Rhode Island, would sail from Boston against Quebec. The British troops were scheduled to arrive in New England by the middle of May. Massachusetts was expected to furnish them with provisions for the campaign and for the first months of garrison duty after Canada's fall. The Bay Colony was also ordered to provide transports for its own men and flat-bottomed landing boats for the sea-borne forces to use in the assault on Quebec. In turn, the arms and ammunition which Vetch had brought from England were calculated to give the New Englanders uniform armament with their British allies.[6]

For the overland attack New York was to furnish a quota of 800 men, including the four companies of Regulars; New Jersey was expected to raise 200 men, Connecticut 350, and Pennsylvania 150. This force was ordered to be ready at Albany by the middle of May. It was to be organized into four battalions, each commanded by a captain of one of the four independent companies of Regulars and including that captain's company. The officers who came over with Vetch were to be distributed among those battalions to leaven them further with leaders of military experience of a more formal sort than that possessed by most colonial militia.

Along with copies of his instructions and the Queen's letters to the governors, Vetch sent a letter of his own to each colonial governor calculated to awaken zeal for the expedition. He

5. Vetch Journal, 1709; Martin to Vetch and Nicholson, Apr. 12, and Vetch and Nicholson to Martin, Apr. 13, 1709, 8 p.m., Vetch Letter Book (Museum of the City of New York); Sewall has Vetch arriving on Apr. 29, 1709; *Diary of Samuel Sewall*, II, 254.

6. Queen Anne's Instructions to Vetch, Feb. 28, 1709 (Museum of the City of New York); Memorandum of Sunderland, P.R.O., C.O. 5, vol. 9, 65 (Lib. Cong. Transcripts). Compare with the data Vetch had submitted to the Board of Trade, above. See also Proclamation of Vetch and Nicholson, Boston, May 9, 1709, Mass. Archives, LXXI, 500-2 (State House, Boston).

flattered Governor Saltonstall of Connecticut with his assumption that Connecticut would co-operate heartily in a project designed to deliver the colony from the terrors and expense of war, "especially when you are at the head." He asked Saltonstall to summon the Assembly and get them started on raising troops, then to join him for a meeting in New York with the heads of all the colonies involved in the advance from Albany.[7]

Governor Cranston of Rhode Island was asked to come to Boston for consultation on the plans for the attack against Quebec, a project "which seemed left by Providence" to complete the wonders of Queen Anne's glorious reign. To Pennsylvania Vetch pointed out that although farthest south of any of the colonies enlisted in the campaign, she would not be the least to share in the victory. She should join the others willingly and bear a share of the expense, the hazard, and the glory. In his letter to Governor Lovelace of New York, Vetch was careful to explain why the ship had taken him first to Boston. Lovelace, of course, had known of the pending scheme before he left England for his post in the colonies and he had expressed his ardent support. He was a man of military experience, who was counted on to take command of the attack on Montreal. Vetch was proud to be able to send him word that the project had become a reality.[8]

New York was expected to furnish storehouses necessary for assembling supplies at Albany and boats to transport men and equipment across Lake Champlain and to contract with the Five Nations for canoes needed to carry the colonial troops along the water courses to Montreal. Lovelace was charged with the task of engaging the Five Nations and the lesser New York tribes for the campaign. The British government promised to supply presents, which were essential to all such negotiations with the Indians.

7. Vetch to Saltonstall, Boston, Apr. 30, 1709, Vetch Letter Book (Museum of the City of New York); also in N.Y. Hist. Soc. Fitzjohn Winthrop, the former governor, had died.

8. Vetch and Nicholson to Rhode Island, Apr. 30, Vetch to the governor of Pennsylvania, Apr. 30, and Vetch and Nicholson to Lovelace, Apr. 30, 1709, *ibid.* Although signed by both men, the last letter uses the first person consistently, and the postscript is signed by Vetch alone, so it is evident that it is the work of Vetch. The same is true of the letter from Vetch and Nicholson to Sunderland, N.Y., June 29, 1709, which is in Vetch Journal, 1709. See also Sunderland to Lovelace, Apr. 28, 1709, which enclosed duplicate instructions in case Vetch's ship went astray; *N.Y. Col. Docs.*, IV, 72 ff.

Vetch suggested that Lovelace relay word immediately to Schuyler and Livingston at Albany to send out Indian spies, the most "sober, trustworthy and sensible Indians, who are known at Montreal and Quebec and won't arouse suspicion." These Indians—two would be sufficient—were to observe the number of troops at Montreal, Trois Rivières, and Quebec, the state of fortifications, and the prices of food. The latter information would serve to indicate how well supplied Canada was this season. As soon as this was done, they were to return to Albany so that the intelligence could be forwarded promptly to the expedition's commander. The Albany leaders were also asked to send scouts to Wood Creek, at the southern end of Lake Champlain, to find a suitable site from which to embark the force and where boats could be built and supplies assembled.[9]

Lovelace was instructed to call the assemblies of New York and New Jersey so they could pass the necessary acts in support of the enterprise. New York was to furnish arms and ammunition out of its magazine for all troops gathered at Albany, but Vetch was able to promise an artillery train equipped with "coehorn mortars, hand grenadoes, blunderbusses, Harquebusses with swivels," and the requisite ammunition. Vetch asked Lovelace to send the station ship, H.M.S. *Maidstone,* from New York to Rhode Island to pick up this equipment, which he would cart down from Boston; it was quicker to transport the supplies to Rhode Island by land.

As soon as they had things under way in Boston, Vetch and Nicholson planned to go to New York. There they would meet with the governors of the provinces responsible for the inland arm of the pincers designed to crush Canada. Vetch's letters stressed secrecy, and he therefore recommended that both New York and Rhode Island impose an embargo on all shipping lest French privateers should capture an English vessel and obtain news of what was afoot. Nor were French Indians to be allowed to leave Albany. Vetch knew that the usual clandestine trade was probably going on between Albany and Montreal, and he feared that

9. Queen Anne's Instructions to Vetch, Feb. 28, 1709 (Museum of the City of New York), and Vetch to Lovelace, Apr. 30, 1709, Vetch Letter Book (*ibid.*); also in N.Y. Hist. Soc. Instructions to be given the two Indians to be sent to Montreal and Quebec (no date), Livingston Papers, box 6.

Canada might learn of the expedition through this channel. To facilitate the co-ordination of the two forces, he recommended establishing stage posts and riders between Albany and Westfield, Massachusetts; Massachusetts would handle communications between Boston and the western part of the colony.[10]

Boston received word of the expedition with joy and thankfulness. Cotton Mather took it as "another matter which I had to spread before the Lord." Massachusetts responded to Britain's orders with alacrity, and Boston was soon swarming with activity. Vetch and Nicholson met with the governor and Council to agree on the organization of the colonial army and the appointment of officers. Arrangements for supply, transport, and other supporting activities were made. Contracts were let for flat-bottomed boats to be used in landing operations. Guides were recruited from among those who had once been captives in Canada. A system of relaying messages between Boston and Albany was established, making use of Indian runners. As Vetch had suggested, this turned out to be more practical than using post riders. An embargo on shipping was established, not only to prevent intelligence from reaching the French but also to prevent the export of provisions which would be needed to feed the troops. Since it was manifestly impossible to keep the design secret in the colonies, it was necessary to prevent whites or Indians from carrying the news to Canada. Scouts were deployed along the Canadian border to stop overland communications.[11]

A proclamation was signed by Vetch, Nicholson, and Dudley, calling for enlistments. Volunteers were assured that they would serve under the command of their own officers and that they would not be subject to occupation duty once Canada was taken. Participation in the expedition, it was pointed out, would give them preference in the land and trade of the conquered area.

By May 12 things were well under way in Boston. As Vetch

10. Vetch to Lovelace, Apr. 30, Dudley to Lovelace, May 2, 1709, Vetch Letter Book (Museum of the City of New York); Vetch and Nicholson to Lovelace, May 2, 1709, Clarendon Mss., CII, 204 (Lib. Cong. Transcripts).

11. Vetch Journal, 1709; Apr. 30, 1709, *Diary of Samuel Sewall*, II, 254; Mather's Diary, Mass. Hist. Soc., *Collections*, 7th ser., 8 (1912), 8; Mass. Archives, LXXI, 527, 529 (State House, Boston); chap. 2, 1709, *Mass. Acts and Resolves*, *1708-20*, IX, 57 ff.

and Nicholson prepared to set out for the colonies to the south, they received devastating news. At the beginning of May Vetch had learned that Lovelace was ill and he had been "not a little concerned." Now came word that the New York governor had died. Vetch grasped at once that this might prove a "retardment" to his scheme, and he hastened to New York.[12]

As he passed through Rhode Island, he was amazed and delighted to find that this usually unruly and independent colony had already taken steps to provide men, transports, and provisions for the expedition and had even made arrangements for raising funds to pay its troops. Its Assembly had appointed a special committee to assist, advise, and manage affairs "for the more speedy expedition of the great design now intended against Canada." The purchase of privately owned vessels was authorized, and a commissary was appointed to provide all arms, ammunition, clothing, food, and transport. Prices were fixed, and eventually it was even voted to use money from land sales in the Narragansett area to finance the expedition. The Assembly took special action to ensure the "kind acceptance of Col. Nicholson and Col. Vetch into our government" and authorized the governor to treat them, charging the general treasury for it. Vetch was careful to report this exemplary performance with unstinting praise in his letter to Sunderland.[13]

Rhode Island's resolution, energy, and efficiency made this semblance of democracy shine in comparison with its neighboring defenders of the royal prerogative. The small size of Rhode Island undoubtedly had something to do with its ability to act quickly and decisively. Its vulnerability as a seaport trading center also may have accounted for the zeal with which it backed the expedition. It would mean much to the shippers of Rhode Island to be freed of the privateers based on Port Royal, that Dunkirk of the New World.

12. Printed copies of the Proclamation are in Mass. Archives, LXXI, 500-2 (State House, Boston); Vetch and Nicholson to Lovelace, May 2, 1709, Clarendon Mss., CII, 204 (Lib. Cong. Transcripts). Lovelace died on May 5, Vetch Journal, 1709; *Journal of the Votes and Proceedings of the General Assembly of the Colony of New York* (New York, 1764), I, 246.

13. John Russell Bartlett, ed., *Records of the Colony of Rhode Island and Providence Plantation in New England, 1707-40* (Providence, 1859), IV, 69-73, 75; Vetch Journal, 1709.

During his three-day stay at Newport, Vetch found Colonel Church, the venerable Indian fighter, raising a force of 200 whaling Indians, dexterous in handling boats. It was Church's suggestion that a fleet of whaleboats, more "nimble" than pinnaces, would prove advantageous for "any sudden or secret design." In accordance with this suggestion, Vetch contracted for thirty-five of them, fifteen at the expense of the colonies and twenty to be paid for by the British government.

After spending Sunday in the colony, Vetch and Nicholson set out with their retinue of officers for Connecticut. Governor Gurdon Saltonstall had just been re-elected and was busy with the legislature at Hartford. Since Connecticut had a record of independency almost equal to Rhode Island's, Vetch also feared difficulties with this province. But the governor had left a letter assuring him that Connecticut would not be lacking in its duty; so Vetch pressed on to New York, asking Saltonstall to follow for the meeting with New York and Pennsylvania leaders. Before he left, Vetch suggested John Livingston, his brother-in-law and the son-in-law of Connecticut's former governor, as commander of Connecticut's regiment. He asked that a vessel be sent to New York to pick up military stores and recommended that Connecticut follow the example of Massachusetts Bay Colony, New Hampshire, and Rhode Island in sending an address of thanks to Queen Anne for her favors.[14]

True to his word, Saltonstall laid Vetch's letters before the Assembly and was gratified to receive a vote signifying the colony's intention to comply with all possible dispatch. The Assembly warned the governor to ascertain that Connecticut troops were commanded by a Connecticut man, that they not be required to furnish any part of a subsequent garrison force, and that Connecticut was not charged for any facilities, storehouses, or other buildings erected in New York territory. Arms and ammunition were voted for the colony's Indians who enlisted, an exchange of Connecticut wheat for Albany bread was requested, and a sloop was ordered off to New York to bring back the promised supplies. With a sharp eye to its sister colony, the Assembly set wages for

14. Vetch Journal, 1709; Vetch to Saltonstall, May 9, 1709, Vetch Letter Book (Museum of the City of New York).

Connecticut soldiers at the equivalent of those paid by Massachusetts. On account of the "great charge that will arise," taxes were levied on all persons whatsoever, "except ministers and the infirm." And Vetch's hopes for his brother-in-law were realized, at least in part, when John Livingston was promoted to major. After this, with the Assembly's authorization, Saltonstall hurried after Vetch to New York.[15]

A day's sail had brought Vetch and Nicholson to New York. It was already past the middle of May, the date set for all to be in readiness. Both Vetch and Nicholson knew the province well enough to be fearful lest its factions prove an obstacle to speedy action. Vetch had counted on the popular and able Lovelace to counteract any such opposition, but now, instead of a man whom he knew to be favorably disposed toward the campaign, Vetch had to deal with Richard Ingoldesby, the lieutenant governor, a man with long experience in the province but with little demonstrated ability. Vetch had known him as undependable, a placeman lacking in imagination and noted for inaction.[16]

Fortunately, Vetch found the situation was not as bad as he had feared. The confusion usually attendant on a change of governor had been minimized, for the lieutenant governor, well known in the province, had been ready to step in. The legislature had been in session when Lovelace died, which obviated the technicalities which might have arisen had Ingoldesby had to call a new session. Moreover, the province had received Vetch's letters, and measures looking toward the expedition were already underway.[17]

The day after their arrival, Vetch and Nicholson met with Ingoldesby and the Council at Fort Anne. The Assembly was called in, Vetch's instructions read, and Vetch acquainted the members with the measures already taken by the New England colonies. Van Rensselaer and Robert Livingston had gone to Albany to send out the Indian spies, but Vetch found many old

15. Charles J. Hoadly, ed., *The Public Records of the Colony of Connecticut from October 1706 to October 1716* (Hartford, 1870), V, 88-103.

16. It was Ingoldesby's command for which Vetch had petitioned Blathwayt after Ingoldesby had been long absent in England.

17. Ingoldesby to Board of Trade, July 5, 1709, *N.Y. Col. Docs.*, V, 82. Some question existed in colonial practice whether a lieutenant governor had the power to call a session of the Assembly without specific instructions from the Crown when he was acting in the place of an absent or deceased governor.

acquaintances present: Schuyler, Wenham, Peartree, Phillipse, Lurting, and others.

Acting with rare unanimity, the Assembly resolved to comply to the utmost, "readily and effectually," with Her Majesty's instructions. A committee was appointed to join with a committee of the Council to concert with Vetch, Nicholson, and the governors on plans. Commissioners to manage details of purchasing supplies were designated. In deference to the Assembly, Ingoldesby declared himself ready to allow the passage of some acts which royal officials in his post had often vetoed, in order that the Assembly would not have grounds for obstructing acts necessitated by the expedition.

The next day the Assembly was afflicted with characteristic misgivings and reported to the Council that it thought the quota set for New York was too high. Vetch and Nicholson hastily offered to address the Queen for reimbursement of some of the expenses to which the expedition would put the province. This satisfied the Assembly, which levied property taxes to raise the sum of £6,000. To meet expenses in advance of tax collections, bills of credit were authorized. An act prohibiting the transportation of provisions out of the province was passed to ensure an adequate supply for the troops. Other acts apportioned men from the various towns for the army, laid a tax on liquor, and prohibited usury. The Council, for its part, ordered Colonel Rednap, the British army engineer stationed in the provinces, to join the forces which were forming and take charge of the artillery and other supplies brought by Vetch. To build boats and storehouses, carpenters were sent to Albany. Finally, John and Abraham Schuyler were appointed to carry presents to the Five Nations with word of the expedition.[18]

Time did not seem to permit Vetch and Nicholson to make personal appearances before the governments of Connecticut and Pennsylvania, but Saltonstall and Governor Charles Gookin of Pennsylvania were interested observers of New York's measures. Gookin had been on hand when Vetch and Nicholson arrived, or

18. May 17-18 and 23, 1709, *N.Y. Assembly Journal*, I, 247-49; *N.Y. Col. Docs.*, V, 82; May 17-21, 1709, *Journal of the Legislative Council*, I, 278-80; Vetch Journal, 1709.

came soon after, and Saltonstall arrived three days later, full of enthusiasm.[19]

Up to this point, Vetch noted, the colonies had "shown such readiness and zeal" in the matter of the expedition "that they have exceeded even what was required of them." New York exhibited co-operation and leadership in the planning and preparation, which went far to offset the charges of inaction leveled against the province by the New Englanders. New York's usual factionalism was notably absent.

According to the army paymaster stationed in New York, the province was "big with expectation of success." Yet even now New York could not match the zeal and spirit of the New England colonies. "Interest, that governs all the world, tyrannizes at New York," observed that official, noting that although a majority of the colony was in favor of the campaign, some remained opposed. The small group of traders at Albany, accustomed to dealing with the French, were loath to see their trade in furs with Montreal disrupted. Without the diversified interests of larger traders such as the Schuylers and Livingstons, they were unable to visualize the long-range advantages of a war which would, if successful, put all the furs of North America in British hands. They were marginal "handlers" who stood to benefit most by the present situation, whereby they gained great advantage through bootlegged goods.[20]

The most serious problem which faced the leaders gathered in New York was the election of a commander for the land forces. Lovelace had been expected to take command or to designate a lieutenant. With Lovelace dead, it was clearly up to Vetch, acting with Nicholson and the various colonial governors, to make a new choice. In his suggestions to the Board of Trade, Vetch had mentioned Ingoldesby, who was then the ranking officer of the Regulars in New York as well as lieutenant governor. But now Ingoldesby was not considered. It may have been because of his lackluster reputation. Or perhaps Connecticut would resent failure to choose a leader from among its officers. Or it may have been

19. Vetch Journal, 1709.
20. Cockerill to Popple, July 2, 1709, *N.Y. Col. Docs.*, V, 80-81; *Journal of the Legislative Council*, I, 279.

simply that Ingoldesby's new responsibilities as governor precluded his undertaking the command. Instead Vetch asked Ingoldesby, Saltonstall, and Gookin to agree on someone with courage, experience, zeal, and known loyalty as military leader.[21]

Colonel Francis Nicholson was the unanimous choice. That Vetch had been active behind the scenes bringing about this decision was reflected in motions originating with his friends in both the Council and the Assembly. Although it was not their choice to make, both bodies urged Nicholson to accept the command. Nicholson showed "a great deal of aversion" to the idea. He knew from experience the difficulties of leading a motley colonial force and making militia from different colonies pull together as a team. It was a heavy responsibility; he doubted his ability. Although he had planned to accompany the sea-borne expedition, he expressed his willingness to go with the army by land. But commanding that army was another matter.[22]

It was Vetch who declared that the expedition could hardly go forward unless Nicholson accepted the post. Schuyler added his urging. In fact, Schuyler, who was slated for the post of second in command and whose ways with the Five Nations made him essential to the scheme, flatly stated that he would not go unless Nicholson would consent to serve.

Nicholson yielded to persuasion. Having promised to spare no pains to make the expedition a success, he could do no less without causing "serious impediments." He was promptly commissioned, and the appointment was confirmed by the action of the Massachusetts General Court. Governor Cranston of Rhode Island sent congratulations and expressed the gratitude of his government at Nicholson's action. He lauded Nicholson as one whose whole course of life "doth bespeak you a man of honor, zeal, and generosity." The Council and Assembly of New Jersey also ratified the action and expressed confidence in Nicholson as

21. *N.Y. Col. Docs.*, V, 72; *Cal. State Papers, 1708-9*, no. 196; Vetch Memorial to Ingoldesby, Saltonstall, and Gookin, May 18, 1709, Webster Papers (New Brunswick Museum).

22. Address of Ingoldesby, Saltonstall, and Gookin to Nicholson, May 23, 1709, Webster Papers (New Brunswick Museum); Vetch Journal, 1709; May 23, 1709, *N.Y. Assembly Journal*, I, 249; May 21, 1709, *Journal of the Legislative Council*, I, 280.

commander of their forces, and Connecticut's legislature followed suit.[23]

Judgments of Nicholson varied, then and later. Future developments lend credence to the possibility that Vetch was already beginning to fear Nicholson's ambition as a threat to his own aspirations. If Nicholson were at Quebec with the conquering British general, Vetch would have to contend with the claims of a man senior to him in age and administrative experience. Tory influence was strong with the Queen, as Vetch well knew. If that party increased its power before the expedition found a successful outcome, Vetch might find his promised governorship withdrawn in favor of Nicholson, who held Tory principles, especially if Nicholson were present at the victory.[24]

With the matter of a commander settled, preparations went forward. Schuyler was unanimously selected as second in command of the forces gathering at Albany. The plan to have one of the companies of Regulars "mixed and incorporated" in each of the four battalions was impractical. Nor could the captains of the four companies be used as the battalion commanders; the companies had dwindled to so few men that it was decided to keep them together as a single battalion, commanded by the only captain on duty with the Regulars. The other three battalions were left to be formed exclusively out of the militia.

On May 25, 400 men, the New York Regulars and some of

23. Vetch Journal, 1709; Nicholson to Sunderland, July 8, 1709 (N.Y. Hist. Soc.); P.R.O., C.O. 5, vol. 9, 70 (Lib. Cong. Transcripts); commissions signed by Ingoldesby, Saltonstall, and Gookin, May 23, 1709, Webster Papers (New Brunswick Museum); N.Y. Colonial Manuscripts, LII, 60 (N.Y. State Lib., Albany); Mass. Archives, LXXI, 526 (State House, Boston); June 27, 1709, Bartlett, ed., *R.I. Records*, IV, 74-75; June 1-5, 1709, Frederick W. Ricord and William Nelson, eds., "Journal of the Governor and Council, volume I," *Documents Relating to the Colonial History of the State of New Jersey* (Trenton, 1890), XIII, 339, 344-45, 352-53 (cited hereafter as *N.J. Archives*, XIII); June 8-11, 1709, Hoadly, ed., *Public Records of Conn.*, V, 108.

24. A biography of Nicholson is greatly needed. Pending a more thorough examination of this complex personality, a fair characterization might admit Nicholson's high temper and surpassing ambition but balance these traits with notice of his zeal and generosity in public undertakings, demonstrated in affairs like this of 1709 and his former efforts on behalf of the Anglican Church in Virginia. Francis Parkman has a good characterization in *A Half-Century of Conflict* (Boston, 1933), I, chap. VII. A near contemporary, Cadwallader Colden, was less charitable; see Colden to his son, N.Y. Hist. Soc., *Collections*, Pub. fund ser., 1 (1868), 201.

the militia from New York and Connecticut, advanced north of Albany to Wood Creek. It was the advance guard, ordered to establish a fort and make ready to receive the subsequent levies. Maintenance of even this force put a strain on colonial treasuries. A soldier's pay was eighteen pence per day, plus an allowance for subsistence. Vetch noted that the rates were four times that received by European soldiery.

In addition, New York had been assigned responsibility for arming the force, and the colony's treasury was, as usual, empty. Cornbury had seen to that; inspection showed "not one sixpence." And the arms in the New York arsenal had been found in serious disrepair. Vetch had no alternative but to draw bills of exchange on the British Treasury for the payment of gunsmiths to put the arms in order. Vetch and Nicholson also met the situation another way. By their proclamation, those who chose to make use of their own arms were assured recompense of their value in money.

Vetch had to authorize bills, too, for the guns and clothing furnished the Indians who enlisted. In lieu of pay they could choose between a gun or three yards of the stuffs called strouds and duffels. Two hundred Indians accompanied the first troops north, drawn largely from Connecticut and the area along the lower Hudson.[25]

It remained for Ingoldesby to enlist the support of his other province, New Jersey. The situation there was complicated by the relations of Council and Assembly, "betwixt whom," wrote Vetch, "there hath been for some time a great variance." These "misunderstandings and feuds," said Vetch, "do not a little retard Her Majesty's service as well as ruin the country." Half of the Assembly members were Quakers—an awkward fact when it came to getting war measures passed.[26]

Faced with an unruly Assembly, the Jersey Council and Governor Ingoldesby asked Vetch and Nicholson to address the legislators personally, as they had in Boston and New York. The Council agreed to comply with Vetch's instructions from the Queen,

25. Vetch Journal, 1709, and a Proclamation, dated May 26, 1709, printed by William Bradford (N.Y. Hist. Soc.).
26. Vetch Journal, 1709; Nicholson and Vetch to Board of Trade, New York, June 28, 1709, *N.Y. Col. Docs.*, V, 78.

acknowledging Ingoldesby's sentiment that "like opportunity was never yet offered nor ever may again if this should be neglected." A committee was formed to make plans for the expedition, arrangements to enlist the Jersey Indians were completed, and the body adjourned to the "great room at Harrison's" to meet with the Assembly.

Vetch found the Assembly adamant in its refusal to raise men. The Quakers were joined by enough others to prevent passage of such an act. It was apparent that the "heats and animosity" which the governor had hoped might for once "be buried in oblivion" had merely been intensified by the requirements of the campaign. However, the Quakers were quite willing to allow a system of volunteers, and although they would not themselves vote money for paying such troops, they planned to absent themselves in sufficient numbers so that an appropriation measure would pass, in the event that their presence offered a threat to it. The Quakers lacked two of a majority, so there seemed no likelihood of that.[27]

At this juncture, however, the "factions and turbulent spirit" of New Jersey government manifested itself. Ingoldesby and the Council, seeing a chance to strike a blow against the Quaker faction, arranged for two of their "tools" in the Assembly to desert to the Quakers on the third reading of the bill, thereby handing it a surprise defeat just when it seemed sure of passage and making it appear the Quakers' fault. The situation was patently one in which the governor's faction was sacrificing the common good and the success of the expedition to satisfy long-standing grudges against the independent spirit of the Assembly. They justified the stroke as affording a demonstration which would bring home to the British government the realization that a people like the Quakers, professing principles so at variance with the interest of the colonies and the home government, had no place in the British imperial scheme and should be kept off the benches of the colonial assemblies.

27. May 26, 30, and 31, *N.J. Archives*, XIII, 329, 331, 333, 362; Ingoldesby to Board of Trade, June 16, 1709, William A. Whitehead, ed., *Documents Relating to the Colonial History of the State of New Jersey, 1703-9* (Newark, 1881), III, 460-61 (cited hereafter as *N.J. Archives*, III). Cockerill to Popple, July 2, 1709, *N.Y. Col. Docs.*, V, 81.

Vetch was in entire agreement with such sentiments, but he had no patience with Ingoldesby's political maneuvering at such a critical time. When the governor adjourned the Assembly, throwing the blame for the bill's failure on the Quakers, Vetch and Nicholson put pressure on him to recall the body. They then allowed the members to pass an act to raise £3,000 "for the Queen," even though it was encumbered with provisions which advanced the Assembly's pretensions and was highly distasteful to the governor and Council. Finally, seeing no further advantage in placating the opposition, Vetch and Nicholson joined in recommendations to the Crown that Quakers be excluded henceforth from colonial assemblies.[28]

After this setback in New Jersey, Vetch had no doubt that matters would be worse in Pennsylvania, where the Assembly was almost wholly Quaker. He left it to Gookin to persuade the province to join the plan, if he could. The proprietor of Pennsylvania, Penn, was caught, as Gookin feared, between the wishes of the British government and the will of his colonists. Gookin was fully aware that failure to win the Assembly's support of the expedition might result in the proprietor's loss of the colony to the Crown. Political tensions in the colony had already gone to extremes. With the "unhappiness" of additional demands, the Assembly would "do no other than give a flat denial."[29]

Nevertheless, Vetch's enthusiasm had been contagious and his arguments and inspiration called forth Gookin's best efforts. Although loath to alienate the Assembly, the governor refused to do any other business with it until it should attend to the matter of the expedition. But to the Quakers of the Pennsylvania Assembly, the arguments against support of the campaign proved to be decisive. They maintained their scruples against raising

28. *N.J. Archives*, III, 464-73; IV, 36-38; XIII, 364-72; Donald L. Kemmerer, *Path to Freedom, The Struggle for Self-Government in Colonial New Jersey 1703-1776* (Princeton, 1940), 84; Nicholson and Vetch to Board of Trade, June 28, and Cockerill to Popple, July 2, 1709, *N.Y. Col. Docs.*, V, 78, 81.

29. Logan to Penn, May 12, Isaac Norris to Benjamin Coole, May 24, and to Henry Goldney, June 3, 1709, Edward Armstrong, ed., "Correspondence between William Penn and James Logan, . . . 1700-1750, with notes by the late Deborah Logan," Historical Society of Pennsylvania, *Memoirs*, 10 (1872), 346; Gookin to Assembly, June 11, 1709, "Minutes of the Provincial Council of Pennsylvania, 1700-1717," *Colonial Records of Pennsylvania* (Harrisburg, 1852), II, 484.

men or money for war. They pointed out that they were in no more danger from the French than was Maryland or Virginia, neither of which had been asked to contribute. Here, it was apparent that Vetch's failure to include all the colonies in his plans had been a serious mistake.

The Pennsylvanians excused themselves further on the grounds of their poverty—the result of declining trade, misapplied revenue, and an unfavorable exchange rate for coinage. Gookin's arguments and denials were unavailing. It was no use to point out that Pennsylvania's meager quota of 150 men could be filled easily from the ranks of non-Quakers. The Assembly would not even consider sending provisions instead of money. The governor's offer to allow the legislators complete responsibility for disbursing the money that it might vote did not move them.[30] Not until several decades later, when the French began to encroach on Pennsylvania interests in the Ohio Valley, would the Quaker colony see that the menace of a foreign Canada was common to all the British colonies.

Finally, the Assembly agreed to vote £500 as a token of its loyalty to the Queen. But Gookin refused to accept a gift of such mean proportions. At this, the body petitioned for adjournment. Gookin also refused that, whereupon the Assembly adjourned anyway, agreeing to vote the £500 at its next meeting in August. Faced with this decision, Gookin retreated. He repealed the general embargo which he had laid on exports in anticipation of the needs of the expedition, and the colony returned to business as usual. Gookin wrote to Vetch and Nicholson that he had done his best and asked them to represent his efforts to the ministry in a favorable light.[31]

By the end of June, Vetch had done what he could in New York and prepared to return to Boston. Nicholson and Ingoldesby planned to go to Albany to look after arrangements and meet with the Indians. Despite the defection of New Jersey and Pennsylvania, it appeared likely that the colonial troops would exceed the quotas which had been set. The Albany forces num-

30. "Minutes of Pa. Council," *Pa. Col. Recs.*, II, 467-81.
31. June 7-15, 1709, *ibid.*, 479, 481-86; Gookin to Nicholson and Vetch, June 17, 1709, *Cal. State Papers, 1708-9*, no. 580; Nicholson to Sunderland, July 8, 1709, encl. no. 3 (N.Y. Hist. Soc.).

bered closer to 3,000 than the appointed 1,500, and word from Boston indicated that the men being readied there would come to 2,000 instead of the 1,200 requested. Volunteers and Indian recruits had more than compensated for the levies refused by New Jersey and Pennsylvania. Clearly the colonists were behind the campaign as never before. Vetch had been even more successful than he had dared hope.[32]

At this stage in the preparations, the New York government sent an address of gratitude to the Queen, and Vetch and Nicholson sent letters apprising the ministry of their accomplishments. Official New York expressed confidence in the undertaking and described the measures it had taken to comply with the Queen's orders. Nicholson's acceptance of the leadership of the land forces was taken as fully compensating for the loss of Lovelace. An accompanying memorial asked sanction for the expenditures to which Vetch had been put.[33]

Vetch wrote that the expedition was "one of the greatest and most glorious enterprises Britain hath been concerned in for many years." In Marlborough's heyday this was an impressive statement. To Britons the "boasting Spaniard" was still the representative of vast and golden empire, so it meant much when Vetch painted his project as one which would bring Britain not only peace but an imperial position rivaling that of Spain.

Nor was Vetch disposed to forget his own claims on the eve of such a success. He reminded Pringle of the assurances he had been given of the governorship of Canada. From Sunderland he asked the command of a regiment to garrison the conquered province. He proposed to raise 1,200 colonials for this duty, considering them more suited for it than Regulars.

Similar remarks were addressed to Boyle, Queensbury, and Somers. He pointed out to Lord Treasurer Godolphin that he had acted within his orders, been as frugal as possible, and kept careful

32. Vetch Journal, 1709; Vetch to Queensbury, Aug. 1-12, Journal continuation, and Vetch to Sunderland, June 29, 1709, Vetch Letter Book (Museum of the City of New York); Nicholson to Sunderland, July 8, 1709 (N.Y. Hist. Soc.); Armstrong, ed., "Penn-Logan Correspondence," Hist. Soc. Pa., *Memoirs,* 10 (1872), 35; Cockerill to Popple, July 2, 1709, *N.Y. Col. Docs.,* V, 81.

33. Address of Ingoldesby, Council, and Assembly to Queen Anne, June 24, 1709 (N.Y. Hist. Soc.); Memorial of Ingoldesby, Nicholson, and Vetch to Queen Anne, July 1709 (Huntington Lib.).

accounts. The expenses which had been incurred were nothing when weighed against the advantages to be gained or compared with the cost of the "long and expensive wars in Europe." After performing his duties with "all the application, diligence, and faithfulness imaginable," Vetch never doubted that so glorious and good a queen and such a great and just ministry would reward his merit.[34]

The auspicious start of the summer's venture emboldened Vetch to embroider his enterprise. It had been the intention, once Quebec fell, to make sure of the recapture of Newfoundland as well. Now, Vetch proposed that the Spanish colonies should be taken, as well as the French. It was apparent that he had in mind Florida, the disputed land between the Spanish holdings and Carolina, and the Spanish islands adjacent to the British Caribbean colonies. Such a course would, as he pointed out, put Britain in a position to dictate peace terms and become the arbiter of the commerce of Europe and America. But further than this he had no very clear idea. New Spain, in contrast to New France, was not familiar ground to Vetch.

The suggestion may have been the outcome of discussions with Nicholson, who was presumably conversant with the point of view of British colonists in the south through his term of service in Virginia. Carolinians had just cause to fear an allied French and Spanish attempt to push back the British colonial frontier in the south. Or it may be that the suggestion was merely an effort to win support of the Tory faction in England for the expedition. The Tories were known to favor British attempts to limit Spanish power, and they were becoming increasingly influential in the British government. At any rate, Vetch did not elaborate upon his proposal, and its future rested with the outcome of the Canadian campaign.[35]

34. Vetch to Sunderland, Godolphin, Board of Trade, Queensbury, Somers, Boyle, Pringle, all dated June 29, 1709, Vetch Letter Book (Museum of the City of New York); Vetch to Pringle, June 28, 1709, Webster Papers (New Brunswick Museum). For his letter to Boyle, see *N.Y. Col. Docs.*, V, 78-79.

35. Vetch to Sunderland, Queensbury, Somers, etc., June 29, 1709, Vetch Letter Book (Museum of the City of New York); Verner W. Crane, *The Southern Frontier, 1670-1732* (Philadelphia, 1929), chap. IV. The French had recently seized the small English settlement on Newfoundland. Sunderland had ordered the expedition to proceed to Newfoundland if Canada was disposed of by the

Another suggestion by Vetch was the nomination of Nicholson for the New York governorship. Vetch put him forward as the man to remedy the violent party divisions of New York and New Jersey and added that the appointment of Nicholson, who was already in the province, would save the expense of sending over a governor. Vetch denied any ulterior motive in this proposal; in this, as in his own claims, he wanted only just reward for a deserving man. To Pringle, whose favor and influence he begged, he promised Nicholson's gratitude, as well as his own. Although the Scotsman did not mention it to Pringle, if Nicholson were awarded the New York post, Vetch need fear no rivalry for the Canadian governorship.[36]

---

end of August or sooner; P.R.O., C.O. 5, vol. 9, no. 65 (25) (Lib. Cong. Transcripts).

36. Vetch to Pringle, June 29, 1709, Vetch Letter Book (Museum of the City of New York).

CHAPTER EIGHT

Enterprise Disappointed

EFORE VETCH LEFT New York, the Indian spies sent out from Albany returned with news of Canada's forts and military dispositions. What they had to say about them was not particularly revealing. Some outlying forts were in disrepair. Quebec itself was strongly held. A war party of French and Indians was reported on its way to attack Deerfield, the Massachusetts outpost beset so often before. Massachusetts had been duly warned, and in addition Schuyler, already at Albany, was sending out a party of his own to intercept the enemy.[1]

But the scouts did confirm the fact that British plans had not remained a secret. Despite frontier scouts and embargoed shipping, it was impossible to keep such a large enterprise under cover. Disputing assemblies discussed the plans openly. Vetch himself knew of the close ties between the Mohawks and their kinsmen in the French "Praying Indian" village of Caughnawaga. With French priests in many of the castles of the Five Nations, with French Indians in Albany constantly trading between New York and Montreal, and with long and amorphous borders which could not be kept under constant surveillance, Vetch could not have been sanguine about keeping his design under cover.

At first, the French leaders had been divided in their assessment of what was intended. One of the bright young men in the army, Charles Le Moyne, Chevalier de Longueuil, concluded that British attempts to get the Iroquois to break their neutrality and join an expedition against Canada were bound to fail, even though he was fully aware of Peter Schuyler's "great efforts to

1. July 2, 1709, N.Y. Council Minutes, encl. 6 to Nicholson's letter to Sunderland, July 8, 1709 (N.Y. Hist. Soc.); Examination of Indians by Commission for Indian Affairs at Albany, June 21, 1709, *N.Y. Col. Docs.*, V, 85; *Cal. State Papers, 1708-9*, no. 621iv(a).

induce them to make war on us." Governor Vaudreuil, on the other hand, took seriously the intelligence he received and rushed to Montreal with 1,000 men, only to hear that a large fleet was sailing for Quebec. His colleague, the intendant, believed that the objective was Acadia or Newfoundland and thought Vaudreuil entertained "exaggerated apprehensions about the fate of Canada." It was a highly advantageous confusion, if the British had been ready at the end of June to take advantage of it.[2]

Indians, as willing to spy for one side as the other, soon gave Vaudreuil a more accurate, if not reassuring, conception of what he might expect. Largely because no other course was open to him, the governor resolved to remain inactive. He was in no position to initiate a preventive action and could not expect France, hard pressed on the Continent, to send timely reinforcements. Fearing to arouse the Iroquois, he put his faith in continued Indian neutrality and the hope that New York would not relinquish the inactivity which had preserved peace between the two colonies so far in the war. He sent word to Schuyler that he intended to adhere to the earlier French promise and await the first blow.[3]

But the French governor failed to gauge the temper of the Albany leader. As far as Schuyler was concerned, New York's policy of inaction had been one of convenience, strategically advantageous as long as intercolonial co-operation and aid from Britain were not to be relied on. But it was a stalemate increasingly irksome to him. Sensitive to the complaints of New England, sympathetic with those whose outposts the French had continually ravaged during the war, he had protested to Vaudreuil just a year before, "You will pardon me if I tell you I am disgusted when I think that a war which is carried on by Christian princes . . . should degenerate into savage and reckless barbarity." When the opportunity of the expedition offered, Schuyler engaged heartily in the enterprise, accepting the post for which the Queen's instructions had recommended him. With his unparalleled influence over the Five Nations, his vast acquaintance with the terrain over which the land forces would have to move, his unique talents in forest

2. Richard, ed., *Canadian Archives Supplement*, ser. D, XLVII, XLVIII, 26, and ser. C, II, vol. 4, 220, 223.
3. *N.Y. Col. Docs.*, V, 85-87; Munsell, *Annals of Albany*, IV, 129-30; Richard, ed., *Canadian Archives Supplement*, ser. B, XXIII, 360-68.

transportation and communication, and his experience in military leadership gained during the first colonial war, Schuyler was an opponent New France could not take lightly.[4]

By mid-July, the French governor knew further details of the British threat. Herter de Rouville, returning from the Deerfield raid, brought back two English prisoners. Interrogated separately, they both told the same story. Vetch had spent a considerable time in England, they related, where his perseverance had won him an audience with the government and resulted in a large grant of money and the promise of a fleet of ships for the capture of Canada. The captives made it good. Eight warships, two bomb ketches, and thirty lesser vessels would strike by sea; four thousand men were advancing by land. They boasted that they knew Canada would get no help from France and that their Queen would dictate peace terms.

Toward the end of July, news from Acadia confirmed the story and added other details. A French privateer had reportedly captured a vessel from Boston and learned that almost two thousand men were gathered in the Bay Colony awaiting a fleet of sixteen large warships from Britain. Vetch was named as leader in the scheme. He was known to have a map of Quebec and its environs, and he had boasted that he had many friends in Canada who would help him. Daniel d'Auger de Subercase, in charge of the garrison at Port Royal, wrote that he had sent out a privateer to keep watch on the Boston area so that the arrival of the British fleet would be promptly reported. He had also placed lookouts to report the arrival of hostile vessels in the Gulf of St. Lawrence. It was rumored that the expedition would be cancelled unless the British fleet came by the middle of August. People in Boston were already saying that the season was too far advanced, Subercase learned, but it seemed to be the consensus that the scheme would go forward if the ships arrived before that deadline.[5]

The Canadians received little comfort from these reports. Vaudreuil must have wondered uneasily at the hint of disloyalty among those of his subjects who were "friends" of Vetch. His

4. *N.Y. Col. Docs.*, IX, 818-19, V, 70-73; N.Y. Colonial Manuscripts, LIII, 60-70 (N.Y. State Lib., Albany).

5. Subercase to Vaudreuil, July 23, 1709, *Documents historiques relatifs à la Nouvelle France*, I, 504-6, and see 502.

peace of mind was not improved by the fact that an Indian brought in to give him information turned out to be one of those sent from Albany to spy.[6]

Back in Boston, Vetch found preparations proceeding auspiciously when he arrived the first week in July. Transports had been hired and fitted out, storeships bought, and Captain Belcher's little brigantine *Hope* had been sent off to Newfoundland to reconnoiter French dispositions there.

Sir Charles Hobby, whose quarrel with Dudley was now patched up, had been appointed to command one regiment of Massachusetts men, Colonel William Taylor the other. Colonel William Wanton led the Rhode Island regiment and the New Hampshire forces. John Walley, who had accompanied Phips' expedition in 1690, commanded the artillery; his position was comparable to that held by Colonel Rednap in the land forces. Lieutenant Paul Mascarene, who accompanied Vetch from England, had been entrusted with the training and command of the artillery train, the expense of which was to be met by the British government. Vetch had made credit arrangements with Borland before he left Boston so that Mascarene could attend to paying this force.[7]

It was a matter of course that controls should be invoked by the colonial government in a time of emergency. Prices for provisions were set at the level current the day before notice of the expedition had been received. Pork was to sell at between three pounds and three pounds five shillings a barrel. Beans were set at from five shillings to five shillings sixpence a bushel. Since bills of credit had been voted in the amount of £30,000, of which £25,000 were emitted at once, price control had been necessary to prevent an inflationary rise in campaign necessities. Necessary, too, had been the law to discourage counterfeiting of the bills which was passed at the same time.

6. Richard, ed., *Canadian Archives Supplement*, ser. C, II, vol. 4, 223.

7. Chap. 2, 1709, *Mass. Acts and Resolves, 1708-20*, IX, 58; Vetch Journal, 1709; Vetch to Mascarene, May 10, Dudley to Vetch, May 1, Vetch and Dudley to Capt. Pickering, May 4, Vetch to Nicholson, Aug. 12, 1709, and Commission to Walley, Vetch Letter Book (Museum of the City of New York). Mascarene was destined for a long and honorable career in Nova Scotia; see John Bartlet Brebner, "Paul Mascarene of Annapolis Royal," *Dalhousie Review*, 8 (1929), 501.

During the debates, the lower house of the legislature had been aroused momentarily by an act for the payment of billeting money to the soldiers assembling in Boston. The representatives, with Yankee frugality, suggested that the men enlisted for the expedition be left in their own towns until the fleet arrived. They rationalized their position by arguing that Boston had a shortage of provisions, that the men were needed to work in their own localities, and that the "mortal fever" raging in Boston made it dangerous to gather a larger force there prematurely. Dudley remained adamant. He wanted to get the troops together, look them over, and be sure they were fit and in sufficient number. The House gave in, allowing eight pence a day per man for lodging, ordering them to be quartered on private households, but requiring not more than two men per family without the householder's consent. Some were provided for in public buildings.[8]

The legislature set the pay of officers at three pounds fifteen shillings a week for colonels, three pounds ten for lieutenant colonels, and two pounds ten for majors. It also designated a committee to appoint physicians and surgeons for the campaign and establish their rate of pay. Provisions for a period of four to five months were ordered as the amount necessary to supply the forces during the campaign.

Although gratified that enlistments rose steadily, the representatives protested against "nefarious enlistment practices." Men were being bribed to enter the service. Some were released from jail to join the troops. Serious dislocations in the civilian life of the colony had been expected, but the House petitioned strenuously against one practice, the enlistment of children and servants without the consent of their parents or masters. It had occasioned "extreme disorders," destroyed "family government," and violated the Fifth Commandment.

Vetch must have been pleased to find that, in his absence, the General Court had removed the slur on his loyalty occasioned by his trial for illegal trading and resolved that the fine and costs which he had paid should be restored. In addition, the legislature

8. Mass. Archives, LXXI, 527-28, 513-15 (State House, Boston); chaps. 3, 8, 11, 15, 18, and 25 ff., 1709, *Mass. Acts and Resolves, 1708-20*, IX, 58 ff., 65-70.

voted Vetch a present of sixty pounds toward furnishing his table during the campaign in recognition of his exertions which had "very much forwarded" the expedition. A present had also been provided for the general of the forces when he should arrive.[9]

The refund of the fine and the award of the present were doubly welcome, because Vetch's travels had occasioned great expense. Despite frugality and careful accounting, costs had been larger than anticipated, but Vetch had steadfastly refused to weigh costs against imperial benefits. In asking the British ministry for reimbursement, Vetch pointed out the necessity he had been under to hire a "good clerk" at five shillings a day to carry on his extensive correspondence and make copies of letters sent. It might sound expensive in England, but it was a common laborer's pay in the colonies. Then, too, the seven officers who had accompanied Vetch and Nicholson had expenses, the horses' hire mounted up, as did the advances Vetch made for guns and Indian presents and the repair of arms in New York's armory.[10]

Despite the fatigue and the expense he had undergone, Vetch was well pleased with the way his plans were turning out. The colonial troops were numerous and well drilled. They were in better health and appeared better in bodily build than European troops usually were. Vetch hoped their courage would prove correspondingly greater. They were better paid than European soldiers, too, about four times as well. The colonials received a minimum of eighteen pence a day, plus their subsistence and a ten-pound advance for enlisting. For once the colonial governments were paying their soldiers both punctually and cheerfully. They hoped this would be the final campaign they would have to undertake, that it would put an end to the drain on their treasuries occasioned by twenty years of border skirmishing.

Just one disturbing factor shaded the prospect of success. Where was the promised fleet from Britain? The colonies would hardly have been ready if it had come by the middle of May, as scheduled. But it was now the end of June. Vetch did not try to

9. Mass. Archives, LXXI, 531, 534, 541 (State House, Boston); chaps. 2, 7, 31, 41, and 47, 1709, *Mass. Acts and Resolves, 1708-20*, IX, 57, 59, 72.

10. Vetch Journal, 1709; Vetch to Queensbury, Aug. 1, 1709, Journal continuation; Vetch to Godolphin, June 29, 1709, Vetch Letter Book (Museum of the City of New York).

conceal his worry and impatience in his letters to the ministry. "Only the late arrival of the fleet," he wrote, "will disappoint the design." Canada, forewarned, was being allowed precious time to prepare. Indians and colonials alike were growing impatient. Whatever the French thought, Vetch himself had decided that if the expedition did not reach Quebec by the end of September, it would not succeed.[11]

Although the colonists were slow to complain, the period of waiting was difficult. Vetch occupied his time in Boston reviewing the troops and writing long letters to England, reminding those in authority of the great issues at stake and keeping them posted on developments. Harvard had its commencement on July 6, and Vetch may have taken part in the exercises. His wife was with him in Boston, and the social life of the provincial capital, enlivened by the officers and their ladies gathered there, pursued its accustomed round.[12]

By the middle of July, Boston authorities had decided upon the best chart of the St. Lawrence and ordered a plate engraved so that a sufficient number of copies might be struck off to supply the fleet. Two sloops were hired and equipped to guard the coast while the province galley *Marlborough* under the doughty Cyprian Southack was away on the expedition. Bread for the troops was increased from five to six months' supply as it became more apparent that the lateness of the season might prolong the return of the forces, particularly if bad weather were encountered.[13]

While the New England forces waited for the English fleet, word came that the army was ready at the foot of Lake Champlain. A wagon road had been built from Albany to the camp at Wood Creek. Indians from Long Island had been rounded up and sent to Albany, after Ingoldesby had thwarted attempts made by the

11. Vetch Journal, 1709; and Journal continuation, Vetch Letter Book Museum of the City of New York).

12. Vetch to Nicholson, Aug. 12, 1709, *ibid.*; Henry Douglas to Philip Livingston, Aug. 8, 1709, Livingston Papers, Group 3, box 1; *Cal. State Papers, 1708-9*, nos. 409-10. The possibility that Vetch took part in commencement activities was advanced by Samuel Eliot Morison in a letter to Dr. J. Clarence Webster, Oct. 2, 1935, Webster Papers (New Brunswick Museum) and Morison states it as a fact, without indicating the basis of his statement, in *Harvard College in the Seventeenth Century* (Cambridge, 1936), II, 470n.

13. Chaps. 54, 56, and 60, 1709, *Mass. Acts and Resolves, 1708-20*, IX, 74-75, 76.

independent Long Islanders to hinder the move. The Indians were promised rewards and threatened with being turned over "to the resentment of the Mohawks and the rest of the Five Nations" if they did not obey. Some two hundred Mohawks and Oneidas, the tribes nearest to Albany, had already arrived. The Onondagas and Cayugas were reported on their way. But the Senecas, farthest west of the Five Nations, were cowed by the attacks of the "Far Indians" and were not coming; the French were using their Indians with as much effect as possible to discourage the British allies.[14]

A delegation of Mohawks arrived in Boston early in August from Albany. Dudley and Vetch did their best to impress the visiting Indian leaders with the might of the English force. Colonel Hobby's regiment was mustered for their review. Sir Charles feted the officials and their Indian guests at an evening entertainment. The governor took the Mohawks on a round of the fortifications and gave them a view of the men-of-war *Dragon* and *Guernsey* lying at anchor in the harbor with the three colonial warships readied for the campaign.

Every day of delay made the colonists more restless and pessimistic about their plans. Vetch, sensitive to public feeling, knew his reputation was hanging in the balance. Samuel Sewall was already critical of his influential position. It rankled the old judge to have Vetch sitting at the head of the council table with Dudley, "leaning his elbow on the arm of the Governor's chair." Sewall and other councilors resented the pretensions of the executive and his friends in the military forces. The struggle for political control of the colony went on even during this time of emergency and special effort, in Massachusetts and New York alike.

Sewall took occasion to protest a proposal to send a flag of truce to Port Royal for the exchange of prisoners. He masked his annoyance with Dudley and Vetch by protesting that the Council had been called without adequate notice. He pointed out that since the French knew of the expedition, they would not be likely

14. Journal continuation, Vetch to Nicholson, Sept. 12, 1709, Vetch Letter Book (Museum of the City of New York); N.Y. Council Minutes, July 2, 1709 (N.Y. Hist. Soc.); Wraxall, *Abridgment*, ed. McIlwain, 68.

to want to treat. An offer would only expose the English to ridicule. Sewall was joined by the secretary of the Council, who suggested that sending to Port Royal might only serve to let the French know that the fleet had not come. But Sewall went too far when he referred to the possibility that the province might be parting with men, sloops, and provisions in vain. Sewall might be perspicacious enough to guess that the fleet was not coming, but some of his fellow councilors were not ready to admit that possibility. Colonel Foster reproached him heatedly. Vetch and Dudley rejected his demurrers with disdain. When Sewall protested that a present of strong beer to Subercase was out of order in view of the Acadian governor's having "dealt basely" with them, Vetch stated that Massachusetts would know how to deal with its French captives if Subercase refused to send home his English ones. Sewall could but retire to a secluded part of the river and soak his weary frame in the soothing waters of the Charles.[15]

He was further piqued at seeing Vetch swagger around behind the governor "with his sword at his side," but his resentment stemmed from an incident of the morning. He had seen Monsieur Bernon, a French resident of Boston whom he suspected of espionage. Running across Vetch just afterward, he accusingly said, "Mr. Bernon is in town, as I told you he would." It had come as a shock when Vetch made light of it and even informed Sewall that he had been buying cider from the Frenchman.

But Sewall was not alone in his uneasiness. Trade was at a standstill in the colonies until the expedition was over. In addition, the hope of future trade in the rich produce of Canada was vanishing, along with the dream of happiness and tranquility. Had the colonists expended thousands of pounds, embargoed their trade, and aroused the French all for nothing? One explanation of the delay came with the arrival of H.M.S. *Guernsey* the first week in August. General McCartney, designated to lead the expedition, was a prisoner of the French. When it proved impossible to arrange an exchange for him, Brigadier Whetham replaced him in the plans; revised orders for Whetham had been issued early in May. Word came, too, that preliminaries of peace

15. July 21, 1709, *Diary of Samuel Sewall*, II, 259-60.

were being discussed. Vetch began to fear that the war might be over before his Glorious Enterprise was accomplished.[16]

Vetch pointed out in a letter to Queensbury that failure of the fleet would be "the last disappointment to all her Majesty's colonies . . . and would render them much more miserable than if such a thing had never been projected or undertaken." Vetch stood to lose not only his reputation in the colonies but his promised rewards as well. He hoped that whatever the reasons for the failure of the fleet, he would not go without the "just reward" which his service merited at all events. But even now, Vetch could not consider the expedition as more than postponed to another season, at the worst. His lively strategic sense asserted itself; he wished that he might have known how long the fleet would be in coming so that he could have been employed in taking Acadia with the forces at hand. Port Royal was still a little Dunkirk— French privateers had captured eight or nine New England vessels.[17]

Throughout August, hope for a last-minute attempt on Quebec remained alive. But before the middle of September, Vetch concluded that it was too late. He therefore turned to a new and depressing problem: What to do with the assembled colonial force? He had suggested at the end of August that Colonel Wanton take his Rhode Island troops for a "small cruise" to allay their restlessness and boost their morale. Now both Rhode Island and Massachusetts were urging demobilization. But Vetch did not want to act precipitously when orders of some kind were daily expected from the British government. Nor did he wish to waste the summer's preparations. If the plan to take Canada was not to be dropped altogether, new offensive plans had to be worked out. In the meantime, measures to assure the protection of the frontiers against French retaliation were pressing. And it was absolutely necessary to hold the Five Nations to their allegiance. Vetch communicated his fear to Nicholson of the "fatal consequences to

16. Aug. 9-11, 1709, *ibid.*, 261-62; Vetch to Nicholson, Aug. 12, 1709, Vetch Letter Book (Museum of the City of New York); May 7-9, 1709, *Cal. State Papers, 1708-9*, nos. 492, 497, 498; P.R.O., C.O. 5, vol. 9, 27-29 (Lib. Cong. Transcripts); Aug. 5, 1709, *Diary of Samuel Sewall*, II, 260.

17. Vetch to Queensbury, Aug. 1 and 12, Vetch to Nicholson, Aug. 12, 1709, Vetch Letter Book (Museum of the City of New York).

all the British continent" if the failure of the expedition occasioned
the loss of the Indians' loyalty.[18]

Acting in a capacity very like that of the later British office of
commander-in-chief in the colonies, Vetch proceeded to frame a
policy and enlist the co-operation of the several governors. His
first goal was the maintenance of the advance base at Wood Creek
for frontier protection and quick renewal of the expedition when
possible. The second was the capture of Port Royal, using the
military and naval forces at Boston. Like the first goal, this would
serve an immediate purpose, that of putting the assembled armament to work eliminating a troublesome nest of French privateers,
and it would also achieve the long-range objective of establishing
an advance base in the immediate neighborhood of the Canadians.

Letters went out to the governors asking them to meet with
Vetch and Nicholson to consult on these matters. Vetch proposed
a conference at New London early in October and suggested that
it would be well for the governors to bring along representatives
of their councils, assemblies, and their "chief officers." At the
same time, he wrote to Sunderland. Hopeful for so long, he now
let his pent-up discouragement pour out. He had used the best
he had in "both rhetoric and politics" to keep up the spirit of the
colonists, hard as it had been to keep his own spirits up. He did
not hesitate to say that he considered himself and the colonists
deserted and neglected. Neither a fleet nor even a letter of explanation had arrived. Vetch acknowledged the probability that
some "solid and substantial reason" was behind the failure, but
people were becoming "uneasy" with him, blaming him for their
disappointment. He had hoped that he was "raising to myself a
lasting monument amongst them"; instead he found himself
blamed for the expensive and futile effort which the colonies had
lavished on the undertaking. Vetch reminded the minister of the
need for instructions. He dared not disband the forces for fear
the French would descend on the colonies and wreak their resentment for the summer's disturbance. He urged that the project be
renewed, that Her Majesty's honor might be upheld, and he reminded Sunderland that it still remained an undertaking which

18. Vetch to Nicholson, Boston, Sept. 12, Vetch to Wanton, Aug. 30, Rhode
Island Assembly to Vetch, Sept. 3, Dudley to Vetch, Sept. 8, 1709, *ibid.*

might favorably be weighed against any European military undertakings. And he insisted that whatever happened, he wanted suitable reward for his services. He was already casting about for vacant governorships to which he might lay claim.[19]

Plans for Vetch's proposed "congress" of colonial leaders went forward rapidly. It was well that they did, since word from Wood Creek spoke of sickness, cold, worn-out clothing, and provisions coming to an end. Vetch hoped that the meeting would gain time in which orders from England might arrive. At least, it would give him a chance to show that he was not to blame for the miscarriage of the plan. He encouraged Nicholson with praise for the superb service he had rendered in attaching the Five Nations more securely to the British interest. He agreed with the recommendations of the field officers at Wood Creek that the three forts built for the advance—"Wood Creek," "Ingoldesby," and "Nicholson" —should be maintained and garrisoned through the winter at all costs. He warned that they should stay on the alert, although he hoped those officers who could be spared would be present at the meeting.[20]

Saltonstall and Cranston notified Vetch of their willingness to meet. A lack of accommodations at New London caused Vetch, at Saltonstall's suggestion, to transfer the proposed site of the gathering to Newport. But Ingoldesby was recalcitrant. His Assembly balked at doing anything further for the expedition and had adjourned. He wanted the meeting held at New York, as the government "more immediately under the Crown." To this suggestion Dudley refused assent—the rivalry between Boston and New York could never be left out of account. For himself, Dudley was willing to go anywhere, even to Philadelphia, but he knew that his own Assembly would not send representatives further than Rhode Island. It considered Massachusetts and New Hampshire as the "senior governments."

Vetch rebuked Ingoldesby for his reluctance. It would be all right to consider New York halfway between the northern and southern colonies, if Pennsylvania were included, but since the

19. Vetch to the various governors, Sept. 12, and Vetch to Sunderland, Sept. 12 and 22, 1709, *ibid.*

20. Schuyler, Rednap, and Whiting to Vetch, Wood Creek, Sept. 2, Vetch to Nicholson, Sept. 22, 1709, *ibid.*

latter province had offered no co-operation in the enterprise, it was not to be considered in plans for the assemblage. In Vetch's view, the fact that New York was more immediately under the Crown should only make Ingoldesby more zealous. He concluded that it was nothing to him whether the colonists held a congress or not; he had planned it in keeping with what he considered their best interests.[21]

Now, after long months of waiting, affairs moved fast toward a culmination. A small vessel arriving in Boston brought word that H.M.S. *Enterprise* had sailed from England on August 4 with important dispatches for the expedition's leaders. It would sail into the harbor any day. This information came just as Vetch was writing to Ingoldesby on Monday, October 3.[22] On Thursday, Saltonstall, already at Newport, received word from Wood Creek that the outpost was overwhelmed by sickness and desertions. A French attack was momentarily expected, and aid was sorely needed. It was nearly midnight when the message arrived; Saltonstall hurriedly forwarded it to Vetch. It was obviously urgent that the congress convene, and yet Vetch hoped for the arrival of the *Enterprise* before he left Boston, so that the leaders could have knowledge of what the British government intended. He finally decided to leave for Newport on Saturday noon, unless the ship were actually in sight. Dudley, remaining in Boston, could bring the dispatches as soon as they arrived.[23]

Vetch traveled to Newport on Sunday, October 9, and immediately sent John Livingston to Wood Creek with orders to hold that outpost at any cost. Livingston had been on the frontier

21. Saltonstall to Vetch, Sept. 22, Cranston to Vetch, Sept. 23, Ingoldesby to Vetch, Sept. 26, Dudley to Vetch, Oct. 3, Vetch to Ingoldesby, Oct. 3, 1709, *ibid.*

22. The ship which brought this news was a French prize taken by the *Enterprise* off Newfoundland and sent in ahead under English officers. Vetch to Ingoldesby, Boston, Oct. 3, 1709, *ibid.*

23. Vetch to Ingoldesby, Oct. 3, Saltonstall to Vetch, express, Newport, Oct. 6, Vetch to Saltonstall, Boston, Oct. 7, 1709, *ibid.* No evidence exists to bear out the story that members of the Five Nations poisoned the water supply at Wood Creek by throwing dead animals into the stream above the camp, causing the outbreak of pestilence among the troops. The story was that the Iroquois took this means to avoid breaking their neutrality with the French, on condition that the eastern Indians would forego aiding the French in their raids against New England. See *N.Y. Col. Docs.*, IX, 842, and the Rev. P. F. X. de Charlevoix, *History and General Description of New France*, ed. John G. Shea (New York, 1871), V, 220-23.

during the summer, but he had come to Boston early in September. Nicholson was also in Newport, and, together with Vetch, he sent peremptory notice to Ingoldesby to insist on the New York troops' remaining at their posts in the forts. They also repeated their "earnest desire" that Ingoldesby come to Newport or send a delegation from his legislature. In Boston, Dudley awaited the *Enterprise* and chafed at the contrary winds which prevented the vessel's arrival. He offered to come to Newport anyway, if his presence were required, and added his voice to the request that Wood Creek be held.[24]

Finally, on Tuesday, the awaited dispatches came ashore from the tardy *Enterprise*. Dudley forwarded them to Vetch and prepared to follow with members of his Council. The message from Sunderland was the expected one. The expedition had been "laid aside." The Queen's intentions remained the best, and opportunity would not be neglected to renew the project. What was unexpected was the date of the message. It had been written July 1. Yet with it were further instructions dated July 27, and the *Enterprise* had not sailed with the dispatches until August 4. Even then the ship had not been ordered to sail directly for America but had spent the intervening time cruising the Atlantic on routine naval patrol, taking a French prize, and finally coming into port more than two months later. Vetch, aware of the limitations imposed by distance and time in working so far from the center of government, was nevertheless aghast at the indifference and negligence exhibited by British bureaucracy.[25]

Had he known the actual timetable that the government had followed in the dissolution of the British force against Canada he would have been even more dismayed. By the end of May, the

24. Vetch and Nicholson to Dudley, Oct. 11, Vetch and Nicholson to Ingoldesby, Oct. 11, Vetch and Nicholson to Schuyler or other officers at Wood Creek, Oct. 11, Dudley to Vetch, Oct. 10 and 11, 1709, Vetch Letter Book (Museum of the City of New York). Livingston had brought word to Vetch about Wood Creek, letter from officers at Wood Creek to Vetch, Sept. 2, 1709, *ibid*.

25. Dudley to Vetch, Roxbury, Oct. 11, Sunderland to Lovelace, July 1 and 27, 1709, *ibid.*; Dudley to Sunderland, Oct. 1709 (Huntington Lib.); Memorandum of Sunderland to Vetch, July 1, Sunderland to Dudley and Lovelace, July 27, Sunderland to Dudley, Aug. 4, 1709, *Cal. State Papers, 1708-9*, nos. 612, 658, 670; Memorandum of Sunderland to Vetch, July 1, 1709, in full, P.R.O., C.O. 5, vol. 9, 33 (Lib. Cong. Transcripts); Vetch to Sunderland, Oct. 24, and Vetch to Pringle, Oct. 25, 1709, Webster Papers (New Brunswick Museum).

ministry had reached the decision to call off the expedition. The naval squadron intended for Quebec was diverted to Spanish waters early in June. By June 11, Brigadier Whetham had received orders to disband his command. But not until late June did Sunderland ask the Admiralty for a vessel to carry the disappointing news to America, and then no ship was made available until August.[26]

He would have been even more irritated to learn that Pennsylvania had been apprised in August that an "unhappy blow in Portugal" would, "as it is supposed," cause diversion of the forces designed for Canada. Unco-operative as Pennsylvania had been in the affair, it was incredible that such knowledge was not shared with the northern participants. Pennsylvania may have assumed that those most concerned would have been notified first. At any rate, this knowledge, current in Pennsylvania over a month before the arrival of Sunderland's packet, might have saved the northern colonies much expense or at least allowed alternative plans to be set in motion early enough to be effective.[27]

Vetch was right in his belief that reasons unknown to America had occasioned cancellation of the expedition. But Sunderland's letters to the colonists contained no explanation of the action. Whatever the reason, Britain had found use for the fleet in its peninsular campaign, meeting the reverses which its forces had suffered there. Godolphin, who was in a position to know, said later that the Canadian venture was called off because the preliminaries of peace, which were being formulated in the summer of 1709, required restitution of captured colonies. Such an article in the peace treaty would, of course, mean that the conquest of Canada would be wasted effort. With this in prospect, it was only good sense to forego the attempt.[28]

26. Godolphin to Marlborough, May 31 and June 5, 1709, Brit. Museum Add. Mss. 9105, f. 63v and 81; May 30, 1709, P.R.O., S.P. Domestic, Anne, S.P. 44/108, pp. 91, 97v; Sunderland Letter Book in Blenheim Mss., II, 290, 295; Blenheim Mss., C.I. 16; Brit. Mus. Add. Mss. 32694, f. 110v; Sunderland to Admiralty, June 24, 1709, P.R.O., Adm. 1/4093, no. 78, all cited in Bond, *Queen Anne's American Kings*, 114-15n.

27. Logan to Penn, Aug. 29, 1709, Armstrong, ed., "Penn-Logan Correspondence," Hist. Soc. Pa., *Memoirs*, 10 (1872), 357.

28. Godolphin to Marlborough, Apr. 20, 1710, *The Private Correspondence of Sarah, Duchess of Marlborough* (London, 1838), II, 423.

But to the colonists, betrayed in an enterprise which meant so much to them and to which they had contributed their staunch support, the decision highlighted Britain's lack of consideration, its total failure to appreciate their point of view. The result was not conducive to good imperial relations. This incident was one of the many instances which sowed seeds of colonial dissatisfaction with the mother country and which had an incalculable but nonetheless real bearing on the eventual breakdown leading to the Revolution. The chance to accomplish the conquest of Canada was only postponed, but the cost of the postponement in lives and money weakened and embittered the colonists.

CHAPTER NINE

Enterprise Limited

HE COLONIAL OFFICIALS gathered, disillusioned but grimly patient with the overseas ministry which had played them false. Vetch viewed the ministry's failure to act as a "dark circumstance" of such importance "that it required the mature and deliberate consultation of all the governors concerned." New York might consider it an "unintelligible proposition" to consult with the other colonies in the crisis, but the other governors of the northern provinces found their justification in Vetch's dictum that the "supreme law was the safety of the whole." Even at this late hour, the colonial leaders were resolutely determined to save what they could from their great effort. The meeting had been moved from Newport to Rehoboth to make it easier for Dudley to attend, now that New York officials had declined. On Friday, October 14, the congress got underway.[1]

The Massachusetts House had been reluctant to send representatives, but two members did attend, probably in an unofficial capacity. Even with these two, and three members of his Council, Dudley was not empowered to act for the colony. Rhode Island, on the other hand, sent a committee composed of members of both houses to assist Cranston. They were empowered to act "as if the whole Assembly were present."[2] Two members of the Connecticut legislature accompanied Governor Saltonstall, although it was ap-

---

1. Vetch to governors, Sept. 13, Vetch to Pringle, Oct. 25, Vetch to Ingoldesby, Oct. 3, 1709, Webster Papers (New Brunswick Museum); Nicholson and Vetch to Ingoldesby, Oct. 15, and Minutes of the Congress, Oct. 14, 1709, Vetch Letter Book (Museum of the City of New York); Oct. 19-20, 1709, *N.Y. Assembly Journal*, I, 262-63.

2. Sept. 16, 1709, Mass. Archives, LXXI, 543 (State House, Boston). The three members of the Massachusetts Council who attended were Addington, the secretary of the General Court, John Higginson, and Nathaniel Paine. Five deputies from the lower house of Rhode Island were there with two councilors; Minutes of the Congress, Vetch Letter Book (Museum of the City of New York). Also see Sept. 30, 1709, Bartlett, ed., *R.I. Records*, IV, 77-78.

parent that any action taken by these delegates would have to be ratified by the Connecticut government. New Hampshire, Dudley's other government, sent Mark Hunking, speaker of the House, and Samuel Penhallow of the Council. Here again, Dudley's commitments would be subject to final approval insofar as they affected the colony.

Nicholson represented the forces at Wood Creek. The New England army designed for Quebec sent its three colonels, Sir Charles Hobby, William Taylor, and William Wanton. In addition to these governors, military leaders, and legislators, John Moody, prospective governor of Newfoundland, was at the Rehoboth deliberations.[3] Despite this able representation, the congress was seriously marred by the absence of delegates from New York and New Jersey. Ingoldesby made a last-minute attempt to attend, but the Assembly could not justify his going, and the governor knew that anything which required "men or money" needed legislative concurrence. Vetch had to rely on the hope that New York would "think fit to come into the same measures" which the congress should propose.[4]

The first order of business was to present the dispatches from England, but the government's orders were singularly ill-suited to assuage colonial irritation. Stating only that Britain had been "obliged to lay aside the project," the dispatch from Sunderland failed to do the colonials the courtesy of an explanation. Even the Queen's generous permission to proceed with the forces at hand to attack Port Royal had a hollow sound so late in the season. In view of the problem which shortly arose when that course was decided upon, the suggestion was doubly ironic.

3. Minutes of the Congress, Vetch Letter Book (Museum of the City of New York).

4. Vetch to Ingoldesby, Oct. 15, Ingoldesby to Vetch, Oct. 11, 1709, Vetch Letter Book (Museum of the City of New York); Oct. 20, 1709, *N.Y. Assembly Journal*, I, 263. This gathering was an important one in the history of colonial co-operation. Usually overlooked, it belongs with the similar meetings before and after the expeditions of 1710 and 1711, in the account of colonial congresses antecedent to the more famous Albany congresses later in the century. See F. C. Stone, "Plans for the Union of the British Colonies of North America, 1642-1776," in Hampton L. Carson, ed., *History of the Celebration of the One Hundredth Anniversary of the Constitution of the United States* (Philadelphia, 1889), II, 429-503, and Richard Frothingham, *Rise of the Republic of the United States* (Boston, 1872), 107-21.

But if Sunderland's first dispatch showed a certain lack of appreciation of what the abandonment of the expedition meant to the colonists, a second one was strikingly deficient in discernment of the colonial dilemma. After the astonishing declaration that it was "absolutely necessary for the security of Her Majesty's Dominions in America and the trade of her subjects thither that the Bahama Islands should be recovered from the enemy if possible," Sunderland conveyed the Queen's request that the governors use their best endeavors to accomplish that project. He added that the commanders of Her Majesty's men-of-war already in America had orders to co-operate in such a design.[5]

Faced with the encroachments of the French, the immediacy of bloody raids on the frontier, and the ruthless privateers along their coast, the colonial leaders could hardly view an expedition against the Bahamas as "necessary for the security" of their establishments. The French on their own borders posed a more urgent problem than any in the West Indies. Moreover, they were fully aware that no French were in the Bahamas, although those islands had been raided by French privateers on occasion. Vetch himself had suggested originally that the fleet might spend the winter profitably in resettling the Bahamas, after the reduction of Canada and Newfoundland. It had been part of his vague recommendation that Spanish holdings in North America might well be dealt with while Her Majesty's forces were engaged in that part of the world. But it was not nearly the pressing matter that Port Royal was, and Vetch's suggestion was probably made only to enlist the support of British West Indian interests. Since Sunderland's orders did not mention forces to garrison the islands—a measure necessary to ensure their resettlement—sending the available men-of-war seemed a useless proceeding.[6]

With the dispatches out of the way, the congress agreed on three measures. Saltonstall and Addington drafted a memorial

5. Sunderland to the governors of New York, Virginia, and New England, July 27, 1709, *Cal. State Papers, 1708-9*, no. 658. A copy of the letter to Lovelace is in Vetch Letter Book (Museum of the City of New York).
6. *Cal. State Papers, 1710-11*, no. 421; Vetch, Nicholson, Dudley, and Moody to Ingoldesby, Oct. 18, 1709, Webster Papers (New Brunswick Museum). It doubtless reflected rising Tory influence in the government's counsels.

to the Queen which expressed the conviction of the assembled colonists that the expedition must be revived for the next year. It thanked the Queen for her good intentions, assured her of the efforts put forth by her American subjects, and stressed the great expense they had incurred. Concluding, the memorial expressed the hope that England would insist on possession of Canada and Nova Scotia in any peace negotiations. The colonists knew that otherwise a European peace would not end the struggle between the two powers in America. A second resolution proposed the maintenance of the three forts at Wood Creek. New York and Connecticut troops were requested to garrison those points, looking toward resumption of the campaign in the spring. Finally, the congress voted to prosecute the attack against Port Royal, utilizing the regiments of Massachusetts, New Hampshire, and Rhode Island, the colonial flotilla of transports and storeships, and the six British men-of-war presently in colonial waters.

Colonel Moody presented the congress with a memorial concerning Newfoundland and asked that the colonists consider doing something to help reinstate British control of that beleaguered place. But the New Englanders decided that their present distress and disappointment would allow them to entertain neither this scheme nor the Bahamas project.[7]

Practical men, the delegates also laid plans to implement their decisions. The congress agreed with Schuyler and the military leaders at Wood Creek that the best means of presenting the home government with the request for a renewal of the Glorious Enterprise was to send representatives of the several colonies to England to present their case to the Queen. They also recommended that sachems of the Five Nations should go along, accompanied by an interpreter. This was not a new idea, for the French had used the device successfully to bind their Indians more securely to their interests. It had been proposed at least as early as 1696 in the English colonies, and an Indian had occasionally been carried to the Old World earlier. But no member of the Five Nations had ever been prevailed on to go. The Rehoboth congress resolved

7. Minutes of the Congress, Vetch Letter Book (Museum of the City of New York); and *Cal. State Papers, 1708-9*, nos. 922, 922i.

to send Nicholson to England with an agent from each colony and sachems from each of the five Iroquois tribes.[8]

To Vetch the meeting was "a great and honorable congress." No doubt it would have become a landmark in the development of colonial co-operation, if all its resolves had been carried out. If even the capture of Port Royal in the fall of 1709 had stemmed from the deliberations at Rehoboth, as was intended, that gathering would have marked the initiation of a vigorous and united colonial effort carried through independent of all but the remotest British government supervision. Such an unprecedented effort would have stamped the proceedings as momentous.

But none of the intentions of the Rehoboth congress was fulfilled entirely; most failed utterly. Despite the urgent protests of the New England leaders, the forces at Wood Creek were disbanded, the forts dismantled, and frontier defense left to the Regulars, who were withdrawn to Albany. The New York Assembly considered the forts too costly to maintain. The New York militia, suffering from disease in that "unwholesome situation," its morale shattered by disappointment, could not be kept in camp. Even Connecticut recalled its levies, already in "sorrowful circumstances." Massachusetts and Rhode Island had consented to furnish quotas for the defense of the Lake Champlain outpost if the Port Royal expedition did not go forward, but with the collapse of the land army, the situation reverted to one of jealous bickering between New Englanders and New Yorkers. Massachusetts turned a deaf ear to New York's request for help in guarding its frontiers against the vengeful French and Indians. In New York, gleefully wrote the French governor of Montreal, "they all swear against Mr. Vetch and wish him hanged, he being, according to them, the cause of all this Expense."[9]

8. Schuyler probably suggested that sachems accompany the delegation. For a discussion of the origin of the idea, see Bond, *Queen Anne's American Kings,* 33-38; Schuyler, Whiting, Rednap, John Schuyler, and John Livingston to Vetch, Sept. 2, 1709, Minutes of the Congress, Vetch Letter Book (Museum of the City of New York).

9. Vetch and Nicholson to Schuyler, Mathews, and Whiting, Oct. 11, Vetch and Nicholson to Ingoldesby, Oct. 11 and 15, 1709, Vetch Letter Book (Museum of the City of New York); Oct. 18-19, 1709, *N.Y. Assembly Journal,* I, 262; Hoadly, ed., *Public Records of Conn.,* V, 123-24; Saltonstall to Sir Henry Ashurst, Jan. 30, 1710, Mass. Hist. Soc., *Collections,* 6th ser., 5 (1892), 207-12;

The projected attack on Port Royal fared no better. The plan depended on the willingness of the British naval units to support the colonial arms. Sunderland's instructions seemed to put the ships in colonial waters at the disposition of the colonial leaders. But when Dudley attempted to convene the captains to consider the attack, they refused. The *Kinsale* and the *Maidstone* had tarried at Nantasket until Dudley could inform them of the import of Sunderland's packet. Now Captain Clifton, senior officer of the two ships, refused to delay longer in taking regular station at New York. Nor could Ingoldesby be persuaded to order these two men-of-war to join an expedition against Port Royal.[10]

The captains of H.M.S. *Dragon,* which had brought Nicholson and Vetch to New England, of the *Guernsey,* which had come in during the summer, and of the *Enterprise,* which had brought Sunderland's dispatches, were no more co-operative. Captain Martin stated that the *Dragon* and the *Guernsey* had orders for Newfoundland and thence to England. The colonials pointed out that Port Royal was on the way to Placentia—a mere twenty-four-hour stop to support the attack would be a sufficient service to their forces. But Martin refused even this concession. Captain Smith of the *Enterprise* interpreted Sunderland's orders as authorizing the Bahamas expedition. If he were not required for that, he intended to take up his assigned station cruising off Virginia. Only the *Chester,* assigned as New England station ship, would accept Dudley's orders. But this ship and Southack's little province galley were hardly enough for the purpose. The project of assailing "that nest of spoilers and robbers who are so great a plague to all Her Majesty's plantations" had to be dropped.[11]

Address of Assembly to Ingoldesby, Oct. 12, 1709, *Cal. State Papers, 1710-11,* no. 1581; Dudley, Nicholson, Vetch, and Moody to Sunderland, Oct. 24, 1709, *ibid., 1708-9,* no. 794; also in P.R.O., C.O. 5, vol. 9, 75 (Lib. Cong. Transcripts). For description of ruins of forts at Wood Creek, see de Ramesay to Vaudreuil, Montreal, Oct. 1709, *N.Y. Col. Docs.,* IX, 846, 838-39.

10. *Cal. State Papers, 1708-9,* nos. 794v-viii; Vetch, Nicholson, Dudley, and Moody to Ingoldesby, Oct. 8, 1709, in both Webster Papers (New Brunswick Museum) and Vetch Letter Book (Museum of the City of New York); P.R.O., C.O. 5, vol. 9, 84-89 (Lib. Cong. Transcripts); and exchange of letters between Dudley and ship captains in Vetch Letter Book.

11. *Cal. State Papers, 1708-9,* no. 794ix-xii; and Dudley, Vetch, and Moody to Sunderland, Oct. 25, 1709, *ibid.,* no. 798; Mass. Archives, LXXI, 561 (State

Even the proposal to send delegates to England to press the colonial case was not carried out as projected. Nicholson hurried off on the *Dragon* with Colonel Moody, bound for Newfoundland and England, without waiting for agents from the other colonies or the Indian sachems. New Hampshire, Rhode Island, and the Bay Colony were content to entrust their cause to Nicholson. Saltonstall, whose Assembly urged him to go as the Connecticut representative, missed the boat. Nicholson had left, he complained, in such haste that "there was no overtaking him." Added to that, the Connecticut governor became ill, and, after the delays occasioned by straightening out the affairs of the summer, he finally decided not to make the trip.[12]

The unique feature of the plan, the idea of sending representatives from the Five Nations to England, was one which appealed to New York as much as it did to the leaders at Rehoboth, and it was not allowed to miscarry. But the process of selecting sachems capable of the assignment and making the necessary arrangements for their transportation was not one which could be accomplished hurriedly. The Indian embassy did not follow Nicholson to London until late in the winter.

Taken altogether, the year's project of putting all of North America in Her Majesty's hands had been a dismal failure. What had set out to be of "unspeakable benefit to the British nation," as Dudley somewhat infelicitously put it, had turned out a "vast loss and disappointment" for all the British colonies concerned. Massachusetts had incurred expenses just short of forty thousand pounds. New Hampshire had spent some three and a half thousand in vain, and Rhode Island nearly twice that. Connecticut was out twenty thousand pounds. Ingoldesby estimated New York's expenses at eighteen thousand pounds, noting that "never people went more cheerfully on any design than they have done

House, Boston). Also see P.R.O., C.O. 5, vol. 9, 75, 84-89 (Lib. Cong. Transcripts).

12. Dudley to Popple, Oct. 25, Dudley, Vetch, and Moody to Sunderland, Oct, 25, Addington to Popple, Oct. 26, Resolution of the Massachusetts House of Representatives, Oct. 27, 1709, acknowledging Nicholson as agent, *Cal. State Papers, 1708-9,* nos. 797, 798, 803, 806; Saltonstall to Sir Henry Ashurst, Jan. 30, 1710, Winthrop Papers, Mass. Hist. Soc., *Collections,* 6th ser., 5 (1892), 212. Nicholson sailed about the end of October.

on this," only to awaken an enemy which had left New York alone up to that time.[13]

In one respect the colonies could blame themselves for what had happened. Not one of them had been represented at court by an able agent who favored the scheme to reduce Canada. Although they could never know to what extent a representative might have influenced the ministry to support the undertaking, an agent might at least have been expected to keep them abreast of developments and thereby to have spared them protracted hopes and belated notification. Timely information might have allowed an alternative use of the colonial forces. Yet, neither New York nor Massachusetts had an active agent in London during the summer of 1709; and Connecticut's agent, Sir Henry Ashurst, had been indefatigable in his efforts to procure Dudley's ouster, so obviously he was not one to rely on.[14]

Massachusetts, at least, took the lesson to heart and hastened to appoint a colonial agent. Dudley was not convinced of the necessity, fearing, perhaps, that his opponents in the colony would utilize such a representative to undermine his position at court. He had grounds for his fears because the legislature proposed Sir William Ashurst, Sir Henry's brother, who, as the governor said, had "injuriously pursued him these twenty years." When Dudley tried to maintain that Sir William was seldom at court, Sewall opposed him, and "a great deal of warm discourse" followed.

To prove his "interest" with the British leaders, Sir Henry was boasting that he would get Dudley removed. Nor had he any use for Nicholson, Vetch, or Sir Charles Hobby. Ashurst pointed to the Whig junto as responsible for the continued favor

13. P.R.O., C.O. 5, vol. 9, 74 (Lib. Cong. Transcripts); Vetch to Pringle, Nov. 18, 1709, Webster Papers (New Brunswick Museum); Mass. Archives, XX, 124 (State House, Boston); Addington to Popple, Oct. 26, Resolution of House of Representatives of Massachusetts to the Queen, Nov. 18, Quary to Board of Trade, Dec. 2, 1709, *Cal. State Papers, 1708-9,* nos. 794, 803, 806, 860, 888; New Hampshire legislature, Dec. 6, 1709, Dudley to Board of Trade, Jan. 31, Ingoldesby to Board of Trade, Mar. 15, 1710, enclosing Assembly's Address of Oct. 12, 1709, *ibid., 1710-11,* nos. 81xvi and 158. All the colonial legislatures addressed the government asking for a renewal of the expedition, the acquisition of Canada in any forthcoming peace settlement, and help in meeting their financial losses. Sixty-six of the "principal inhabitants" of Massachusetts asked for help in freeing America from French tyranny; *ibid., 1708-9,* no. 794iii.

14. Mass. Hist. Soc., *Collections,* 6th ser., 5 (1892), 213-20.

enjoyed by the governor and his clique, as well as "money and something else kept him in which I dare not write." It was no wonder that Dudley pleaded, "Would none do but Sir William?" Quite apart from his personal opposition to the Ashursts, it seemed foolish to appoint a man who would thereby be forced to oppose his own brother in supporting the interests of Massachusetts against Connecticut claims. The General Court stood firm, however, and Ashurst was duly appointed. Fortunately for Dudley, Sir William declined to serve, and Jeremy Dummer received the post late in 1710. But the delay meant that Massachusetts spent still another year without official representation apart from the special emissaries sent to urge the case for imperial expansion.[15]

Dummer was active in behalf of the colonists long before his appointment; he was not one of Dudley's backers, but he had become convinced of the necessity of eliminating the French from North America. Even before Nicholson arrived to urge resumption of the expedition, Dummer had submitted a memorial for the use of the British peace negotiators which set forth the British claims to French possessions "on the River of Canada" based on territorial discoveries and conquests by the English since the time of the Cabots.

He echoed Vetch's arguments more than once, pointing out the French threat to English settlements by virtue of Indian alliances all along the "back side of New York and Virginia." He used Vetch's phrase in describing Port Royal's threat to New England shipping, a Dunkirk continually sending privateers against English trade. He stressed the value of Canada's naval stores, particularly in view of the increasing scarcity of supplies from Sweden. And he added at least one new idea, that of renaming Nova Scotia "New Brittain" in honor of the union between England and Scotland. When Nicholson arrived, Dummer gave unremitting aid to the effort to have the expedition renewed.[16]

15. Feb. 7, 1710, *Diary of Samuel Sewall*, II, 273, 275, 283; Sir Henry Ashurst to Wait Winthrop, Increase Mather, and Saltonstall, Mass. Hist. Soc., *Collections*, 6th ser., 5 (1892), 213-22; appointment of Sir William Ashurst, Feb. 10, 1709, Mass. Archives, XX, 129, 130, 144, 160 (State House, Boston); Addington to Popple, Nov. 14, 1710, *Cal. State Papers*, *1710-11*, no. 488.

16. Sept. 10, Oct. 6, 1709, Egerton Mss., no. 929, f. 119, 121 (Lib. Cong. Transcripts); Sanford, "Jeremy Dummer," 131.

While Nicholson pursued his design with vigor in England, Vetch wrote unflaggingly from Boston. Like others presenting the point of view of the colonists, he stressed their discouragement and resentment and made it evident that the ministry was held at least partly to blame for the failure of the naval officers to support even a thrust against Port Royal. This final blow had been "prejudicial in more respects than one," making the charges incurred by both Crown and colonies a total loss. Vetch, who had initially warned the British government to provide for unified command of land and sea forces, now made the point again. In a renewal of the expedition to Canada, or a lesser one against Port Royal, the ships must be under the commander-in-chief or a council of war so that "no more misunderstanding between land and sea captains" could arise, such as had "ruined hopeful designs in the West Indies before." Vetch had never forgotten his experience at Darien.[17]

Vetch also hoped that a perusal of the accounts of his summer's work and the reports of Nicholson and Moody "will do me justice in recommending me to Her Majesty's favor." If peace should intervene, he asked "some settled employment in these parts" and reminded his correspondents that several governorships in America were vacant. His choice remained the Glorious Enterprise, however, "which I dare still recommend to your Lordship as one of the greatest piece[s] of service to the British Empire in general, as well as to the American parts in particular." If the Port Royal expedition were decided upon, he hoped to command that whole affair. And he still hoped to be left in command of any conquered territory.

In his letters to various officials in England, Vetch reverted to these topics again and again. He was aware of impending changes, but there was little actual indication of what would be the outcome. Negotiations for peace were taking place; if they were successful, the Americans must place their hopes on terms which would end the menace of Canada. Vetch also knew that if "all our expeditions are at an end," he must look for other employment. It was

17. Vetch, Dudley, Nicholson, and Moody to Sunderland, Oct. 24, Vetch, Dudley and Moody, Oct. 25, 1709, *Cal. State Papers, 1708-9,* nos. 794, 798; Vetch to Pringle, Oct. 25, Nov. 18, 1709, Webster Papers (New Brunswick Museum).

a foregone conclusion that Ingoldesby would not be continued in his New York post. In fact, Colonel Robert Hunter had already received a commission for the New York governorship, although the colonists had not yet been notified. Vetch was still urging Nicholson's availability for that position, however, writing Pringle that since Lovelace's death New York had suffered from "no government at all" because of the "insufficiency" of the lieutenant governor. Nor was he averse to accepting the New York office himself, if it pleased British leaders to consider him. He informed Pringle that James Douglas, the London merchant who served as Vetch's agent, would furnish the necessary funds to advance Vetch's interests, and Vetch vowed himself "gratefully to acknowledge your friendship and favor."

The governorships of Maryland and Virginia were also vacant, and Vetch considered himself acquainted with both colonies. Governor Seymour of Maryland had died, and Hunter, slated for Virginia, was rumored to want Jamaica instead. The Earl of Orkney was the nominal governor of Virginia, but he never came out to his post, delegating the actual administration to a lieutenant governor. Vetch was sure that he could make himself acceptable to Orkney, and he set about cultivating that gentleman in letters to his influential friends.

It was also rumored that Dudley would be replaced, but this was probably only the wishful thinking of his opponents. The Massachusetts governor was still firmly entrenched in the favor of British leaders. Vetch let Sunderland know that he would like that post if Dudley were going to be removed, adding, "I doubt not but I should be found as capable to serve Her Majesty in that station, and as acceptable to the people here, as anybody."

He put his case before the Duke of Queensbury, his old "patron and protector," and introduced himself to Lord Stairs, the Scottish nobleman whose father and grandfather had always been ready to favor the elder Vetch with their patronage. The Duke of Argyll was another Scottish leader whose family had reason to return favors once rendered by Vetch's father. Vetch outlined his capabilities for a colonial governorship to him.[18]

18. Vetch to Sunderland, Oct. 24 and 28 and Nov. 18, Vetch to Pringle, Oct. 25 and Nov. 18, proceedings to revoke Ingoldesby's commission and appoint

To Godolphin he again set forth his application for an administrative post in the colonies, assuring the Lord Treasurer that he would "rather have that of Canada with blood and blows" than the governorship of Virginia, Maryland, or New York with peace. Vetch knew that Godolphin was closest to Marlborough of any of the ministry and probably wedded to the latter's continental policy. So he made it clear that more than Canada was at issue. Freed from the northern threat, colonial arms could be turned against the West Indies, where French and Spanish power posed a menace equally serious, if not more so, in the eyes of Englishmen at home.

Here Vetch was speaking with bland indifference to the colonial attitude toward this use of their forces. But he was also taking account of the fact that in the imperial view Canada and the West Indies were part of the same strategic area. He knew that cutting off the treasure fleets from the Caribbean would appeal to the leaders of the European alliance against France. They would thereby eliminate the source of revenue which continued to stoke the fires of conflict on the French and Spanish side. Louis XIV would be forced to accede to British terms. That Vetch could use such an argument indicates a remarkable breadth of insight; few colonists possessed such a total view of the struggle.[19]

It was a good argument but hardly realistic for 1709. Colonists would never consent to participating in wider prospects of the war; nor would Godolphin be sympathetic to what amounted to the Tory approach to the use of British sea power, especially if he was, as he seemed to Vetch, the "primum mobile" of the continental alliance. Nevertheless the point was worth stressing. The lack of geographic knowledge about the Americas was widespread in Great Britain, but it was not merely geographic confusion which resulted in references to the "West Indies" when areas in con-

---

Hunter, Popple's notice of the revocation, Oct. 25, 1709, *Cal. State Papers, 1708-9*, nos. 738, 751, 753, 800; Board of Trade to President of Virginia Council, Oct. 12, 1709, *ibid.*, no. 771; Vetch to Queensbury, Nov. 16, Vetch to Stairs, Nov. 18, Vetch to Mason, Nov. 18, 1709, Vetch Letter Book (Museum of the City of New York).

19. Vetch to Godolphin, Nov. 18 and Dec. 9, 1709, Vetch Letter Book (Museum of the City of New York); W. T. Morgan, "The South Sea Company and the Canadian Expedition in the Reign of Queen Anne," *Hispanic-American Historical Review*, 8 (1928), 143 ff.

tinental North America were meant. Canada and the West Indies were interrelated parts of the problem of imperial defense. Colonists were affected as much by privateers operating off the coasts of America between the Caribbean and the Port Royal refuge as they were by frontier Indian massacres. Similarly, the Canadian threat to the English colonies on the mainland was a threat to the bread basket of the island plantations.

Provincially minded colonists on the frontiers might not be expected to realize this larger concept of the struggle, and Britain's European allies could not be counted on to welcome increased use of her available sea power in areas overseas. But some of the more cosmopolitan leaders in the colonies and in England were coming to see the war in imperial terms and to recognize more effective uses for Britain's strength afloat. Vetch was later to appreciate the use the rising Tory leaders made of this concept.[20]

His cosmopolitan outlook and understanding prevented him from straying very far from essentials which could meet with little argument. Still, it was characteristic of the period that rational motivation was mixed with personal and political considerations. Colonists, as well as Whigs and Tories in England, were alike the prisoners of their own public and private interests when it came to shaping the strategy of the struggle against France and Spain. Party politics or personal pique determined events at least as often as overriding concepts of imperial benefit. Vetch could write one letter urging the capture of Canada for the highest reasons of state and on the same day pen another, such as the one to his London acquaintance Mason, noting alarm at the possibility of peace and asking to be referred to the Earl of Orkney for the Virginia governorship if the Canadian expedition should be cancelled. For this service, Vetch offered to give "a handsome present, oftener

20. W. T. Morgan has outlined the connection between the projected conquest of Canada and the war as a whole in "Some Attempts at Imperial Cooperation During the Reign of Queen Anne," Royal Historical Society, *Transactions*, 4th ser., 10 (1927), 171-94. Morgan's articles imply more conscious and rational motivation for the expeditions than contemporary evidence suggests, but contrariwise, he remedies the omissions of most historians who fail to see that there was a logical connection between the major efforts in the colonies during the war and the British conduct of the war as a whole. For an early advocacy of the use of Britain's sea power, see "A New Model at Sea," author unknown, in Historical Manuscripts Commission, *Report on the Manuscripts of His Grace the Duke of Portland, Preserved at Welbeck Abbey* (London, 1919), X, 20.

than once"—gifts were likely to be as effective as rational and lengthy arguments in moving the ministry to action.[21]

It had been "a very hurrying year" for Governor Dudley and his collaborator in imperialism when he and Vetch sat down together to review the unhappy circumstances of the colonies and plan for the year to come. Schuyler had arrived in Boston with four sachems (or Indians who would do just as well) during December, ready to sail for England to aid Nicholson with firsthand information of the northern colonies. News from Albany had followed him that the French were again stealing upon the New England frontiers; "the Good Lord stop them!" was Sewall's injunction.

And Vetch wryly noted that French privateers were daily taking their toll of New England vessels, almost in sight of the very captains who had been in haste for other duties when they refused the Port Royal venture. Instead they waited at Boston, careening their vessels, and "durst not go out of the harbor for want of orders." Latest word from Albany confirmed earlier reports that all the summer's building had been in vain. The forts were in ruins and the defenders dispersed. But this situation would be tempered if, as Vetch hoped, the Crown had already determined upon renewing the Canada expedition or sending a force to take Port Royal. It would not do to paint a hopeless picture which might jeopardize these plans.

Vetch hoped that Schuyler and his Indians would add further strength to the colonial petition and that news of continued adversity might "quicken their motions" in England. Schuyler's Indians were not representative of all the Five Nations; they were three Mohawks and a member of the "River tribe," but Schuyler had doubtless picked those best suited for his task, and England would not know the difference. Vetch recommended them to Sunderland as "true philosophers that carry all their treasure along with them, taking no care for more than their present subsistence." He asked that they be given clothing, subsistence, presents, and a good time. And to make sure they were provided for, Vetch arranged for credit to be furnished by his faithful kins-

21. Vetch to Mason, Vetch to Godolphin, Nov. 18, 1709, Vetch Letter Book (Museum of the City of New York).

man James Douglas in London, who would see that they were suitably garbed for an audience with the Queen, in addition to his assignment of waiting frequently upon Sunderland's secretary in the matter of Vetch's own preferment.[22]

The New York legislature authorized Schuyler to add its plea to that of the other colonies. His Indians would urge renewal of the campaign and add their own testimony of the Five Nations' appreciation for the past summer's efforts and the "wise and generous treatment" accorded them by Nicholson and Schuyler. Since Schuyler was a stranger to Europe, Vetch arranged to send Major Pigeon with him. Pigeon's commission was granted by the New Englanders, and he hoped that his trip with the Indian embassy would also allow him to solicit his rank as a Regular. Schuyler, too, had the further mission of collecting arrears of the sums he had advanced for provisioning and equipping the Albany forces.[23]

When the Massachusetts Council was apprised of Pigeon's imminent departure, Sewall and others were critical. Here was another of Dudley's supporters who might thwart the colonial opposition to the governor at court. The Council resented the failure to consult it in the matter; Sewall warned Dummer that although Schuyler had often befriended Massachusetts with timely advice of approaching danger, "yet he cannot be supposed to be an equal arbiter, when the Massachusetts interest shall come in competition with that of New York." Even when faced with a common menace, the two colonies continued to exhibit jealousy of each other.[24]

22. Bond, *Queen Anne's American Kings*, 38-44, and notes, 158-59, traces the movement of Schuyler and the Indians before sailing. Bond agrees with the arguments of contemporaries that the four Indians were not sachems and were not drawn from all five, or even four, of the Iroquois tribes. The evidence is unmistakable that however well suited to their role, they were Albany adherents rather than leaders in their own tribes. Also see Vetch to Pringle, Feb. 10, to Nicholson, Feb. 2, and to Sunderland, Feb. 2, 1710, Webster Papers (New Brunswick Museum); Dudley to Popple, Jan. 3, 1710, *Cal. State Papers, 1710-11*, no. 82; Mass. Hist. Soc., *Collections*, 6th ser., 6 (1893), 272.

23. Vetch to Sunderland, Feb. 2 and 10, 1710, Webster Papers (New Brunswick Museum); Vetch to Sunderland, Jan. 9, and Vetch to Godolphin, Feb. 10, 1710, Vetch Letter Book (Museum of the City of New York). Pigeon had accompanied Vetch from England in the spring of 1709.

24. Feb. 4, 1710, *Diary of Samuel Sewall*, II, 273; Sewall to Dummer, Feb. 13, 1710, Mass. Hist. Soc., *Collections*, 6th ser., 1 (1886), 389.

If Vetch had any fear that Nicholson might not be working for his interests, he did not show it. "I doubt nothing of your friendship to me in all within your power," he wrote his colleague and admitted that although he would always endeavor to be deserving, he could never repay Nicholson's loyal support. He wished Nicholson "all health, happiness, and success, and a safe return here if you design it." Nevertheless, when Schuyler and Pigeon sailed for London late in February on H.M.S. *Reserve,* Vetch could rest assured that he was adding two more loyal advocates of his cause to the agency in London.[25]

Before the four sachems could make their colorful appearance before Queen Anne, Nicholson accomplished his mission. On March 18, he received a commission to command British and colonial forces in the reduction of Port Royal "or any other place in those parts now in the possession of the enemy." His instructions ordered him to Boston along with 500 marines, stores of war, and a "bomb ketch." These were to be joined by the militia of New Hampshire, Massachusetts, Connecticut, and Rhode Island, according to the quotas of the previous summer. Final decisions rested with a council of war which included Nicholson, Vetch as "the eldest colonel," the governors of the colonies concerned, the senior marine commander, and the four senior sea captains. The colonial governments were instructed to furnish their own transports and provisions, landing boats (the whaleboats built for the intended expedition against Canada), and pilots, including the indispensable Captain Southack with his province galley.

To encourage support of the expedition, the Crown promised preference in the land and trade of the conquered area to the colonists who participated and urged the governors to enlist the services of any and all "gentlemen volunteers." Vetch was designated to be the commander of the conquered area with the necessary garrison to hold it. As an afterthought, Nicholson's instructions warned against indiscriminate disposition of plunder. Only perishables were to be divided among the victors, as the

25. Dudley and Vetch to Sunderland, Feb. 3-4, 1710, *Cal. State Papers, 1710-11,* no. 103; Vetch to Nicholson, Feb. 2, 1710, Webster Papers (New Brunswick Museum).

council of war determined. Anything else must await the orders of the British government.[26]

Notices of these plans were prepared for Dudley, Saltonstall, and Cranston. A commission similar to Nicholson's was drawn up for Vetch, allowing him to act in Nicholson's absence. Sunderland informed Vetch that the Crown was unable to spare troops and supplies in sufficient numbers to launch a full-scale attack against Canada; the conquest of Port Royal would be all that they could undertake this year. But this decision, made in March, remained unknown to the colonists until Nicholson returned to Boston in mid-July. It was just as well, since alterations in the new scheme impended during the spring.[27]

The arrival of the four Indians so excited London that the ministry, after hearing them, was half inclined to reconsider the attack on Canada. The four savages were wined, dined, and lionized; their portraits were painted by the Queen's order; impresarios of plays and sporting events contended for their presence. Literary effusions reflected their visit. The Indians addressed the Queen herself, on April 20, paying tribute to their three mentors, Quedar, Anadagarjaux, and Anadiasia (Schuyler, Nicholson, and Vetch) and expressing their appreciation for the attempted campaign of 1709. Describing their sorrow and humiliation at the failure of that attempt, the Indians made it clear to the court that they considered the enterprise one of "great weight." It would solve their problems of hunting and trading; otherwise they would be forced to move to other habitations or "stand neuter." According to all reports, the Indians were highly pleased with their reception. They returned home laden with presents when Nicholson sailed for America.[28]

Although Nicholson received his orders in March, he lingered in London for the Whigs' trial of Dr. Sacheverell. With the resultant clamor against the Whigs, the Tory Nicholson may

26. P.R.O., C.O. 5, vol. 9, 97, 88 (Lib. Cong. Transcripts), and Nova Scotia Historical Society, *Collections*, 1 (1879), 59-62; also in Society of Colonial Wars in Massachusetts, *Year Book*, Publication No. 3 (Boston, 1879), 82 ff., and Mass. Archives, LXXI, 617, 620 (State House, Boston).

27. P.R.O., C.O. 5, vol. 9, 103-4, 108 (Lib. Cong. Transcripts).

28. *Cal. State Papers, 1710-11*, nos. 194, 210. Bond, *Queen Anne's American Kings*, chap. I, describes the visit in detail from a wealth of sources. Chapter III traces the various literary manifestations, then and later.

have hoped for a political upset which would bring even greater advantages than the command of the Port Royal expedition. With the attention of London on the trial, the routine business of out-fitting ships and personnel must have suffered interference. When he finally arranged to sail early in May, contrary winds delayed his departure. Not until the twenty-second did the two ships get to sea. A convoy of heavier naval vessels accompanied them 100 leagues from Land's End as protection from the French fleet, rumored to be on the prowl, and the summer's campaign was underway.

The *Falmouth* and the *Dragon* were to be joined by the two station ships assigned to New York, H.M.S. *Feversham* and H.M.S. *Lowestoft*, along with H.M.S. *Chester* stationed at Boston. These five vessels of the regular navy, with the British and colonial transports and auxiliaries, would compose a formidable fleet. Although Nicholson had been unsuccessful in getting his full complement of five hundred marines, he had nearly four hundred to augment the colonial forces. But he was apprehensive that these marines, "nigh half" of whom were "new raised men," would be less effective than veterans in action. His main worry was his long-delayed departure, for, as he noted, "summer draws on apace and they will be very impatient in New England to have us there."[29]

Even as Nicholson sailed, Vetch was sending word to Sunderland that when the offensive was not promptly renewed in March, as had been planned, the French had become bold. They had taken nine vessels within fifteen leagues of Boston in the last five days. "The season being so far advanced without my having the least orders relating to the expedition's being renewed," he wrote, "mightily discourages all the people who had so readily complied with Her Majesty's orders last year."[30] Unfortunately, colonial enterprises usually were delayed by the procrastination of British bureaucracy, the threat of enemy action, or the weather. Slowness of communication remained a vexation to the colonists; nothing had been done to effect Vetch's plan for establishing a number of

---

29. *Cal. State Papers*, *1710-11*, no. 241iv, and nos. 211, 215, 240, 241, 246.
30. P.R.O., C.O. 5, vol. 9, 98 (Lib. Cong. Transcripts); and May 15, 1710, *Cal. State Papers*, *1710-11*, no. 237.

fast packet boats to keep Britain and her colonies informed about latest developments. As spring wore into summer, Vetch, Dudley, and the members of the Massachusetts Council had to bide their time, treating each other at the Green Dragon Tavern and hoping for favorable word from the seat of empire.[31]

Although Nicholson's departure from England had initiated the alternative to a full-scale expedition against Canada, the British ministry still toyed with the idea of going ahead with the original plan. Backstairs intrigue between Harley and the Queen heralded a Tory resurgence, as did the popular outcry aroused by the Sacheverell affair. The Whigs had nothing to offer but failure of the peace preliminaries, military deadlock in the Lowlands, and military reverses in Spain. For years the plan to attack France and Spain through their outlying colonies in the West Indies and the American mainland had found favor in some Tory quarters. Certainly the war in Europe was unpopular with the Tories, and their leaders might try to exploit an American campaign if they could not bring hostilities to an end otherwise. So the Whigs had good reason to consider this final effort to prolong their hold on the government.[32]

But it was too late for the Whigs in the spring and summer of 1710. Sunderland fell from office, and Dartmouth replaced him as Secretary of State. In early July, Dummer suddenly was asked whether it was too late in the season to reconsider the expedition against Canada. The assiduous New Englander assured Dartmouth that time enough did indeed remain. He cited Phips' expedition of 1690 which did not arrive in the St. Lawrence until October and, although unsuccessful against Quebec, returned safely to Boston in November. In fact, he noted, New England ship captains held to the belief that contrary winds usually pre-

31. Vetch to Sunderland, Feb. 15, 1710, Vetch Letter Book (Museum of the City of New York). For an earlier occasion, see the entry for Feb. 6, 1710, on the Queen's birthday, *Diary of Samuel Sewall*, II, 273.

32. Nicholson had proposed such an approach as early as 1702; *Cal. State Papers*, 1702-3, nos. 567-68. Dummer, who also found himself closer to the Tories than the Whigs, favored it; Sanford, "Jeremy Dummer," 122-23, and see also *Proposals for Carrying on an Effectual War in America Against the French and Spaniards* (London, 1702). The slippery Shrewsbury, sometime Whig but soon to reappear in the Tory ministry, had been receptive to the idea; Hist. Mss. Comm., *Duke of Buccleuch and Queensbury Mss.*, II, 792-93.

vented ships from going up the river to Quebec until September. October and even November should be possible months for an assault; an earlier attempt was to be preferred, but it was not yet too late. Besides, he pointed out, if Nicholson should run into difficulties at Port Royal, the timely arrival of a larger fleet would at least assure attainment of that objective.

Dummer had the Glorious Enterprise very much at heart. If it were revived, he told Dartmouth, he wanted to go with it. A few days later, he found that it was in motion and applied for the position of judge advocate and secretary to the commander. Viscount Shannon had been commissioned as general and commander-in-chief and ordered to Portsmouth with five regiments, there to board ships for Boston. Once in America, Shannon was to concert with the principal land and sea officers, including Vetch, Nicholson, and the new governor of New York, Robert Hunter. New York forces were to be added to those already gathered by New England for the Nova Scotia campaign, and the Five Nations were to be offered suitable presents and engaged for the undertaking. Shannon was to be over-all commander of the land forces, although his orders merely specified co-operation with the sea captains. Vetch's wise suggestion that the commander be given control of his supporting naval force was again overlooked. But provision was made for alternative or additional operations if the force arrived too late to undertake the main attack or had time left afterward for another project.[33]

This last effort of the Whigs, or first venture of the Tories, however it may be interpreted, found no favor with Marlborough, who still held his position as Britain's great director of the war effort. Working closely with the Whig junto, yet often suspected of Tory sympathies, if not outright Jacobitism, Marlborough now appeared to believe with the Tories that a prompt peace would gain more than further conquests. He cited the expense of such an expedition and the injudiciousness of diverting naval vessels from European waters. Godolphin, in desperation, suggested another new approach to break the military deadlock, an amphibious

33. Dummer to Dartmouth, July 6, Shannon's Commission and Instructions, July 14, 1710, *Cal. State Papers, 1710-11*, nos. 290, 297, 301, 302, also in P.R.O., C.O. 5, vol. 9, 107 (Lib. Cong. Transcripts).

landing against some French seaport. But Marlborough opposed this too.[34] Despite the extensive preparations for the expedition, therefore, the time was not propitious for a renewal of the mammoth attack against Canada. In the spring, Godolphin had feared an invasion of Scotland by the Pretender. Under such circumstances, he was unwilling to release troops for service elsewhere.[35]

Without the support of their military idol, Marlborough, it is doubtful that the Whigs could have gone through with the Canadian offensive. To make matters worse, Godolphin went out of office before the campaign could be launched. The new ministry needed more time to get the reins of government in hand before carrying out anything so ambitious; nor could it dispense summarily with Marlborough's military genius. It would be folly to disregard his recommendations before considering all the elements of Britain's wartime dispositions. At the end of August, Dartmouth wrote to Dudley that although the expedition had been prepared, it was now laid aside. A late start, delay in sailing because of contrary winds, and the final determination that the force was needed for other service—all had contributed to the decision to call off this second attempt to attain Vetch's great aim. Tardily begun, it had been pressed sincerely and without stint; yet conditions had made it unlikely from the start.[36]

Rumors of the contemplated expansion of Nicholson's forces for the larger objective had reached America before Dartmouth wrote, but expectations had not been raised too high. Dudley, Vetch, Nicholson, and the other leaders pinned their hopes for the summer on the capture of Port Royal, realizing that the situation in England could not be expected to yield much more. But Vetch seemed to sense the changes in viewpoint which a Tory

34. Bond, *Queen Anne's American Kings*, 47-48, and notes, 124, cites the Godolphin-Marlborough correspondence in the Blenheim Mss., and Coxe's copies in Brit. Mus. Add. Mss. Marlborough's judgment seems to have been based on his assessment of the situation as a military leader and not on his adherence to either party.

35. Godolphin to Marlborough, Apr. 20, 1710, *Private Correspondence of Sarah, Duchess of Marlborough*, II, 423.

36. *Cal. State Papers, 1710-11*, no. 380. Historians have largely ignored the preparations for Shannon's expedition, despite the fact that British records are fairly full on the subject. Osgood, for instance, omits mention of Shannon, and Parkman has the details of the intended expedition confused. See Bond, *Queen Anne's American Kings*, 47-48, and notes, 124.

administration might bring. Even with peace, he hoped Britain might proceed against Spain and suggested that the provisions and supplies already gathered be used in a "reduction of New Spain." He acknowledged himself "very ready to contribute my mite of advice and assistance, having been formerly upon that coast." Ever ready to unite his private interests with advantages to his country, Vetch was always shrewd enough to trim his sails to the freshening breeze. In this case, however, it was evidence of growing desperation.[37]

With Nicholson's arrival at Boston on July 15, active military preparations got underway. The marines were brought ashore where they could be kept together. With the exception of the unhappy independent companies who had languished in garrison at New York for so many years and who served quite a different purpose, these were the first British Regulars to land on American shores for military duty in the cause of the colonists. Commissary agents Belcher and Steele were kept busy finding provisions for the force. Prices were high, especially for pork and beef. The leaders were forced to pay dearly for guns, gun carriages, and other military stores, because the Board of Ordnance had failed to furnish all the items which had been ordered. Vetch and Nicholson, on the Queen's account, shouldered the cost of provisions and supplies for the seamen, marines, and the artillery company, which Vetch had maintained since the failure the year before. The colonial administrations met the expenses of their militia. As before, the colonists were assured that conquered territory would not be garrisoned by militiamen. But volunteers were offered a new coat, "worth thirty shillings," a month's wages in advance, and exemption from impressment for three years if they would consent to serve at Port Royal after its capture. Maintenance and pay of the garrison was left to the British government, as Nicholson and Vetch reminded the Secretary of State.[38]

Nicholson and Vetch were distressed that only 400 of the

37. *Cal. State Papers, 1710-11*, no. 237.
38. For the preparations, see July 15, 1710, and following, *Diary of Samuel Sewall*, II, 283-84; Mass. Archives, LXXI, 641-791 (State House, Boston); Nicholson and Vetch to Secretary of State, Sept. 16, 1710, *Cal. State Papers, 1710-11*, no. 396, also in P.R.O., C.O. 5, vol. 9, 110 (Lib. Cong. Transcripts); and Soc. of Col. Wars in Mass., *Year Book*, Pub. No. 3, 96. Despite this agreement Vetch later attempted to get Massachusetts to pay the garrison.

promised 500 marines had been sent on the expedition. The late start also occasioned misgivings, but, as they noted, the colonists had not been eager to act beforehand in the matter of preparations after their previous disappointment. Nevertheless, Nicholson had "with unwearied pains and diligence pushed forward the preparations," and the colonists were able to appear in full number, well clothed, and provided with necessary transports, pilots, chaplains, surgeons, provisions, stores of war, and all the "necessaries and utensils proper for the service."[39]

Massachusetts raised 900 men, provisioned for three months. Rhode Island added 200 men, with transports and military stores; Connecticut filled its quota of 300, and New Hampshire furnished its small force. Although these colonial legislatures memorialized the Queen in gratitude for her allowance of the expedition, their statements lacked the zeal which had characterized their addresses of the previous summer. They took occasion to point out the heavy expenses under which they labored, to complain of the high quotas required from their slender pool of manpower, and to ask that colonies to the south be required hereafter to help in the cause that was equally theirs.[40]

Vetch had done all that was required of him as adjutant general and senior colonel of the force. But he exhibited a disposition to remain in the background, leaving to Nicholson the responsibility of directing the preparations. This conduct was in marked contrast to his pre-eminence during the preliminaries of the 1709 campaign. There the responsibility had been his, but his hopes of "raising to myself a lasting monument" among the colonists had been dashed by the failure of his enterprise. Since then people in New England had been very "uneasy" with him. But the campaign of 1710 had been entrusted to Nicholson, and Vetch,

39. *Cal. State Papers*, *1710-11*, no. 396; Nicholson's Journal, *Boston News-Letter*, Nov. 6, 1710, as reprinted in Nova Scotia Hist. Soc., *Collections*, 1 (1879), 64.

40. Governor, Council, and Assembly of Massachusetts Bay to the Queen, Aug. 22, Cranston to Sunderland, Aug. 23 (enclosing Address of Governor and Company of Rhode Island), New Hampshire Governor, Council, and Assembly to the Queen, Aug. 24, 1710, *Cal. State Papers*, *1710-11*, nos. 356-58. For Massachusetts' Address, see also Public Archives of Nova Scotia, VII 1/2, no. 1 (Dalhousie University, Halifax), and Soc. of Col. Wars in Mass., *Year Book*, Pub. No. 3, 95-105.

although seldom averse to pushing himself forward, with or without authority, was not eager to assume any more responsibility than the discharge of his duty required. A second failure identified with him, should it occur, would work permanent injury to his reputation.[41]

41. The failure of the British fleet to arrive made it apparent that the expedition would not be pursued; Vetch to Sunderland, Sept. 12, 1709, Vetch Letter Book (Museum of the City of New York). Vetch was finding it financially difficult to "maintain the rank and character of a general officer" without the usual pay and allowances. To make matters worse, Pringle had addressed him at the end of the last season's undertaking as "lieutenant colonel," whereas being adjutant general by the Queen's commission, he ranked as senior colonel in the colonial army; Vetch to Pringle, Nov. 18, 1709, Webster Papers (New Brunswick Museum); Vetch to Sunderland, May 15, 1710, P.R.O., C.O. 5, vol. 9, 98 (Lib. Cong. Transcripts).

Outpost Governor

HE PUSH AGAINST Port Royal could have started in August but for the failure of the New York station ships to arrive. When H.M.S. *Feversham* and *Lowestoft* finally put into Nantasket on September 9, the commanders of the force made immediate preparations to sail. Captain Mathews set out first in the *Chester* to reconnoiter, and at noon on Monday, September 18, Commodore Martin in H.M.S. *Dragon* led the rest of the fleet out of Nantasket. The flotilla numbered thirty-six sail and several small open sloops carrying bulky stores.[1]

With fair wind and weather, the force coasted northeast to "the Wolves" at the entrance to Passamaquoddy Bay, but fog, bad weather, and the "extraordinary currency of the tide" forced it to anchor. The *Chester* joined up, bringing four French deserters, and reported having been fired on by Indians at the entrance to Port Royal Harbor. Its cannon had "feared them away." After a delay of three days, the fleet set sail at four in the morning on Sunday, September 24, crossed the Bay of Fundy, and arrived off Port Royal at noon. An ebbing tide brought them again to anchor. When the small ship *Caesar* attempted to negotiate the narrow entrance to the bay, she ran aground and was battered by the rising winds. Although thirty-three men swam ashore, nineteen others, including the master of the ship, drowned.

Better luck followed the rest. With a fair wind, the ships sailed through the "gut" and up the tapering bay to its end, where they anchored off the French fort. Sunset over the low hills

---

1. *Cal. State Papers, 1710-11*, nos. 392, 395; Nicholson's Journal, Nova Scotia Hist. Soc., *Collections*, 1 (1879), 65. See Mass. Archives, LXXI, 662, 674 (State House, Boston), for lists of transports and tonnage of supplies carried. P.R.O., C.O. 5, vol. 9, 102 (Lib. Cong. Transcripts), lists the officers of each regiment and their distribution on board H.M.S. *Falmouth* and *Dragon*.

which fringed the placid basin found the officers gathered in council to plot their strategy. Ashore, the French fired off a beacon to warn the inhabitants to take shelter in the fort. Two Frenchmen, less valorous than their fellows, deserted to the British fleet, but three Irishmen and a Dutchman, lacking in zeal for the British Empire, more than redressed the balance by jumping ship under cover of night.[2]

On Monday morning the siege commenced. Opposing Nicholson's forces of nearly two thousand were two or three hundred cowed and terrified French troops under Subercase. It was a vast credit to this plucky French commander that he doggedly held off the British for over a week, largely by the force of his own resolute spirit and despite constant desertions by his panic-stricken soldiers.[3]

After the preliminary scouting by a force of marines, the British army landed and took positions along two sides of the French stronghold. With drums beating and flags flying, Vetch, accompanied by Engineer Forbes and Mascarene's grenadiers, marched with the regiments of Walton and Taylor to his campsite on the north flank as the French bastions kept up a steady fire. Nicholson led the main body, comprising the regiments of Reading, Hobby, and Whiting, to positions on the south side, with Engineer Rednap and Major John Livingston's Indian scouts in support. Nicholson's forces had to cut their way through heavy brush to camp in woods adjoining the fort on the south, while French fire "beat up the marsh near us." At nightfall, the ketch *Star Bomb* sailed up and dropped seven shells on the French fortifications, and the enemy's west bastion answered with a cannonade.

Skirmishing on Tuesday was confined to brushes between Livingston's Indian sentinels and the French Indians, led by French officers. Whenever they exposed themselves, the British forces came under fire from the fort and from the houses, fences, and gardens of the nearby village; however, few casualties were reported, except from a small force which entrenched itself

2. Nicholson's Journal, Nova Scotia Hist. Soc., *Collections*, 1 (1879), 65-66, 100; Mass. Archives, LXXI, 787-88 (State House, Boston).

3. Subercase to Pontchartrain, Oct. 26, 1710, *N.Y. Col. Docs.*, IX, 927-29.

400 paces from the enemy earthworks. Vetch and his engineer tried to set up the coehorn mortars for Mascarene's artillerymen at Spurs Point, but they found the lay of the land unsatisfactory. The next morning brought rain. Stores were landed from the ships, cannon were mounted, and the flat-bottomed whaleboats brought artillery and ammunition ashore in the face of "warm" fire from the French. Rain drenched the exposed soldiers on Thursday, and dark and cloudy weather hindered the bomb ketch in its customary evening bombardment of the fort. Back in Boston, the hopeful citizenry observed a day of fasting and prayer for the success of its absent army.

British control of the high land around the fort put Subercase at a disadvantage, but he did not dare launch an attack for fear of exposing his meagre garrison and because it might give his men an opportunity to desert. At best, he could only keep the besiegers at bay by shelling British gun positions and forcing relocation of their cannon. His Regulars and militia alike, as well as the women gathered in the fort, were "rendered crazy" by the constant shelling from the bay. Subercase's men petitioned him to surrender, his officers conferred, and a rumor spread that the French defenders planned to blow up the fort and surrender themselves.

As the British officers lingered after dinner on Friday night, a French officer accompanied by a sergeant and a drummer suddenly appeared with a flag of truce and a letter from Subercase. Translating, Nicholson read that the enemy commander asked a favor of his opponent, the "gallant and honest gentleman." Women in the fort, some of noble lineage and some pregnant, had thought that they could stand the British bombardment. Now they found they had been mistaken and begged sanctuary in the British camp.[4]

This Nicholson was quite ready to grant. But he suspected, not without justice, that Subercase had sent his men primarily to ascertain how great the odds really were against the defenders and to search out any weaknesses which would allow the French to turn the tables against opponents who so greatly outnumbered

4. Nicholson's Journal, Nova Scotia Hist. Soc., *Collections*, 1 (1879), 66-70, 102-3; *N.Y. Col. Docs.*, IX, 928.

them. Ostensibly because the French had failed to beat their drum and obtain permission to enter the British camp blindfolded, Nicholson detained the officer and sent one of his own to Subercase. Returning the compliments, "which I value . . . the more upon coming from so good a judge as yourself and so old a soldier," he stated that he had not been sent to make war on women; he would protect any French ladies who were sent across the lines. But the old French veteran pretended indignation and told the English messenger that never in his thirty-six years as a soldier had he heard of arresting the bearer of a flag of truce. Furthermore, pleading inability to read English, he requested Nicholson to put his future letters in French. Stubbornly, he sent the English officer back to Nicholson, although the hour was nearly midnight.[5]

It was a bold defiance, but it postponed Subercase's inevitable decision only briefly. The British had their cannon mounted on strategic heights, and surrender could be put off for only a short while longer. On Saturday morning, the last day of September, Nicholson replied brusquely to Subercase's appeal. Noting that the French commander seemed more anxious to get his officer back than to provide for the fainting females in the fort, Nicholson concluded that the previous evening's exchange had indeed been for purposes of espionage. He added that he would write in French when Subercase addressed him in English. The arrested officer would be given civil treatment, and in return Nicholson expected the honorable Subercase to accord his British hostage the same.

This exchange was enough for the French commander, who asked for surrender terms in accordance with the rules of war. But he continued to put up a bold front before the English messengers. They were informed that 500 men were on their way to relieve Port Royal. The French cannon were larger than the mortar on the bomb ketch, boasted the French garrison. Subercase sent word to "Colonel Vetch that he came of an indifferent errand," for he, Subercase, would still be governor. "I have your officer and you have mine, we are equal," wrote Subercase to

5. Letters between Subercase and Nicholson, Nicholson's Journal. Nova Scotia Hist. Soc., *Collections*, 1 (1879), 69-72.

Nicholson. Eliot, the British officer who had brought Nicholson's reply, was queried as to the location of Nicholson's headquarters. Subercase magnanimously offered to spare that area if he were informed of its whereabouts. Eliot's reply was in a classic vein: "Sometimes in a bottom, sometimes in a hill, sometimes in a house, sometimes in a hedge, and sometimes betwixt two bear skins." Asked how the British liked the cold weather and how long they expected to be able to stand it, Eliot answered that "cold weather was most agreeable to the English."

On Sunday, Nicholson sent Colonel Reading to negotiate with Subercase, and at the same times Forbes and Rednap began a sustained shelling, which the French endeavored to return. Nicholson soon dispatched two more officers to the fort with a demand for surrender. Subercase reluctantly agreed to treat, and a cease fire was ordered on both sides. On Monday, hostages were exchanged, articles of capitulation agreed on, and Nicholson sent out a party to find the French ladies who had fled the fort when the final shelling began. They were brought back Tuesday morning and breakfasted with Nicholson before they returned to their own lines. While final arrangements for the ceremony of surrender were completed, the British rested in camp, and the French inhabitants came out of the woods and returned to their homes.

The next day the British army formed itself. Taking his place at the head, Nicholson advanced to the fort with Vetch on his right, Hobby on his left, and the French officers with whom he had treated following. Subercase emerged from the stronghold he had so staunchly defended, followed by the other French officers and the British negotiators. Meeting on the little bridge leading into the fortifications, the two groups saluted. Subercase gracefully offered the keys of the fort to Nicholson, declaring that he was sorry the French King had lost such a brave fort but happy it fell to so noble and generous a commander. Nicholson delivered the keys to Vetch as rightful governor by the Queen's orders. Then the little force of French soldiers marched out, guns shouldered, drums beating, and colors flying, as the terms of surrender provided, saluting Nicholson as they passed. The British raised the Union Jack and drank to the Queen's health. Mascarene with sixty men mounted the first guard, Nicholson renamed the place Annapolis Royal, and the guns of the fort thundered a salute, answered by the cannon of the ships in the basin.[6]

With his assumption of the governorship, Vetch achieved his highest post. In the more than twenty years left to him, he was to work constantly toward the solution of the problems of an expanding empire. His discouragements would have blighted the hopes of lesser men, but Vetch never gave up the attempt to achieve greatness.[7]

As he faced the problem of administering a military outpost amid an alien and hostile populace, Vetch, at forty-one, faced problems which would test all of his innate ability and his store of experience. No standards existed, with which he was familiar, for governing by military occupation. Furthermore, he had to contend with the antagonism of a people still loyal at heart to a powerful European monarch and professing adherence to a faith which was the antithesis of English Protestantism. No parallel existed on the American colonial scene. When England had taken New Amsterdam from the Dutch, little religious difference had existed. Holland had not been able to offer more than temporary opposition, and the settlers had stolidly acquiesced. Civil government and English colonists had come to New York almost at once. Yet, even there the admixture of nationalities had been troublesome. Vetch could expect worse from the French.

The articles of capitulation settled the immediate problems. The French garrison was allowed to keep its arms and baggage. The British promised to transport the French Regulars to France. Religious ornaments in the chapel were to be returned to the church. Officers might sell their effects if they did not want to take them home, and Subercase was allowed to keep six cannon, which he promptly sold back to the British in order to pay govern-

6. *Ibid.*, 73-86; articles of capitulation, Oct. 2, 1710, *Cal. State Papers, 1710-11*, no. 412.

7. The Historic Sites and Monuments Board of Canada, under the chairmanship of Dr. J. Clarence Webster, in 1928 erected a monument to Samuel Vetch on the ramparts of the old fort at Annapolis Royal. The inscription reads: "Samuel Vetch. Adjutant-general of the force under Colonel Francis Nicholson which captured Port Royal, capital of Acadia, in 1710. First Governor and Commander-in-chief. A notable figure in Colonial history. An able soldier and administrator. With imperial vision he strove to extend the realm of Britain beyond the seas."

ment debts owed to the inhabitants surrounding the fort. The unhappy ex-governor was also forced to sell his plate, furniture, and other personal belongings to meet royal charges for which Louis XIV had failed to provide. Those French who resided within gunshot of the fort (this *banlieue*, as it was called, occupied approximately a three-mile area) were promised protection from molestation for two years, if they wished to remain, provided they swore loyalty to the British. The rest of the population of Nova Scotia was to be considered "prisoners at discretion."

The fall of the fort gave the British the opportunity of claiming the entire territory of Acadia, once an English possession; reprisals were threatened against those who offered harm to the conquerors, although it was recognized that possession of Annapolis Royal alone hardly put the British in a position to make good their claim by effective control. In fact, the British asserted sovereignty over the entire maritime region below the St. Lawrence, from the bounds of the British claims in Maine along the northwest shores of the Bay of Fundy, including Acadia and Cape Breton Island, and extending to Cape Gaspé. It was more than the French were to allow in the future peace treaty and more than the British were able to guard and utilize for many years to come.[8]

At the end of the first week in October, 200 marines were detached for garrison duty at Annapolis Royal, and 250 of the New Englanders consented to join them. The able Paul Mascarene was promoted to major, as was the engineer, Forbes, and the Reverend Mr. Harrison was appointed chaplain for the garrison. The next week, the remaining forces embarked for New England and old, and the French soldiers boarded the three transports designated to carry them to Europe. Tuesday was observed as a day of thanksgiving.

On Thursday evening, Baron Saint-Castin, a colorful half-breed, appeared from Pentagoet at the mouth of the Penobscot River. This son of a French baron and a Penobscot princess had a lonely trading outpost on the French frontier in Maine and wielded influence important for the French with the people of his

8. *Cal. State Papers, 1710-11,* nos. 412, 429; *N.Y. Col. Docs.,* IX, 928; Public Archives of Nova Scotia, VII 1/2, nos. 4, 12 (Dalhousie University, Halifax); see especially no. 8, "The English Bounds of the seacoast of Nova Scotia . . ." as set forth in a memorandum of Cyprian Southack, Oct. 16, 1710.

mother's tribe and related members of the Abenaki group. Suber-case sent Saint-Castin as his agent to Vaudreuil, to inform the governor of Canada that Port Royal had fallen. The Baron accompanied Major John Livingston, whom Nicholson had designated to carry a similar message warning Vaudreuil to respect the new British claims. He was requested to return British captives in Canada lest Nicholson make good his threat of turning over the newly conquered French subjects to the Five Nations as slaves.[9]

These arrangements completed, the fleet prepared to sail. In a final exchange of compliments, Nicholson sent Subercase two barrels of beer. He received the thanks of the French commander, who expressed the hope that Vetch would treat the inhabitants of the region as well as Nicholson had treated Subercase.

Nicholson and his officers drew up an announcement of their success for the Queen, begging preference in the soil, trade, and fishery of the new colony, as promised in Nicholson's instructions, and suggesting that the old order of baronets of Nova Scotia be revived for them. They asked for further instructions about the treatment of those inhabitants not covered in the terms of surrender. Inventorying Vetch's garrison of 200 marines, 250 New England troops, and 50 matrosses, they appealed for a fourth- or fifth-rate frigate to guard the coast. It was also suggested that the garrison be regularized as a single regiment, with Vetch as the colonel.

For those French who could never be expected to become loyal British subjects, the council of officers anticipated the solution which was finally arrived at only much later in the century. They suggested that these people should be deported. Vetch thought that they could be settled in the French colonies in the West Indies and Newfoundland; since most of them were women and children, it would not strengthen those places unduly.[10]

At mid-month, the outgoing vessels were on their way, stopping

9. J. Clarence Webster, *Acadia at the End of the Seventeenth Century* (St. John, N.B., 1934), 194-96; Nicholson's Journal, Nova Scotia Hist. Soc., *Collections*, I (1879), 86, 89, 98; Nicholson to Vaudreuil, Oct. 14, 1710, *Cal. State Papers, 1710-11*, no. 427; Oct. 11, 1710, Public Archives of Nova Scotia, VII 1/2, no. 4 (Dalhousie University, Halifax). Pentagoet is now Castine, Maine.

10. *Cal. State Papers, 1710-11*, nos. 425, 426, 460; Public Archives of Nova Scotia, VII 1/2, nos. 6, 12 (Dalhousie University, Halifax).

for wood and water before leaving Annapolis Basin. The New England fleet arrived in Boston on the afternoon of Thursday, October 26. Governor Dudley promptly proclaimed a general thanksgiving, and the General Court moved an address to Queen Anne exulting over her newly gained riches of land, naval stores, furs, and fish and hailing the prospects of safer commerce and more protection for their frontier on the east. "Annapolis Royal," said Dudley, was a name which "hears pleasantly." Seconding the application of the council of war for preference in land and trade for the campaigners, Massachusetts nevertheless asked for the reservation of rights to catch fish and whales in the waters of Nova Scotia and to land on its shores to dry fish or extract whale oil. Coal was an important resource of Nova Scotia, and Massachusetts also wanted permission to dig and fetch "sea cole" without tolls or duties.[11]

The New England colonists further advised that the capture of Port Royal was only the first step toward the goal which they sought. Happy as they were at the outcome of the summer's efforts, they did not neglect to ask for more. The design against Canada should be renewed, but this time Massachusetts did not want to bear so much of the expense. Since all the colonies would enjoy the results, why should not they all contribute men and money, as far south as Virginia? The northern colonies, so they thought, had already furnished the sinews of war beyond their slender capacities. It was time for colonies such as New Jersey, Pennsylvania, Maryland, and Virginia to bear their share. Nicholson once again sailed for England with letters of this import from the New England colonies.[12]

The news of the fall of the French fort was not received cheerfully in Canada. Livingston and Saint-Castin arrived in Quebec early in December after a harrowing trip of over a month and a half. They found Vaudreuil neither surprised nor par-

11. Nicholson's Journal, Nova Scotia Hist. Soc., *Collections*, 1 (1879), 101, 103-4; Public Archives of Nova Scotia, VII 1/2, no. 2 (Dalhousie University, Halifax); Governor, Council, and Assembly of Massachusetts, Nov. 11, 1710, *Cal. State Papers, 1710-11*, no. 482.

12. *Cal. State Papers, 1710-11*, nos. 435, 482, 488, 492, 503-5. Samuel Sewall composed a poem in honor of Nicholson and wrote him a personal letter of gratitude; Oct. 31, 1710, Sewall Letter Book, Mass. Hist. Soc., *Collections*, 6th ser., 1 (1886), 399-400.

ticularly sympathetic with Subercase. Quebec had heard in August that an expedition was projected against Port Royal. Twenty-seven men and officers, along with some Indians, had been sent to Subercase as reinforcement. But he had sent the men back, with an earlier reinforcement of seventy others, insisting that he was capable of repelling any British assault. For Vaudreuil this was carrying bravery too far. He realized that the overwhelming force which finally reduced the fort was one which Subercase could not have hoped to resist, even with the reinforcements which had been offered. And he admitted that the terms of capitulation which the intrepid commander had earned were generous. But he feared for the rest of Acadia's inhabitants, left to the mercy of the conquerors.[13]

Livingston made the most of his time in Quebec. He was treated handsomely, and English prisoners there were allowed to see him frequently. He advanced them money to comfort their captivity and in exchange extracted whatever they had been able to learn of the state of Canada's defenses. In addition, he thoroughly surveyed Quebec in his walks. On his return to Boston, he was able to draw up an extensive account of the fortifications and general strength of New France. But two could play at that game. Vaudreuil grasped the opportunity of sending an answer to Nicholson's letter with officers instructed to do a similar job of espionage in the New England colonies. He also sent Baron Saint-Castin back to Nova Scotia to organize resistance among the Indians and sound out the sentiments of the French toward their British conquerors.[14]

With the departure of Nicholson, Vetch took stock of his situation. A list of the inhabitants who came within the terms of capitulation was drawn up. It came to 481 persons, some 84 families. A similar list of British officers and soldiers was made, as was an inventory of supplies and provisions left by Nicholson. Vetch ordered his engineer Forbes to draw up a plan of the fort

13. Vaudreuil to Pontchartrain, Aug. 10, 1710, and Apr. 25, 1711, *N.Y. Col. Docs.*, IX, 846-49, 853; *Cal. State Papers, 1710-11,* no. 673. Subercase may have feared that he would not have food sufficient to maintain a larger garrison, although the British found him well supplied.

14. Livingston's view of Canada, Dec. 27, 1710, *Cal. State Papers, 1710-11,* nos. 569, 673; *N.Y. Col. Docs.*, IX, 853-54.

for transmission to the Queen and then to set about making the necessary repairs. It was evident that between Subercase's neglect and the bombardment of the British the fort was in poor condition. Forbes surmised that Subercase had not received adequate supplies from France or had been overconfident of his opposition.[15]

Annapolis Royal was the sole fortified place held by Great Britain or France in the maritime area. It stood on a tongue of land projecting westward into the basin at a point where the bay narrowed and became a mere stream, which was referred to as the River Dauphin. Facing the bay, the fort was flanked by this river on the north and a low, swampy area on the south. It was constructed in the classic system of Vauban, the French military engineer, a square with four projecting bastions, one at each corner. In addition, a large, detached bastion, or ravelin, mounting a twelve-gun battery guarded the west side exposed to the bay. This "half-moon," as the British called it, was connected to the fort by a covered passageway. The entire fortification was surrounded by a ditch and earthworks and was approached by a bridge, on the landward east side, leading to the gates of the fort.[16]

Forbes faced a task beyond the abilities of the garrison in restoring the fortifications and providing adequate housing. The enemy had left no barracks standing, and it was necessary to convert most of the chapel into sleeping quarters. Bricks were needed in virtually limitless quantities for the fireplaces and chimneys which warmed the buildings in the cold climate of Nova Scotia. The brewhouse, ovens, bakehouse, and windmill needed repairs. The wells around the fort were clogged. The conduit in the ditch which carried off the "ordure from the necessary house" was not sufficiently deep to "carry all into the river"; it had become "noisome." The necessary house itself would have to be rebuilt. The guard house in the "half-moon" had fallen down, and sentry boxes

15. Public Archives of Nova Scotia, VII 1/2, nos. 9, 10, 11 (Dalhousie University, Halifax); *Cal. State Papers, 1710-11,* nos. 433-34; Forbes' account of his work, Nova Scotia Hist. Soc., *Collections,* 4 (1884), 99.

16. Public Archives of Nova Scotia, VII 1/2, no. 10 (Dalhousie University, Halifax), has a map of town and fort copied from an orginial preserved in P.R.O. as calendared in *Cal. State Papers, 1710-11,* no. 434. See also *ibid.,* no. 460, for the description of Port Royal by Nicholson's council of war. For the plan of the fort, see facing page.

THE FRENCH FORT AT PORT ROYAL, 1710

The Fort projected westward into Annapolis basin and was flanked by the River Dauphin on the north and by a low, swampy area on the south. After its capture by the British in 1710, the settlement was renamed Annapolis Royal in honor of Queen Anne. The River Dauphin became the Annapolis River.

KEY

1. Bastion du Roy containing a storehouse and a cavalier
2. Bastion Dauphin containing a bakehouse, a smith's forge, and a small cavalier
3. Bastion de Bourgogne containing a powder magazine and above that a magazine for small arms
4. Bastion de Berry containing a powder magazine
5. Barracks and over it a storeroom
6. The governor's house
7. The lieutenant governor's house
8. The chapel
9. Detached bastion to defend the river
10. Houses of inhabitants

had slid off the ramparts into the ditch. The bridges, magazines, and earthworks had been seriously weakened during the siege. It was more than enough to keep the garrison busy during the winter. Carpenters, smiths, and bricklayers had to be recruited from among the inhabitants and considerable sums expended for tools, nails, lumber, and glass.

Supplies of firewood, coal, lumber, and provisions brought from New England were soon exhausted. The French were willing to sell firewood by the cord, but it had to be brought across the river, which meant paying additional hands to man the flat-bottomed boats employed in bringing it; the risk of Indian attack was too great to allow the British to work in the woods. French residents had to be paid to burn charcoal in their homes to conserve the dwindling sea coal. Likewise, Vetch had to depend on local residents for the enormous quantities of spars, planks, beams, and large timbers required in renovating the fort. He encountered difficulties at once on this problem. The inhabitants were to help their conquerors make themselves more secure, and even if they did so, the work of felling trees and floating them down to the basin was constantly jeopardized by the hostility of Indians instigated by French leaders to overturn the British conquest.[17]

At the outset, a proclamation to the French of Acadia declared the country British. Good treatment was promised so long as the residents co-operated with the new regime. They were ordered to have no dealings with other Frenchmen or Indians in the French interest. Trade with Canada was prohibited, and no trade with other British colonies was allowed except through Annapolis Royal. Violation of these terms, which was frequent, nullified any claims the French had to better treatment than they received. According to the articles of capitulation, only the residents of the immediate neighborhood of Annapolis Royal were assured friendly treatment. Until the Queen's pleasure could be known, Vetch was left to deal with other inhabitants at his own discretion.[18]

Representatives of settlements outside the *banlieue* soon arrived at Annapolis to discover Vetch's intentions. Conspicuous among

17. Forbes' account, Nova Scotia Hist. Soc., *Collections*, 4 (1884), 99-102.
18. Public Archives of Nova Scotia, VII 1/2, no. 7 (Dalhousie University, Halifax); *Cal. State Papers, 1710-11*, no. 419.

them were those from Minas, a relatively prosperous and well-settled farming area at the head of the Bay of Fundy, some sixty miles northeast of Annapolis. Rather than negotiate with them at Annapolis, Vetch sent Paul Mascarene, his senior officer, to investigate the region, including the neighboring settlements at Chignecto and Cobequid. Vetch hoped to find out how much the inhabitants could afford to contribute as a sort of indemnity; he wanted at least 6,000 livres. Mascarene was also to require of them a monthly contribution toward the expenses of Vetch's table in the amount of twenty pistoles. Vetch justified this exaction on the grounds that both the persons and effects of the French outside the *banlieue* were at British disposal. He had protected them from the plunder and destruction which his conquering army might have meted out, and they had been spared the losses of those inhabitants who had suffered in the reduction of the fort. He considered it only just that they offer some kind of tribute. In return, he offered freedom to trade at Annapolis and, indeed, was eager to encourage it.[19]

Mascarene carried out his mandate, sailing with fifty men from the garrison on November 8. The mission went off smoothly. The residents of Minas were respectful; they provided him with comfortable quarters and appeared anxious to comply with any reasonable requirements. Mascarene exhibited the mixture of tact and firmness which was to characterize his long and successful career in Nova Scotia, and his men earned praise for their "civil behavior."

But the sum demanded by Vetch distressed the French. They pleaded poverty, occasioned by Subercase's previous "tyranny," and pictured themselves "actually beggars." This was obviously far from the truth, but after some discussion, Mascarene accepted half the alloted sum, 3,000 livres, and allowed the inhabitants to petition Vetch for a remission of the other half. A part was furnished in furs immediately and cheerfully. More was con-

19. The articles of capitulation termed the French inhabitants "prisoners at discretion," *Cal. State Papers, 1710-11*, no. 412. A census of Acadia in 1707 listed Port Royal as having 554 inhabitants, Minas, 577, and Cobequid, 81. Vetch estimated that the whole of the maritime area held five hundred families or twenty-five hundred people. He counted their cattle, sheep, and hogs in the several thousands; Nova Scotia Hist. Soc., *Collections*, 4 (1884), 22-23. Also see Nov. 1, 1710, *ibid.*, 70, 85-87.

tributed over a period of time, but probably never the full amount, even of the reduced figure. Part of the exaction was paid in produce and part was met with bills drawn by Subercase on Vetch for money which Vetch owed the former French governor for the purchase of cannon. Mascarene observed that "the sum due by Colonel Vetch to Mr. Subercase must have been considerable since there was abundance of those bills."

Lack of adequate food supplies became a serious matter very shortly. The workmen employed in the fort demanded the best available food and helped consume the meagre rations. Little could be had from the surrounding area, which itself depended upon supplies from Minas. When a sloop laden with peas and wheat arrived from Minas, the citizenry claimed the protection of the surrender terms and refused to spare part of it for the garrison. A second sloop was seized by the English, "which caused a great deal of clamor and noise" and contributed to the spirit of insurgency which began to possess the conquered residents as they recovered from the shock of their defeat. Seeing the British suffering from shortages, the fort falling into increasing disrepair with the winter frosts, and the sick lists growing day by day, the inhabitants began to hope for early relief.[20]

Nor was Vaudreuil slow in nourishing this spirit. He had been pleased to receive word from the Acadians complaining of "the harsh manner in which M. Weische [Vetch] treats us, keeping us like negroes, and wishing to persuade us that we are under great obligations to him for not treating us much worse, being able, he says, to do so with justice and without our having room to complain of it." Indications that Vaudreuil was taking steps toward relief of the inhabitants came when Vetch's commissary officer was seized and held for ransom while on a trip up the river looking for provisions. This action put the supposedly loyal French under suspicion, for the commissary had been in their company. He was promptly ransomed, and Vetch immediately acted to prevent further molestation of the British. Four of the principal inhabitants of the upriver area and the priest of a French chapel were seized and held, pending delivery of the "banditti" who were responsible for the crime.

20. *Ibid.*, 70-73, 75-78.

Many of the French residents were willing to remain at peace under the terms of the surrender or, alternatively, desired to be aided in removing to Canada. But Vaudreuil sent agents to urge resistance, ordered them to remain on their land pending his dispatch of a force to drive out the British, and he encouraged the priests to keep the Indians stirred up against the conquerors. Further evidence of his efforts came from the reluctance of the inhabitants to cut trees for repairing the fort. At first, they seemed willing; but delay followed delay as they protested, first, that they must wait until the creeks were clear of ice and, then, that their animals were too weak from lack of fodder to drag the timbers. It became evident that the French inhabitants who were willing to work were being intimidated by those opposed to the British. Work parties were prevented from floating felled trees down the river by Indians who promised the "murdering and burning of them if they offered to carry a single tree towards the repair of the fort."

Vetch's treatment of the inhabitants was clearly far from oppressive. Workers were paid for their labors, and the men of the garrison were strictly controlled in any dealings with the French residents. As a conqueror who had been promised rights in the land and as a colonial governor, Vetch's first obligation and interest was to secure his position. With his hold on the country still most tenuous, he exhibited remarkable moderation, particularly in view of French efforts at subversion.

Just as the problem had begun to reach really serious proportions, a sloop from Borland in Boston, laden with provisions, came into the harbor. Borland's captain, John Alden, with the help of Providence, as it seemed to the afflicted garrison, had made his way through the wintry seas at a time when aid could not be counted on. This brought temporary relief, and Vetch determined to return with Alden in order to arrange a regular supply for the troops. It was evident that Annapolis Royal could not be self-sustaining, at least this first season, but must rely on victualing from New England. Moreover, Vetch wanted to keep in touch with plans for the renewal of the Glorious Enterprise, for he knew that Nova Scotia would not be secure as long as the French held Canada. He was also anxious to see his wife and children again, and he longed to escape to Boston for a time, away from the dreary isolation of Nova Scotia in the winter. The arrival of supplies had eased the situation for the garrison. Vetch could leave in good conscience, trusting Sir Charles Hobby with the government in his absence.[21]

The governor arrived in Boston at the end of January and found his family in good health. Never one to discourage help by painting a disheartening picture of conditions, he reported that the Annapolis garrison was happy and that he was generally satisfied with the newly acquired region. Perhaps Vetch's story was lent credence by his physical condition, which remained strong despite the rigors of the campaign and the weather. Two matters claimed his first attention. He wanted to arrange for the payment of his forces and then to establish a regular supply of food for them. His first step was to memorialize the Massachusetts General Court for the prompt payment of that part of the garrison made up of New England volunteers.[22]

But before he could proceed, he was faced with an accusation which, coming as a total surprise, thoroughly distressed him. Some of his enemies in the colony, remembering the old charge levied against him for trading with the enemy at Port Royal, had spread the rumor that he was again trading with the French Indians for arms which they would use against the English colonies. No doubt his possession of the skins received from Minas, along with the bills of exchange dating back to his former transactions with Subercase, seemed to substantiate the charges. Dudley's opposition was still active in the legislature and may have hoped to damage the governor by this attack on his friend.

The imputation aroused Vetch's wrath. After months of struggle to maintain his men and fortify the British hold on an area whose capture meant so much to New England, he could not hear such aspersions calmly. Far from benefiting from his dealings with the Acadians, he had pledged his own slender resources as security for the vast expenditures which had been required to begin strengthening the British position at Annapolis Royal. He

---

21. *Ibid.*, 23-24, 28, 74-79.

22. Vetch to Robert Livingston, John Borland to Livingston, Feb. 2, 1711, Livingston Papers; Jan. 31, 1711, *Diary of Samuel Sewall*, II, 298; Mar. 14, 1711, Mass. Archives, LXXI, 767 (State House, Boston).

had been forced to put his faith in ultimate reimbursement by the Crown. And no one knew better than Vetch the struggles which men like Robert Livingston had endured in attempting to get repayment for funds advanced in the public interest.

It was no wonder that he served a notice on the Council to shake its sanctimonious complacency. Flatly denying the charges, he "withall in a vile manner" accused New England not only of old sins, "a spirit of witchcraft," but now "sevenfold a spirit of lying." They were "haters of monarchy" who regretted Her Majesty's success in taking Port Royal and rejected the vast service done for them. New York, so often the object of New England's strictures, would have gloried in his caustic rejoinder, and the New England worthies were visibly disturbed.

Fearing that the bitter indictment might find its way into print, Sewall urged retraction. Sewall was quite willing to join in a certification that Vetch was not guilty of the rumored trade, but he considered the reflections on New England dishonorable to both Nova Scotia and New England; it was "raillery unbecoming a government." He had no wish that Vetch's denunciation be aired along with his vindication. But Vetch was adamant. If he could not get his statement printed in New England where those who had made the charges could see his answer, he would have it printed in England. He told the Council that copies of it were already on their way to Britain. With this, Vetch left the Council chamber. Sewall begged the governor to forbid the printing, but Dudley, solidly behind Vetch, stated that he could not hinder it, although he admitted the justice of Sewall's argument.[23]

On a later occasion, Vetch attended a meeting of the Council when Vaudreuil's agents were present, bringing the French governor's reply to the news of the fall of Port Royal. The earlier exchange still rankled; when Sewall attempted to exclude the French officers from the session, Vetch turned to the visitors and warned them that "the people of New England were generally given to lying." Dudley did not intervene. It was evident that the hardships which Vetch had undergone left him without his customary discretion. This display of authority on the part of an upstart governor would avail him nothing in a colony long ac-

23. Feb. 1, 1711, *Diary of Samuel Sewall*, II, 298-99.

customed to opposing the royal prerogative in the person of its own governor. Flamboyance was not calculated to attain the objectives of Vetch's visit.[24] His attempt to persuade Massachusetts to pay the volunteers at Annapolis Royal failed. To Vetch's request, the New Englanders answered that the volunteers who had gone to Nova Scotia would find their pay for the expedition ready for them whenever they came to claim it. But they were now considered in the Queen's service and would no longer be paid by the colony.[25] This had been the original arrangement, so Vetch's hopes that he could get Massachusetts to assume the burden had likely not been high. His attempt probably reflected his fear that the royal credit could not be strengthened much farther. Eventually, the bills on the British government might all be honored—Vetch expected they would—but until that time they would meet with a progressively greater discount. Also, soldier's pay in the royal establishment was less than that to which the colonists were accustomed. This, he thought, would make his troops "very uneasy," but no alternative appeared, and he could only do his best to keep them in moderately good spirits.[26]

The expense of victualing the men at Annapolis was similarly a matter which had to be left to the British government. Vetch planned to order supplies through Borland at Boston at the rate of seven halfpence a day per man. The going rate in Boston was seven pence, and the added amount would cover the cost of shipping the provisions to Nova Scotia. Vetch was sure the rate conformed so closely to colonial practice elsewhere and to the rate for provisions furnished the seamen on Her Majesty's ships that it could not "be thought too dear at home." By order of the council of war at the time Vetch took over the government, victualing at the Queen's expense had been authorized for eight months. Only three more months remained, and Vetch considered this too small a margin. On his own authority, he extended the account for three additional months and hoped that the Queen's orders for additional subsistence would be forthcoming. As he pointed out in his appeal to the ministry, at the present time "all

24. Feb. 26, 1711, *ibid.*, 301.
25. Mar. 17, 1710, Mass. Archives, LXXI, 775 (State House, Boston).
26. Vetch to Dartmouth, Mar. 20, 1711, *Cal. State Papers, 1710-11*, nos. 742, 396; Public Archives of Nova Scotia, V, no. 24 (Dalhousie University, Halifax).

. . . [the soldiers'] pay will not go near to purchase them provisions, especially in a country where the coldness and sharpness of the air contributes so much to their good appetites." Supplies must be shipped in, as had been the case in all new colonies, until settlers in sufficient numbers came to cultivate the country. Then, he hoped, the cost of rations could be commuted to pay by which the soldiers could subsist themselves. At the end of another year, "we shall want no provisions from any place."[27]

Robert Livingston had submitted a proposal to Nicholson for victualing the garrison which Vetch thought either too extravagant or too cheap. He wrote his father-in-law that he was making other arrangements and hoped Nicholson would be wiser than to show Livingston's proposal to anybody in England. Victualing troops was profitable, and Vetch probably wanted to keep arrangements in his own hands. His letter to Livingston breathed confidence in the future of his colony and described the domestic operations which Vetch believed would interest the New Yorker. Vetch planned to brew beer at Annapolis and had imported malt, hoping to achieve the excellence of the product of Livingston Manor. But he took Livingston to task for a recent shipment which had not come up to form. At twenty shillings it had proved inferior to Boston's six-shilling beer and had embarrassed Vetch's wife, who had confidently made Nicholson a present of several barrels of it.

While Vetch was in Boston, Major John Livingston returned from his arduous trip to Canada, and Vetch decided to send him on to England. With his recent information about Canada, he would be highly useful to Nicholson in persuading the court to renew the expedition. Vetch hoped that he would also see that bills drawn on Britain for the expenses of the last campaign and the maintenance of the fort were honored. In earlier letters, Vetch had urged the political and economic advantages of conquering Canada and had reminded important ministers of the promise the former regime had made to him of the governorship of such newly won territory. Livingston would take additional reminders

27. Vetch to Robert Livingston, Feb. 1711, Livingston Papers; Vetch to Lords of the Treasury, Mar. 12, 1711, Public Archives of Nova Scotia, VII 1/2, no. 15 (Dalhousie University, Halifax); *Cal. State Papers, 1710-11,* nos. 721, 742.

and would serve to guard Vetch's interest if Nicholson should be forgetful.[28] After a short visit with his wife in New London, John Livingston prepared to depart for England. Still fatigued from the long months of overland travel he had recently undergone, he was probably glad when weather prevented his sailing. By the time another opportunity offered, word from England that another expedition was underway made his trip unnecessary.[29]

Toward the end of April, Vetch returned to Annapolis Royal. During his absence, the garrison had once again run out of provisions, but it had been rescued by the arrival of another small vessel from Boston with stores. Vetch brought more, and "everything now was plenty." After Mascarene had led a detachment of fifty men into the woods to investigate the French hesitancy in supplying timbers for repairing the fort, enough trees had been felled and floated down to Annapolis to enable the completion of the task. Then the workmen struck again, and work on the fort was halted once more. An increasing number of "skulking Indians" were noted. The French were in ferment, those willing to work threatened by increasing numbers of those hopeful of the settlement's early recapture.[30]

The winter, the hard work, and the constant fear of attack had taken its toll of the British. Illness, death, and desertion left Vetch with only 200 effectives. He calculated that 500 men and a forty-gun frigate were the minimum force required as long as the French held the neighboring territory. His position was becoming increasingly precarious, especially with the fort in its ruined state. Forbes finally became desperate for timbers and persuaded Vetch to let him take an armed force out to bring pressure on the French who had contracted to cut trees. The inhabitants were to be promised protection from French retaliation if they complied; if they did not, the British planned to make a show of killing their livestock. Vetch ordered his men not to kill anything but chickens,

28. Vetch to Livingston, Feb., and John Livingston to Robert Livingston, Mar. 21, 1711, Livingston Papers; Vetch to Rochester, and to Dartmouth, Jan. 22, Vetch to Dartmouth, Mar. 20, 1711, *Cal. State Papers, 1710-11*, nos. 611, 613, 741.

29. Livingston to Nicholson, May 25, 1711, *Cal. State Papers, 1710-11*, no. 855.

30. Mascarene's account, Nova Scotia Hist. Soc., *Collections*, 4 (1884), 79.

if that were necessary, and to pay for those before returning to the fort.[31]

The party of seventy men, under the command of Captain Pigeon, set out early in June with Forbes. It was a strong group; too strong, as it turned out, for its very strength made it over-confident. Proceeding without proper precautions, it was ambushed at a narrow place in the river. Forbes was killed, along with everyone else in the leading boat except the fortunate Ensign Coxsedge, who suffered seven wounds before the rest of the force arrived on the scene. Unable to see their well-concealed attackers, the British rashly exposed themselves on the riverbank. Surrounded by an estimated one hundred and fifty Indians, the badly outnumbered force surrendered after losing fifteen or sixteen men. Fortunately, the Indians treated their captives better than usual; they offered to let Vetch send surgeons to care for the wounded and were willing to exchange the prisoners for ransom. They knew that Vetch could easily mistreat French hostages if they committed outrages against the English soldiers.

More French and Indians were on the way, and Vetch shortly found himself "entirely blocked up" in Annapolis Royal by a force he estimated to number nearly six hundred. The inhabitants of the *banlieue* became "extremely uppish" and were revealed as "all our enemies, at the bottom." They left their homes, and the workmen who had been helping to restore the fort disappeared. To make matters worse, desertions from the garrison mounted. Many of the marines in the British force who were "Irish papists" were prevailed on by the French to change sides. Vetch was bitterly critical of the wisdom which had allowed a force designed against French Catholics to be made up of these men. Through death mainly, but also through desertions, 116 men had been lost since Annapolis had been taken.[32]

Vetch did not consider the situation desperate, but it clearly

31. *Cal. State Papers, 1710-11*, no. 879; Vetch to Dartmouth, May-June 1711, Public Archives of Nova Scotia, V, no. 19 (Dalhousie University, Halifax).

32. Vetch's orders to Pigeon, June 9, Vetch to Dudley, June 24, Vetch to Hunter, June 19, 1711, Public Archives of Nova Scotia, VIII, nos. 1, 8-11, 83-85 (Dalhousie University, Halifax); Nova Scotia Hist. Soc., *Collections*, 4 (1884), 91-92, 95-96, 103; Vetch to Dartmouth, June 14 and 18, 1711, *Cal. State Papers, 1710-11*, nos. 879, 887.

needed strong measures. Convening his council of war—his two senior colonels, Hobby and Whiting, and the majors and captains— he decided to ask all the neighboring colonies for at least one hundred men to reinforce the dangerously small garrison of approximately two hundred; he recognized, however, that five hundred men were actually needed to resist any serious French attack. Vetch also asked that Colonel Rednap be sent to replace Forbes so that the engineering work on the fort could be resumed. Finally, he requested the immediate assistance of H.M.S. *Chester,* but if the Massachusetts stationship were not available, he hoped that Dudley would send the province galley until a frigate could be ordered.[33]

Accordingly, Vetch wrote to Dudley, using his most persuasive arguments. He assured the Massachusetts governor that he "should not wish to survive the loss of this place while I have the honor to command it." He believed that the fort could be held. Appealing to the pretensions of the Massachusetts legislature, which thought of itself as an independent parliament, Vetch expressed the hope that the General Court would send speedy relief, "in imitation of the present worthy British Parliament who are so far from being discouraged by the great disasters . . . in Spain that all the enemy's successes only whet or enrage . . . [its] zeal." He suggested to Dudley that this was a good opportunity to send his son, young Major Dudley, at the head of 100 men, thereby getting him a post in Her Majesty's establishment, "if he inclines to follow the sword." He made it clear that copies of his appeal were being sent to England, knowing the sensitivity of Massachusetts to British allegations of disobedience.

Vetch sent a similar letter to Governor Hunter at New York, pointing out that Massachusetts would not be able to send troops without the Assembly's order, which would take time. Therefore, he hoped for speedy assistance from New York first. He suggested that New York enlist a party of 100 Iroquois and send them to Annapolis under the command of Major Livingston.[34]

33. June 15, 1711, Nova Scotia Hist. Soc., *Collections,* 4 (1884), 98.
34. Public Archives of Nova Scotia, VIII, nos. 7, 8-12, 183-85 (Dalhousie University, Halifax).

After his reception in Massachusetts a few months earlier, Vetch had little confidence that these appeals would bring action from the other colonies. The alternative was help from Great Britain, or at least emphatic orders to the colonists of Massachusetts and New York to give aid. Vetch again wrote Dartmouth and others in the ministry and the Board of Trade, enclosing a detailed plan for the establishment of a regiment of Regulars under his command, designed to end the "heats and disputes" about chain of command, precedence, and "other nicities." To the Treasury he observed that by incorporating the colonial volunteers Britain was spared the expense of raising that number of additional men and transporting them to Nova Scotia. He was sure that "regimentation" would improve morale and aid administration, as well as cut costs by eliminating duplication of officers. Vetch expressed his fear that he could hope for little help from the other colonies without positive commands from the home government. He described his plan for a force of Indians recruited from the Five Nations and suggested that, failing this, the best of the four Regular companies in New York be transferred to Annapolis Royal. He pointed out that New York had so far been "in perfect peace" with Canada and did not need the soldiers.

In all these letters, he harped on the need for the reduction of Canada if real security were to be had. He repeated his hopes for preferment and for the pay usually accorded to his station. With his usual thoroughness, he described the plight of the garrison, the need for a man-of-war to protect the colony, and the importance of getting his force on a regular footing. But above all, he was anxious for definite instructions from the British government, so that he, the garrison, and the French would know what to expect. Until he had these instructions he could never be sure that his actions would be supported or that the expenses which he was incurring would be paid.[35]

Finally, at the end of June, when the spirit of the men at Annapolis Royal was at its lowest ebb, news came of Nicholson's arrival in Boston with orders for a resumption of the attack on

35. Vetch to Dartmouth and Popple during the period of June 14-18, 1711, *Cal. State Papers, 1710-11*, nos. 879, 884, 887; see also Vetch to Dartmouth and to Lord Treasurer, Public Archives of Nova Scotia, V, nos. 18-19 (Dalhousie University, Halifax); and Vetch to ministry, June 15, *ibid.*, VIII, nos. 6-7.

Canada. Despite the virtual blockade of the fort—access was limited to the approach by sea—the defenders were cheered by the prospects of an early victory over the French. Vetch was ordered to turn over temporary command of the fort to Sir Charles Hobby and then hurry to Boston to assume command of the New England troops destined to attack Quebec.[36]

36. Vetch's instructions to Hobby as deputy governor, July 5, 1711, Public Archives of Nova Scotia, VIII, no. 131 (Dalhousie University, Halifax); Minutes of Council of War, New London, June 21, 1711, Nova Scotia Hist. Soc., *Collections*, 4 (1884), 83, 104; *Cal. State Papers, 1710-11*, no. 893.

CHAPTER ELEVEN

Tory Design

WHILE NICHOLSON AND VETCH had busied themselves in the summer of 1710 reducing Port Royal, the Tories had come into power in England. Soon after Nicholson sailed for England to urge resumption of the Canada expedition, Vetch heard from Popple that the general would face a whole new ministry. Godolphin was out, the Treasury had been put in commission with Harley as its leading figure, Dartmouth had succeeded Sunderland as Secretary of State for the Southern Department. Shrewsbury, Rochester, and Buckingham were all back in office.[1]

In this situation, no better man than Nicholson could have been delegated to present the colonial case. Although he had never allowed political sympathies to interfere with his own interests, Nicholson was a staunch High Churchman and would inevitably find dealing with the new ministry congenial. In addition, sentiment in Great Britain for an attack on Canada had been raised by past efforts, and appeals favoring Nicholson's representations flooded in from America. Dudley again reminded Whitehall of the rich supplies of naval stores, fish, and lumber "sufficient for all Europe." Vetch, who knew neither Dartmouth nor the Queen's uncle Rochester, nevertheless addressed both of them. Similar petitions in favor of the project went from Connecticut, Rhode Island, and New Hampshire; and even Hunter, in New York, was hopeful that something of the sort could be undertaken again, although he was pessimistic about the role New York would be able to play.[2]

1. Popple to Nicholson and Vetch, Nov. 18, 1710, *Cal. State Papers, 1710-11,* no. 497.
2. Dudley to Board of Trade, Nov. 15, Saltonstall to Secretary of State, Nov. 21, Rhode Island's Address to the Queen, Dudley to Boyle, Nov. 15, 1710, New Hampshire's Address to the Queen, Jan. 5, Vetch to Rochester and Dartmouth,

In England, Jeremy Dummer presented his credentials as Massachusetts agent early in January and hastened to solicit Dartmouth's aid. After making a strong case for the retention of Annapolis Royal in any pending peace, he went on to develop the argument for the Glorious Enterprise. To the old points, Dummer added several new ones. Canada was too cold for sheep; therefore Britain need not fear that the colony might become a rival to the British woolen industry. Lumping the American plantations under the general term "West Indies," as was often done, Dummer predicted that possession of Canada would make Great Britain as opulent and powerful in the West Indies as Holland was in the East Indies. To the list of epigrammatic comparisons headed by Vetch's description of Port Royal as the Dunkirk of North America, Dummer added the characterization of Canada as the "American Carthage." Summing up the mercantile argument for colonies, he succinctly concluded: "The wealth of the Plantations is the riches of Great Britain, and as the former thrive and prosper the latter must increase with 'em in a double proportion."[3]

The efforts of Nicholson and Dummer, joined with the continued solicitation from America, had the desired effect. The conquest of New France appealed particularly to Henry St. John, Secretary of State for the Northern Department, as a method to offset the prestige of Marlborough's triumphs, which continued to bolster the Whigs. Such a victory would redound solely to the benefit of Great Britain, whereas Marlborough's gains, it might be argued, did more for Britain's continental allies than for the English. The Tories were willing to advance a strategic concept of the use of sea power, Britain's strongest suit, to strike at her enemies in their distant colonies, where they were most vulnerable. The idea was a precursor of the course Pitt was to follow so effectively several decades later.[4]

Jan. 20 and 22, 1711, Hunter to Dartmouth, Nov. 26, 1710, *ibid.*, nos. 491, 503, 504-5, 571i, 583, 611, 613, 512.

3. Memorial of Jeremy Dummer, Gentleman, Agent for the Province of Massachusetts-Bay, to Lord Dartmouth, Jan. 3, 1711, Public Archives of Nova Scotia, VII 1/2, no. 3 (Dalhousie University, Halifax), and also *Cal. State Papers, 1710-11*, no. 579.

4. Morgan, "Imperial Cooperation During the Reign of Queen Anne," Royal Hist. Soc., *Transactions*, 4th ser., 10 (1927), 171-94; and also Morgan, "South

The main burden of arranging for the expedition fell on the two Secretaries of State, Dartmouth and St. John. St. John considered the "whole design" as one formed and managed by himself alone. Harley, on the other hand, favored another project, which was proposed by the South Seas Company and involved an attack in the West Indies. But he was stabbed by a mad Frenchman in the spring of 1711. The attack took him out of politics for a time, although it earned him the Queen's sympathies and elevation to the nobility as Earl of Oxford.[5]

Already, rivalry between St. John and Harley was developing into a struggle for control of the Tory party. Harley favored an attack on Spanish holdings and, in addition, he was unwilling to risk the expedition against Canada just after the death of Joseph I, the Holy Roman Emperor, knowing that this loss of one of the allied leaders might give France an advantage. He knew, too, that St. John was conducting secret peace negotiations with the French and he suspected ulterior motives on the part of his colleague. He sought to use his wound, which was alleged to be serious, to gain an advantage. Through his brother, he sent word to Rochester to advise the Queen that it was "his dying request" that the expedition be laid aside. This melodramatic attempt was unavailing, but Harley's opposition later became a source of great difficulty to Vetch. Furthermore, evidence subsequently appeared to both Harley and Vetch that St. John's enthusiasm for the campaign against Canada may well have been the product of personal avarice.[6]

Whatever his other reasons, St. John proceeded secretly in order that the French would have no opportunity to reinforce

Sea Co. and the Canadian Expedition," *Hispanic-Amer. Hist. Rev.*, 8 (1928), 143 ff., and Morgan, "Queen Anne's Canadian Expedition of 1711," in Queen's University, *Bulletin of the Department of History. . . ,* no. 56 (Kingston, Ontario, May 1928); Parkman, *Half-Century of Conflict,* I, 156-57. Jonathan Swift was enlisted as an active pamphleteer in presenting the Tory views.

5. Gilbert Parker, ed., *Letters and Correspondence Public and Private of the Right Honorable Henry St. John, Lord Viscount Bolingbroke* (London, 1798), I, 68-69, 142-43, 161.

6. Earl of Rochester to Harley, Apr. 18, 1711, Hist. Mss. Comm., *Report on the Manuscripts of His Grace the Duke of Portland* (London, 1897), IV (*Harley Papers,* II), 675; Oxford's account, and Edward Harley's "Memoirs of the Harley Family," Hist. Mss. Comm., *Portland Mss.,* V (*Harley Papers,* III), 464, 655; Hist. Mss. Comm., *Portland Mss.,* X (*Harley Papers,* VIII), 335.

Quebec. How far the French were deceived is open to question; certainly Vaudreuil in Quebec feared the worse on the basis of intelligence which had reached him from New York. As for Great Britain, most people, even in high places, remained oblivious to the purpose of the preparations. Admiral Walker later charged that even the Navy and Ordnance Boards had been kept in the dark. Overzealous security, according to the admiral, resulted in disastrous omissions in the supply of the forces.[7]

All through March, Nicholson labored at Portsmouth to ready the British forces. The problem which had beset the previous expeditions and had bedeviled Vetch at Annapolis afflicted Nicholson: bills drawn on the government for necessary expenses were not promptly honored. Moreover, the ships for the expedition arrived late to begin loading. The naval and military commanders were also tardy. Admiral Walker and General Hill were not ordered to Portsmouth to take command until April, and Walker struggled until early May with the task of preparing his fleet. To shepherd a large and motley assemblage of ships of the line, auxiliaries, transports, and supply vessels across the North Atlantic called for a high order of leadership and seamanship, but these were qualities which Walker did not possess. Nicholson sailed ahead of the main fleet in April to apprise the colonists of the plans and begin preparations in America. He arrived on June 8, too late, as Dudley noted, to assure adequate provision for a campaign of such magnitude. At the outset, then, the expedition of 1711 was handicapped by a late start.[8]

Nevertheless the colonial leaders went to work with a will. A council, called at New London to enable the governors to hear the instructions which Nicholson brought and to concert plans for carrying them out, met on June 21. Nicholson and Dudley were

7. Vaudreuil to Pontchartrain, Apr. 25, 1711 (NS), *N.Y. Col. Docs.*, IX, 854; Sir Hovenden Walker, *A Journal or Full Account of the Late Expedition to Canada* . . . (London, 1720), 10-11; Arthur Moore to St. John, Mar. 4, Nicholson to Dartmouth, Mar. 14, 1711, *Cal. State Papers, 1710-11*, nos. 699, 724.

8. Mar. 3, 1711, Public Archives of Nova Scotia, VII 1/2, no. 14 (Dalhousie University, Halifax); Walker, *Journal*, 49-56; Dudley to Popple, May 22, Dudley to St. John, July 25, Nicholson to Dartmouth, Portsmouth, England, Mar. 3, 1711, *Cal. State Papers, 1710-11*, nos. 850, 45, 701; June 8, 1711, *Diary of Samuel Sewall*, II, 313-14.

joined by Governor Hunter and Colonel Schuyler from New York and by Saltonstall and Cranston from Connecticut and Rhode Island. Hunter was informed of the plan of attack, similar to that proposed in 1709, whereby his forces and those of Connecticut, New Jersey, and Pennsylvania would gather at Albany for a descent on Montreal under the leadership of Nicholson. New York was asked to furnish 600 men, Connecticut and New Jersey 360 each, and Pennsylvania 240. A thousand men from Massachusetts, New Hampshire, and Rhode Island, commanded by Vetch, would accompany the British army against Quebec. The council dispatched a sloop to Annapolis Royal to bring Vetch to Boston and designated Sir Charles Hobby to serve as deputy governor in his absence.

The governors hurried back to their respective colonies to carry out the war council's orders. Saltonstall had been asked to supply his forces with three months' provisions and to furnish carpenters for boatbuilding at Wood Creek. Hunter and Dudley agreed to share the expense of establishing an express service between Albany and Boston for the co-ordination of communication between the two forces. Embargoes on commerce were voted, and it was agreed that colonists would eat fish twice a week instead of once so that more salt provisions would be available for the army.[9]

This time there was no waiting for the fleet from Great Britain. All through April, Walker had received frequent urging from St. John to get started, and his convoy finally sailed early in May. Walker made an unusually fast crossing, just over seven weeks, arriving off Nantasket on June 24, while the governors were still at New London. Boston was immediately faced with an unprecedented problem when the fleet arrived. On short notice it had to provide for six thousand British Regulars and the sailors from over sixty ships, in addition to the thousand or more colonial troops gathering for the expedition. Food and water were required for the stay at Boston, and additional provisions had to be gathered for the campaign and the occupation of Quebec. Fresh

9. Minutes of the New London Council of War, June 21, 1711, *Cal. State Papers, 1710-11*, no. 893; Saltonstall to Oxford, Sept. 10, 1711, Hist. Mss. Comm., *Portland Mss.,* V (*Harley Papers*, III), 89.

produce was only beginning to be available at that time of year in colonial gardens and farms. The winter's salt provisions had been largely depleted. Even in the best of times, Boston depended to a large extent on its neighboring provinces for food, particularly for staples like flour, bread, and salt meat.

The colony was in for a difficult month, made worse by the disagreements which arose between the British officers and the colonists. Colonel Andrew Belcher, who had undertaken to provide supplies for military forces on the former occasions, refused to act as commissary. Even when offered higher rates, he would not take the job. What Admiral Walker and General Hill did not know was that he already had a contract to supply the New York forces with provisions, including 50 butts of wine and 10,000 gallons of rum. He could get better prices in New York and would be busy enough with that commission. The admiral finally found another merchant, Andrew Faneuil, who was willing to accept the task.[10]

Next, the British commanders found fault with the rate of exchange. The colonists valued their pounds only slightly less than sterling, offering to give the British only 20 per cent more advantage for their money. After "many days' commissary solicitation," the rate was finally raised so that the British commissary could get one £140-worth of goods, colonial value, for their £100 sterling. There were bitter accusations against the "perverseness of these people," but the rate had to be accepted, even though Walker and Hill still thought it less advantageous than it had been before the fleet's arrival. When General Hill discovered that New Yorkers were allowing sterling only a 30 per cent premium, 10 per cent less than at Boston, he concluded that the British forces were indeed "prey to the merchants of North America."[11]

Even with the exchange rate set, or perhaps because of it, the British quartermaster Colonel King had trouble getting supplies. Walker and Hill decided that they needed more money than the

10. King's Journal, May-July, 1711, *Cal. State Papers, 1711-12*, no. 46i; St. John to Walker, Apr. 17, 20, and 23 and May 1, 1711, Walker, *Journal*, 41-68, 177-79, 185, 192; *Cal. State Papers, 1710-11*, no. 893.

11. Walker, *Journal*, 36, 83; King's Journal, June 28, Hill to Dartmouth, July 31, 1711, *Cal. State Papers, 1711-12*, nos. 46i, 61; June 8–July 4, 1711, *Diary of Samuel Sewall*, II, 312-18.

British Treasury had provided. Dudley informed them he could not give it to them without an act of the Assembly, which was not then sitting. A loan of several thousand pounds was finally negotiated after some hesitation, which caused Walker to comment on New England's "unaccountable backwardness." "I did not imagine things would have moved so heavily in this place towards an undertaking so beneficial for themselves," he grumbled.

The British officers admitted, however, that Governor Dudley showed a zealous concern for the expedition and acted with firmness and resolution. The colonial press worked overtime printing proclamations in furtherance of the affair. The governor and General Court took almost dictatorial action in enlisting men, assessing fines against derelict colonists, regulating prices and the rate of exchange, and confiscating provisions and supplies wherever they might be found.[12]

Hoarding and gouging existed, but much of the shortage could be blamed only on the unexpected arrival of so large a force at a difficult time of year. Nor could the colonists be blamed for demanding ready money before they would make goods and services available. They had already spent lavishly in their previous undertakings and received scant thanks, let alone reimbursement. The British officers who criticized them knew only that the expedition was obviously to the colonists' advantage; they could not yet realize the discouraging effect of Britain's failure in 1709 to live up to its promises. They complained of the slackness and delays encountered in New England; but the colonists' relationship with the generally inefficient and corrupt Whitehall administration had given them little precedent for speedy and methodical administration.

Nicholson arrived from New York on July 14, just as Vetch came in from Annapolis Royal, and things began to go more smoothly. Walker admitted that Nicholson's authority and influence had been much missed, and he noted that Vetch's presence was very useful. Nicholson personally put up a reward of

12. King to St. John, July 25, King's Journal, July 2-12, Proclamations and Orders, and Dudley to St. John, July 25, 1711, *Cal. State Papers, 1711-12,* nos. 46, 46i, 44ii-v, 44ix, 44x, 45; Walker, *Journal,* 72-73. For copies of Proclamations, see Douglas C. McMurtrie, *Some Massachusetts Broadsides of 1711* (Metuchen, N.J., 1934), 7-15.

£100 sterling for the recovery of deserters, an "insupportable grievance" of which the British commanders complained, and offered five pounds to encourage the town marshal to proceed with his business of impressing seamen to replace those who had deserted. It was evident that neither Hill nor Walker had shown much initiative in expediting preparations. Nicholson and Vetch, who knew their colonists, realized that money could iron out most difficulties of the kind which had been afflicting the British authorities.

Despite their problems, the British forces encamped on Noddles Island presented a brave show. They had arrived in better condition than expected after the sea voyage, and they behaved well while guests of the colonists. A review of the troops on July 10 saw them "making a fine appearance, such as had never before been seen in these parts of the world." Negroes in the town were so struck by the sight that they volunteered to fill the vacancies caused by illness and desertion. Some of the officers would have willingly accepted them, but General Hill considered it improper.

New England put on its best show for the visitors, too. On July 4, the little college at Cambridge held its annual commencement exercises. General Hill and Admiral Walker went out to take part in the customary celebration, "to put people in a humor to comply with our needs," as Hill put it. Walker reported a "great concourse of people" present, and Judge Samuel Sewall noted the presence of the British officers with approval. Perhaps the commencement helped the expedition, for an increase in the quantity of provisions being supplied was immediately evident.

Another diversion occurred when a group of Indians from the Five Nations arrived to satisfy themselves that this time a British fleet was actually present. Walker realized that the Indians' adherence to the enterprise was important and gave them a thorough look at the British fleet. The troops had already been re-embarked, and another review was out of the question, but the Indians were received aboard the flagship and entertained with wine and music. Sailors danced their hornpipes for them, and the Indians reciprocated. While one sachem capered, Walker reported, the rest "hum'd and hollow'd at distinct periods of his dance, with a tone very odd and loud but yet in time." The Indians expressed their thanks for the expedition and assured the British that the Five Nations would do their part. To Walker they appeared "people of thought and understanding, sincere and devoid of levity." When they left the ship, he ordered cheers and a salute from the guns.

Nevertheless, the long stay at Boston was making the commanders uneasy. King still blamed the "indolence, indifference," and the "thousand scruples and delays" of the New Englanders for preventing the fleet from sailing sooner. He thought they must want to defeat the expedition. When the Massachusetts General Court presented its final memorial thanking the British commanders for their efforts and assuring them of Massachusetts' good intentions, Walker tartly replied that he hoped they would make their good intentions evident in action.[13]

While preparations for the descent on Quebec pursued their troubled way at Boston, similar preparations were going forward at New York for the overland attack against Montreal and in support of the forces at Boston. Robert Hunter's arrival as governor had served to quell the factionalism of New York. The tone of his first pronouncements made it evident that the province had at last a governor of ability, tact, and fairness. When he received word of the expedition of 1711, he was just returning from Albany where, at a meeting with the Five Nations, he had confirmed the Indians in their traditional relationship with New York. Within a short time after the conference at New London, he received assurances from the Indian commission at Albany that the Five Nations would enlist themselves again in Nicholson's force to go against Montreal. Iroquois support was, if anything, stronger this time. The Indians who visited Boston reported that at last a force with strength enough to accomplish the mission was at hand. On August 24, over eight hundred warriors arrived at Albany and were reviewed by Hunter, who reported them "a jolly

13. This account is based on Walker's *Journal*, 82, 90, 102-4; King's Journal, July 14, 22, 24, Hill's Journal, July 4, 10, 14, 22, King to St. John, and Hill to Dartmouth, July 31, 1711, *Cal. State Papers, 1711-12*, nos. 44ix, 46i, 61; and June 8–July 4, 1711, *Diary of Samuel Sewall*, II, 312-18.

crew . . . very likely men, with all marks of a hearty disposition for the service."[14]

Hunter was able to raise the remainder of the required New York force, although the time was short. The Assembly voted £10,000 for the expedition, grumbling "much at the proportion," and agreed to equip its quota of 600 men. Connecticut furnished its required force of 360, but Hunter could enlist only 200 of the similar number required from New Jersey, and those were raised only with difficulty. Pennsylvania, as usual, flatly refused to furnish the men requested, although, with Virginia, it contributed provisions.[15]

With the help of the colonial leaders, who spared no pains in their efforts to co-operate fully, the colonial forces in New York and New England were enlisted and equipped, and the British troops were provided with the necessary supplies. However, the difficulties encountered on a lower level indicated a spirit of unrest in the colonies. The general grumbling and hesitations in assemblies and among the people, although not as disruptive as Colonel King's complaints alleged, were indicative of suspicion and hostility toward outside authority. The spirit of independence manifested in the struggle of assemblies for power had been growing in the colonies for many years, and it had reached a point where it forced more serious notice. The attitude was probably intensified by the demands of the expedition. Certainly the failure of plans in 1709 hurt relations between the colonies and the mother country. Doubtless, too, the party struggles in Great Britain added uncertainties in colonial policy which encouraged the colonists to assert themselves.

Many of the colonial leaders raised frank warnings about imperial relations. New governors were particularly sensitive to the situation; Hunter, for one, grasped the problem clearly. But with all his considerable abilities, he was unable to bring the New York Assembly into line, except in large matters of intercolonial consequence. Even in the case of the enterprise against Canada, where colonial interests and the commands of Britain coincided,

14. Quary to Pulteney, July 5, Hunter to Board of Trade, July 24, 1710, *Cal. State Papers*, *1710-11*, nos. 288, 317; Hunter to St. John, Sept. 12, 1711, *ibid.*, *1711-12*, no. 96. See also Hist. Mss. Comm., *Portland Mss.*, V (*Harley Papers*, III), 89.

15. *Cal. State Papers*, *1711-12*, nos. 42, 47, 48.

many assemblymen exhibited a sullen mood.[16] Hunter was a practical and level-headed administrator, not one to become alarmed over trifles or to shirk a difficult task. Despite this capability, he believed that "the general aversion to the support of government" was a matter requiring the thoughts of the "greatest council in the realm." Without a remedy, he prophesied that "all must run into confusion here." Nor did he fear for his own province alone. "For anything I can learn," he asserted, "they are driving the same way in most of the other provinces."

The solution, Hunter knew, would be a lengthy process, embracing nothing less than unification of the colonies under one government. Yet, without some speedy and effectual remedy, "in a little time the disease may prove too strong for the cure." The highly literate governor quoted Harington's *Oceana* and understood it better than any of the colonial administrators: "The colonies were infants, sucking their mother's breasts, but such as, if he was not mistaken, would wean themselves when they came of age."[17]

Ample confirmation of Hunter's diagnosis existed. Vetch had railed at the antagonistic spirit of the Massachusetts legislature. Dudley found that his Assembly took any excuse to avoid settling a salary on him; without his own ample means he could not have stayed in office. Spotswood had to deal with actual revolt in North Carolina. The spirit of the colonists had been protested earlier by government representatives such as Quary, Randolph, and Caleb Heathcote, a prominent New York merchant who wrote at the end of the war that "if some speedy care is not taken to reduce the charter governments and instruct the people in better principles, they may in time be able to put in practice what they now can only talk of."[18] The situation was recognized in England, but the government was too occupied with the war and too distracted by the domestic struggle for political power to take action. To reduce the proprietary and charter governments to

16. *N.Y. Col. Docs.*, V, 269-70.

17. *Cal. State Papers, 1711-12,* nos. 95, 96.

18. Colonial records of this period are full of indications of this problem. See *ibid. passim,* and Dudley to Boyle, Nov. 15, 1710, Cranston's Report to the Council of War at New London, King to St. John, July 25, 1711, *ibid., 1710-11,* nos. 575, 893, 46; Heathcote to Oxford, July 8, 1712, Hist. Mss. Comm., *Portland Mss.,* V (*Harley Papers,* III), 199.

obedience would take time, talent, and money; it was a task requiring attention which Britain could not then give.[19]

From the imperial point of view, England's failure to deal with these problems was most unwise. The colonies were still too divided and too dependent on Britain's military support to have successfully opposed positive action had it been taken. It may well have been the last good chance to establish a colonial system which would have been proof against the later division. The French, however, were quick to capitalize on the situation and tried to drive a wedge between the English colonists and their British defenders—it seemed their only hope to preserve Canada. The governor of Newfoundland sent Monsieur de la Ronde Denys to Boston in the early summer of 1711, ostensibly to offer once more a neutrality between Massachusetts and the French but actually to suggest to the "Bastonnais" that the British forces engaged on the expedition were in reality designed to bring the province back under strict royal control. Dudley detained la Ronde for fear that he might carry intelligence back to the French. The Frenchman had once resided in Boston and was well known, but his arguments, if he had an opportunity to make them, had little effect on preparations for the campaign.

It is notable, however, that the French realized the implications of the spirit of independence in the British colonies. In addition to la Ronde's mission, an anonymous French writer was drawing attention to the "antipathy between the English of Europe and those of America, who will not endure troops from England even to guard their forts." He predicted that if Canada fell, the various colonies "will then unite, shake off the yoke of the English monarchy, and erect themselves into a democracy." It is testimony to their realization of the pressing need to eliminate the menace of New France that the colonists co-operated in 1711 as well as they did. That the colonists were willing to try again after earlier disappointment is also testimony to how well Vetch had performed the job he was entrusted with in 1709.[20]

19. After the war ended, an attempt was made by the Board of Trade to grapple with the problem in 1721. *Cal. State Papers, 1720-21*, nos. ix-xii, 656, 657.

20. Parkman, *Half-Century of Conflict*, I, chap. VIII; Walker, *Journal*, 64, 138.

CHAPTER TWELVE

Inglorious Enterprise

WHILE VETCH AND the other commanders drilled their troops for the attack on Quebec, Admiral Sir Hovenden Walker made arrangements to transport the powerful force into position. The readiness of the army for battle could only be tested when the troops came face to face with the French. Unfortunately, Walker's state of mind was not one calculated to arouse enthusiasm among the soldiers. If the morale of fighting men is a product of their commander's spirit, the morale of the troops bound for Quebec must have been low indeed.

From the beginning, Walker was obviously unhappy about his assignment, and his pessimism deepened as the campaign progressed. At the outset, he did not consider it his project; it had been well underway before he had been named to command. Once in command, he had moved lethargically. St. John had finally written him, "I take it for granted that if you continue any time wind bound, that you will be stopped for good and all, that the whole expense and trouble will be thrown away and that we shall make as little of our fleet this year as we have done in former summers." But the Secretary's blast did not activate the admiral, who shifted the blame to his subordinates, as he was to do continually through the summer.[1]

In Boston, Walker lodged at Captain Southack's so that he could acquaint himself with the navigational lore possessed by that veteran of New England coastal sailing. But his discussions with Southack only gave him a growing realization of the difficulties of navigating the St. Lawrence. Every available chart was provided him, and everyone who had any acquaintance with Canada was enlisted as a pilot, even captains who had not been on the St.

1. Walker, *Journal*, 192, 193.

Lawrence since Sir William Phips' expedition many years before. But Walker remained restive. "By all that appeared to me, every day producing something unexpected," he noted, "I begun to think this expedition would prove difficult and hazardous." His past record—or the lack of it—suggested that he was not likely to accept a challenge but would prefer to take an easy course and exert himself as little as possible.[2]

Although he and Hill were pleased with the troops encamped on Noddles Island, they both had, nevertheless, "a very indifferent opinion" of the enterprise. Hill favored a campaign against Placentia, Newfoundland. But Walker feared to call a council of war to consider the change because he was sure it would decide against the descent on Canada. Since he had explicit instructions to attack Quebec, he believed it necessary to make the attempt.

But even this shaky resolve was soon undermined. Walker was pleased to learn from a French prize brought into Boston that the French ministry did not know of the expedition, but he was upset when the captured sailors predicted that he would lose all his ships if he tried to ascend the river. They pointed out that a great number of ships were cast away in the St. Lawrence every year; just the last season eight or nine French vessels had foundered there. Walker tried to discount this report as an obvious artifice on the part of the French, but he was half-persuaded by it. He only resolved "if possible" to go through with the project because of his "positive instructions." With these overmastering doubts, Walker prepared to sail. Troops boarded on July 20, and deserters who returned by July 27 were promised pardons. Walker intended to depart on the twenty-eighth, but just before he sailed seven provision ships from New York came into the harbor. These supplies were hurriedly loaded aboard the already crowded ships.[3]

Not so welcome was news from Annapolis Royal that Sir Charles Hobby, acting governor, had refused to let the marines

2. *Ibid.*, 55, 67, 71, 74-75, 87. King was a prey to similar fears and foresaw success only "if storms, contrary winds, and the difficult navigation of the river don't defeat us"; *Cal. State Papers, 1711-12*, no. 46.

3. Walker, *Journal*, 90, 110-11, 99, 102, 106-7; King's Journal, May-July, 1711, *Cal. State Papers, 1711-12*, no. 46i; John Winthrop to Wait Winthrop, Boston, June 18, 1711, Mass. Hist. Soc., *Collections*, 6th ser., 5 (1892), 232; June-July 1711, *Boston News-Letter*.

under his command leave the garrison, even though they had been replaced by a company of New Englanders. Nor would he give up the ordnance stores, as he had been ordered. Vetch told Hill that Hobby's excuses were false, and Walker ordered Southack to call at Annapolis and insist on the dispatch of the men and stores. It was an unfortunate choice, for Walker needed the best pilots, and Southack had few, if any, peers.[4]

On Monday, July 30, Walker's flagship, the seventy-gun *Edgar*, sailed out of Boston harbor bound for Quebec. By eight in the morning, when Vetch boarded his vessel, the *Despatch*, the entire fleet was under sail and outward bound with a fair wind from the west. Walker's fleet was a formidable force. Three seventy-gun men-of-war, four of sixty guns, and the two eighty-gun ships *Humber* and *Devonshire* (which Walker did not plan to take up the river) headed a fleet of transports, supply ships, and two bomb ketches. The *Despatch* of twenty-nine guns and the *Lowestoft* of thirty-two also were in company, but seven men-of-war ordered on the expedition were absent. The *Saphire* had gone ahead to pick up the men and stores at Annapolis and, having failed in that mission, was waiting to join the fleet off Cape Breton. H.M.S. *Chester* and *Leopard* had gone ahead to reconnoiter, while the *Kingston, Enterprise,* and *Triton's Prize* were still at New York or Virginia waiting to convoy additional provision ships. H.M.S. *Feversham* was awaiting similar orders; she was destined never to reach the main fleet. These vessels would provide two ships mounting fifty guns, two with forty, two with thirty, and one, the *Kingston*, with sixty, making a total of eighteen men-of-war.[5]

Vetch was in command of all the New England forces, with Colonel Shadrach Walton of New Hampshire serving under him as a commander of the combined contingents from New Hamp-

4. King's Journal, May-July, Hill to Dartmouth, July 31, Hill's Journal, June-July, 1711, *Cal. State Papers, 1711-12,* nos. 46i, 61, 61ii; Walker, *Journal,* 67, 111, 113; "Journal of the expedition against Canada in 1711" (cited hereafter as Vetch's Journal), Nova Scotia Hist. Soc., *Collections,* 4 (1884), 105 (also in *Cal. State Papers, 1711-12,* no. 175v). Walker had only recently persuaded Southack to go on the expedition.
5. Vetch's Journal, Nova Scotia Hist. Soc., *Collections,* 4 (1884), 105; Walker's *Journal,* 108-9, 113; list of ships in Livingston Papers, Group 1a, box 7.

shire and Rhode Island. Commander-in-chief of all the land forces was Brigadier General Hill, who had virtually no military record, unless Marlborough's refusal to give him a command be counted. Familiarly known to his bottle companions as "Honest Jack Hill," he held his present post because his sister Mrs. Masham enjoyed the favor of Queen Anne.

After the fleet had proceeded up the coast to the southern end of Nova Scotia, Walker hove to and sent for Vetch. The admiral asked him to lead the fleet and assigned him a French pilot, who had offered his services. But Vetch distrusted the Frenchman's advice and convinced Walker that he was "an ignorant, pretending, idle, drunken fellow." Vetch therefore sailed "with no pilot aboard save myself" to the rendezvous point off Cape Breton. There, the *Saphire, Chester,* and *Leopard* joined the fleet, and Vetch went aboard the *Edgar* to discuss plans with Walker for the rest of the voyage. They agreed that when Walker made the proper signal, Vetch would again take the lead. The *Despatch* and the *Saphire,* both small and maneuverable ships, would precede the *Edgar.* The force parted company with the large *Humber* and *Devonshire,* but because the commanders feared the possibility of the arrival of a French fleet, the two large men-of-war were ordered to cruise between Cape Breton and Newfoundland, rather than sail for England as Walker had originally planned.[6]

Over ten days had elapsed from the time the fleet left Boston. Vetch considered that they were halfway toward their objective. Even he had succumbed somewhat to the admiral's pessimism; he wrote St. John that the difficulties of navigation were the greatest obstacle in the whole enterprise. He had no faith in the collection of pilots, "being myself if not the only, at least the best pilot ... although none of my province." The dour Colonel King also wrote St. John, "I am persuaded I may assure you that our forces both by sea and land are resolved to succeed or perish in the attempt." If this was indeed resolution, the next few days were to

6. Walker, *Journal,* 108, 116-19; King's Journal, May-July, 1711, *Cal. State Papers, 1711-12,* no. 461; Parkman, *Half-Century of Conflict,* I, chap. VIII; Vetch's Journal, Nova Scotia Hist. Soc., *Collections,* 4 (1884), 105, 106-7, and 31; Walker to Vetch, off Canso, Aug. 8, 1711, Public Archives of Nova Scotia, V, no. 7 (Dalhousie University, Halifax).

see it melt rapidly away. Perhaps King was more convinced of the likelihood of perishing.[7]

Headed by the *Edgar*, the fleet turned westward into the mouth of the St. Lawrence. No orders came for Vetch to resume the lead, and Captain Rouse of the *Saphire* indicated that the *Despatch* was to follow his orders. He sent word that he expected Vetch aboard his vessel. Vetch declined; he had already explained to Walker that he preferred to remain on the *Despatch* with his stores and baggage. It was apparent that Walker put more trust in Rouse than in his other captains, and he may have had some thought that Vetch and Rouse would eventually form an able team to lead the other vessels up the treacherous river. However, Walker did not relinquish the lead to either captain.

Late at night, on August 14 as the ships were sailing west by northwest, guns were heard booming Walker's signal to tack. Vetch could not understand the reason. Instead of making good headway toward the entrance to the river, the fleet was suddenly sent sailing directly back the way it had come. In the morning, after considerable loss of time, the fleet again bore away for the river. But just as the ships had all but reached the point where they could turn and sail directly up the St. Lawrence, the wind veered to the northwest and opposed the fleet. The British ships were forced to lay up in the Bay of Gaspé. Vetch considered that the significant navigational error of the expedition was the decision to backtrack on the night of the fourteenth, when so much time was lost "of the fair wind which would have carried us into the river."

Vetch went aboard the *Edgar* to inquire into the reason for the admiral's strange change of course. Walker told him that it was a whim of Captain Paddon, commander of the *Edgar*, and of old Captain John Bonner, Walker's chief pilot. They were afraid of running into shoals off Anticosti Island in the dark. Bonner had been reluctant to go on the expedition at all, and Vetch had been almost forced to drag him aboard the *Edgar* in Boston. Now he could regret his trouble. Walker had also been listening to his French pilots, and they had been effusively discouraging.

On the evening of August 20, the fleet cleared Anticosti Island

7. *Cal. State Papers, 1711-12*, nos. 71, 73.

and started west in the broad mouth of the river. The St. Lawrence is over seventy miles wide at this point, and by the twenty-second Walker was lost, out of sight of land, facing fog and gathering darkness. After consultation with his pilots, he decided that he was somewhere near the northern shore. Fearing that he might run onto the rocks if he failed to exercise extreme care, he set a course for the south. Vetch, trailing the fleet, became increasingly uneasy. Frequently during the evening he asked his companions, Colonel Paul Dudley, the son of the Massachusetts governor, and Captain Perkins of the *Despatch*, what Walker could mean by such a course. The three paced the deck, and the *Despatch* cautiously kept well astern of the main fleet. Vetch believed that a course west and west by south, directly up the river, was preferable.

After several hours, Captain Paddon of the *Edgar* told Walker that he thought he saw land to the south; Walker made the signal which swung the fleet back on a northerly course. Then, about ten o'clock, with a careless assurance which contrasted strangely with his frequently expressed fears, Walker went below to turn in. He had hardly changed into his dressing gown and slippers before Captain Goddard, one of the army captains, reported land to the north and urged him to change course again. Walker refused to believe the captain and climbed into his bunk. Within minutes Goddard was back, insisting that the admiral come on deck. At the same time shouting and the sound of running on deck told Walker that something was amiss. Arriving topside in slippers and gown, and peering through the darkness, Walker could see breakers. His French pilot was nowhere to be found. Paddon, in a panic, ordered the anchor let go, but Walker took command, issued orders to cut the anchor cable, and the ship slowly beat its way south again, clear of the shore. The rest of the night was spent running through periods of calm alternated by squalls until daylight disclosed the southern shore.[8]

Aboard the *Windsor*, General Hill and Colonel King had an even narrower escape. Perceiving rocks and shoal water, the ship's captain brought the man-of-war to anchor precariously between

8. Vetch's Journal, Nova Scotia Hist. Soc., *Collections*, 4 (1884), 105-8; Walker, *Journal*, 118-25; Hill to Dartmouth, Sept. 9, 1711, continuing Hill's Journal, *Cal. State Papers, 1711-12*, no. 92.

two shoals. Violent waves, wind, and rain fortunately were followed by a calm, or the anchors would not have held. By five in the morning, after a harrowing night, the *Windsor* made its way clear of the rocks and reached open water. Colonel Lee, in command of the men from Rhode Island on board the *Leopard*, also thanked divine providence for his deliverance. The *Leopard* found herself in the midst of the breakers but managed to stay clear of the rocks until daylight. Then she returned to the scene, and Lee saw the bodies of men, women, and children strewn in heaps along the shore. Eight of the transports and a provision ship had not been so fortunate as the rest of the fleet: they had foundered among the rocks. With the help of two sloops detailed from the fleet, the *Leopard* spent the next two days rescuing the more than two hundred survivors who had made their way ashore and taken shelter in the woods. An estimated eight or nine hundred men and officers of the military force had been lost, along with perhaps a hundred sailors. The regiments of the British Regulars had been the ones to suffer, with no colonials lost. Thirty-five women accompanying the regiments were included in the totals; the "children" reported by Colonel Lee probably were drummer boys, unless some of the women camp followers had brought small children with them. None of the men-of-war was damaged, and the military force remained a strong one despite the losses.[9]

The next three days were spent gathering the fleet together. The ships tacked back and forth in the mouth of the river until August 25, when Hill signalled for a council of war. Vetch came aboard Hill's ship and learned for the first time of the extent of the disaster. He had heard guns firing in distress during the fatal

9. The fleet had run into the rocks and shoals off the north coast of Lower Canada at the Isle aux Oeufs. The Isle aux Oeufs is about halfway between Pointe de Monts and the Seven Islands, near the mouth of the Pentecost River. Far from being near the south shore of the St. Lawrence, Walker had been coasting along the northern shoreline on a course south, and then north, most of the evening. Either way he ran the danger of running aground on points of land or inshore islands. Prudence would seem to have dictated standing off on an easterly course until daylight. The course west and then southwest suggested by Vetch would have been feasible if adopted before the fleet reached as far north as it must have been by mid-evening. Hill to Dartmouth, Sept. 9, King's Journal, Aug.-Sept., George Lee to Lord Fox, Sept. 12, 1711, *Cal. State Papers, 1711-12*, nos. 92, 94i, 98; list of men lost, Sept. 17, 1711, P.R.O., C.O. 5, vol. 9, 4 (Lib. Cong. Transcripts), and Livingston Papers, Group 1a, box 7; Walker, *Journal*, 127-28.

night, "which we did conclude to be the ships near the shore, yet we did not until the day know that there had been any totally lost." The account of the tragedy both surprised and affected him.

All the military leaders, according to Vetch, did not doubt that sufficient forces remained to carry out the attack on Quebec; they seemed eager to proceed. The colonels of the various regiments showed no sign of wanting to alter the plans. But the assembled captains and pilots, meeting without the army officers, came to the conclusion that the ignorance of the pilots made it impractical to attempt to sail up the St. Lawrence. The captains pointed out that they had lacked confidence in the pilots from the start.[10]

Vetch had not been invited to attend the meeting. When he learned that the difficulties of navigation had discouraged the pilots from continuing, he immediately protested that Phips had made the voyage successfully at an even later date with no one aboard who knew the river. Walker asked Vetch if he would undertake the assignment of leading the force—a request which seems unnecessary in view of Vetch's previous proposal to guide the fleet. Vetch's answer was not strong enough, perhaps. The presence of so many captains of the Royal Navy and the memory of their recent disaster may have muffled the usually outspoken Scot. But he offered to do the best he could, and he was quite willing to claim an expert knowledge of the river.

But it was no use. Walker had never been enthusiastic about the design, and the catastrophe was more than enough to convince him that, having made the attempt, he was now free to abandon the enterprise. With no one else in authority willing to side with Vetch and Vetch's stand less strong than it might have been, the decision to return was not altered.

Back aboard his own vessel, Vetch realized that he had not been sufficiently firm. After coming so far, a retreat would have "vast disadvantages and fatal consequences." He was not at all convinced that the navigation offered insurmountable difficulties. And he was sure that he could have avoided the misfortune which had befallen the fleet if Walker had only let him take the lead earlier. Vetch would never have steered the course which piled

10. Walker, *Journal*, 131; Hill to Dartmouth, enclosing Resolution of the Council of Sea Officers, Aug. 25, 1711, *Cal. State Papers, 1711-12,* nos. 92, 92ii.

the transports on the rocks; nor would he have proceeded without sending three sloops ahead to warn of dangerous waters, as he had done off Cape Breton.

He sat down that evening to write the admiral, hoping that he might persuade Walker to reconsider. He urged that another consultation with the captains and pilots be called. Navigation up the river, he wrote, was no more difficult than the return to Cape Breton. By sending the transports ahead to buoy the passage, the men-of-war could proceed safely, and "once we got up to the town [Quebec] I look upon the greatest part if not all the difficulty to be over." He reminded Walker that General Hill and the other military leaders considered the remaining force adequate to the attack. To return on the pretense that the pilots had been found wanting would expose the admiral to ridicule, "the averseness and insufficiency of the pilots being known before we left Boston." He stated flatly that the "fatal disaster" which had occurred must be blamed on steering the wrong course and not imputed to difficulties of navigation. "Who directed that course," he boldly added, "you best know." Realizing that a failure would have serious consequences for both Britain and the colonies, Vetch was willing to take liberties in addressing Sir Hovenden which he would not have dared if the matter had not been of much concern.[11]

Walker remained unmoved. As far as he was concerned, the disaster had been a timely warning of Providence. If the expedition had not been warned off by the accident, "more fatal mischiefs" might have befallen. Walker had an exaggerated notion of the Canadian winter, and Vetch himself had suggested that the French could employ a highly effective defense: They might simply retire, deserting Quebec and leaving the British to starve or freeze. No indication exists that the French thought of such a thing, but Vetch had said this was what he would do if he were Quebec's defender. The tactic seemed all too plausible to Walker, who had become obsessed with the dreadful probability that his force might find itself trapped in a web of its own making. "How dismal must it have been," he wrote in retrospect, "to have beheld the seas and earth locked up by adamantine frosts, and swollen

11. Vetch's Journal, Nova Scotia Hist. Soc., *Collections*, 4 (1884), 108-10.

with high mountains of snow, in a barren and uncultivated region, great numbers of brave men famishing with hunger, and drawing lots who should die first to feed the rest." It was a fantasy of despair—the nightmare of a man with an overwrought imagination, excessive caution, and a total lack of dash and fire. The easygoing Walker had no stomach for a difficult task, and for him the St. Lawrence had become more than that; he considered its navigation virtually impossible. Far from blaming his pilots, he had concluded that the river was simply too treacherous, too beset with unknown depths and currents to be known by any man.[12]

The day after the consultation, the fleet headed out of the St. Lawrence, bound for the bay of Spanish River at Cape Breton.[13] There, further deliberations were to be undertaken concerning the possibility of an alternative attack on Placentia. The *Saphire* was sent back to New England to carry word of the disaster and warn Nicholson's forces against proceeding further. Walker was admittedly afraid to return to England without accomplishing something. If Placentia was out of the question, he proposed to winter at Boston with the fleet and attack Newfoundland in the spring.

Colonel King was also anxious to attempt some alternative action. After his active disparagement of the colonists, he had become surprisingly sensitive to their point of view. Writing to Secretary St. John after the fleet's arrival at Spanish River, he spoke feelingly of the blow that the expedition's failure would be to "our poor American colonies." He feared that it would hasten the depopulation of their frontiers, diminish their trade, and discourage them mightily. With the great effort to succour them "thus ruffled and defeated," they would not dare hope for relief from the mother country in the future.

General Hill, on whom no blame for the failure could fall, was indifferent. He saw no reason why the force should not return to England if an alternative venture did not seem promising. He was willing to leave the decision up to a council of war, but it was apparent that he had no great wish to spend the winter in New England if he could enjoy the comforts of London.

12. Walker, *Journal*, Introduction, 25-29.
13. The area is the present Sydney Harbor, still well known for its coal mines.

The council of war met early in September and decided against any further projects. Hill refused to give the uneasy Walker the comfort of his acquiescence in the proposal to remain in America. Vetch objected to an attack on Placentia so late in the year and suggested military reasons why it was not practical. Then H.M.S. *Kingston, Enterprise,* and *Triton's Prize* arrived from Massachusetts without the provision ships which were expected, and Dudley sent word that he could not furnish additional victualing ships until October. The commanders were afraid that provisions sent so late might never get through the winter weather to them. Vetch and Colonel Walton testified that no food would be available at Placentia. With only ten weeks' subsistence available, even on short rations, it was finally determined that the British ships should return to England, while the New England transports and the men-of-war assigned to American stations should make their way to Boston.[14]

After the failure of the attempt on Quebec, Vetch became concerned about the fate of his fort at Annapolis Royal. While the fleet lay at Spanish River, he applied to Hill for part of his force to be ordered to the Nova Scotia garrison. Outlining the problems of defense against the French Indians, he noted his plan to bring in a band of Iroquois who would be "a terror" to the Acadians and their Indian allies. But until Livingston could be recalled from Nicholson's force, Vetch suggested that some of the New England Indians presently with his troops might be detailed for the garrison. He needed a military engineer, along with bombardiers, gunners, and matrosses, to make up the artillery train which had become depleted during the past year. He also requested a man-of-war to be stationed at Annapolis to keep communication with New England open.[15]

Hill co-operated fully with Vetch's request. A force of 350 men and officers was detached for duty at Annapolis. Captain Vane, an engineer, was ordered to duty there, as were the ordnance men that Vetch had requested. Walker drew up orders for H.M.S. *Saphire* to attend Vetch's government as soon as it re-

14. Walker, *Journal*, 132-37, 142; King's Journal, Council of War of Sea and Land Officers on H.M.S. *Edgar*, Sept. 8, Hill to Dartmouth, Sept. 9, 1711, *Cal. State Papers, 1711-12,* nos. 94i, 92iii, 92.

15. Vetch to Hill, Sept. 11, 1711, *Cal. State Papers, 1711-12,* no. 175iv.

turned from New England, and he sent H.M.S. *Enterprise* to convoy the transports carrying the troops for Annapolis. The marines then at the fort or on board the province galley en route to join the expedition were to be sent back to England, and the arms furnished by the Queen for the use of New England troops were directed to be stored in Dudley's care until it was known whether the attack on Canada was to be renewed at some future date.[16]

With the conclusion of these arrangements, the fleet broke up, the British ships making their way to England and the New England flotilla proceeding to Annapolis Royal on its way to Boston. Unfortunately, the *Enterprise* was unable to keep the New England ships together. Some broke away and sailed directly for Boston. Vetch, with about two hundred of the soldiers assigned to garrison duty, landed at Annapolis, exchanged the troops, and went on to Boston, leaving Thomas Caulfeild as deputy governor. Caulfeild replaced Hobby, whose disobedience had incensed the British leaders. By the time he arrived in Boston, Vetch found the force disbanded, those designed for the fort at Annapolis along with the rest. The Indian company had dispersed and melted into the forest, and the demobilized militia could not be brought back. He had no choice but to release the soldiers of the old garrison and to raise replacements as he could.[17]

The "dismal and awful account of our fleet's miscarriage in Canada River" burst upon New England unexpectedly. Judge Sewall, on circuit at Rehoboth, was "stunned." When the proud fleet sailed, no one thought that Canada could resist such military and naval might. By the time Vetch arrived, the first shock had worn off, but New Englanders had not been slow to place the blame. Some in Boston remembered Walker's unimpressive showing off Guadaloupe, where his excessive caution had been evident some years before—he had considered his mainmast to "be of more value than the whole island." Dudley hotly defended the ability of New England pilots to negotiate the St. Lawrence and pointed out that the decision to abandon the enterprise had been taken

16. *Ibid.*, no. 175iii.
17. Vetch to Dartmouth, Boston, Nov. 16, Hill to Dartmouth, Sept. 9, 1711, *ibid.*, nos. 175, 92.

after only six of Walker's thirteen pilots had been asked for their opinions. Two of the best pilots had not even been questioned. Walker was also blamed for sending Southack to Annapolis Royal when his general seafaring ability and specialized knowledge of North American winds and currents might have stood the fleet in good stead.[18]

The unlucky Walker reached England on October 9 and anchored the *Edgar* at Spithead. Hurrying to London, he was dismayed to hear a few days later that his flagship had blown up with 500 men on board. Disaster, not always of his own making, seemed to dog his footsteps. General Hill did not lose his favored position, but Walker was later dismissed from the naval service and found himself unable to collect even the half-pay usually offered to retired officers. Although an investigation was never held, Walker was left in no ignorance of the blame attached to him. St. John had been profoundly upset by the failure of his scheme; as its backer, he wrote that he had "a sort of paternal concern for the success of it." But he was even then seeking to achieve his ends another way, by secret peace negotiations with the French.[19]

The British authorities who read the reports of General Hill, Colonel King, and others concerning the summer's difficulties in outfitting the fleet at Boston could be expected to lay blame for the failure on the colonists. Tories were quick to attribute what had happened to the Whiggism of the Americans. It was "all owing to the avarice or treachery of the godly at New England," wrote Matthew Prior, commenting that the Dissenters, a similar party, were "doing all the mischief they can in Old England." Writing to Dudley, Sir William Ashurst expressed his concern at the "re-

18. Lechmere to Wait Winthrop, Sept. 18, 1711, Mass. Hist. Soc., *Collections*, 6th ser., 5 (1892), 246; Sept. 17, 1711, *Diary of Samuel Sewall*, II, 322; Dudley to St. John, Nov. 13, 1711, *Cal. State Papers, 1711-12*, no. 164; see also Hist. Mss. Comm., *Portland Mss.*, IV (*Harley Papers*, II), 482, noting Walker's undue caution off the French coast in 1708.

19. Walker, *Journal*, 155-56; Parkman, *Half-Century of Conflict*, I, chap. VIII. Parkman quotes Swift, who noted Walker's return and the catastrophe in the Thames in his *Journal to Stella*. Swift heard that the *Edgar* had been destroyed by the carelessness of "some rogue who was going . . . to steal some gunpowder." The original journal of Sir William Phips' expedition against Quebec, which Walker had taken along with him, was lost along with all the other papers Walker had; Parker, ed., *Letters of St. John*, I, 161.

flections which were cast upon New England and the other colonies, by those who to excuse their own ill-conduct would have thrown the blame off themselves and laid it upon you." He added that he thought people were now "sensible that nothing was wanting on your parts," but he reminded Dudley that he had enemies at court "who would have been glad of such an occasion to have quarreled with you and done you any diskindness [sic] in their powers." Ashurst warned Increase Mather that "all blame of the Canada miscarriage is laid on your backs" and hoped that Nicholson would be able to vindicate New England from the "scandalous accusations" of its enemies. To allay criticism of this kind, Jeremy Dummer published his *Letter to a Noble Lord*, which set forth the arguments Dudley furnished, along with his own general observations on the situation of the British colonies.[20]

Some years later, when Walker was finally called to account for the failure, he published an account of the expedition replete with excuses and recriminations against Governor Dudley, Colonel Nicholson, and the New Englanders who had been so ungenerous as to "condemn my conduct with bitter invectives and to charge me wholly with the miscarriage of that expedition." Even taken at its face value, it revealed the admiral's shortcomings more strikingly than the testimony of any witnesses might have done.[21]

20. Prior to Hanmer, Oct. 9, 1711, Sir Henry Bunbury, ed., *The Correspondence of Sir Thomas Hanmer, Bart.* . . . (London, 1838), 131; Sir William Ashurst to Gov. Dudley, Jan. 15, to Increase Mather, Jan. 31, 1712, John W. Ford, ed., *Some Correspondence Between the Governors and Treasurers of the New England Company in London and the Commissioners of the United Colonies in America . . . 1657-1712* (London, 1896), 94-95, 96-97; Jeremy Dummer, *A Letter to a Noble Lord Concerning the Late Expedition to Canada* (Boston, 1712). Sanford, "Jeremy Dummer," points out that most of the problems which arose in the relationship between the colonies and the mother country were a result of Great Britain's failures to furnish effective aid in the colonial struggle. The extra expenses of war led to financial exhaustion in the colonies. Their effort to recover resulted in land bank schemes, excessive issues of paper money, and intensified struggles over appropriations between assemblies and governors. To re-establish their economy, the colonists attempted variously to levy duties on imports from England, to establish their own manufactories, to exploit their own resources, and to bypass the Acts of Trade and Navigation. Great Britain countered with its attack on the charters of the independent colonies and with the establishment of vice-admiralty courts with added powers; eventually, under the stress of the next struggle with France, she renewed the attempt to conquer Canada and established the post of commander-in-chief in the colonies. It is significant that these years of struggle growing out of Queen Anne's War coincided with the youth of many leaders in the Revolution.

21. Walker, *Journal*, 15-23; Hist. Mss. Comm., *Portland Mss.*, V (*Harley*

Some of the blame for failure is certainly attributable to delays in England before he was appointed. And bad weather was something else over which the admiral had no control. But Walker went too far when he insisted that navigation of the river was impossible and that the "people of Boston knew nothing of what they proposed when they laid schemes for such expeditions." Also, there is no escaping the fact that his was the sole responsibility for running the ships on the rocks. He had determined the course and spurned the aid of men, like Vetch, with firsthand experience.[22]

In the colonies, the leaders were left to make the best of a bad situation. Nicholson heard the news at Wood Creek and at once gave vent to his rage. Bystanders saw him tear off his wig, throw it to the ground, and stamp on it, crying "Roguery! Treachery!" Hunter advised that the Indians be told the truth and sent home quietly. When he had recovered from his anger, Nicholson withdrew his forces to Albany, disbanded them, and prepared to return to England to be on hand if any chance offered for further military aid from the mother country; but no one really thought that Britain would renew the attempt on Canada.[23]

The French government sent word to Vaudreuil that it was confident he could have repulsed the attack had it come and advised a continued neutrality with the Iroquois, even though the Indians had broken faith. The governor was urged to make the Indians "thoroughly sensible of the fault they have committed," however, "so that they may not in future again fall into it." Quebec indulged in wild rejoicing when news of the British ship-

---

Papers, III), 537. Jeremy Dummer decided not to answer Walker's arguments, which were generally considered indefensible; Apr. 8, 1720, Mass. Hist. Soc., *Collections*, 3rd ser., I (1825), 141-42.

22. Walker, *Journal*, 141, 46.

23. Peter Kalm, *Travels Into North America* (London, 1772), II, 135; Sept. 18, 1711, N.Y. Colonial Manuscripts, LVI, 94 (N.Y. State Lib., Albany); Dudley to St. John, Nov. 13, 1711, *Cal. State Papers, 1711-12*, no. 164. Like the New Englanders, leaders in the southern colonies were threatened by the French as well as the Spanish. John Stewart writing from his plantation on the Carolina frontier saw the reasons for the failure of the Canadian expedition as primarily a matter of starting too late in the season. For his expansionist arguments, economically phrased but aptly relating the Glorious Enterprise to the reasons which brought it forth, see P.R.O., C.O. 5, vol. 9, 53 (Lib. Cong. Transcripts). Stewart was one of several Carolina leaders urging expansion as the only alternative to French encirclement and strangulation of the English colonies; Crane, *Southern Frontier*, 103.

wrecks reached the city, and stories of enemy losses were elaborated far beyond the facts. In France, Pontchartrain correctly guessed that England would not soon fit out another expedition.[24]

The New England governors, along with Vetch and Nicholson, met together in another conference, similar to the one held after the failure of the 1709 expedition, to see if anything could forestall what they believed almost certain attack from the French. Hunter was unable to attend or to promise New York's co-operation.[25] In the fall of 1711, therefore, each colony again went its own way, the summer's united effort only a nightmare to be forgotten. Massachusetts addressed the Queen, expressing sorrow over the failure and stressing the good faith with which the colony had pursued the design. It urged a renewal but made it clear that Britain's next effort could not count on its support. Two attempts and two disillusionments had left the colonists without any desire for further British help of the kind they had received. New Hampshire wrote in similar terms.[26]

In Boston, Vetch took up the problems of Nova Scotia again, disheartened almost as much by the continued lack of notice from the ministry as he was by the second failure to realize his dream of the conquest of Canada.

24. Pontchartrain to Vaudreuil, June 28, 1712, *N.Y. Col. Docs.*, IX, 862.

25. Mass. Archives, II, 126, 187, 448, 453 (State House, Boston); *Journal of the Legislative Council*, I, 331.

26. *Cal. State Papers, 1711-12*, nos. 123, 147. See also Sewall's account of feeling in the Massachusetts Council, Oct. 17, 1711, *Diary of Samuel Sewall*, II, 324.

Trials of a Governor

A ANNAPOLIS ROYAL approached its second winter in British hands, all the old problems still pressed for solution. The fort continued in a state of considerable dilapidation. The garrison remained without a clearly defined organization; it was a motley assemblage of men, its officers contending for authority. No regular provision for pay and supplies had yet been made, and expenses already incurred had not been met by the Crown. No instruction of any sort had come from England.

Perhaps for these reasons, Vetch decided to stay in Boston for the winter. He had no taste for another dreary season shut up within the confines of the fort, where he would be insecure, out of contact with the other colonies and England, without the assurance of even the bare necessities. From Boston, he could at least see that regular shipments of victuals went to Nova Scotia and renew his pleas to the ministry and the Board of Trade for attention to his government's needs.

Furthermore, the society of Boston was attractive to the gregarious Vetch. He had enjoyed all too little home life during his absence in England, three summer campaigns, and the past winter in Nova Scotia. His official position and his friendship with Governor Dudley made him a member of the inner circle of the colony. Entertainments were frequent in the provincial capital: dinners at the governor's house, celebrations of holidays at the "Castle," excursions into the country, the excitement of election days, and the very considerable social events which New Englanders made of their frequent funerals.

In April, Vetch paid £400 to Edward Willey for an impressive house fronting on what is now Tremont Street along the Common.

To help in furnishing it, Mrs. Vetch had him write to England for an easy chair upholstered in blue satin, along with two "new fashioned hearths with tongs and shovels" for the fireplaces.[1] Vetch spent considerable time with Dudley and his sons William and Paul, who had recently accompanied the Nova Scotia governor on the voyage to the St. Lawrence. He saw much of Samuel Sewall, Colonel Elisha Hutchinson and his son Captain Thomas Hutchinson, Lieutenant Governor William Tailor, and leaders of the legislature such as Colonel Penn Townsend, Edward Bromfield, Captain Andrew Belcher, and Isaac Addington. Officers of the militia and other military figures were members of the group. In addition, sessions of the General Court brought leaders from the western part of the colony into town, who, along with other frequent visitors, were part of the winter's social scene. Vetch took pleasure in gatherings at Boston's various taverns, where Madeira and flip warmed the discussion of politics and the colonists speculated over the latest news from Whitehall or the allied forces in Europe.[2]

Vetch's first task was to pay and dismiss the New England troops under his command. Then he turned to the job of finding supplies and reinforcements for the Annapolis garrison and dispatched them by Captain Rouse of H.M.S. *Saphire* early in November. At the same time, he sent detailed instructions to Caulfeild for the management of affairs during his winter's absence. He forwarded bills of exchange to pay French laborers, "thus keeping them in our interest better than all the oaths they can take," but he warned against the use of currency in payments to the inhabitants, for silver money would be sent to Canada. Otherwise, the French were to be allowed liberty to trade with the garrison and live on their land so long as they took the oath.

1. Vetch's house stood on the north corner of Winter and Common streets (now Tremont) on a large lot measuring more than 150 feet along Common Street. Vetch bought it for £400; after he returned to England he sold it to Captain Thomas Steel in 1714 for £1,050. See Suffolk Deeds, Lib. 26, f. 159 (Apr. 18, 1712); Public Archives of Nova Scotia, VIII (Vetch's Letter Book, June 1711–Oct. 1713), nos. 62-63 (Dalhousie University, Halifax). Also see *Diary of Samuel Sewall*, III, 9-10, 156, and Annie H. Thwing, *The Crooked and Narrow Streets of the Town of Boston, 1630-1822* (Boston, 1920), 154, 157.

2. Feb. 6–May 28, 1712, *Diary of Samuel Sewall*, II, 333-49; Vetch to Douglas, Feb. 10, 1712, Public Archives of Nova Scotia, VIII (Vetch's Letter Book, 1711-13), nos. 62-63 (Dalhousie University, Halifax).

Indians were to be treated civilly if they behaved. However, Vetch warned the deputy governor to trust neither the French nor their Indians.[3]

Before he left Annapolis Royal, Vetch had ordered the new engineer, Captain Vane, to repair the fortification. Having secured additional men to replace those carried to Boston, Vetch had now to find a similar replacement for the Indian troops who had been disbanded by mistake. He turned to his earlier plan of having John Livingston raise a company of men from the Five Nations. Iroquois warriors would strike fear into the hearts of the French Indians, and they would furnish the British in Nova Scotia with scouts who could be trusted to warn the garrison of any approaching French force. By January, Livingston had raised over fifty Indians. They sailed for Annapolis early in February.[4]

With Livingston's departure went further orders to Caulfeild to supervise the Indians carefully, making sure that they committed no depredations on the Acadians. Vetch assured him that Livingston knew the Indian temperament and would be able to control them. Raising the company had been a remarkable feat, possible only because of Livingston's prestige among the Five Nations, the result of his leadership and close association with the Indians for many years. Livingston's friends often referred to him as "the Mohawk." Vetch hurried to write Dartmouth, requesting that the company be made part of the regular establishment and that Livingston himself be commissioned by the Queen as Vetch had promised him.[5]

Livingston performed his mission at real personal sacrifice. His wife was dying of cancer in New London, and he had been forced to leave her there, under the care of her mother, the

3. Vetch to Dartmouth, Nov. 16, 1711, *Cal. State Papers, 1711-12*, no. 175; Vetch to Caulfeild, Oct. 22, Vetch's Orders to Captain Rouse, Oct. 18 and Nov. 12, 1711, Public Archives of Nova Scotia, VIII, nos. 33-36, 68 (Dalhousie University, Halifax).

4. Vetch to Dartmouth, Jan. 5 and Feb. 9, 1712, *Cal. State Papers, 1711-12*, nos. 253, 303. Additional men and supplies for the garrison were sent to Annapolis Royal in Apr. 1712; Public Archives of Nova Scotia, VIII, nos. 82-83, 60-63 (Dalhousie University, Halifax).

5. Instructions to Livingston, Nov. 12, 1711, Vetch to Caulfeild, Mar. 12, Vetch to William Alden to carry the Indian company to Annapolis Royal, Mar. 1, Vetch to Dartmouth, Feb. 9, Vetch to Hill, Feb. 11, 1712, Public Archives of Nova Scotia, VIII, nos. 70, 71, 74, 75, 76-77 (Dalhousie University, Halifax).

widowed Mrs. Winthrop, and Livingston's younger sister Johanna. Writing to his mother at Livingston Manor, he confessed to being lonesome and homesick and acknowledged that "a little of the manor beef would go down here very well." Cordially received by Caulfeild, Livingston and his Indians proved themselves an important accession during the following year.[6]

Having provided for the welfare of his command, Vetch turned to the task of getting attention from the British government for his neglected outpost. Throughout the fall and winter, he wrote pleadingly to Dartmouth, Oxford, the Board of Trade, and the Ordnance Board asking for instructions, the establishment of the garrison on a regular footing, with pay and subsistence, and payment of the expenses of the colony. From his friends and erstwhile associates, he begged intercession with the British leaders, requesting news of the peace negotiations so that he might know what to expect for Nova Scotia. He also needed information about the party struggles to guide him in his applications for help.[7]

Unknown to Vetch, the Treasury was then asking the Board of Trade whether there were not revenues in Nova Scotia which might be applied against the bills amounting to almost eight thousand pounds which Vetch had drawn for money spent in supporting Annapolis Royal. The Treasury reported that it had no authority from Parliament to meet "such extraordinary expense." The Board, struggling with a backlog of business, confessed its ignorance and referred the Treasury to Blathwayt, who at that juncture probably knew even less than the Board about Nova Scotia. Dartmouth, whom Vetch had kept regularly apprised of the colony's desperate straits, apparently found it too much trouble

6. Public Archives of Nova Scotia, VIII, nos. 112-15 (Dalhousie University, Halifax); John Livingston to Alida Livingston, Apr. 17, 1712, Livingston Papers, Group 2; John to Robert Livingston, Aug. 7, Johanna Livingston to Robert Livingston, Nov. 19, Gurdon Saltonstall to Robert Livingston, Sept. 3, 1712, *ibid.*, Group 1a, box 7. Livingston left Annapolis in Nov. 1712, depriving the fort of the officer best able to control the temperamental savages. The Indian company was returned to Boston, paid, and dismissed in the spring of 1713; Public Archives of Nova Scotia, V, no. 34 (Dalhousie University, Halifax), and Ottawa Transcripts of Nova Scotia Archives, IV, 92, 94 (Public Archives of Canada, Ottawa).

7. *Cal. State Papers*, *1711-12*, nos. 175, 192, 253, 304, 457; Public Archives of Nova Scotia, V, nos. 21, 27, VIII, nos. 48-49, 51-55, 57-64, 76-83, 86-89 (Dalhousie University, Halifax).

to relay his information to Harley at the Treasury. Even if he had, the Earl of Oxford was doubtless too busy with greater affairs to take a hand in straightening out the confusion in his own department. And evidence was soon to reach Vetch that the Lord of the Treasury did not particularly want to pay bills incurred in the enterprises against Canada.

Vetch was careful to point out that he had exercised the utmost care in making expenditures. He had not taken to himself the perquisite of the pay of those who had died or deserted, as commanders regularly did in that time. He begged Dartmouth to use his influence with Harley to get the garrison's bills paid, so that credit might be re-established in Boston. Finally, for details of his circumstances, he referred Dartmouth to Nicholson, whose "zeal to serve his Sovereign and his country hath been without a parallel."[8]

In writing to Harley, Vetch was more specific. He pointed out that the failure of the British government to honor the obligations which his instructions had authorized him to enter into was wrecking the public credit, ruining his agent, and making the rate of exchange between colonial issues and sterling highly disadvantageous to the British government. As it was, food had become very dear after the exhaustion of supplies by the summer's campaign. Vetch complained particularly about the price of rum, six shillings a gallon instead of the customary two or three. Perhaps stretching a point, he noted that rum was essential to the welfare of his garrison, since beer was frozen by the severity of the winter "in that cold country."

But his hopes received a severe blow when he learned from his agent in London that the Lord Treasurer would not even look at bills drawn for the support of the forces in Nova Scotia. Sir William Ashurst reported to Increase Mather that Harley would be glad to find the New Englanders guilty of causing the

8. Vetch to Dartmouth, Nov. 6 [16?], Lowndes of the Treasury to Popple, Board of Trade, Aug. 31, Popple to Treasury, Sept. 13, 1711, *Cal. State Papers, 1711-12,* nos. 175, 84, 99. Blathwayt's answer, if he was applied to, is not known. The Board of Trade was rapidly falling behind in its business, because of the great amount of extra work occasioned by the peace negotiations. Nor was its efficiency increased by the political uncertainties arising from the struggle between the Tories and Whigs; *ibid.,* xx.

failure of the Canadian campaign, thus giving him a plausible pretense for not passing their bills. The truth was that Harley, secretive and dilatory, was resisting every effort of St. John's to get him to pay the cost of an expedition with which Harley had no sympathy. He sought to find evidence of fraud in the accounts which were submitted to him and threw aside letters from Vetch without opening them. Once again, Vetch found himself the victim of partisan struggles which were none of his making; his accounts were hopelessly involved in Whitehall politics and he was charged with having "built a city at Her Majesty's charge."[9]

Vetch immediately attempted to answer the charges against himself. In a long and reasoned letter to Harley, he pointed out that he had instructions from Queen Anne to do everything necessary to prepare for the expedition of 1709. He held Her Majesty's commission to command the garrison at Annapolis; Borland had been legally appointed to act as Her Majesty's agent in meeting the expenses of the campaigns and the occupation of Nova Scotia. The governors and Nicholson had possessed authority from the Queen to act, when, as a council of war, they had authorized Vetch to incur the expense of maintaining the military forces and repairing the fort at Annapolis. Careful accounts had been kept and submitted, and no needless expense had been entered into—contrary to the charge that he had built a city, no new houses had been constructed at Annapolis. Few, he justly claimed, would have been so unsparing in their efforts to serve the Crown. He requested leave to return to Britain to render a full accounting, if objections to his bills were still sustained, and he begged for some kind of instructions concerning what bills he was authorized to incur.

Vetch had already written the Board of Trade about the resources of Nova Scotia in an attempt to persuade it of the value of the new colony. He was not only interested in the immediate support of the garrison but was anxious that some means be devised to settle the country so that a permanent solution to its problems could be worked out. In the fall of 1711, he wrote again to sug-

9. Nov. and Dec. 1711, Public Archives of Nova Scotia, VIII, nos. 51-52, 57-60, 77-82 (Dalhousie University, Halifax); Parker, ed., *Letters of St. John*, I, 154; Ford, ed., *Correspondence of the New England Company*, 96.

gest that Britain subsidize six or seven hundred prospective settlers with free passage, tools, and a year's subsistence. He cited the arrangements which had been made in behalf of the Palatines who were sent to New York, conveniently overlooking the expense and ultimate failure of that venture.

Such a group would contain enough able-bodied men to provide the colony with a militia, making the continued expense of a garrison unnecessary. Without a populace of loyal, Protestant Englishmen, Vetch foresaw no peace in a country inhabited by French Roman Catholics and "savages yet more bigotted than they." Oaths made little difference; as long as the French sought to recapture Canada, their priests would order the inhabitants to break their oaths and would give them absolution.

A second means by which Vetch proposed to make the new acquisition prosperous was to declare Annapolis Royal a free port for trade with all Britain's subjects. Such a proposal, cutting across the regulations of the Acts of Trade and Navigation, would provide traders with startling opportunities. The laws were already ambiguous. A port without regulations, where goods could flow without customs duties or inspection, would indeed attract business. Vetch intended this opportunity to be offered for only approximately seven years, after which time the regular revenue schedules would be reinstated. He assumed that revocation of Nova Scotia's special status would not seriously alter the patterns of trade which had developed; he believed that within a year of the expiration of the special arrangement the port would attract more revenue than it would in twenty years of regular development. Such a provision would attract settlers and render Nova Scotia strong and secure. As a matter of fact, Vetch had already reopened trade with the French at Annapolis in an effort to give the garrison some support and gain the allegiance of the Acadians.[10]

In a letter to Nicholson, Vetch credited the French with inciting the Indian uprising in Carolina. It was all part of a single pattern to Vetch, and he hoped that Nicholson could impress the authorities in England with the need for supporting every effort to

10. Vetch to Lord Treasurer, Feb. 26, 1712, Public Archives of Nova Scotia, VIII, nos. 76-82, V, no. 21 (Dalhousie University, Halifax); *Cal. State Papers, 1711-12*, no. 175.

combat the French threat; certainly the outpost at Annapolis was of considerable importance in the struggle. Vetch depended heavily on Nicholson's interest at court with the Tory St. John. He gave explicit instructions to his agents to show Nicholson all his letters to other leaders before they were delivered.[11]

Others in England had given Vetch repeated assurance of support, and he asked James Douglas, who was acting for him in London, to remind them of their pledges. With Scots caution, he broached another possibility. "If there wants money to move the wheels" in the matter of getting the establishment of a regiment with a commission as colonel for himself, he wrote, "you may advance what you think necessary towards the same." But, he added, "as I never yet gave any money that way, so I hope the reasonableness of the thing itself will prevail with the Ministry." In moving the grand affairs of years past, Vetch had bestowed the usual small gratuities on lesser functionaries. But he had never found it necessary to buy a commission or to bribe the principal servants of the Queen, and he could hardly afford to do so now, unless it was the only solution. Douglas was supposedly receiving Vetch's pay for the office of adjutant general, if not as governor and commander-in-chief at Annapolis. So sums were apparently available if needed.[12]

Vetch was avid for news of what was going on and urged Douglas to send him newspapers and pamphlets. Information about an impending peace settlement was constantly filtering through to the colonies. Vetch heard that a congress of plenipotentiaries was meeting at Utrecht in January 1712, and he scanned the papers anxiously through the following months to find out what it might mean for him and his colony.[13] After a year of secret negotiations, St. John's efforts had borne fruit. In December 1711, the Tories had felt strong enough to dismiss Marlborough from his command. The creation of twelve new Tory peers had given the Queen's party control in the House of Lords

11. Vetch to Nicholson, Nov. 12, to Casswell, Aug. 10, and to Douglas, Annapolis Royal, Aug. 10, 1712, Public Archives of Nova Scotia, VIII, nos. 66-67, 90, 100-2 (Dalhousie University, Halifax).

12. Vetch to Douglas, Nov. 1711, and June 27, 1712, *ibid.*, nos. 54-55, 89.

13. Feb. 10, 1712, *ibid.*, nos. 62-63; Vetch to Caulfeild, Mar. 12, and to Casswell, Feb. 10 and Aug. 10, 1712, *ibid.*, nos. 71, 63-64, 90.

and carried the motion to make peace. It remained to set the terms and bring Britain's allies to accept them. The peace terms were of great concern to Vetch. Nova Scotia had been in British hands before but had been subsequently given up in treaties. If the colony were lost again, the meagre gains of a great expenditure of colonial effort would be lost; the colonists would not be able to claim even partial success for the Glorious Enterprise. Vetch knew that it was important to get as much territory in the peace treaty as possible if the colonists were to be freed of their burden of defense against French expansion. At the least, Canada's boundaries should be clearly defined.

At Utrecht, England and France debated Canadian concessions. In April 1712, St. John asked the Board of Trade whether Canadians should be allowed to fish on the Newfoundland banks and dry their catch on the great island's shore. He also asked whether Cape Breton Island might not be ceded to the French in return for keeping Nova Scotia and Newfoundland. The Board of Trade promptly advised the Secretary against such a move. Allowing the French any rights in Newfoundland would defeat the object of possessing it. Furthermore, the Board pointed out that Cape Breton had always been considered a part of Nova Scotia. Subercase had considered it so and had surrendered it along with the rest of Acadia. The Board advised strongly in favor of insisting on a strict and careful description of the boundaries of Nova Scotia in any peace treaty. Nicholson, shortly after, urged the Board to recommend that the bounds of the whole French claim in America be as strictly drawn.[14]

Louis XIV put up a strong fight to regain Acadia. He was prepared to give it up rather than to break off negotiations, but he urged his representatives to yield only as a last resort and offered several West Indian islands in exchange for the northern province. When that offer was refused, he added Newfoundland and the fishing rights to the banks which France had treasured for over a hundred years.[15]

14. *Cal. State Papers, 1711-12*, nos. 365, 374, 385.
15. Parkman, *Half-Century of Conflict*, I, chap. IX. Matthew Prior, negotiating with Torci on peace terms in Paris in July 1711, had noted that British possession of Nova Scotia gave him an advantage in the proceedings; Hist. Mss. Comm., *Portland Mss.*, V (*Harley Papers*, III), 34-41.

By August 1712, Vetch was beginning to suspect that the government intended to return Nova Scotia to the French. Almost another year had gone by without instructions for the colony. The Treasury had still not accepted any of the bills drawn for its support. Vetch knew that the two parties in England were locked in "a mighty ferment . . . still, about peace and war." In addition to newspapers and pamphlets sent by Douglas, he had also received a letter from his father. The old minister, who was still serving his parish at Dumfries at the age of seventy-two, observed the frenzied efforts of the Whigs to head off an easy peace with France and "insinuated that the clouds gather apace and [there is] great appearance of a storm."[16]

In actual fact, St. John, now Viscount Bolingbroke, had aroused the opposition when it became apparent that in his eagerness for peace he would not hesitate to conclude a settlement unsatisfactory to Britain's allies. The colonists were to find in the years to come that such a settlement was no more satisfactory to them; but for the time, the prospect of peace was welcome, and they would have been cheered to know that the British plenipotentiaries were standing firm in their insistence on the retention of Nova Scotia, along with Newfoundland and Hudson Bay.

After his winter in Boston, Vetch returned to Annapolis Royal on June 6, 1712, and found that the fort had been strengthened; Caulfeild reported it able to "withstand any force the enemy can possibly bring against it in this part of the world." The French inhabitants appeared satisfied, the garrison was in good health, and the Indian company was well established in its little fort a quarter of a mile from the main works. Indians under French influence were reported gathering for an assault, but Vetch was confident that a siege would merely "confine us to salt provisions."

Nevertheless, he had much to worry him. Despite his fear that his frequent pleas would weary the Secretary of State, he wrote again to say that he had received no orders. He had no knowledge of whether provisions had been made for the pay and subsistence of the garrison nor whether the outstanding accounts

16. Vetch to Douglas, Annapolis Royal, Aug. 10, 1712, and Jan. 28, 1713, Public Archives of Nova Scotia, VIII, nos. 100-2, 137-39 (Dalhousie University, Halifax); Vetch to Robert Livingston, Nov. 20, 1712, and Jan. 25, 1713, Livingston Papers.

had been honored. Without a regular regimental organization, "endless trouble among the garrison's officers" prevailed. They were constantly contending about their relative rank and commands. Repairs to the fort had been held to a minimum, but expenses were still very great. Settlement was obstructed because of lack of instructions about how land was to be parceled out. He begged again for Dartmouth to intercede with Her Majesty and the Lord Treasurer and again referred the British authorities to Nicholson, who could "best inform you of what methods are properest to the civil and military establishment of this country."[17]

Vetch was more outspoken in letters to his agents. He confessed that he was at a loss to know what to do until he saw whether the bills would be paid. Yet, expenses had to be met, and he had not been able to wait for explicit orders. Instead, he had depended on the good faith of the home authorities to stand behind his proceedings in Nova Scotia, and he had informed the ministry of his actions at every opportunity. However, Whitehall had done nothing for two years.

Vetch was finding out what other colonial governors knew: Little credit adhered to those public servants who attempted to follow their instructions and advance the royal cause. But woe betide any unlucky governor who aroused complaints, real or fancied, from colonists or interests in England. Even though he was working for the Crown's advantage, if the complaints were loud and sustained, he would reap royal censure and shortly find himself without support from the very authorities who had appointed him.

To Vetch it seemed very likely that with credit rapidly being exhausted in Boston he might have to abandon Annapolis Royal. He wondered how a ministry could possibly think a garrison of 500 men could be subsisted "without one farthing being paid for either victualing or pay for above two years—they may equally suppose they can subsist without breathing." Although he urged his friends to redouble efforts in behalf of his accounts and those of

17. Public Archives of Nova Scotia, V, no. 29, VIII, nos. 86-88 (Dalhousie University, Halifax); Caulfeild to Dartmouth, Dec. 6, 1711, Vane to Dartmouth, May 5 and June 18, Vetch to Dartmouth, June 24, 1712, *Cal. State Papers, 1711-12*, nos. 208, 403, 452, 457.

Borland, he hoped to be given leave to go to England, where he could help clarify the situation.[18]

By August, Vetch was in despair. An attempt to salvage arms and stores from the wreck of H.M.S. *Feversham* and the three transports which had foundered off Cape Breton had failed.[19] The garrison was becoming almost mutinous, and desertions were mounting. One group of eight men was returned to the fort by the French, who had been offered a five-pound reward. Of these, a court-martial condemned five men to death. Vetch reprieved four, and had the fifth one shot as an example. Another group was recaptured only after two of its number had been killed by lurking Indians. Vetch noted that Irish Catholics in the garrison who fell sick often deserted to seek the comfort of the French priests in the area.

At this troubled time, he discovered that British authorities had been receiving adverse reports of him. The "surmises of some malicious people," he did not know whom, would doubtless be seized on as further warrant to put off meeting his needs. Consequently, Vetch considered it even more important to obtain permission to return to England in order to defend his character from these "scandalous, underhand informers." He asked Nicholson to help in getting him leave and assured both Nicholson and the Lord Treasurer that his innocence was "as clear as the sun." It seemed to Vetch that he "labored under the greatest difficulties and hardships that perhaps any person in such a post ever did," but he was certain that he could make the truth evident to the ministry "notwithstanding any surmises [which] may have been made . . . to my disadvantage."[20]

18. Vetch to Douglas, June 27, and to Casswell, Aug. 10, 1712, Public Archives of Nova Scotia, VIII, nos. 89-90, 136-37 (Dalhousie University, Halifax). Vetch hoped that Dummer might be able to help him and was also anxious to hear from Mr. Newman, of the Society for the Propagation of the Gospel, "from whom I've not heard this age."

19. The attempt had been suggested by Hunter and Dudley, since the wreck lay within the limits of Vetch's authority, and they thought fast action was necessary to get the stores before the French did. Vetch's efforts failed because the wreck lay among rocks and shoals with no convenient anchorage nearby. One of the salvage vessels became lost in the fog and was captured by a French privateer; *ibid.*, nos. 90 ff., 104-5.

20. Vetch to Dartmouth, Aug. 8, to Harley, Aug. 8, to Nicholson, Nov. 20, 1712, *ibid.*, nos. 90, 102-4, 126-27.

His fears were far from paranoiac. Early in May, the engineer, Captain Vane, had sent Dartmouth a series of bitter charges against Vetch, based almost entirely on hearsay and the allegations of French inhabitants who had every reason to foment division among the British. After citing the care of Caulfeild, "who has gained the affections of the people here by his affable and just government," he went on to say that "Governor Vetch . . . had raised excessive contributions and committed abundance of extortions, using the people more like slaves than anything else." He alluded to the complaints which the French had made to their own government and brought out the old charge, which was apparently quite true, that "Governor Vetch has effects still in Canada that have remained there ever since he was in trouble about the smuggling trade." Vane had heard from one of Vetch's erstwhile French factors that he wished directions for sending some of Vetch's goods to the governor. Vane concluded that Vetch was a "very good governor for his own profit but not for the public good; nor will the country ever flourish whilst he commands." He asserted that there was a cloud in every face at the thought that Vetch would be returning soon to Annapolis Royal. The inhabitants were making plans to abandon their homes and leave the country. Vessels hired to bring provisions to Nova Scotia were generally a third loaded with merchandise for Vetch and Borland, Vane noted, and added that "were I to write half of what they do, I should never be finished."[21]

It was always easy to bring such charges against royal officials, whose public duties and private interests were inextricably mixed and often identical. Vetch's former trade connections at Annapolis Royal had, in fact, facilitated maintenance of the post, making his private credit available for the public service. The bills had given Annapolis a meagre currency for a time.

Vane's motives are obscure. Perhaps he was dissatisfied about his low salary; Vetch had noted that he claimed to rate more pay than his predecessor, Captain Forbes. The engineer was also writing home hopefully about the possibilities of silver mines in Nova Scotia, and he may have hoped to displace Vetch in favor of someone from whom he could expect consideration in getting a

21. Vane to Dartmouth, May 5, 1712, *Cal. State Papers, 1711-12,* no. 403.

share of such wealth. At any rate, when he wrote his accusation Vane had almost no personal acquaintance with Vetch, and he was not in a position to assess his motives nor to appreciate the difficulties under which he had labored. As long as credit held out, the garrison and Vetch would not be reduced to poverty. But it should have been apparent to Vane that Vetch had risked his entire personal fortune on the good faith of the ministry and stood to lose heavily if he became discredited.

On the other hand, if all his bills were paid, Vetch would gain not only what he could legitimately expect as the chief enterpriser of the assault on New France and as Her Majesty's royal governor in Nova Scotia but also interest on his advances and profit from the victuals and stores for which he had acted as supplier.[22] Vetch may not have guessed that it was Captain Vane who was his traducer, but by November he had reason to complain of his engineer. Rumor had reached him that Vane was the man who had earlier betrayed the British garrison at Newfoundland to the French. Furthermore, the other officers of the Annapolis garrison were complaining of him as a publicly professed Jacobite who reflected against King William and the Revolution of 1688. Vetch could not know that Bolingbroke was already hedging in the matter of the Protestant succession, and views such as Vane's were being increasingly voiced in England. Indeed, his complaints against Vane were to serve him ill with the government. In any event, Vane's discourses had finally become so objectionable to Captain Armstrong of the garrison that this officer, "not being able longer to bear it, broke a large glass decanter full of wine upon his head, and had very near sent him to the other world."

As the mellow stillness of brilliant late autumn days warned of the approach of Annapolis Royal's third winter under the British flag, Vetch wearily set about preparing for another season isolated from the other colonies. Still without encouragement from London, his officers drew up a memorial setting forth the needs of their troops for pay and subsistence, pointing out that unlike the militia of New England they could neither be fed from the surrounding country nor find work on the side to piece out their

22. *Ibid.*, no. 452; Vetch to Board of Ordnance, Nov. 10, 1711, Public Archives of Nova Scotia, VIII, nos. 53-54 (Dalhousie University, Halifax).

small pay. In support of Vetch's contentions, they cited the extra expense involved in paying shipping costs for the supplies they received from New England, in addition to the Boston prices which were so extravagant because of Vetch's and Borland's attenuated credit.[23]

This statement, along with one from Vetch to Dudley, was entrusted to Captain Armstrong. Since he had not received permission to return to England, Vetch had decided that he must do the next best thing and send a representative to press the case for Nova Scotia. His pleas to Nicholson and his London agents apparently were not doing any good. Vetch addressed an appeal to Dudley, signed by himself, Caulfeild, and the other officers, relying on New England's interest in the maintenance of the outpost. They pointed out that Massachusetts was the nearest colony and the one most concerned that Annapolis Royal be held. Depending on Britain had been "slim reliance"; now, with Borland's credit exhausted, the colonies would have to help each other. Vetch suggested privately to Dudley that the proceeds of the liquidation of ships and supplies returned from the Canada expedition might be used. He assumed, with evident validity, that instructions from England were being held up, pending settlement of the great questions at issue in the peace. But he noted that New England could not afford to let Nova Scotian credit lapse. The bills and currency of New England were in use there, and New England's credit would suffer along with Nova Scotia's.

Armstrong was instructed to present the case to the Massachusetts Assembly, if it were sitting. If not, he was to proceed to England immediately after waiting on Governor Dudley. In a letter to Nicholson, Vetch asked his friend to support Armstrong's mission and arrange for introductions to the proper authorities. The captain was to seek an audience with the Queen herself and to use all possible diligence to obtain favorable answers to the garrison's requests. Vetch also expressed his satisfaction with the news that Nicholson might shortly arrive in the colonies on "honorable and beneficial employment."[24] It was rumored that Nicholson

23. Vetch to Board of Ordnance, Nov. 20, 1712, Public Archives of Nova Scotia, VIII, nos. 117-19, 121 (Dalhousie University, Halifax).
24. Instructions to Captain Lawrence Armstrong, Nov. 20, Memorial of Governor, Lieutenant Governor, and Officers to Dudley, Nov. 20, Vetch to

was to be governor of a reconstituted "Dominion of New England," a development which promised Vetch stronger aid from his southern neighbors and might eliminate the independency always manifest in the legislatures of Massachusetts, Connecticut, and Rhode Island. Although Whig in his general attitude toward English politics, Vetch, along with other royal leaders in America, was quite in sympathy with Tory efforts to bring the colonies into conformity with royal authority. Like many of his Whig contemporaries in Britain, he did not realize that encroachments on the power of the sovereign in England would weaken royal authority in colonial affairs as well.

Before winter set in, Vetch sent for his wife, who had spent the summer in Boston nursing Billy through an illness and parrying rumors about her husband. Mrs. Vetch had denied that he was beset by a mutinous garrison or had been recalled by the British government. Although she was sorry to leave their daughter Alida at home, presumably to continue her schooling in Boston or at the Manor, Mrs. Vetch was not reluctant to leave the rumor-ridden colonial capital.[25]

The Nova Scotian winter was an exceptionally stormy and violent one. But for Vetch the vigor of the elements was offset by the credit he had gained in Boston to subsist the garrison until the following May. He also learned that more than half of his bills had finally been cleared for payment. It was little enough, and late, with still no provisions for the future. Vetch, reportedly, had been seven thousand pounds in debt, and Borland owed nearly two thousand; both men were still seriously overextended in terms of colonial fortunes at the time. Vetch continued to press for permission to return to England to vindicate himself and asked his agent to set aside money which he would need when he arrived in London. Perusing the latest newspapers and pamphlets, he could still make little of the course of British affairs, but the reading

---

Dudley, Oct. 16, Vetch to St. John, Nov. 20, Vetch to Board of Ordnance, Nov. 20, Vetch to Secretary of War, Nov. 20, 1712, *ibid.*, nos. 125-27, 119-21, 110-12, 122-24.

25. Margaret Vetch to Robert Livingston, Aug. 25, and July 25, 1712, Livingston Papers, Group 2 and Group 1a, box 7; Vetch to Douglas, Nov. 20, 1712, Public Archives of Nova Scotia, VIII, no. 127 (Dalhousie University, Halifax).

"very much diverted" him.[26]   Less diverting were the French privateers operating off the coast of Nova Scotia.[27]

In order to facilitate financial transactions at Annapolis, Vetch proclaimed that his own bills of exchange were to circulate as current tender, payable in six months in New England bills or bills on Great Britain's Treasury.   The move was made necessary by the almost total lack of revenue and commercial dealing in the colony, which left Nova Scotia without even the meagre circulating currency enjoyed by New England.   But it was almost certain to meet with objection from the neighboring colonies and the British government.

Vetch was also beset by the difficulty of clothing the garrison. The soldiers had been "almost naked" at the onset of winter; yet they rebelled at the prices put on the clothing which Vetch ordered from New England.   Actually, the prices which Vetch intended to charge were the bare cost of the clothing in New England money, but apparently the officers had been raising the prices and pocketing the difference.   Vetch was forced to issue a proclamation to the garrison setting forth the facts and giving the prices, so that the soldiers could protect themselves against the rapacity of their officers.[28]

The winter monotony of barracks life was enlivened occasionally by efforts to apprehend the French privateers.   In addition, Vetch could look forward to spring.   Mrs. Vetch was expecting a third child in July, and Vetch planned to send her to Boston in April; he would follow in time to be on hand for the baby's birth. He wrote to Douglas "to drink our healths" with his other friends

26. Vetch to Casswell, Jan. 20, to Douglas, Jan. 28, 1713, Public Archives of Nova Scotia, VIII, nos. 136-37, 137-39 (Dalhousie University, Halifax); Vetch to Robert Livingston, Apr. 24, 1713, John Livingston to Robert Livingston, Aug. 7, 1712, noting the extent of Vetch's and Borland's debt, Livingston Papers.

27. Vetch to Lord Treasurer, Jan. 22, Vetch to Dartmouth, Jan. 22, to Casswell, Jan. 20, 1713, and to Costebelle, Sept. 26, 1712, Public Archives of Nova Scotia, VIII, nos. 130-33, 134-36, 136-37, 171 (Dalhousie University, Halifax). Vetch complained to the French governor of Newfoundland about the privateers, and also to Vaudreuil; *ibid.*, nos. 176-79.   The cessation of arms had been proclaimed in the colonies Oct. 27, 1712; Thomas Lechmere to Wait Winthrop, Mass. Hist. Soc., *Collections*, 6th ser., 5 (1892), 262.   British troops had actually been withdrawn from active operations in June.

28. See Vetch's Orders on current tender and his proclamation on clothing prices, Public Archives of Nova Scotia, VIII, nos. 143-44 (Dalhousie University, Halifax).

in London and added that he hoped to get to England himself in the fall. Late in April, Captain Southack arrived at Annapolis Royal in the province galley and returned Mrs. Vetch to Boston the first week in May. Johanna, her sister, who had nursed Mrs. John Livingston in New London during her last illness, traveled to Roxbury, where Mrs. Vetch met her. Johanna was homesick, but she intended to stay with her sister in Boston until the baby came. Shortly after Mrs. Vetch's arrival, she and Johanna were distressed that John Livingston, their brother, announced his impending remarriage. When he wrote his father for parental consent, John noted that he had known the girl's family for several years. Madame Sarah Knight, the indefatigable traveler and diarist, was her mother, and the girl herself was, he noted, a marvel of character and breeding. Madame Knight wrote to Robert Livingston to express her hopes that the marriage would meet with his approval. In a casual aside, she let drop the consideration that all her fortune would go to her daughter.[29]

Margaret Vetch and Johanna flatly opposed their brother's marriage. Johanna esteemed Miss Knight "a very stony character" and was angry with her brother because he was disparaging his family in order to make it appear that Miss Knight's was its equal. Mrs. Vetch was even more outspoken. She considered it too soon after the death of John's first wife for him to marry again. More than that, she had been shocked to have him tell her, even before Mary's death, that he meant to marry Miss Knight, which, she said, "I shall always think on with abhorrence, for in my opinion a woman that will encourage a man in such a matter during the life of his wife is not to be looked on as one of very good principle!" Miss Knight, continued the sharp-tongued Margaret, was a woman of neither note nor good family; she had a "very indifferent reputation in the town either for honor or modesty, yea, I may say, of a stained character." In fact, she wrote her father, some people "talk very odd of unlawful familiarities" between Miss Knight and John Livingston; but Margaret con-

29. *Ibid.*, nos. 130-33, 136-39, 176-80; Vetch to Robert Livingston, Apr. 24, Johanna to her father, May 13, 19, and 20 and June 1, John Livingston to his father, June 1 and 15, Sarah Knight to Robert Livingston, June 22, 1713, Livingston Papers. Madame Knight had very little fortune, according to Margaret Vetch.

cluded that was a matter best known to John himself. She said
that she had told John her mind fully in the matter, as she thought
it her duty to do, but he had stalked out of the house and refused
to speak to her any longer.

Robert Livingston informed his son that he did not think well
of John's choice, but John referred his father to Increase Mather,
minister of the North Church, for an evaluation of the girl's
character and pursued his design. He was persuaded that "Sister
Vetch" had prejudiced his father, and he hoped to live to retaliate
with a similar favor. But the Livingstons always got over family
quarrels. Despite this sharp flare of temper, the marriage went
on, and no perceptible coolness lasted between John and the
Vetches.

In June, word reached Boston that the Treaty of Utrecht had
been signed in April and that Nicholson had been selected as governor of Newfoundland and Nova Scotia. Margaret and Johanna
heard the somewhat depressing news that Vetch was merely to
have his commission as adjutant general to Nicholson, a commission as captain of a company of Indians, and a present of £500
from the Queen.[30] Meanwhile, Vetch informed Dartmouth that
he intended to trouble the Secretary no more with complaints of
the state of the garrison but would await Nicholson's "longed-for"
arrival. Although he had not yet heard of Nicholson's appointment as governor, news of the Utrecht peace terms came to him
from Gaulin, the priest who had led the siege of the fort in the
winter of 1710-11 and had been active as a missionary to the
French Indians in Acadia.

Gaulin was apparently aware of the struggle which Louis XIV
had made to keep Acadia, but he attributed its loss to the French
authorities' lack of awareness of its value. Vetch was dismayed to
learn that Cape Breton was to remain in French hands, and he
warned the Board of Trade that the French would now build up
that island to take the place of the forts they had lost at Port
Royal and Placentia. He heard from Gaulin, who had it from the
governor of Newfoundland, that Pontchartrain was embarking im-

---

30. Johanna to her father, June 22 and 29, Margaret Vetch to her father,
June 29, John to his father, July 1 and 9, 1713, Livingston Papers.

mediately upon the construction of a fortress which would be strongly manned by French Regulars.[31]

Vetch left it to the Board, "whose job it is to judge how far this will affect the British interest and trade in those parts," to consider further action. But he hoped to wait on the Board in person before many months to show it the mistake which had been made in ceding this part of Nova Scotia to the French. He could not know of the Board's effort to impress Bolingbroke with the importance of the French claim on Cape Breton as a part of its Acadian province. Britain and the American colonies were to expend much worry and considerable blood in regaining this rocky island which commanded the Gulf of St. Lawrence and had been surrendered so needlessly by the Tory peacemakers.[32]

Nor had the peace terms defined the limits of Canada or even the newly won Nova Scotia, apart from ceding the island of Cape Breton. Gaulin frankly admitted that the French would exert themselves to claim part of the territory west of the Nova Scotian peninsula, the area north of the British posts in Maine, extending to the Cape of Gaspé.[33] If they were successful in this, as well as in fortifying Cape Breton, the British would have but a slender hold on Nova Scotia, an outpost cut off from the mainland of North America and existing precariously under the constant threat of superior force which might descend on it. On his return to England, Vetch was to find his knowledge of this dangerous situation greatly in demand in the subsequent negotiation over boundary lines.

While Vetch fretted over the peace terms, Francis Nicholson prepared to assume his new duties. In addition to his commission as governor of Nova Scotia, he received a commission as general and commander-in-chief of all British forces in Newfoundland

31. Vetch to Dartmouth, May 22, Vetch to Board of Trade, Dec. 12, 1713, Public Archives of Nova Scotia, V, no. 34, VIII, nos. 180-83 (Dalhousie University, Halifax).

32. Exchange between St. John and the Board of Trade in Apr. 1712, *Cal. State Papers, 1711-12*, nos. 365, 374; Bolingbroke's secretary to the Board and the Board's reply, Dec. 9-10, 1712, Public Archives of Nova Scotia, V, no. 32 (Dalhousie University, Halifax), and Ottawa Transcripts of Nova Scotia Archives, IV, 54, 55 (Public Archives of Canada, Ottawa).

33. Public Archives of Nova Scotia, VIII, nos. 180-83 (Dalhousie University, Halifax).

and Nova Scotia. Although the commissions were granted in October 1712, Nicholson did not sail for America until July 1713.[34] His instructions gave him the power to inquire into the conduct of government in all the British colonies, evidence that the Tory ministry was at last interested in moving from the chaos of independency exhibited by the separate assemblies in America toward uniformity and adherence to royal instructions. It remained to be seen whether Nicholson's efforts at enforcing principles in the face of disparate actualities would be any more successful than those of former agents of the Crown.[35]

Since Nicholson did not arrive in Boston until September, Vetch stayed at Annapolis Royal throughout the summer. Late in October, the new governor sent Lieutenant Governor Caulfeild orders to take over the government from Vetch. Nicholson reminded the soldiers and inhabitants that they should realize the Queen was preoccupied with greater affairs—the implication seemed to be that constant communications from Nova Scotia were not welcome in England. Although this seemed a not-too-gentle rebuff to Vetch's persistent efforts, it may have reflected Nicholson's reluctance to allow his subjects recourse to higher authority, should they become dissatisfied with his measures.

The new governor also reversed Vetch's policy in outfitting the garrison. Clothing designed for the expedition against Canada was made available to the troops, the same clothing on which Moore and St. John had allegedly turned a handsome profit. Now the garrison was to be allowed to buy it from the officers. And Nicholson stated that he would back whatever prices the officers charged. He also nullified Vetch's policy of encouraging trade between the British and French by ordering that all trade must be licensed.[36]

From inquiries reaching Caulfeild and Mascarene at Annapolis,

34. Nicholson's Commissions, Windsor, Oct. 20, 1712, *ibid.*, V, nos. 10, 11; Ottawa Transcripts of Nova Scotia Archives, IV, N.S.E. 7, 57, 71, 73, 74-78, 80-85 (Public Archives of Canada, Ottawa).

35. Nicholson seems to have remained for a time in Cork, Ireland, before sailing; see correspondence between June 25 and July 19, 1713, in Ottawa Transcripts of Nova Scotia Archives, IV, 96, 116 (Public Archives of Canada, Ottawa).

36. Caulfeild to Nicholson, May 27, 1714, *Nova Scotia Archives* (Halifax, 1900), II, 7.

Vetch surmised that Nicholson was investigating the record of his administration. He promptly decided that his presence in Boston was necessary. His last letter to Dartmouth had pictured once again the miserable state of the garrison, noting that the troops were "wholly naked," without bedding, and victualed through the end of the year only with the "utmost difficulty imaginable." Vetch considered it a miracle that the garrison had been kept together, one made possible largely by the constant promise that help from Britain could be expected. Hearing nothing for three years, Vetch had been moved to "freedom and warmth" in his expression. Had he written later, after receiving the shipment of clothing from Nicholson, he might have expressed himself even more freely. It was sleazy stuff, priced exorbitantly, and furnished originally under the impression that it was intended for troops bound to the tropical West Indies.[37]

Arriving in Boston in November, Vetch was shocked to hear of the political situation in London. The Tories sought to put all civil and military positions in the hands of extremists in their party, even down to the lowest office. Bolingbroke was struggling to secure the Queen's party before her death in order to bring back the Catholic Pretender or at least to assure continued control of the government under a Protestant successor. Nicholson, as a High Churchman and Tory, had been favored. Vetch, after his critical remarks about Vane's Jacobitism, had been marked as no man to represent Bolingbroke in a colonial governorship.

Even more astonishing was the personal animus Nicholson at once exhibited toward his former comrade-in-arms. Vetch had all along been confiding his affairs trustingly to Nicholson but he now found that Nicholson had become "so violent a party man that every man must fly very high that expects any favor or recommendation from him." On the pretense that Vane's charges were true, Nicholson accused Vetch of maladministration and peculation in Nova Scotia. Vetch was convinced that his lack of enthusiasm for the Tory ministry was at the bottom of the treatment he was

---

37. Nicholson to Caulfeild, Oct. 20, 1714, Nicholson to Board of Trade, Dec. 14, 1713, Ottawa Transcripts of Nova Scotia Archives, IV, 135, 252 (Public Archives of Canada, Ottawa); Oct. 5, 1713, Public Archives of Nova Scotia, V, no. 35 (Dalhousie University, Halifax).

receiving.[38]   Nicholson's behavior recalled the willful perversity
he had exhibited at the time of Leisler's revolt in New York and
the flaring temper he had shown when news of the failure of the
expedition of 1711 had reached him.   It should have been no
surprise to Vetch that Nicholson was subject to fits of passion in
which he lost all reason.   The story was told that after one of his
outbursts, while he was in command of the army on the New York
frontier, an Indian had commented that "the general is drunk."
The Indian was told that Nicholson never took strong liquor.
"I do not mean that he is drunk with rum," replied the Indian.
"He was born drunk."[39]

Vetch could only conclude that Nicholson had become a
"malicious madman," who was studying "all he can to find pretense of complaint against me to excuse his unfair dealing in supplanting me."   He would leave "nothing unattempted against
me," Vetch reported, "that fury, malice, and madness could inspire."   Although he despaired of adjusting his accounts to Nicholson's satisfaction under these circumstances, Vetch vowed he would
be the instrument of lowering the governor, just as he had been
in raising him.   Observing that Nicholson was bullying Governor
Dudley, Vetch warned Governor Hunter of New York that he
was suspect as a Whig.   Nicholson's instructions included a warrant to investigate Hunter's management of the Palatine settlers,
as well as the general situation in New York, and Vetch was sure
that Nicholson would seek to discredit Hunter at every opportunity.   Vetch also warned his father-in-law Robert Livingston that
Nicholson might interfere with the collection of sums due him for
advances made on behalf of the Palatines.   "I wish it may not cost
you a voyage to Britain before you get your money," wrote Vetch,
who was determined to present his own case before the home
authorities at the first opportunity.   John Livingston and Borland's son planned to go with Vetch to "tell our own story in
Britain," and they did not doubt that they could convince the

38. Vetch to Robert Livingston, Dec. 28, 1713, and Jan. 25, 1714, Livingston
Papers.
39. Cadwallader Colden to his son, no date, but between Sept. 25 and Dec.
31, 1759, N.Y. Hist. Soc., *Collections*, Pub. fund ser., 1 (1868), 201.

government to render justice to those who had labored so arduously and faithfully in the cause of empire.[40]

For Vetch it was a season of adversity. His third child had not lived. Both Alida and Billy had been very ill with measles, and Vetch himself had been sick with a severe cold after his arrival from Annapolis. He could well exclaim, "God be thanked" for the recovery of his children—the measles epidemic was virulent and many people were dying of it.[41] But Vetch was not easily overcome by misfortune. He fought back against Nicholson's extravagant charges and found that he still had allies in Boston. Nicholson brought Vetch before the Massachusetts Council to justify his accounts and explain why he had exercised the right of granting commissions and warrants to the officers at Annapolis Royal. He held Vetch accountable for almost nineteen thousand pounds disbursed for the expenses of the outpost between the time of its capture and the fall of 1713. When he heard that Vetch intended to return to England, he put every possible obstacle in his way. But the angry Nicholson quickly learned that he would need more power to deal with Vetch; he had turned up no evidence to which the Council would listen.

Vetch then decided not to remain within reach of any measures which Nicholson might employ. He refused to attend further Council hearings and arranged with John Livingston during the first week in March to remove to New London, whence they could sail to England. To Livingston he wrote that there was little news in Boston except "what the old madman G—N— makes"; Nicholson seemed to be railing at all mankind and attacking the Livingstons, as well as Vetch. Mrs. Vetch reported that

40. Vetch to Robert Livingston, Dec. 28, 1713, Jan. 25, Apr. 6, John Livingston to Robert Livingston, Jan. 1, 1714, Livingston Papers.

41. According to the correspondence in the Livingston Papers, mainly the letters of Johanna, who was with Mrs. Vetch during the summer of 1713, the baby was not premature. On June 29 she wrote that her sister was ready to "lie in." There is no record of the birth, so it is presumed that the child was stillborn or died soon after birth. The other two children are mentioned frequently afterward and it is assumed that a third child would also have been mentioned if it had lived. The illnesses are mentioned in Vetch to Robert Livingston, Jan. 25, 1714, and Dec. 23, 1713, and John Livingston to his father, Jan. 1, 1714, *ibid.*

nobody in Boston approved of Nicholson. He seemed, indeed, to be a lunatic.[42]

But there was method to Nicholson's madness. Vetch's house was attached for the sum of £30,000 and the sheriff instructed "for want thereof to take the body of the said Samuel Vetch" and hold him for the justices of the inferior Court of Common Pleas. The sheriff's deputy made the attachment and left the summons for Vetch. But the victim had escaped, and at the April session of court Nicholson found himself without evidence to make a case. He lamely asked Paul Dudley, the attorney general, to continue the action until Her Majesty's pleasure could be known. With a futile gesture of authority, he sent Vetch's unfortunate clerk to prison—but the keeper refused to shut him up.[43]

When Vetch sailed on April 9, his friends were glad to see him escape, and Borland noted that few men were of a contrary sentiment. Before he left, Vetch wisely confided his papers to his wife, and she promptly sent them off to the Manor for safekeeping so that Nicholson would not be able to seize them and deprive Vetch of the evidence he might need to prove his rectitude. Mrs. Vetch and her children temporarily moved—she was having her house redecorated anyway, and it seemed best to keep out of the way of the painters and the furious Nicholson. Frustrated in his attempt to get Vetch, Nicholson brought Vetch's agents Borland and Steel before the Massachusetts Council to give an account of their dealings with Vetch and to produce their account books for examination. He hoped to seize any "effects or credits" of Vetch's which might be in their hands. But neither one would testify against Vetch or give up his records, and the Council refused to proceed against them.[44]

42. Margaret Vetch to her father, Apr. 26, Vetch to John Livingston, Mar. 8, Nicholson's accusation, Feb. 24, 1714, *ibid*.

43. Margaret Vetch to Robert Livingston, Apr. 26, David Jamison to Robert Livingston, Mar. 30, John Livingston to Robert Livingston, Apr. 21 and 27, 1714, *ibid.;* Nicholson to Paul Dudley, Her Majesty's Attorney General, Apr. 8, and attachment, Feb. 24, 1714, Misc. Bound Mss., VIII (Mass. Hist. Soc.). A copy of the last item, along with the Account of the Deputy Sheriff and the Order for Continuance, Dom Regina vs. Vetch, Suffolk County Court of Common Pleas, Apr. 1, 1714, is in the Livingston Papers. See Apr. 6, 1714, file no. 9575, and May-Sept. 1714, file no. 9734, Book 93; July 6, 1714, file no. 9751, Book 94; May 1715, file no. 10310, Book 98, Records of the Clerk of the Supreme Court, Suffolk County Court House, Boston, Mass.

44. Margaret Vetch to Robert Livingston, Apr. 26 and May 30, Vetch to

Nicholson was confined to issuing orders in Nova Scotia and Newfoundland against honoring Vetch's bills or furnishing Vetch with any sort of certificates of good conduct. He instructed Caulfeild to open and hold any letters written by Vetch, hoping that they might contain evidence which could be used against him. Nicholson feared that Vetch might try to represent him as having designs against the garrison and counseled that such insinuations were not to be credited, coming from such a "lying fellow." The new governor appeared convinced that Vetch had acted arbitrarily and illegally, assuming powers to which he had no right, appointing officers without authority, and in general using "all means to cheat Her Majesty and her subjects in the affairs of the garrison as far as it was possible for him to do."[45]

Robert Livingston, Apr. 6, Borland to Livingston, Apr. 19, Council Meeting, Mar. 24, 1714, Livingston Papers; Philip Verplank to Robert Livingston, transmitting papers from Mrs. Vetch, Apr. 19, 1714, Webster Papers (New Brunswick Museum). For an abstract of bills drawn by Vetch after the reduction of Port Royal, submitted to Nicholson, Jan. 7, 1714, see Ottawa Transcripts of Nova Scotia Archives, V, 1 (Public Archives of Canada, Ottawa).

45. Nicholson to Moody at Placentia, June 15, 1714, Public Archives of Nova Scotia, VII, no. 7 (Dalhousie University, Halifax); Nicholson to Caulfeild, Apr. 6, 1714, *Nova Scotia Archives*, II, 3.

CHAPTER FOURTEEN

End of the Enterpriser

ETCH ENTRUSTED HIS WIFE and children to the care of Robert Livingston and slipped off quietly to England. He left America with regret and misgivings. Although he had no doubt that everything would work out well eventually, he was afraid that he might encounter difficulties which would take time, trouble, and money to surmount. Neither he nor anyone else, however, realized that he was leaving America for the last time; nor did it occur to him during the next eighteen years that he would not be returning within just a few months in some official capacity.

In England Vetch found that "party violence precludes doing any business yet—everybody's time is taken up by politics." He evaluated the situation and decided that the summer of 1714 was a most inauspicious time to press a case either for the clearance of his accounts or for his reinstatement as governor. It was apparent that the Queen had little longer to live. Bolingbroke had split with Oxford and the moderates and was making frenzied efforts to put all the offices of the government and the military establishment into the hands of Tory regulars who could be trusted to maintain the party and insist on a succession on their own terms. Obviously, Vetch could hope for little consideration from Bolingbroke's faction.[1]

But British sympathies which had supported Bolingbroke in his efforts to bring peace were not likely to back him if it came to seeking the return of the Catholic Pretender. The Tories had already forfeited favor with the Hanoverians, and, if Vetch waited, there

1. Vetch to Livingston, Apr. 6 and June 7, 1714, Livingston Papers. Vetch well knew that it had taken months and years of solicitation in England on two prior occasions for Livingston to get payment of amounts advanced in the public service and the interest thereon.

was a good chance that he might find the Whigs back in power under a Protestant king. He feared, however, that the death of the Electress Sophia, which occurred just as he arrived in England, might impede the settlement of political affairs.[2]

Vetch's father wrote to the Earl of Oxford from Scotland in his son's behalf, laying it "much at your lordship's door to clear him" in the public accounts with which he was charged. He begged Oxford to allow the expenses "and not expose him and his family to destruction." Another Scots minister, the Reverend William Carstares, wrote in a similar vein, describing the elder Veitch as "a very worthy, reverend, and aged minister whom I have particularly known for many years," and noting that the old man was "greatly concerned for . . . his only son now alive, and looking upon him as entirely ruined as to worldly concerns if he shall not get his arrears."[3]

Patiently waiting for the political situation to jell, Vetch refrained from pressing his case before a Tory ministry. However, he co-operated with the government on colonial matters. Soon after his arrival in England, he rendered service in an affair of great moment. According to the Treaty of Utrecht, British and French commissioners were to decide on colonial boundaries left unsettled by the treaty. Bolingbroke ordered the Board of Trade to prepare instructions for the British commissioners based on its knowledge of the American situation. When Vetch applied for an audience before the Board, the members asked him to join Dummer, Lodwick, and others in England who knew the colonies in preparing memorials setting forth their views concerning the proper boundaries between Great Britain and France in the New World. Vetch drafted a general report but noted that it would take time and detailed research to draw up a scheme to adjust colonial boundaries to Great Britain's advantage.[4]

As Vetch understood the recent treaty, the line of the British colonies ran in a southwesterly direction from the Gut of Canso at the northeast end of Nova Scotia to the boundary between South

2. June 7, 1714, *ibid.* This raised a question of the validity of Hanoverian succession.

3. Hist. Mss. Comm., *Portland Mss.*, X (*Harley Mss.*, VIII), 262, 318.

4. June 15-17 and July 28, 1714, *Board of Trade Journal, 1709-15,* 542-43, 555.

Carolina and Florida. The British held the entire coastline, but the French, he pointed out, had run a line of pretended settlement behind the whole length of the thickly inhabited British colonies, as far as the mouth of the Mississippi. Although they had actually established only a few small forts, the French claimed "to entirely environ, upon the land part, all our British settlements." This backcountry, not yet settled, was not highly regarded, but Vetch warned that its value was increasing daily and that it behooved the British to advance claims in that direction.[5]

Alluding "without vanity" to his own perfect knowledge of America, the equal of any British subject's, Vetch moved on to consider the colonies separately. As far as Nova Scotia was concerned, it was important to clarify the allegiance of the French inhabitants and the Indians. Indian trade and loyalty were given to the French, which meant that Nova Scotia existed with "many enemies in our bosom." Trade was not developing, he pointed out, and French encroachment on the valuable Nova Scotian fisheries was seriously undercutting the British fishing enterprises. In case of war, the colony would be seriously exposed.

Vetch thought that New England's major problems were declining trade and commerce and frontier attacks in which "whole towns are barbarously butchered." The fishery, fur trade, and naval stores industries were all affected by the fact that Indians, properly tributary to New England, were employed by the French against the British. A similar problem beset New York, occasioned by the French success in winning the Iroquois over to their interest. In case of another war, Vetch believed, "it might go near entirely to win the upper part of that colony, so valuable not only for the fur, peltry, and naval stores trade, but for being one of the best granaries in the world for supporting our West India Company's colonies." French influence over the savages had lately become serious in the Carolinas, and this influence was a matter which concerned Virginia, although to a lesser degree. In the Carolinas, the French had succeeded in "debauching over to their interest" the Indians, "whom they hounded out underhand to destroy our people and settlements there, to such a degree as had almost en-

5. Vetch to Board of Trade, Aug. 3, 1714, Public Archives of Nova Scotia, V, no. 36 (Dalhousie University, Halifax).

tirely unpeopled and ruined the two flourishing young colonies of North and South Carolina."

The remedy was clear. Great Britain's commissioners must set boundary lines, regulate the fisheries, agree on the extent of inland trade and commerce to be allowed between the French and British colonies, and make a formal agreement with each tribe of Indians, specifying "under whose government they shall hereafter be esteemed to be, together with their trade." Vetch urged quick action while the two Crowns were in "so perfect and good an understanding" and insinuated his own abilities for executing the plan. He delivered his memorial only a few days after the death of Queen Anne. In the attendant excitement, he was probably justified in going into no more detail than he did.[6]

In the fall of 1715, Vetch presented the Board of Trade with a résumé of the situation in Nova Scotia, pointing out the error of having permitted France to retain Cape Breton and stressing the continued neglect of the garrison, the necessity of reviving the Indian trade, and the potentialities of the fishery. During the winter, the Board also considered the broad issues of trade and commerce in the colonies, and Vetch appeared several times to inform its members about the state of his colony. Dummer, representing Massachusetts, Joshua Gee, agent for Pennsylvania, and Boon and Beresford for the Carolinas appeared along with Vetch and Borland.[7]

Vetch also attempted to settle the accounts of his father-in-law, whose creditors were clamoring for payment. Commenting on a family quarrel over money matters, Vetch made an observation which also applied to Livingston's accounts: It was hard, he protested, "that the exorbitant love of money should rob mankind of natural affection, reason, and religion." "Had I money," Vetch wrote Livingston, "I would have satisfied them for your reputation's sake, and shall when I get money tho I should never receive it again." For the moment, Vetch promised to do the best he

6. Memorial from Colonel Vetch relating to the settling of limits between the French and British Colonies on the Continent of America, Webster Papers (New Brunswick Museum).

7. Feb. 10 and 16, Mar. 28, 1716, *Board of Trade Journal, 1715-18*, 113-15, 127; Ottawa Transcripts of Nova Scotia Archives, VII, 51, 141, 184, VIII, 5 (Public Archives of Canada, Ottawa); *Nova Scotia Archives*, II, 24-38.

could; he hoped to be free of his own financial difficulties after the government settled Nova Scotian affairs.[8]

With the accession of George I, in the fall of 1714, Vetch decided to request reinstatement in his governorship and payment on his accounts. Elections in January 1715 returned a decisive Whig majority to Parliament in support of a preponderantly Whig ministry. Bolingbroke and Oxford were out. Vetch's old friend, Sunderland, was back in office as lord-lieutenant of Ireland. Marlborough was again commander-in-chief of the British army, and the two Secretaries of State were Charles, Lord Townshend, a leader in the negotiations at Utrecht, and James Stanhope, who had played a brillant role as minister to Spain. Stanhope had returned to England in 1712 and with Robert Walpole had taken a leading part in building up Whig power in the House of Commons. Walpole was shortly to become First Lord of the Treasury and George's leading minister. For the moment, Stanhope, Townshend, and Marlborough were in chief control of affairs.

Under these circumstances, Vetch had no great difficulty in asserting his pre-eminent qualifications as governor of Nova Scotia and his claim for proper recompense. Nicholson, as a Tory, fell into disfavor and lost influence at court. In December, Secretary Townshend was persuaded to submit Vetch's application to the Board of Trade, which took up the case early in January.[9]

Vetch put himself forward as the one who had formed the scheme for the reduction of Canada and who had played a leading role in the conquest of Port Royal. With his instruction from Queen Anne to prepare the expedition of 1709, he produced his letters tracing the events of the intervening years. He referred the Board to his correspondence in the office of the secretary of state and the war office as evidence of his contention that he had regularly petitioned the ministry for orders to guide him in the administration of Annapolis Royal but had received no instructions whatever. To support his argument that the British government

8. Vetch to Robert Livingston, Aug. 25, Robert Livingston to Philip Livingston, Apr. 23, 1716, Livingston Papers.

9. Dec. 20, 1714, Ottawa Transcripts of Nova Scotia Archives, V, 175 (Public Archives of Canada, Ottawa); Vetch's Memorial stating his services, asking payment for himself and Borland, and a second Memorial praying reinstatement as governor on the basis of his record, *ibid.*, 189.

had only itself to blame if his actions had not been satisfactory, he referred the Board to his agents, Douglas and Borland, who could testify to his efforts.

The Board of Trade sent an inquiry to Pringle, secretary to the successive ministers who had been charged with colonial affairs, and he duly affirmed that no orders had been sent to Vetch. Borland, who had come to England, and Douglas appeared before the Board to add their evidences. Douglas stated that he had received a letter by every ship from Vetch addressed to the Queen's ministers, but he had no answers from any of them. The Lord Treasurer, he added, had refused to read letters which had Vetch's name on them, even when delivered personally by Nicholson.

Borland's testimony struck a savage blow at Nicholson. He had informed Nicholson of the suffering and neglect of the Annapolis garrison occasioned by the failure of British support or aid from New England and had pointed out that the outpost would have been lost without the money he advanced. Nicholson's comment, according to Borland, was that it would have been better if it had been so.[10]

Two weeks later, the Board again considered Vetch's affairs. Jeremy Dummer was present to declare that Vetch was "a man of good sense, well affected to the government, and a good soldier." Dummer had heard no complaints against him except those of Nicholson and he considered them "no way related to his character or courage." A number of London merchants also came before the Board to state that they knew only of Nicholson's complaints and that they looked upon these as "very violent and arbitrary." They pointed out that Nicholson had attached Vetch's property before he had examined Vetch's accounts. As far as they were concerned, "Col. Vetch always had a very good character for integrity, sense, worth, honor, and military abilities," and no one knew North America better than he did. A letter to the Board from Vetch's old friend, John Chamberlayne of the Society for the Propagation of the Gospel, put the matter succinctly when it noted that Vetch had not only won Nova Scotia from the French

10. Jan. 3 and 4, 1715, *Board of Trade Journal, 1709-15,* 582, 584-85; Jan. 13, 1715, Ottawa Transcripts of Nova Scotia Archives, VI, 120 (Public Archives of Canada, Ottawa).

but had also kept it in spite of all that the French had attempted and the British had left unattempted.[11]

Vetch's testimony in his own behalf was the most damaging of all against Nicholson. When Vetch first returned from Nova Scotia, Nicholson had begun to apologize for superseding him as governor; but when Vetch had urged that strenuous efforts be made to preserve the Annapolis garrison, Nicholson had told him "in his passionate way" that those efforts were considered Vetch's greatest crime by the Tory ministry. When the Crown sent neither money nor orders, Nicholson thought that Vetch should have realized it intended to abandon Nova Scotia. That the colony had not been given up vitiated this argument, but Nicholson seemed unaware of the fallacy of his reasoning.

Vetch had been surprised at Nicholson's attitude until he heard of an incident in Ireland, where Nicholson had tarried on his way to America. Some of his retinue had been imprisoned for drinking the Pretender's health, whereupon Nicholson was reported to have labeled the Irish in Cork "a damn'd nest of Whigs." He had gone further to "repute it a crime to drink the succession in the House of Hanover" and swore in public that whoever was not for "indefeasible hereditary right" was to be accounted an enemy of Church and Crown. That Nicholson exposed "his errand and designs in all companies" Vetch attributed to his "violent natural temper which is a continued degree of madness" and his being "entirely illiterate (having but lately learned to sign his name)." Although Vetch considered that Nicholson's temper and slight education rendered him incapable of any political undertaking, he had heard that the Tories justified his appointment as governor, saying "he was very fit for the errand, since by his madness and indiscretion he might irritate those people to commit some irregularities as might prove a handle to forfeit their charters."[12]

The other side was presented by Sir Charles Hobby. With General Hill, the Tory favorite, no longer on the scene to bear

11. Jan. 17, 1715, *Board of Trade Journal, 1709-15,* 590-91; Ottawa Transcripts of Nova Scotia Archives, VI, 24 (Public Archives of Canada, Ottawa).

12. Vetch's Petition to Lord Townshend, forwarded to the Board of Trade, Dec. 20, 1714, *Cal. State Papers, 1714-15,* no. 122ii.

witness to Hobby's recalcitrance during the expedition of 1711, the ex-deputy governor of Nova Scotia was now eager to claim the governorship of the province for himself. He had invested heavily in land around Annapolis Royal and apparently had high hopes for the future of the colony. He charged Vetch with harsh treatment of the Acadians, citing the occasion when Vetch had sent a detachment of seventy men to compel the French to cut trees for the repair of the fort. According to Hobby, the British force had been ordered to kill the inhabitants' swine and poultry to enforce obedience, and this practice had so angered the French that they had committed the notorious massacre of the force in June of 1711. Hobby said that Vetch had ordered the inhabitants to furnish timber for the fort without pay. The testimony of the merchants who had appeared in Vetch's behalf was discounted as "fulsome flattery he received . . . drawn up by a parcel of mercenary fools and pedlars which is as scandalously false as it is foolish." Vetch's administration was characterized as "arbitrary and loose."[13]

Dummer was quick to refute Hobby's charges. Vetch himself, called before the Board, was able to show the complete untruthfulness of every item. The French had been paid for their labors in behalf of the garrison. Sir Charles had not seen Vetch's orders to Forbes and therefore did not know that the party which had gone out to oversee the cutting of timber had explicit orders to kill only poultry in its demonstration and then only if necessary to intimidate the French. In addition, they had been told to pay for any chickens killed. Actually, the party had been ambushed by Indians, who had just arrived in the area from Canada, and knew nothing of Forbes' mission. The British had never reached the place where the inhabitants were supposed to be cutting trees and had never had a chance to make their threats against the Acadians' livestock.[14]

13. Jan. 17, 1715, *Board of Trade Journal, 1709-15,* 591; Ottawa Transcripts of Nova Scotia Archives, V, 133 (Public Archives of Canada, Ottawa). For deeds of land to Hobby, see Public Archives of Nova Scotia, VIII, nos. 144-45 (Dalhousie University, Halifax).

14. For the account of the Forbes massacre, see Chap. VIII above, and Mascarene's account in Nova Scotia Hist. Soc., *Collections,* 4 (1884), 69 ff. The British government had long since been informed of the facts; Vetch to Dartmouth, June 18, 1711, *Cal. State Papers, 1710-11,* no. 887.

Vetch was supported by four of his former Annapolis officers, Captain Blackmore, Lieutenant Erskine, Commissary Jackson, and the surgeon of the fort. Vetch, they affirmed, was universally beloved by all the officers and soldiers of the garrison for his humanity and good treatment, whereas Hobby treated them badly and had their hearty ill-will. They cited the incident of the supply ship which had arrived at Annapolis while Hobby was commanding. The deputy governor had confined the officers to the fort and bought all the vessel's liquor and provisions, selling them later to the officers at his own price.

Hobby reasserted his arguments and also declared that Vetch's attempt to levy an indemnity on the inhabitants outside the area around the fort was contrary to the articles of capitulation which the British had signed with the French. But the text of the surrender agreement easily refuted this contention, and Vetch flatly contradicted Hobby's other allegations. Hobby was reduced to lame pleading that he could produce evidence if given time and, finally, to admitting that he had no proof in support of his statements. To this the Board speedily agreed; he had offered nothing of sufficient weight to warrant holding up approval of Vetch's nomination for the governorship. With the conclusion of the hearings on January 18, the Board of Trade recommended Vetch to Secretary Stanhope.[15] Two days later, George I signed Vetch's commission as governor of Nova Scotia. For the first time Vetch had an official directive from the Crown for the administration of the outpost. It remained to determine a policy for the colony and to arrange its support and settlement.[16]

Hobby immediately petitioned for the lieutenant governorship. Vetch magnanimously agreed to accept him, or to retain Caulfeild, as the Board should determine. Despite their recent dispute before the Board, Vetch maintained that he harbored no resentment against Hobby and believed that they would get on well together. He agreed that Sir Charles had done a great deal to further the settlement of Nova Scotia and had laid out money

15. Jan. 17, 1715, *Board of Trade Journal, 1709-15*, 592-93; Ottawa Transcripts of Nova Scotia Archives, VI, 26, 34 (Public Archives of Canada, Ottawa).

16. Vetch's Commission, Jan. 20, 1715, Public Archives of Nova Scotia, V, no. 15 (Dalhousie University, Halifax).

for land and buildings to that end. The Board of Trade accordingly decided to present no objection to Stanhope's appointing Hobby to the post if he so desired, but it warned that it would not tolerate further quarreling with Vetch which would prejudice the public service.[17] It was a vain hope for Sir Charles; he did not receive the office. Instead, it remained in the hands of Thomas Caulfeild during the remainder of Vetch's tenure. The outcome was important for Nova Scotia, because Caulfeild was unquestionably a steadier man, who got along well with both the garrison and the neighboring inhabitants. Since Vetch never returned to America to take up his governorship personally, it was left to Caulfeild to manage alone. Under the circumstances of continued neglect and uncertainty, the outpost probably would not have proved attractive to Hobby.[18]

During the spring of 1715, the Board of Trade continued to sit frequently to consider the situation in Britain's new colony. Earlier, Vetch, in response to its queries, had testified concerning the attitude of the Acadians after the fall of Port Royal. He outlined the disloyalty which had been manifest when, after swearing allegiance to Her Majesty, the inhabitants had risen in arms and blockaded the fort during the winter and spring of 1711. Only the end of the war had made Annapolis safe for the British, and Vetch was sure that the French would not prove trustworthy if another conflict broke out.

Three months later, Vetch reported to the Board on the French proposal that the inhabitants of Nova Scotia be permitted to move; most wished to go to Cape Breton. Vetch had once advocated the deportation of the French inhabitants, assuming that they would be removed to a much more distant location and replaced by loyal British settlers. Now he saw the matter in a different light. The peace terms had returned Cape Breton to the French, and the inhabitants would be a potential danger to Annapolis. At the least, their departure would leave the garrison without the labor force and the local farmers' provisions which it needed. Also, the British government showed no sign of attempting to attract set-

17. Feb. 7, 1715, *Board of Trade Journal, 1709-15*, 596; Ottawa Transcripts of Nova Scotia Archives, VI, 52, 65 (Public Archives of Canada, Ottawa).

18. For Caulfeild's correspondence as lieutenant governor, see Governor's Letter Book, 1713-17, *Nova Scotia Archives*, II, 1-50.

tlers to Nova Scotia. If the French left, Vetch feared that the colony would be permanently depopulated.

He estimated that Nova Scotia contained approximately five hundred families, about two thousand five hundred people. They would double the population of Cape Breton. With their skills at woodcraft, agriculture, and fishing, the Acadians and their Indians would make Cape Breton the most powerful French colony in America, a constant threat "to all British colonies as well as to the universal trade of Great Britain." By removing their livestock to Cape Breton, the French would give that settlement an initial advantage of thousands of black cattle, sheep, and hogs, already acclimated to the severe climate. It would cost £100,000 to stock the colony in a like manner from France. To replenish Nova Scotia would take time and thousands of pounds, and the question of whether New England-bred livestock could survive and produce in the colder climate would have to be considered.

The inhabitants who proposed to leave Nova Scotia, it was reported, intended to sell their holdings to the British. Vetch questioned this procedure. In the first place, British colonists could obtain free land in the other British colonies, so they would be unlikely to buy land in Nova Scotia; the area would remain unsettled. Moreover, according to the royal instructions to the army which originally captured Port Royal, the land was to be given to those who shared in its conquest. Vetch found nothing in the terms of the peace treaty which provided the French an opportunity to sell. They had been granted the right to stay or leave the colony within a year, but there was no provision to indemnify those who chose to depart. Vetch was of the opinion that most of them would remain in Nova Scotia if it were not for the pressure which the French government was putting on them to cross to Cape Breton and build up that settlement.[19]

The problem of how to treat the Acadians was one which had troubled Vetch from the beginning. After the peace, French efforts to reclaim their subjects and resettle them in Cape Breton made it even more difficult to administer a firm British policy.

19. Aug. 13, Nov. 23, and Dec. 22, 1714, *Board of Trade Journal, 1709-15,* 559, 573-77; Vetch to Board of Trade, Nov. 24, received and read Dec. 22, 1714, Public Archives of Nova Scotia, V, no. 40 (Dalhousie University, Halifax).

No easy solution existed. If the French were allowed to depart, the consequences would very likely be those which Vetch outlined. If they were held against their will, they would be a constant source of trouble and, in wartime, completely unreliable. It was a matter which was to concern the British for many years to come.

Evidence began to come in indicating that Nicholson's record offered little which would have argued his continuance in office even had he been of the ruling political persuasion. After his arrival in America, he had not gone to Annapolis Royal until late summer, 1714, and then he had remained only a few months. Nicholson's sojourn at Annapolis had been long enough, however, to disillusion those who had been inclined to take his part against Vetch. "As he used to curse and damn Governor Vetch and all his friends," wrote one of the members of the garrison, "he is now served himself in the same manner." On his arrival he had pulled down the fort, driven off the French, and carried away the English so that the place had been left desolate. He passed his time in implacable malice against Vetch, the writer concluded, and did more mischief in two months than Vetch could have done in a lifetime.[20]

Soon after Vetch's departure for England, Nicholson sent clothing remaining from the expedition against Canada for the use of the Annapolis garrison and for sale to the Acadians. The goods were shoddy, entirely unfit for the cold climate of Nova Scotia. Caulfeild reported a great many of the items "damnified . . . rotten and useless" and discovered that coats which Nicholson sold for twenty-one shillings could be bought elsewhere for six—Nicholson himself was selling the same articles in Boston at half the price. Neither the French nor the Indians would buy from the Annapolis traders when they could get items cheaper from Boston merchants. The consequence was serious for the garrison; Caulfeild wrote that there were "neither shoes, stockings, nor watch coats in store to keep our men from perishing."[21]

20. Adams to Steel, Vetch's agent in Boston, Jan. 24, 1715, Ottawa Transcripts of Nova Scotia Archives, VI, 50 (Public Archives of Canada, Ottawa). Nicholson left Boston for England late in Dec. 1714, *Nova Scotia Archives*, II, 8; also see Nicholson to Moody, Dec. 20, 1714, Public Archives of Nova Scotia, VII (Dalhousie University, Halifax).

21. Correspondence of Caulfeild concerning the clothing situation, Apr. 20, 1714, to Nov. 1715, *Nova Scotia Archives*, II, 4, 6, 9, 15, 30-31; Hunter to

In his treatment of the French inhabitants, Nicholson had presumably been guided by a letter he had received from Queen Anne just before he departed for America. In exchange for Louis XIV's promise to release his Protestant subjects who had been condemned to the galleys, the Queen offered to allow her French subjects in Nova Scotia to remain there without dispossession or to sell their lands to the British if they chose. Under urging from French emissaries sent by the governor of Cape Breton, a large number of the inhabitants determined to avail themselves of this opportunity. Nicholson, who was present at the meeting of the Acadians when this plan was decided, gave his consent. But when the French living near Annapolis attempted to remove, Nicholson refused to let them sell even their personal effects.[22]

Outside the immediate area of the fort, the French were free to go or stay, as they saw fit, and there was little that Nicholson or anybody else could do to keep them in Nova Scotia. Actually, according to the reports of the French authorities at Cape Breton, the Acadians were extremely reluctant to leave their homes; during the following years, attempts to induce them to migrate were largely unsuccessful.

Nicholson's unfriendliness actually drove away some of the French who would have stayed. His policy was unaccountable to Caulfeild. He agreed to let the French sell their homes and land, then reversed himself, and finally shut the gates of the fort against the inhabitants, declaring to his soldiers that "the French were all rebels, and would certainly cut . . . [your] throats if . . . [you] went into their houses." Nicholson knew full well that the British could subsist only with the help of the neighboring farmers.

If Vetch had not dispatched a ship from England with nine months' provisions soon after regaining his governorship, Caulfeild would have been in sore straits because of Nicholson's "malicious neglect of the province and garrison." Caulfeild concluded

Nicholson, Oct. 26, 1713, Ottawa Transcripts of Nova Scotia Archives, IV, 145 (Public Archives of Canada, Ottawa).

22. Queen Anne to Nicholson, June 25, 1713, Public Archives of Nova Scotia, V, no. 12, and see nos. 37-38 (Dalhousie University, Halifax); Ottawa Transcripts of Nova Scotia Archives, V, 16-33, 35, 39 (Public Archives of Canada, Ottawa); Parkman, *Half-Century of Conflict*, I, chap. IX.

that it would puzzle the wisest head in Europe to find anything Nicholson had done of the least benefit to the garrison or colony. Had his designs been carried into effect, the deputy governor was convinced that "there would not be an inhabitant of any kind in the country nor a garrison on foot." To cover his neglect, Caulfeild wrote Walpole, Nicholson was representing Nova Scotia as not worth maintaining. Indeed, such a belief on Nicholson's part seemed the only way to account for his actions.[23]

But Nicholson, like Vetch, had returned to England to defend himself. When Borland complained in February that Nicholson had questioned his accounts and was blocking payment, the Board called in Nicholson, who had just arrived in England. Nicholson coolly offered no objections to Borland's accounts. But he was not to get off so easily. The departure of the French settlers from Nova Scotia was worrying Vetch, and he asked the Board to prevent the ruin of the province which would ensue if all the Acadians removed to Cape Breton. Thereupon, the Board asked Nicholson to appear again and defend his policy toward the inhabitants.[24]

This time Nicholson arrogantly defended his actions. Better to let the French go, he said, than harbor such disloyal elements within the colony. He pointed to the Acadians' subversive activity against the British, instigated by the Jesuit agents of the French rulers. Vetch contended that the departure of the French should be stopped, and Hobby and Shirreff, a member of the Annapolis garrison who had come to England to settle Caulfeild's private accounts, appeared before the Board in support of Vetch. Shirreff suggested that Caulfeild, as one well affected to the French and held by them in high esteem, was quite capable of stopping their exodus and repairing the damage done by Nicholson.[25]

23. Caulfeild to Vetch, Nov. 1, 1715, *Nova Scotia Archives*, II, 15-17, 28-29, 31.

24. Mar. 9, 1715, *Board of Trade Journal, 1709-15*, 617; Ottawa Transcripts of Nova Scotia Archives, VI, 81 (Public Archives of Canada, Ottawa).

25. Nicholson had received the appeal of La Ronde Denys and Pensens "that justice be done all the inhabitants for the vexations which were inflicted on them under the rule of Lord [*sic*] Vetch and Colonel Hobby in the interval between the capitulation and the peace"; Aug. 23, 1714, Public Archives of Nova Scotia, VII, no. 1 (Dalhousie University, Halifax); Mar. 15, 1715, *Board of Trade Journal, 1715-18*, 4, 15; Ottawa Transcripts of Nova Scotia Archives, VI, 84, 92, 107 (Public Archives of Canada, Ottawa).

Finally, early in May, the Board of Trade considered measures for the support of the garrison at Annapolis. Here, Nicholson underwent his most severe questioning and emerged at last discredited. During the course of discussions on provisioning and supplying the soldiers, Vetch brought up the clothing fiasco. He testified to the poor quality, insufficient amount, and exorbitant prices of the clothing and was supported in his remarks by a number of others acquainted with the situation. Nicholson was forced to agree that the clothing was not fit for northern climates. When pressed, he admitted that he had not reported its inadequacy and then went on to add, loftily, that he could not be bothered to "charge his memory" with complaints of the soldiers. This feeble excuse was not allowed to stand, however; evidence was made available that the complaints about the clothing had been presented in writing to Nicholson.

Nicholson denied that the Annapolis garrison was in difficult circumstances for lack of provisions. He boasted that he had fed the soldiers for five pence less a day per man than had Vetch. But Vetch knew better: The British soldiers still needed pay and provisions, as they had during most of the years since Nova Scotia had been taken. Shirreff had recent firsthand knowledge of the situation and supported Vetch. Caulfeild's brother presented a letter he had received from the lieutenant governor which told of the hardships of the men and ascribed them to Nicholson's ill-treatment. If the Board remained in any doubt on which side the truth lay, its doubts would presently be banished. Letters from Caulfeild were even then crossing the ocean recounting the "unhappy circumstances of this, His Majesty's garrison," and enclosing the accounts which proved "the straits we are put to, having lived a considerable time on half allowance, and I am at this time obliged to send a sloop to represent our case to the governor of New England."[26]

On May 20, the Board held its final hearing on Nova Scotia. Vetch presented his commission as governor of the province and a

26. May 10-16, 1715, *Board of Trade Journal, 1715-18*, 26-32; Ottawa Transcripts of Nova Scotia Archives, VI, 169, 175, 179, 183, 198-99, 203 (Public Archives of Canada, Ottawa); Caulfeild to Privy Council, to Secretary of War, and to Secretary Stanhope, May 3, 1715, *Nova Scotia Archives*, II, 12, 14.

letter which set forth in detail the counts against Nicholson's actions. He reiterated the need of the Annapolis garrison for a provisions allowance in addition to pay until such time as the colony became self-subsisting. He recommended victualing the troops on a contract basis and suggested Borland as the best agent for the task; if his arrears were paid he could possibly be persuaded to assume the responsibility again. In its report, the Board summed up the situation in Nova Scotia and largely followed Vetch's policy recommendations.[27]

One result of the Board's months of consideration was the dispatch of a nine months' supply of provisions to the garrison. Back pay was more of a problem, for Nicholson had thoroughly entangled the pay accounts of the men and officers. Caulfeild was compelled to spend additional weary months of correspondence to get the garrison its back salaries—if, indeed, the full amount was ever paid.[28]

Yet for all his faults, Nicholson possessed a devotion to duty and the welfare of Britain's colonies which was all too rare among early eighteenth-century officials. A hasty and overmastering temper led him into great excesses, but his real contributions to colonial America cannot be denied. His zeal for party and the egotism fostered in him by the Queen's broad commission to investigate colonial affairs doubtless explain his highhanded attitude in 1713. In his arrogance as an instrument of Tory policy, he had been guilty of rash actions. Essentially, however, his views and those of Vetch corresponded closely in matters of general colonial policy. With Vetch, he was to appear frequently before the Board of Trade in the following years to give advice in colonial matters. He had before him the discharge of one more important assignment in the colonies, that of governor of South Carolina.[29]

27. May 11, 20, 1715, *Board of Trade Journal, 1715-18,* 27, 34; May 18-20, 1715, Ottawa Transcripts of Nova Scotia Archives, VII, 1, 6 (Public Archives of Canada, Ottawa).

28. See Caulfeild's acknowledgment of receipt of provisions, but continued complaints about pay and the need for adequate clothing and bedding; *Nova Scotia Archives,* II, 22-39. The latter was furnished late in 1716, *ibid.,* 44.

29. Nicholson's treatment of Vetch is similar to his unaccountable actions on previous occasions. Nicholson's important role as a "professional" colonial governor deserves treatment in a full-length biography; his illiteracy explains the lack of any body of correspondence that might have called forth an earlier biography.

The Board of Trade's lengthy deliberations about Nova Scotia resulted in Vetch's reappointment as governor, Caulfeild's warrant as his deputy, the establishment of the garrison as independent companies in the Regular army, and the eventual dispatch of clothing and food supplies. There were far more weighty problems: how best to provide for the settlement of the country and the development of its resources; how to define its boundaries; how to regulate its trade and its relations with other colonies; and what to do with the French inhabitants. But they were all too complicated for officials new in office, busy establishing the Hanoverian line. Many of these matters were still to be negotiated with the French, and some depended on large questions of colonial policy yet to be considered.[30]

Moreover, the Board of Trade was a strictly advisory body. Evidence brought out in hearings could lead to action only as it was incorporated in recommendations on specific measures which had been referred to the Board. It could not initiate policies or recommend actions, no matter how necessary its hearings disclosed them to be. It was not advisable to neglect the Board of Trade, since it was invariably called upon for an opinion in matters concerning the colonies. But Vetch knew, as his past actions had indicated, that application must be made to an appropriate Crown officer in order to initiate any measures of consequence. Colonial policy originated with the Secretaries of State, the Treasurer, or, to a lesser extent, the lords of the admiralty and the war office. These officials constituted an inner circle of the Privy Council—in effect, an early cabinet. Under the authority of the King and Council, or, increasingly, the acts of Parliament, they originated specific measures. That Vetch neglected these other officials is most improbable; nevertheless, he undoubtedly realized that their time was taken up with a multitude of things, details concerned with the recent party change and the Treaty of Utrecht.

With his reappointment as governor of Nova Scotia, Vetch's work was largely done. He was not to return to America, however. Until he was superseded by Governor Philipps in August 1717, he left the administration of Nova Scotia to Caulfeild.

30. They were part of the over-all situation included in the Board of Trade's review of the colonial system in 1721.

That conscientious deputy struggled as best he could with an always difficult situation. He died at his post in March 1717. In England, Vetch busied himself with attempts to make better provision for his colony and to devise further schemes of his own. Time and again, he gave valuable advice to the government in matters with which he was well acquainted. He remained close to the center of colonial affairs, but his appearance before committees became more and more infrequent. Of the details of his existence, little is known.[31]

In Boston, Margaret Vetch grew increasingly impatient over Vetch's continued absence. It was September 1717, and she had given up hopes of seeing her husband for another winter; his absence was "a very great affliction" for the family. By October, Mrs. Vetch had received news of Vetch's loss of the governorship. "Not knowing when he may return to this place," she decided to go to London with her family. It was a resolve she had made before, only to delay in the hope that Vetch would soon return. Borland had written from England that she should remain in Boston with the children, saying that Vetch had difficulties enough without having to care for his family in London. But Mrs. Vetch had different views. She planned to take both children and sold most of her household goods. At the last minute, "considering the hazard of a winter voyage and Mr. Vetch being unsettled," she decided to leave Alida in Boston. She and Billy sailed in November to join Vetch.[32]

Reunion with his family must have been one of the few bright spots in Vetch's last years, when his hopes were often raised high and just as often dashed. The Board of Trade still relied on the former governor's advice and often requested it on broader

31. Commissions of Governor Philipps, Aug. 17, 1717, and Lieutenant Governor Doucett, May 25, 1717, Public Archives of Nova Scotia, V, nos. 13, 14 (Dalhousie University, Halifax); report of Caulfeild's death on Mar. 2, 1717, Ottawa Transcripts of Nova Scotia Archives, VIII, 73 (Public Archives of Canada, Ottawa).

32. Margaret Vetch to Robert Livingston, Boston, Apr. 22, Sept. 16, Oct. 15 and 21, and Nov. 4, Borland to Robert Livingston, Jan. 1717, Livingston Papers. Nothing more is known about Vetch's son. He may not have survived the voyage, or he may have succumbed to the smallpox which was raging in London at the time. It is assumed that he died before his parents did, since no mention of him is found in Mrs. Vetch's later correspondence or in her will.

problems of colonial policy.[33] In the summer and fall of 1719, two members of the Board, Bladen and Pulteney, were empowered as His Majesty's commissaries to treat with the French in the matter of colonial boundaries, one of the issues remaining from the peace treaty. Vetch urged a comprehensive settlement of the whole thorny question and offered his views concerning the proper boundaries of New York and Nova Scotia. The St. Lawrence, he suggested, had always marked the northern boundary of the latter province, and he recommended maintaining that line, excepting Cape Breton and other islands specifically reserved to the French by the treaty. Cape Breton, he feared, was growing year by year into a more formidable threat to the British colonies, but it was too late now to rectify the errors of Utrecht.

But it was not too late, Vetch believed, to insist that the French cease their persistent encroachment on the lands they had ceded to the British. The French had established a fishery at the Strait of Canso, on the islands which lay in the eastern end of the Gut; under the ambiguous wording of the Treaty of Utrecht, they insisted that these islands were in the mouth of the St. Lawrence and were therefore French possessions. For the British, this was opening the mouth of the river too far. After studying the colony's original charter of James I to Sir William Alexander, the Board agreed with Vetch and ordered Bladen and Pulteney to insist on the old boundary and the clearer wording of the Latin text of the treaty rather than the French version. It was a difficult order—one that proved impossible to carry out—and Bladen had brusque words for Vetch's advice.[34]

Early in 1719, Vetch undertook an entirely new project.

33. Osgood, *Eighteenth Century*, II, Part II, chap. I. The Board's concentrated attention resulted in the famous report of 1721; *Cal. State Papers, 1721*, nos. 656, 657.

34. Instructions to Pulteney and Bladen, *Cal. State Papers, 1719-20*, no. 443; July 30–Aug., 1719, *Board of Trade Journal, 1718-22*, 88-91; June 9, 1719, Ottawa Transcripts of Nova Scotia Archives, X, 111, 113 (Public Archives of Canada, Ottawa); Bladen to Craggs, Nov. 25, 1719, P.R.O. (Foreign Office Papers), France, 166, f. 77. The following year negotiations were still going on, and Vetch added to his previous testimony on the Nova Scotian boundaries, particularly in the matter of the little islands which lay off the southern end of Cape Breton in the Strait of Canso; Aug. 9, Sept. 13 and 14, and Dec. 6, 1720, *Board of Trade Journal, 1718-22*, 196, 208, 209, 236; Ottawa Transcripts of Nova Scotia Archives, XI, 208, XII, 50 (Public Archives of Canada, Ottawa).

Along with his agent Douglas, Sir Alexander Cairns, an erstwhile member of the Annapolis garrison named Capon, and other officers who had been concerned with the capture of Port Royal, he petitioned the Board of Trade for grants of land on the Lahave River, opposite Annapolis on the east coast of Nova Scotia. Such grants involved the customary rights of fishermen to land and dry fish along the coast; the request also brought up the whole question of how land should be parceled out in the new colony. The Board of Trade did not attempt to solve these problems, for land could not be granted until the whole colony had been surveyed. Nevertheless, Vetch renewed his application the following year and managed to get the Privy Council to give it consideration. He brought the matter up again early in 1723, and the Board finally agreed to refer the matter to Governor Philipps. The surveyor of the King's Woods in New England was ordered to Nova Scotia to survey the whole area so that settlement might proceed. But in May 1724, nothing had been done, and Vetch requested still another hearing on his petition for land.[35]

Vetch and his fellow petitioners originally proposed to establish at least four hundred families within three years of the grant and to build one or more stockaded towns. The Board was convinced that it would be advantageous to have Nova Scotia settled only "upon proper conditions," with extensive tracts reserved for naval stores, a strict understanding about the governing authority, reservation of fishermen's rights, and provision for an annual quitrent payable to the Crown after the first four years. It therefore suggested that Vetch's group reduce the size of its requested tract and agree to restrictions which it advocated.[36]

35. Feb. 5, 1719, May 19, and July 1, 1720, *Board of Trade Journal, 1718-22,* 34, 166, 172-78; Mar. 5-20, 1723, May 13, June 4, 6, and 10, and July 15, 16, and 21, 1724, *ibid., 1723-28,* 13, 15, 91, 98, 100, 106-8. Also see Ottawa Transcripts of Nova Scotia Archives, X, 138, 141, XVI, 30-33, 75 (Public Archives of Canada, Ottawa). Jeremy Dummer wrote Massachusetts Bay officials in Apr. 1720 indicating that this group intended to monopolize the fishing grounds rather than settle towns and plantations, warning that Vetch and his friends hoped "to sit lazily at the receipt of custom, to gather in their toll and grow rich at our expense." He also noted the interest of Thomas Coram in Nova Scotia lands. Mass. Hist. Soc., *Collections,* 3rd ser., 1 (1825), 141-42.

36. *Cal. State Papers, 1719-20,* no. 219; Sept. 4, 1723, *ibid., 1722-23,* nos. 708, 709. The recommended quitrent was designated as hemp, in specified amounts, the amount to be doubled after twelve years and trebled after twenty,

Although the petitioners accepted both recommendations, they met with no success. Meanwhile, the South Sea Company asked for land in Nova Scotia. Vetch and his associates protested against any grant to that group, fearing that it might include the better part of the area they were interested in. The South Sea Company met with no better luck than Vetch. When the South Sea Bubble burst, Vetch hurriedly pledged that any lands his group received would not become the object of speculation.[37]

By 1724 Vetch had launched an even more ambitious project: He sought the governorship of Massachusetts. For nearly a decade, the British government had tried sporadically to revoke the charters of the independent colonies in America. A parliamentary attempt to recall the charters by legislative act had failed in 1715, but in 1721 the Board of Trade compiled an elaborate report calling for colonial reorganization. Drawing on reports received as answers to a questionnaire sent to the colonies, the Board outlined problems of government, defense, boundaries, and trade which required urgent attention. Stressing the necessity for more centralized administrative machinery which would eliminate the divided authority in colonial affairs exercised by the King's Council and secretaries, Parliament, and the Board of Trade, it suggested more closely co-ordinated administration in the colonies, unification of the colonial military command, and accurate delimitation of territorial claims. Accurately mirroring the recommendations which Vetch and other colonial leaders had long been urging, it also proposed measures to define and enforce the commercial statutes and to encourage the colonists in industries such as naval stores which would benefit the empire. Unfortunately, the Board was unable to gain status as an independent executive department, which would have given it centralized authority in colonial affairs. Unification of the colonial military establishment was defeated when Lord Stairs declined the proffered post of commander-in-chief. In America, the colonists, fearing for rights and privileges

---

so that it would remain a valuable consideration rather than become a mere gesture as had happened with quitrents assessed on lands granted in other colonies.

37. Ottawa Transcripts of Nova Scotia Archives, XIII, 5, 9 (Public Archives of Canada, Ottawa). See also the earlier application for land in this region by Thomas Coram in June 1713; Hist. Mss. Comm., *Portland Mss.*, V (*Harley Papers*, III), 297.

they had long enjoyed, fought back. Jeremy Dummer's trenchant *Defense of the New England Charters* was no small factor in heading off revocation of the charters of the "independent" colonies. A split among British authorities also helped prevent action in 1721. As Dummer pointed out, "My Lords Cadogan and Carteret draw one way, and My Lord Townshend and his brother Walpole another."

Nothing was settled in 1721. Two years later, Governor Shute, who had succeeded Vetch's friend Dudley in Massachusetts, returned to England after the General Court refused to vote him a regular salary, and Vetch applied for the post. The colony was struggling along in the throes of renewed Indian warfare, and the Assembly was asserting its right to complete control of the colony's finances. In addition, it voted issues of paper money, redeemable after a period of years, instead of managing the colony within the limits of the yearly revenue from taxes. The spirit of independence abroad in the colony was not only a blatant denial of the royal prerogative, but it also challenged the power of the upper house.[38]

In pushing himself forward as the man most likely to solve the problem of royal control in Massachusetts, Vetch addressed his appeal directly to the Secretary of State, the Duke of Newcastle. After citing his past services in the colonies, Vetch informed him of the promises of previous ministers to provide for him in a colonial government. Carteret, he asserted, had indicated that he might be chosen as governor of Massachusetts Bay in the event that Shute did not return to that colony. "Considering the vast breach that is now betwixt Mr. Shute and the whole body of the people and government there," Vetch concluded that Shute's return was "next to impossible." As for his own qualifications, he ventured "without vanity" to say that "no person is more capable of serving the interest of the Crown in that country" and that no one would be more acceptable to the New Englanders. He recognized the problem which Shute had rebelled against; he knew that little salary would be voted by the Assembly. It was a situation which

38. Vetch to Duke of Newcastle, Jan. 22, 1724, P.R.O., C.O. 5, vol. 12, f. 8 (Lib. Cong. Transcripts); Osgood, *Eighteenth Century*, II, 293-98; Jeremiah Dummer to Timothy Woodbridge, Sept. 10, 1723, Colonial Society of Massachusetts, *Publications*, 6 (1904), 197 ff.

made the post unattractive to anybody except one like Vetch who had "some interest in the country."

In recommending himself, Vetch cited an impressive list of supporters, referring to such peers of the realm as the Archbishop of Canterbury; the Duke of Argyll (to whom Newcastle was then obliged for personal support, as Vetch probably knew); Lord Stairs, Britain's ambassador to France at that time; and "almost all the Scots peers." He could also call on the support of Townshend, Newcastle's colleague in the dual office of secretary of state, as well as Walpole, with whom Vetch had corresponded at the outset of the campaign of 1709, when Walpole was war secretary. The Board of Trade was also suggested as a body of men well acquainted with Vetch. Vetch was frank in his acknowledgment of Newcastle's proclivity to handle appointments himself: "I could not judge it proper," he wrote, "to apply myself to any of the above named persons before I had the honor to wait upon Your Grace in person and lay my most just pretensions before you."[39]

In fact, however, rumors about his appointment were current, for before addressing Newcastle, Vetch had submitted his application to Carteret, who was then in attendance on George I. New York heard that there was a possibility of his appointment early in January. By summer Robert Livingston was expecting the return of his son-in-law in some official capacity, and throughout the following months rumors about Vetch's departure continued to reach America. A ship reached Boston in July 1725 with news that Vetch had "kissed the King's hand" and had been designated governor of Massachusetts, but a letter from Vetch to his daughter said nothing about it.[40] Indeed, nothing ever came of it. Shute remained in England but retained the governorship until November 1727, when it was finally decided to make Burnet the governor of Massachusetts and send Colonel John Montgomery to replace Burnet in New York.

Vetch's final appearance before the Board of Trade took place in May 1727, when the Board again asked him for knowledge of Nova Scotia, particularly for suggestions of means to induce set-

39. P.R.O., C.O. 5, vol. 12, f. 8 (Lib. Cong. Transcripts).

40. Philip Livingston to Robert Livingston, Albany, Jan. 4 and June 10, 1724, Stephen Bayard (Vetch's son-in-law) to Robert Livingston, July 8, 11, and 25, 1725, Livingston Papers.

tlers to go to the colony. Vetch had offered his advice on this subject before, and he wearily did so again. Give the colonists adequate protection against the French and their Indians, he said, free transportation to the colony, and an initial grant of land, tools, and supplies. He urged the establishment of forts at Canso, Lahave, and Cape Sable to provide defenses and focal points of settlement. The Board asked him to consult with others proposing settlement in Nova Scotia and bring in further ideas, but he never did.[41]

The years in England had been hard ones for Vetch. Beginning with his loss of the governorship of Nova Scotia in 1717, he suffered a series of heartbreaking discouragements. In 1722, his mother and father had died within a day of each other. The same year Margaret Vetch gave him another child, a daughter, but the baby died within ten days. The land grant for which he continually petitioned never materialized, and the frustration of near success must have reduced him to despair. His disappointment in not getting the governorship of Massachusetts followed.

Vetch had continually hoped for a turn in his fortunes, a turn which never came. When he died on April 30, 1732, he was a prisoner in King's Bench for debt. He was buried at St. George's Church, in Southwark, on the first day of May. The dream of the Glorious Enterprise was over.[42]

The grieving Mrs. Vetch, loyal and proud, returned to New York. She lived to read of Washington's defeat at Great Meadows, Braddock's defeat, the final exile of the Acadians, and the beginning of the upturn in the final struggle against New France, when, in the spring of 1758, the British advanced on

41. May 17-19, 1727, *Board of Trade Journal, 1723-28*, 332-33.

42. Stephen Bayard to Robert Livingston, July 8 and Dec. 16, 1725, Livingston Papers, Group 1a, box 10; Margaret Vetch to her mother, London, Feb. 22, 1723, Alida Vetch Bayard to Mrs. Robert Livingston, Dec. 27, 1725, *ibid.,* Group 2. See also *Veitch Memoirs,* 219; Nova Scotia Hist. Soc., *Collections,* 4 (1884), 54. For Vetch's death, see Bradford's *New York Gazette,* no. 353, dateline London, May 2, 1732. The church of St. George-the-Martyr, Southwark, has extensive burial records, but for these years the books have no entry of Vetch's interment. The church was being rebuilt and many burials resulted in hasty recording, sometimes only with an entry that "a man" or "a woman" had been buried. The burial ground is now a garden; letters to the author from the Rev. C. E. V. Bowkett, rector of St. George's, Mar. 31 and June 19, 1953.

Louisburg. She had lived through the uneasy years of ever-increasing French encroachment on the British colonies, and she must have watched with anguish as the British suffered defeat and delay in the first years of the great war for empire, reminiscent of the difficulties in the earlier war with France. Her death, probably in the summer of 1758, prevented her from knowing of the attainment of the goal which Vetch had dreamed of years before.[43]

Samuel Vetch must be accorded a place with those lamentably few prescient Britons of his time who saw the imperial scene as a whole. Synthesizing the ideas of this small, farseeing group and applying them to the current situation, Vetch was able to draw colonists and Crown together in a plan of action which could command the support of both. His tact and insight played a large part in bringing about more co-operation among the mutually jealous northern colonies and between them and the mother country. The military efforts and the diplomacy of the war mirrored the success with which men like Vetch had impressed contemporary authorities with some concept of the over-all nature of the imperial problem. The correct utilization of Great Britain's sea power in the struggle for empire became clear to some who could grasp the principles, even though Britain did not at once take the lesson to heart. The campaigns against Canada made the North American theater the scene of major British military and naval action for the first time; but colonial provincialism and the mother country's preoccupation with the continental war and domestic party politics put obstacles in the way of realizing an

43. Samuel Vetch died intestate, and in New York Mrs. Vetch was appointed executor of his estate. She inherited the handsome house on Dock Street and was also beneficiary of her father's will. She outlived both her daughter Alida and her son-in-law Stephen Bayard. On her death, Vetch's grandsons William and Robert, who had inherited extensive property from their father, received all of her property. The house was left to William as the eldest heir, entailed. Its total worth was computed at a thousand pounds; she left that amount to Robert, after which the rest of the property was shared. A great grandson of Vetch, Samuel Vetch Bayard, was appointed surveyor and searcher of customs of the port of New York in 1777. The family remained loyal to the king during the Revolution and fled America when the British left New York. See N.Y. Hist. Soc., *Collections*, Pub. fund ser., 29 (1896), 244, for the will of Margaret Vetch, proved June 23, 1758; and letters of administration granted to Mrs. Vetch for the estate of Samuel Vetch, July 26, 1732, *ibid.*, 27 (1894), 71; George III's commission to Samuel Vetch Bayard, *ibid.*, 33 (1900), 11. For the will of Robert Livingston, Aug. 2, 1728, see *ibid.*, 26 (1893), 341.

efficient colonial policy which would provide adequately for the defense and development of British America. Nevertheless, those who could see through the maze of apparently unrelated administrative, financial, military, and legislative problems, as did Vetch, and perceive the underlying necessity of co-operation rendered inestimable service toward maintaining British strength against the formidable French threat.

Vetch was not one of those who foresaw more serious problems that might arise between England and her provinces. He was confident that once France was eliminated from the New World the colonies would enjoy unhampered commercial opportunities. They would gain new resources of forests and furs, and with an improved economic situation they would become profitable to the mother country. He doubtless believed that this development would go far toward solving the conflicts of authority, the destructive rivalries, the illegal trading—all things he knew from experience to promote differences within and between the colonies, and between colonies and metropolis. He never doubted that efficient management by the royal government would be in the best interest of the empire and advantageous to the colonies.

The effort to achieve the goals which Vetch envisioned was bungled. This failure made it all the more difficult to achieve the goals later. But his effort set the pattern for the later success. At the same time, the bungling laid the ground for much of the colonial discontent with Great Britain which, taken with Britain's further failure to achieve a satisfactory relationship with her colonies, resulted in the final separation of the colonies from the empire. The eventual success of Vetch's enterprise, the conquest of Canada, freed the Americans of the threat which had bound them in dependence to the mother country and occasioned the expense which forced Britain to impose taxes unacceptable to the colonists. In retrospect, Vetch, the staunch imperialist, had spent his energies in an effort to accomplish an objective which, when achieved, made possible a revolution and deprived Great Britain of a sizable part of her empire. But that was the imperial irony of history.

Bibliographical Note

I. *Manuscript Sources*

Without the extensive Livingston-Redmond Manuscripts Collection now deposited with the Franklin D. Roosevelt Memorial Library, Hyde Park, New York, this biography would have been almost entirely lacking in glimpses of Vetch's family, his personal life, and the thoughts he privately expressed to relatives which are so important in evaluating his actions. Vetch's letters and those of his wife and daughter are scattered through the boxes of Robert Livingston's correspondence. The entire Livingston-Redmond Collection is rich in material for the history of New York. Livingston's personal correspondence, for example, furnishes many valuable insights into the period covered by this study.

Vetch was a prolific letter writer. Copies of his official correspondence for the year 1709, with a few items for 1710 and the period when he was in command of Annapolis Royal, are found in his Letter Book, formerly the possession of Mrs. Robert Weeks Kelley and her brother, Mr. Julian R. Speyers, of New York. The Letter Book, now in the Museum of the City of New York, was indispensable for this study, not only for letters not preserved elsewhere but also because it contains the full text for Vetch's "Canada Surveyed." A photostatic copy of the Letter Book is deposited in the Nicholas Murray Butler Library, Columbia University.

Other collections of manuscripts bearing on Vetch's career are to be found in the small but valuable group of papers gathered by Dr. J. Clarence Webster and now deposited in the New Brunswick Museum, St. John; among the Miscellaneous Bound Manuscripts and the Parkman Manuscripts of the Massachusetts Historical Society; in the Henry E. Huntington Library and Art Mu-

seum, San Marino, California, especially in the collection of
Blathwayt Papers; and in the Newberry Library at Chicago and
the New-York Historical Society. The Manuscripts Division of
the Library of Congress has transcripts of British records from
the British Museum (Additional Manuscripts, Lansdowne Manuscripts, Stowe Manuscripts, Egerton Manuscripts, Sloane Manuscripts), the Bodleian Library (Rawlinson Manuscripts, Clarendon
Manuscripts), and the Public Record Office (Colonial Office
Papers).

For Vetch's activities in Nova Scotia the Public Archives of
Nova Scotia, located on the campus of Dalhousie University in
Halifax, contain original manuscripts and transcripts from British
and French archives. Volumes V, VII, VII 1/2, and VIII were
particularly valuable for this study. Transcripts of the Nova
Scotia collection are available in the Public Archives of Canada
at Ottawa.

The New York Colonial Manuscripts in the New York State
Library at Albany provided some material, although many of the
records are charred and illegible, and the collection has unfortunate gaps where volumes were totally destroyed in the 1911
fire. Something of the contents of these manuscripts is indicated
in E. B. O'Callaghan, ed., *Calendar of Historical Manuscripts in
the Office of the Secretary of State, Albany, New York* (Albany,
1866). Used in conjunction with the New York State Library
Report of 1911, which tells what was burned and the condition of
the remaining volumes, it is a convenient guide to the New York
Colonial Manuscripts. An invaluable supplement to the printed
New-York Colonial Documents, these manuscripts are too seldom
used by students of New York's colonial period.

Massachusetts is one of the few states which has not provided
a printed collection of its colonial records. These records are
readily available, however, in the Massachusetts Archives in the
State House at Boston. Well indexed, they constitute a source of
much material on the affairs in Massachusetts with which Vetch
was concerned. Supplementing these are records and briefs scattered through the archives of the Clerk of the Supreme Court,
Suffolk County Court House, for the years 1700-1715.

II. *Printed Sources*

Historians and biographers of the colonial period would spend much more time, and would probably have less to show for it, were it not for the host of editors who have compiled the printed collections of colonial documents and the calendars which serve as guides to manuscript collections. Much of this work is of relatively recent date. In 1918 Herbert L. Osgood complained that more than one-half of his source material still existed only in manuscript, scattered through the archives of the thirteen original states or procurable only in London. Thanks to the patient drudgery of copyists, compilers, editors, and indexers, a great deal of the material for the history of the early eighteenth century in America is now more easily available. Historians are vastly in their debt.

Probably the single most useful collection for this study of Vetch was W. N. Sainsbury *et al.*, eds., *Calendar of State Papers, Colonial Series, America and the West Indies, Preserved in the Public Record Office, 1574-1733* (33 vols.; London, 1860-1939). The volumes for the period of Vetch's life were edited by J. W. Fortescue and Cecil Headlam, who provided in the introduction to each volume an excellent brief history of the events of the period covered. I also relied on William John Hardy, ed., *Calendar of State Papers, Domestic Series, of the Reign of William and Mary* (11 vols.; London, 1895-1937); Robert Pentland Mahaffy, *Calendar of State Papers, Domestic Series, of the Reign of Anne, 1702-4* (2 vols.; London, 1916-24); Joseph Redington, ed., *Calendar of Treasury Papers, 1557-1728* (6 vols.; London, 1868-89); Leo Francis Stock, ed., *Proceedings and Debates of the British Parliaments respecting North America, 1542-1754* (5 vols.; Washington, 1924-41); *Acts of the Privy Council of England, Colonial Series, 1613-1783* (6 vols.; London, 1908-12).

The minutes of the Board of Trade are included in the *Calendar of State Papers* for the years before 1704. After that date they are separately printed in the *Journal of the Commissioners for Trade and Plantations, April 1704–May 1783* (14 vols.; London, 1920-38). These volumes contributed the bulk of what could be ascertained about Vetch after he left the colonies for England, a time when he repeatedly appeared before the Board of Trade.

Important manuscripts are to be found in the Historical Manuscripts Commission, *Report on the Manuscripts of His Grace the Duke of Portland, Preserved at Welbeck Abbey* (10 vols.; London, 1891-1919); this report also contains the *Harley Papers* (vols. II-X of the *Portland Mss.*), which accounts for the complicated citation I have had to use in references, for example, Hist. Mss. Comm., *Portland Mss.*, III (*Harley Papers*, I). Also useful was the Historical Manuscripts Commission, *Report on the Manuscripts of His Grace the Duke of Buccleuch and Queensbury* (3 vols.; London, 1903), II.

As a supplement to the manuscripts and transcripts in the Public Archives of Nova Scotia and as a guide to additional material in the Public Archives of Canada, I used Douglas Brymner, ed., *Report on the Canadian Archives, 1894* (Ottawa, 1895). In a typical reference to Brymner the series and volume numbers refer to the archival arrangement of material; the page numbers cited refer to the *Report* itself. However, the calendar of the Nova Scotia transcripts is incomplete in this volume, so I followed a copy with corrections and additions, made by Professor John Bartlet Brebner. Edouard Richard, ed., *Supplement to Dr. Brymner's Report on the Canadian Archives, 1899* (Ottawa, 1901), is especially full on the subject of relations between the French colony and the British colonies. Additional material gathered by Francis Parkman and lodged in the Massachusetts Historical Society, as well as other records from French archives, are to be found in the *Collection de Manuscrits contenant lettres, mémoires, et autres documents historiques relatifs à la Nouvelle France* (Quebec, 1883-85).

Another unusually valuable source is Peter Wraxall's *An Abridgement of Indian Affairs . . . in the Colony of New York . . . 1678-1751*, edited with a suggestive and scholarly introduction by Charles Howard McIlwain, *Harvard Historical Studies* (Cambridge, 1915), XXI. A near-contemporary account by Cadwallader Colden, *The History of the Five Indian Nations of Canada which are dependent on the Province of New York and are a barrier between the English and the French in that part of the World* (2 vols.; New York, 1904), is subject to the same limitations as Wraxall, in that the original records are used to support the political strategy of the author, but the factual material fills many gaps where the original records have been lost. Colden's "Continuation," mentioned below, begins in 1707, leaving the years from 1698 to 1707 unaccounted for. Additional Indian records are in Lawrence H. Leder, ed., *The Livingston Indian Records, 1666-1723* (Gettysburg, Pa., 1956).

Vetch's New York affairs get full coverage in E. B. O'Callaghan's monumental edition of *Documents Relative to the Colonial History of the State of New-York, procured in Holland, England, and France by John Romeyn Brodhead* (15 vols.; Albany, 1853-87). Volumes III, IV, and V, drawn mainly from New York and London records, and Volume IX, consisting of documents found in the French archives, were particularly useful. Joel Munsell's *The Annals of Albany* (Albany, 1850) is a useful supplement to the *New-York Colonial Documents*, printing many of the Albany records for this period. *The Yearbook of the Holland Society of New York, 1905,* also contains Albany records.

The second volume of the New York State Library *Report* of 1902, Bulletin No. 58, contains a calendar of the twenty-eight volumes of the manuscript New York Council Minutes, 1668-1783, in the New York State Library. Printed sources for the New York legislature are the *Journal of the Legislative Council of the Colony of New York Began the 9th Day of April, 1691 and Ended the 27th of September, 1743* (2 vols.; Albany, 1861), and the *Journal of the Votes and Proceedings of the General Assembly of the Colony of New York Began the 9th Day of April, 1691 and Ended the 27th of September, 1743* (2 vols.; New York, 1764).

An idea of early New York may be obtained from the descriptions of Charles Wooley, *A Two Years' Journal in New York,* edited by E. B. O'Callaghan (New York, 1860) and by Edward Gaylor Bourne (Cleveland, 1902); John Miller's "Description of the Province and City of New York in 1695," *Library of American Literature, Gowan's Bibliotheca Americana* (5 vols.; New York, 1862), II; and I. N. Phelps Stokes, *The Iconography of Manhattan Island* (6 vols.; New York, 1915), which reproduces early views of the village. The *Journal of the Voyage of the Sloop Mary from Quebec, together with an Account of her Wreck off Montauk Point, Long Island, Anno 1701* (Albany, 1866), edited by E. B. O'Callaghan, also includes a note on Vetch by the editor.

The *Collections* of the New-York Historical Society include "The History of the Late Province of New York, from its discovery to the appointment of Governor Colden in 1762," by William Smith, 4 (1829) and 5 (1830). Colden's letter to his son is in Publication Fund Series, 1 (1868); additional letters and papers of Colden and the "Continuation" of his *History of the Five Indian Nations* from 1707 to 1720 are in the John Watts De-Peyster Publication Fund Series, 68 (1935). *The Case of William Atwood, Esq.* (London, 1703) is reprinted in 13 (1880). The volumes on wills, edited by William S. Pelletreau for 1885, 1893-96, and 1900, were valuable. The DePeyster Publication Series, 45 (1913), has the records of the Supreme Court of Judicature of New York. The *Collections* include three additional volumes of Supreme Court records edited by Paul M. Hamlin and Charles E. Baker, *Supreme Court of Judicature of the Province of New York*, DePeyster Publication Fund Series, 78-80 (1959).

Like the *Collections* of the New-York Historical Society, the *Collections* of the Massachusetts Historical Society contain many volumes of records of the colonial period. The *Diary of Samuel Sewall* from 1674 to 1729 takes up three volumes of the Fifth Series; 5 (1878) covers 1674 to 1700; 6 (1879) covers 1700 to 1714; and 7 (1882) covers 1714 to 1729. The Sixth Series contains Sewall's Letter Books in 1 (1886) and 2 (1888). The correspondence of Fitzjohn Winthrop is in 3 (1889) and that of Wait Still Winthrop is in 5 (1892). Cotton Mather's diary and some of his letters are in the Seventh Series; for the years 1681-1708 see 7 (1911); the period from 1709 to 1724 is in 8 (1912). For three tracts which marked the attack by the Mather faction on Governor Dudley, the governor's rebuttal, and the rejoinder, see "A Memorial of the Present Deplorable State of New England," "A Modest Enquiry into the Grounds and Occasion of a Late Pamphlet, etc.," and "The Deplorable State of New England by Reason of a Covetous and Treacherous Governor and Pusillanimous Counsellors" in the Fifth Series, 6 (1879).

Material in the Massachusetts Archives is supplemented by the printed *Acts and Resolves, Public and Private, of the Province of the Massachusetts Bay* (21 vols.; Boston, 1869-1912), of which Volume IX contains records pertaining to Vetch. The *Year Book of the Society of Colonial Wars in Massachusetts*, Publication No. 3 (Boston, 1897), reprints Nicholson's "Journal of the Expedition against Port Royal" from the *Boston News-Letter* and other material pertaining to that campaign and to the expedition against Canada in 1711. The Journal is also found in Nova Scotia Historical Society, *Report and Collections*, 1 (1878). The *Boston News-Letter*, first regularly issued colonial newspaper, was studied from the photostat copies in the Columbia University Library. Unfortunately, it suspended publication during the summer of 1709 when the first expedition against Canada was forming. Its predecessor, the *Campbell News Letter*, issued in Boston, is reprinted in part in Lyman Horace Weeks and Edwin M. Bacon, eds., *An Historical Digest of the Provincial Press, Massachusetts Series*, I, 1689-1707 (Boston, 1911).

A near-contemporary record which, like Colden's, is valuable because it is based in part on records which have not survived is Thomas Hutchinson's *The History of the Colony and Province of Massachusetts-Bay*, edited by Lawrence Shaw Mayo (3 vols.; Cambridge, Mass., 1936).

Contemporary broadsides and pamphlets include Jeremy Dummer's *A Letter to a Noble Lord Concerning the Late Expedition to Canada* (Boston, 1712) and *A Letter to a Friend in the Country* (London, 1712), both available in the John Carter Brown Library at Brown University, as is also Sir Henry Ashurst's *The Deplorable State of New England due to the covetous Governor Dudley and an account of the miscarriages of the late expedition against Port Royal* (London, 1708). Other broadsides are printed in Douglas C. McMurtrie's *Massachusetts Broadsides, 1699-1711* (Chicago, 1939) and *Some Massachusetts Broadsides of 1711* (Metuchen, N.J., 1934). Two printed proclamations, one by Ingoldesby and the other by Vetch and Nicholson, are owned by the New-York Historical Society.

The Darien venture is documented in John H. Burton, ed., *The Darien Papers* (Edinburgh, 1849); George Pratt Insh, ed.,

Papers Relating to the Ships and Voyages of the Company of Scotland Trading to Africa and the Indies, 1696-1707, Scottish History Society Publication, Third Series (Edinburgh, 1924), VI; and the extensive collection of pamphlets reflecting the repercussions of the Darien affair which are in the possession of the John Carter Brown Library.

For Vetch's family background, I depended on Thomas McCrie, ed., *Memoirs of Mr. William Veitch and George Brysson written by themselves with other narratives illustrative of the History of Scotland from the Restoration to the Revolution* (Edinburgh, 1825), for which the editor's notes are not completely reliable, and the *Memoirs of Mrs. William Veitch, Mr. Thomas Hog of Kiltearn, Mr. Henry Erskine and Mr. John Carstairs*, issued by the Committee of the General Assembly of the Free Church of Scotland for the publication of the works of Scottish Reformers and Divines (Edinburgh, 1846).

The Nova Scotia Historical Society *Report and Collections*, I (1878), reprints Nicholson's "Journal of the attack on Port Royal," along with letters exchanged between Nicholson and Subercase, the French commander. Vetch's "Journal of the expedition against Canada in 1711" is in 4 (1884), along with letters and orders bearing on Vetch's administration at Annapolis Royal during the winter of 1710-11 and a narrative of events of that period as seen by Paul Mascarene. The whole is preceded by a short biographical essay on Vetch written by the Rev. George Patterson, D.D., inaccurate in some respects. A fairly full calendar of the letter books and a commission book for the period 1713-41, compiled and edited by Archibald M. McMechan from the records in the Public Archives of Nova Scotia, is found in *Nova Scotia Archives* (Halifax, 1900), II. For the attitude taken by the British naval commander toward the expedition of 1711, it is necessary to read Admiral Sir Hovenden Walker's fretful and tactless *A Journal or Full Account of the Late Expedition to Canada with an appendix containing commissions, orders, instructions, letters, memorials, courtsmartial, councils of war etc.* (London, 1720), along with the journals of General Jack Hill and Colonel Richard King printed in the *Calendar of State Papers, 1711-12*. A convenient collection of documents concerning the expedition is found in *The Walker Expedition to Quebec, 1711,* edited with introduction by Gerald S. Graham, in *The Publications of the Champlain Society* (Toronto, 1953), XXXII.

Records of colonies other than New York and Massachusetts that were concerned in the enterprise against Canada may be conveniently consulted in: *The Public Records of the Colony of Connecticut 1636-1776* (15 vols.; Hartford, 1850-90), particularly Volume V, edited by Charles Jeremy Hoadly (Hartford, 1870); William A. Whitehead, ed., *Documents Relating to the Colonial History of the State of New Jersey, 1703-9* (Newark, 1881), III, and *ibid., 1709-20* (Newark, 1882), IV, and Frederick W. Ricord and William Nelson, eds., "Journal of the Governor and Council, volume I," *ibid.* (Trenton, 1890), XIII, cited as *New Jersey Archives,* III, IV, and XIII; "Minutes of the Provincial Council of Pennsylvania, 1700-1717," in *Colonial Records of Pennsylvania* (Harrisburg, 1852), II; Edward Armstrong, ed., "Correspondence between William Penn and James Logan, Secretary of the Province, and others, 1700-1750, with notes by the late Deborah Logan," Historical Society of Pennsylvania, *Memoirs,* 9 and 10 (1872); John Russell Bartlett, ed., *Records of the Colony of the Rhode Island and Providence Plantation in New England, 1707-40* (10 vols.; Providence, 1859), IV.

Other printed sources utilized in this study were: John W. Ford, ed., *Some Correspondence Between the Governors and Treasurers of the New England Company in London and the Commissioners of the United Colonies in America, etc., 1657-1712* (London, 1896); Sir Henry Bunbury, ed., *The Correspondence of Sir Thomas Hanmer, Bart., with a Memoir of His Life* (London, 1838); Gilbert Parker, ed., *Letters and Correspondence Public and Private of the Right Honorable Henry St. John, Lord Viscount Bolingbroke* (4 vols.; London, 1798); *The Private Correspondence of Sarah, Duchess of Marlborough* (2 vols.; London, 1838); G. Murray, ed., *Marlborough's Letters and Dispatches* (London, 1845); Joseph Addison's *The Spectator,* edited by Alexander Chalmers, (6 vols.; London, 1864), I; "The Cadillac Papers," in the Michigan Pioneer and Historical Society, *Historical Collections,* 33 (1903); Peter Kalm, *Travels Into North America,* translated by John Reinhold Forster (London, 1772);

The Journal of Madam [Sarah Kemble] Knight (Boston, 1920);
*A Diary of the Land Expedition Against Crown Point in the Year
1711 in the Private Journals Kept by the Reverend John Buckingham* (New York, 1825); and Cadillac's "Memoire Upon L'Acadie
in 1692," edited by W. F. Ganong, in New Brunswick Historical
Society, *Collections*, 13 (1930), 80-97.

III. *Secondary Works*

Samuel Vetch has had no previous full-length biography. He
is given deserved notice in the article by John Bartlet Brebner in
Dumas Malone *et al.*, eds., *Dictionary of American Biography*
(New York, 1936), XIX, 260. Robert Hamilton Vetch, no
relation, wrote the sketch for the *Dictionary of National Biography*. A privately printed pamphlet, *Samuel Vetch* (Shediac, N.B.,
1929), was issued by Dr. J. Clarence Webster on the occasion of
the dedication of a monument to Vetch erected by the Historic
Sites and Monuments Board of Canada in the old fort at Annapolis Royal. James Grant Wilson wrote an article, "An
Acadian Governor," for the *International Review* in 1881. Another
sketch of Vetch's career, by the Rev. George Patterson, precedes
the documents printed in the Nova Scotia Historical Society's
Collections, 4 (1884).

In most histories of the English colonies Vetch has received
only brief mention, with little indication of his importance. An
exception is found in the works of W. T. Morgan, who has characterized him as "the most interesting, and perhaps the ablest,
figure connected with the Canadian expeditions"; see his articles,
"Queen Anne's Canadian Expedition of 1711," in Queen's University, *Bulletin of the Department of History. . .*, no. 56 (Kingston, Ontario, May 1928); "Some Attempts at Imperial Cooperation During the Reign of Queen Anne," Royal Historical Society,
Transactions, 4th ser., 10 (1927), 171-94; and "The South Sea
Company and the Canadian Expedition in the Reign of Queen
Anne," *Hispanic-American Historical Review*, 8 (1928), 143 ff.
Historians of New France have been more generous to Vetch's
memory. Apparently he was more highly regarded by the French
as an opponent than by the English as a leader. William Kings-
ford condemns most of the English as mediocre, excepting Vetch,

whom he calls "preeminently distinguished by ability," one "who early perceived that the power of the English colonies lay in their Union. . . . It was owing in no small degree to his efforts that the first important steps were taken in this direction"; *The History of Canada* (10 vols.; London, 1887-98), II, 423-30, 441 ff. To G. M. Wrong, "it was his energy which now made a beginning of the end of France's Empire in America"; *The Rise and Fall of New France* (2 vols.; New York, 1928), II, 568. And Francis Parkman names Vetch as "prime mover" in the plan to conquer Canada, characterizing him as "impetuous, sanguine, energetic, and headstrong, astute withal, and full of ambition. A more visionary agent for the execution of the proposed plan of conquest could not have been desired"; *A Half-Century of Conflict* (2 vols.; Boston, 1933), I, chap. VII.

Two more works give a distinctive picture of Vetch and his times: Richmond P. Bond, *Queen Anne's American Kings* (Oxford, 1952), and Everett Kimball, *The Public Life of Joseph Dudley, Harvard Historical Studies*, XV (Cambridge, 1911).

Acknowledgments

AS HISTORIANS WELL KNOW, it is more the pleasure of recollection than a sense of duty that impels one to acknowledge the encouragement and assistance he has received in exploring and exploiting affairs of the past. Without the patient, cheerful, virtually indispensable contributions of many others this work would have fallen far short of its present state. But of course it is with no thought of ascribing responsibility for the results that the writer calls the roll of those who have been helpful in large matters and small.

A score of libraries and kindred repositories have made books and manuscripts available. My thanks are due to Dr. Herman Kahn and his staff at the Franklin D. Roosevelt Library, Hyde Park, New York; the personnel of the Manuscripts Division, Library of Congress, in particular to Miss Katherine Brand, who was in charge while I was there; Mr. Ferguson of the Public Archives of Nova Scotia in Halifax; Miss Margaret Evans, in charge of the library and archives of the New Brunswick Museum at St. John, who opened the papers collected by the late J. Clarence Webster, M.D.; R. W. G. Vail, Director of the New-York Historical Society, Charles E. Baker, editor of the Society's *Quarterly*, Miss Dorothy C. Barck, then librarian, and Wayne Andrews, then in charge of manuscripts; the Department of Manuscripts of the Henry E. Huntington Library and Art Gallery in San Marino, California; Miss Edna L. Jacobsen, Manuscripts and History Section, New York State Library, Albany; those in charge of the Massachusetts Archives in the State House, Boston; the personnel of the Massachusetts Historical Society; and those in the office of the clerk of the Supreme Court, Suffolk County Court House, Boston.

The Museum of the City of New York has extended every courtesy in making the handsome portraits of Vetch and his wife available for reproduction, as well as offering access to Vetch's manuscript Letter Book now in its possession.

For the kind of service which has established members of the librarians' guild high in the esteem of all who engage in research, the writer is grateful to the librarians and their staffs of the Amherst College Library, the John Carter Brown Library at Brown University, the Columbia University Library, Widener Library at Harvard University, Mt. Holyoke College Library, Smith College Library, the University of Wisconsin Library, the Library of the State Historical Society of Wisconsin, and the Butler University Library.

Among those who have had words of encouragement and ideas which enriched this study are three who did not live to see its completion, the late Mrs. Robert Weeks Kelley of New York City, a descendant of Samuel Vetch and the owner, with her brother, Julian R. Speyers, of Vetch's Letter Book for the years 1709-1712 and of the two portraits now in the Museum of the City of New York; J. Clarence Webster, M.D., of Shediac, New Brunswick, during his lifetime Vetch's most enthusiastic partisan and chairman of the Historic Sites and Monuments Board of Canada which erected the monument to Vetch on the ramparts of the old fort at Annapolis Royal; and the late Dr. Victor Hugo Paltsits, long of the New York Public Library's manuscript room.

Others who have been especially helpful in their information and interest are Professor Richmond P. Bond, Department of English, the University of North Carolina; the Reverend Cyril E. V. Bowkett, rector of the Church of St. George-the-Martyr, Southwark, London; Leonidas Dodson, Archivist, the University of Pennsylvania; Dr. Lawrence H. Leder; Dr. R. H. Luthin; Professor Bruce T. McCully, The College of William and Mary; Dr. Ruth Messenger, New York City, New York; Henry Allen Moe, President, the New York State Historical Association; Dr. Charles L. Sanford; and Dr. Susan Reed Stifler, Amherst, Massachusetts.

I am especially indebted to two who followed the work from its inception, John Allen Krout, former Professor of History at Columbia University and now Vice-President of the University, and the late John Bartlet Brebner, Professor of History at Columbia University, who first suggested the subject and was enthusiastically interested throughout. I also want to express my appreciation to Lester J. Cappon, director of the Institute of Early American History and Culture, who encouraged me to prepare the book for publication, and to James M. Smith and Frederick A. Hetzel, whose patient editorial labors have given this work much of whatever ease of expression it may have.

To my wife, who had better things to do and did them but who also had much to do with this work as well, goes the deep appreciation which all authors know who are fortunate enough to have such a sympathetic partner in their enterprise.

Index

Abenaki Indians, 76, 81
Acadia, 102, 143, 144. *See also* Nova
  Scotia
Act "For Settling the Recent Disor-
  ders" in New York (1691), 65
Acts of Trade and Navigation, 30, 50,
  51, 64, 241; of 1695, 36; of 1663,
  56, 64
Addington, Isaac, 160, 236
Admiralty Courts. *See* Vice-Admiral-
  ty Courts
Adventure (ship), 37
Albany, New York, trade of, 78, 85,
  132; and Indian attacks, 81, 85,
  171; Canada expedition, 124, 162
Alden, John, 87, 197
Alexander, Sir William, 279
"American Carthage," Canada char-
  acterized as, 208
American Revolution, 157, 218, 286
Anadagarjaux, Francis Nicholson's Indian name, 174
Anadiasia, Samuel Vetch's Indian
  name, 174
Andros, Sir Edmund, 111
Angus, Earl of, 13
Annapolis Royal, 188, 208, 229, 235;
  garrison of, 188, 200, 248-49, 269,
  276; description of, 192, 244; supply of, 194, 196, 200, 202; trade
  proposals for, 194, 241; defense
  of, 203, 204-5; condition of, 203,
  246, 251. *See also* Port Royal
Anne (ship), 87
Anne, Queen, 69, 118, 172, 222, 261,
  264; and British relations with
  Canada, 82, 112; and illegal trade,
  82, 96; addresses to, 129, 138-39,
  160-61; Tory influence on, 134,
  209; and Nova Scotia conquest, 186,
  189, 273
Anticosti Island, 223

Anti-Leislerian party, 42
Argyll, Duke of. *See* Campbell, John
Argyll, Earl of. *See* Campbell, Archi-
  bald
Armstrong, Captain, soldier at Annap-
  olis Royal, 248, 249
Ashurst, Sir Henry, 88, 96, 165-66
Ashurst, Sir William, 165-66, 231,
  232, 239
Atlantic community, ix
Atwood, William, 59, 60, 65; and
  case of the *Mary*, 60, 63, 64

Bahama Islands, 160
Bank of England, 119
Basse, Jeremiah, 20
Bayard, Nicholas, 54, 65, 66
Beeston, Sir William, 26
Belcher, Andrew, 145, 212, 236
Bell, Thomas, 7
Bellomont, Lord. *See* Coote, Richard
Beresford, Richard, 264
Bernon, Monsieur, French resident of
  Boston suspected of espionage, 150
Bishop of London, 95
Blackadar, John, 6
Blackmore, Captain, 269
Blackwood, Bailie Robert, 27
Bladen, Martin, 279
Blathwayt, William, 70, 95, 238
Blenheim, battle of, 118
Block Island, 62
"Bloody Assizes," 10
"Bloody Claver'se," nickname of John
  Graham of Claverhouse, Earl of
  Dundee, 13
Board of Trade, 67, 75, 95, 238, 243,
  277; receives report from Bello-
  mont, 33; investigates illegal trade,
  48-49, 88-89, 97; receives Dudley's
  defense, 92; considers conquest of
  Canada, 106, 109, 111-13; and

Vetch, 109, 263-65, 269, 279; and Nova Scotia conquest, 205, 253-54, 264, 270, 276, 280, 283-84; examines Nicholson, 274-75; report on colonial reorganization (1721), 281

Bolingbroke, Viscount. *See* St. John, Henry

Bonner, Captain John, 223

Boon, Joseph, 264

Borland, John, on Darien colony, 28, 36; trades with Canada, 56, 60, 80, 83, 91; relations with Vetch, 56, 91-92, 145, 200, 259, 266; victuals Annapolis Royal, 197, 200, 240; charges against, by Vane, 247; appears before Board of Trade, 264, 266

Boston, Mass., 123-24, 145, 153, 184, 211-12, 213

Bourbon monarchy of France. *See* Louis XIV

Boyle, Henry, Earl of Shannon, 177

Boyle, Henry, Lord Clarendon, 109, 116, 139

Bradford, William, 31

Brenton, Jahleel, 56

British Navy, naval stores for, 103; to cooperate in attack on Bahamas, 160; in Port Royal plans, 161; in Canada expedition, 1711, 214, 221, 229

British Regulars, in New York, 70; accounts of presented, 71; role in Indian relations, 74; plan to raise an army of, 113; in Canada expedition, 134; withdrawn from Wood Creek, 162; establishment requested at Port Royal, 205; in Boston, 211-12; condition of, 214

Bromfield, Edward, 236

Broughton, Samuel Shelton, 66

Buckingham, Duke of. *See* Sheffield, John

"Burgis View," of New York, 1716, 45

Burnet, William, 283

Cabot, John, 166

Caesar (ship), 182

Cairns, Sir Alexander, 280

Caledonia, colony. *See* Darien colony

Caledonia (ship), 3, 26, 30, 31, 40

Cameronians, 13

Campbell, Captain Alexander, 25

Campbell, Archibald, Earl of Argyll, 9

Campbell, Duncan, 53, 55

Campbell, John, Duke of Argyll, 168, 283

Canada, 76, 104, 175, 218, 208; trade, 72, 79, 194; Indian relations of, 73, 75, 76, 111-12, 149; early rivalry with northern colonies, 94, 100, 101, 102; plans for conquest of, 94, 100, 102, 110, 111, 113, 117, 139; Canada expedition (1709), 101, 124, 132, 142, 143, 148, 150, 151, 155-59, 161, 164-66, 167, 177, 190, 205; in Vetch's "Canada Surveyed," 106-8; British claims in peace negotiations, 161, 166; Canada expedition (1711), 166, 205, 207, 209-11, 215-16, 221-26

"Canada Surveyed," Vetch's report on Canada, 106-8, 115

Canaries, islands, 50

Canso, Strait of, 62, 83, 279

Canterbury, Archbishop of. *See* Wake, William

Cape Ann, 62

Cape Breton Island, Nova Scotia, 62, 222, 228, 270, 274; in peace negotiations, 243, 253

Capon, Mr., 280

Carolinas, 39, 140, 241, 263-64

Carstares, Reverend William, 115, 262

Carteret, John, Earl Granville, 282

Catholic Pretender. *See* Stuart, James

Caughnawaga. *See* Praying Indians

Caughnawaga, village, 142

Caulfeild, Thomas, 260, 273, 274, 275, 278; and government of Annapolis Royal, 230, 236, 244, 247, 255, 269, 276

Cayugas. *See* Five Nations

Chamberlayne, John, 95, 102, 266

Charles II, King of England, 8, 39

Charles II, King of Spain, vii, 19, 69

Charles River, 150

Chester, H.M.S., 163, 175, 182, 204, 221

Chignecto, 195

Church, Colonel Benjamin, 129

Churchill, John, Duke of Marlborough, 13, 113, 115, 265; opposition to Shannon expedition, 177; opposed by St. John, 208; dismissal, 242

Churchill, Sarah, Duchess of Marlborough, 115
Cleghorn, Adam, 27
Clifton, Captain, English naval officer, 163
Coal, 190
Cobequid, settlement in Nova Scotia, 195
Cochran, Sir John, 39
Cockburn, Adam, 32
Coffin, Ebenezar, 84
Colonial charters, 281
Colonial governors, 38, 122; meet at Rehoboth, 152, 158, 160-62; meet at New London, 210
Colonial troops, 48; quotas of, for Canada expeditions, 110, 124, 131, 138-39, 162, 211, 216; pay and supply of, 127, 135, 146-48, 220. *See also* individual colonies
Commander-in-chief, 152
Commissions, 242
Company of Scotland, 3, 15; and Darien Colony, 23, 24, 33, 39
Connecticut, 48, 158-59, 180, 250; role in Canada expeditions, 124, 129, 162, 164, 207, 211, 216
Cooper, Antony, Earl of Shaftesbury, 8
Coote, Richard, Lord Bellomont, and Darien survivors, 30, 31, 32, 37; relations with Robert Livingston, 42, 54; relations with Vetch, 42, 55; relations with Captain Kidd, 43; in New York politics, 48, 52, 53; opposes illegal trade, 49, 56; character, 52; death, 57; policy toward Canada, 78, 100
Cornbury, Edward, Earl of Clarendon, 67, 70, 71, 81, 108, 113; politics of, 65, 66, 67; and Indian relations, 72, 75, 76
Councils of War, Annapolis Royal, 173, 204; Canada expedition of 1711, 225, 229
Counterfeiting, 145
Courtemanche, Sieur de, 80
Court of Common Pleas, 259
Covenanters, persecution of, 7-11
Cox, John, 62
Coxsedge, Ensign, 203
Cranston, Samuel, 51, 125, 153, 174, 211
Cunningham, James, 21

Currency, shortage of, 50, 71
Cutts, John, Baron of Gowran, 95

Dalkeith, 4
Dalrymple, John, Earl of Stairs, 8, 115, 168, 281, 283
Darien, viii, 17, 110; survivors of, 3, 33, 37, 55; early plans for, 15-17; establishment of, 18; opinion of, 19, 20, 22, 23, 24, 28; failure of, 20-26; second attempt to colonize, 33-37; influence of failure on Vetch, 102, 110, 167
Dartmouth, Earl of. *See* Legge, William
Deerfield, Massachusetts, 80, 142
Dekanissore, Onondaga sachem, 77
Delancey, Stephen, 34, 40, 50
Denys, M. de la Ronde, 218
De Peyster, Abraham, 57
Deptford, H.M.S., 84
Despatch, H.M.S., 221
Devonshire, H.M.S., 221, 222
Dolphin (ship), 24
Dominion of New England, 48, 111, 250
Dongan, Thomas, 78, 100
Douglas, James, 122, 168, 172, 242, 244, 266, 280
Douglas, James, Duke of Hamilton, 114-15
Douglas, James, Duke of Queensbury, influence of, 114-15; Vetch asks support of, 139, 151, 168
Dragon, H.M.S., 121, 123, 149, 163, 175, 182
Drummond, Captain Robert, 4, 26, 27, 28, 31, 39, 40
Drummond, Thomas, 4, 27-28, 31, 40; in Darien, 22, 25, 34
Dudley, Joseph, 90, 149, 155, 163, 190; and illegal trading, 80, 82, 84, 87, 92-93, 98; political role of, 80, 88, 90, 153, 217; opposition to, 88-89, 92, 96, 168, 198; and Vetch, 95, 155, 171, 199, 204, 249; role in Canada expeditions, 104, 109, 124, 174, 204, 207, 210-11, 213, 229-31, 249; opposes Sir William Ashurst, 165; and French neutrality offer, 218; and Francis Nicholson, 257
Dudley, Paul, 204, 224, 236, 259
Dudley, Thomas, 51

Dudley, William, 80, 236
Dumfries, Scotland, 11
Dummer, Jeremy, 103, 262, 264;
  Vetch's influence on, 103, 166, 172;
  early efforts for Canada expedition,
  105, 166; appointment as Massachusetts agent, 166; aids Nicholson,
  166; and Canada expedition
  (1710), 176, 177, 208; presents
  credentials as Massachusetts agent,
  208; *Letter to a Noble Lord*, 232;
  on failure of Canada expedition,
  232; defends Vetch, 266, 268; *Defense of the New England Charters*,
  282
Dundee, Earl of. *See* Graham, John
Dunkirk, Nova Scotia compared to,
  102

East India Company, 15, 48
Edgar, H.M.S., 221, 222, 231
Eliot, Mr., British officer at Port
  Royal, 186
Endeavour (ship), 26
England, viii, 12, 103. *See also*
  British Navy; British Regulars; Eng-
  lish colonies; Imperialism; Mercan-
  tilism; Trade
English colonies, ix, 24, 108, 194,
  207; cooperation among, 78, 216-
  17, 234. *See also* Imperialism;
  Mercantilism; Trade
English politics. *See* Whig party;
  Tory party
Enterprise, H.M.S., 154, 155, 163,
  221, 229, 230
Erskine, Lieutenant, testifies for Vetch,
  269

Fairly, Marion. *See* Veitch, Marion
  Fairly
Fallowlees, 6
Falmouth, H.M.S., 175
Faneuil, Andrew, 212
Ferguson, Archibald, 83
Feversham, H.M.S., 175, 182, 221,
  246
Finch, Daniel, Earl of Nottingham,
  95
Fishers Island, 58
Five Nations, 72, 125, 131, 142, 177,
  214; importance of, in colonial ri-
  valries, 72, 73; enmity toward

Canada, 72, 81, 101; neutrality of,
  74, 77, 85, 143; British allegiance
  of, 100, 151; and Canada expedi-
  tions, 110, 125, 149, 204, 215, 237;
  represented in England, 161, 164,
  171, 174. *See also* Indian commis-
  sion of Albany
Fletcher, Benjamin, 34, 42, 53, 78, 100
Florida, 140
Flying Horse (ship), 83
Forbes, Charles, 22, 25
Forbes, Mr., engineer at Annapolis
  Royal, 183, 188, 192, 203
Fort Anne, New York, 130
Fort Ingoldesby, New York, 153
Fort Nicholson, New York, 153
Fortune (ship), 50
Fort William Henry, New York, 31
Fort Wood Creek. *See* Wood Creek
Foster, Colonel John, 150
France, vii, 151, 161, 209, 220. *See
  also* Canada; Imperialism
French, Philip, 54, 65
Fundy, Bay of, 182

Gaspé, Bay of, 223
Gaspé, Cape of, 254
Gaulin, Father, 253
Gee, Joshua, 103, 264
George I, 265, 269
Georgia, ix
"Glorious Enterprise," 100, 119, 151,
  208. *See also* Canada expeditions
Glorious Revolution of 1688, vii, 11-
  12
Goddard, Captain, 224
Godolphin, Sidney, Earl of Godolphin,
  139, 177; political influence of,
  115; on cancellation of Canada ex-
  pedition, 156; Vetch asks support of,
  169; removed from Treasury, 207
Gookin, Charles, and Canada expedi-
  tion, 131, 133, 137, 138
Governors' Congresses. *See* Colonial
  governors
Graham, James, 52, 53
Graham, John, of Claverhouse, Earl
  of Dundee, 13
Grand Alliance, 118
Green Dragon Tavern, 176
Guernsey, H.M.S., 149, 150, 163

Hamilton, Alexander, Darien colonist,
  21

Hamilton, Duke of. *See* Douglas, James

Hamilton, George, Earl of Orkney, 168

Hanover, House of, 261-62

Harley, Robert, Earl of Oxford, 209, 238, 239, 245, 262; and Tory party, 116-17, 176, 207, 265; rivalry with St. John, 209, 261; opposition to Canada expedition, 209, 239-40

Harnamhall, Northumberland, 6

Harrison, Reverend, chaplain for Annapolis Royal, 188

"Harrison's," meeting place of New Jersey legislature, 136

Harvard College, 90, 148, 214

Heathcote, Caleb, 50, 217

Higginson, Nathaniel, 103, 105; opposition to Dudley, 91, 96

Hill, General Jack, 214, 267-68; in Canada expedition of 1711, 210, 212, 220, 222, 225, 228

Hobart, Mr., Long Island justice of the peace, 63

Hobby Sir Charles, 104, 105, 149, 159, 165; in Port Royal expedition, 145, 183; and government of Annapolis Royal, 198, 204, 206, 211, 220-21, 230, 267-68, 269

Holland, 50, 69

Holy Roman Emperor. *See Joseph I*

Honan, Daniel, 67

Hope (ship), 87, 145

Howell, Mr., master of Scottish ship, 38

Hudson Bay, acquisition of, 244

Humber, H.M.S., 221, 222

Hungerford, Ducy, 52

Hunking, Mark, 159

Hunter, Robert, 168, 177, 204, 234, 257; and New York politics, 168, 215, 216-17; and Canada expedition, 207, 211

Huron Indians, 73

Hutchins, John, 65, 66

Hutchinson, Colonel Elisha, 236

Hutchinson, Captain Thomas, 236

Hyde, Laurence, Earl of Rochester, 207

Imperialism, vi, viii, 170, 215, 262-63, 285-86; and Canadian expedition (1711), 216-18. *See also* Canada; English colonies; Mercantilism

Indian Commission of Albany, and Five Nations, 75, 76, 110, 126

Indian Ocean, piracy in, 48

Indian Relations, Canada, 81

Indians, British allies, 72-75; French allies, 72-75, 111-12; evaluate Canada's defenses, 142; oppose British in Nova Scotia, 197, 203

Ingoldesby, Richard, 70, 110, 130, 168; role in Canada expedition, 131-33, 153, 159, 163; opposed by New Jersey legislature, 135-36; replaced by Hunter, 168

Iroquois Indians. *See* Five Nations

Jackson, Commissary, at Annapolis Royal, 269

Jacobitism, 248

Jamaica, 20, 168

James I, 279

James II, 9, 12

Jamison, David, 54

Johnston, Mr., great-grandfather of Samuel Vetch, 4

Johnston, William, assumed name of William Veitch, 5

Jolly, Mr., councilor of Darien colony, 22

Joseph I, of Austria, Holy Roman Emperor, 209

Kidd, Captain William, 43, 94

Killiecrankie, battle of, 13

King, Colonel Richard, 212, 215, 228

King's Bench, court of, 60

Kingston, H.M.S., 221, 229

King William's War, vii, 48

Kinsale, H.M.S., 163

"Kirke's Lambes," 10

Knight, Elizabeth, 252, 253

Knight, Madame Sarah Kemble, 252

Lahave River, 280

Lake Champlain, 126

Lanark, Scotland, 5

Landen. *See* Neerwinden, battle of

Land grants, in Nova Scotia, 280-81

Lauderdale, Duke of. *See* Maitland, John

Lawson, Roger, 84

League of Augsburg, vii, viii, 12

Lee, Colonel, commander of Rhode Island troops, 225

Legge, William, Earl of Dartmouth, 176, 207, 237, 238, 245, 247; role in Canada expedition plans, 205, 208-9
Leisler, Jacob, 78, 100
Leislerians, 65, 67
Leisler's Rebellion, 42, 257
Le Moyne, Charles, Chevalier de Longueuil, 142
Leopard, H.M.S., 221, 225
Letter to a Noble Lord, by Jeremy Dummer, 232
Leverett, John, 90
Livingston, Johanna, 237-38, 252
Livingston, John, father of Robert Livingston, 41
Livingston, John, 41, 42, 44, 55, 57, 237-38; and the *Mary*, 58, 59, 63; with Connecticut forces, 80, 129; at Wood Creek, 154; as Indian leader, 183, 204, 237; in Quebec, 189, 190, 191, 201; proposal to remarry, 252, 253
Livingston, Reverend John, 5
Livingston, Margaret. *See* Vetch, Margaret Livingston
Livingston, Mary Winthrop, 55, 252
Livingston, Robert, 41, 48, 126, 201, 261, 283; and marriage of Vetch, 6, 44, 45; and Darien expedition, 41, 42; and New York politics, 42, 43, 57, 63, 66, 71; in England, 71, 94, 95; as creditor, 71, 257, 264, 265; as victualer, 74, 201; and John Livingston's proposal to remarry, 252, 253
Livingston, William, 6, 41, 44
Livingston Manor, 41, 201, 259
Lodwick, Colonel Charles, 262
Long Island, 62, 148-49
Louis XIV, vii, 72, 273; and war of Spanish Succession, 69, 76; peace negotiations with, 113, 243
Lovelace, Francis, 100
Lovelace, Lord John, 108, 125, 128, 132
Lowestoft, H.M.S., 175, 182, 221
Lurting, Robert, 54, 71, 131

McCartney, General George, 123, 150
Mackay, Mr., councilor of Darien colony, 21
Madagascar, 34, 50, 58
Maidstone, H.M.S., 126, 163

Maitland, John, Duke of Lauderdale, 7, 8
Manhattan, described, 30
Marlborough (province galley), 83, 148, 163
Marlborough, Duchess of. *See* Churchill, Sarah
Marlborough, Duke of. *See* Churchill, John
Martha's Vineyard, 59, 62
Martin, Captain, 123, 163
Mary (ship), 57, 61, 62; seizure of, 63-65; returned to Vetch, 68; sold, 70
Maryland, Vetch seeks governorship of, 168
Mascarene, Paul, 145; and capture of Port Royal, 183, 186; promoted, 188; exacts taxes, 195-96; investigates lumbering, 202
Masham, Mrs. Abigail, 117, 222
Mason, Mr., London acquaintance of Vetch, 170
Massachusetts Bay, 48, 60, 76, 85, 98, 250; Assembly of, 79-80, 86, 88, 90, 158, 249; General Court of, 81, 97; and Vetch's illegal trade, 83, 84, 96, 146; relations with New York, 85, 153, 172; dispute over Dudley's governorship, 87-93; political factions in, 90; role in 1709 Canada expedition, 104, 105, 124, 127, 145, 149, 151, 164; social life in, 148; role in Port Royal expedition, 161, 179, 190; appoints Dummer agent, 166; Council, criticizes Schuyler, 172; and pay of Annapolis volunteers, 198; Council of, and French agents, 199; and aid for Annapolis troops, 200, 204; role in 1711 Canada expedition, 211-15; addresses Queen, 234; Council hears Nicholson's charges against Vetch, 258-59; governorship of, sought by Vetch, 281
Mather, Cotton, 88-89, 92, 104, 127
Mather, Increase, 88-89, 96, 104, 232, 253
Mayflower (ship), 87
Mercantilism, 103, 145, 208. *See also* English colonies; Imperialism; Trade
Merritt, Captain, accepts cargo of *Mary*, 59

Miller, Janet, criticizes Vetch, 44-45
Minas, 195
Moffat, George, 26-27, 32
Mohawk Indians, 142, 149. *See also* Five Nations
Mohawk Valley, 73
Monmouth, Duke of. *See* Scott, James
Montgomery, Colonel John, 283
Montreal, 104, 112, 162, 215
Moody, Colonel John, 159, 161, 164
Moore, Mr., 255
Morrisania, New York, 59
Murdoch, Mr., accepts illegal cargo from Vetch, 83

Nanfan, John, 31, 57, 63; and Darien refugees, 30, 31, 38; and New York politics, 65-66
Nantasket, Mass., 163, 211
Neerwinden, battle of, 13
Negroes, 214
Nelson, John, 87
New Amsterdam, 187
"New Brittain," proposed as new name for Nova Scotia, 166
Newcastle, Duke of. *See* Pelham-Holles, Sir Thomas
New England, vii, 103, 171, 198, 249, 263; illegal trade in, 56; and conquest of Port Royal, 173, 180; and Canada expeditions, 175, 190, 230
Newfoundland, 58, 76, 159, 248, 253; illegal trade from, 50; plans for attack on, 143, 161, 228; in peace negotiations, 243, 244
New France. *See* Canada
New Hampshire, 48, 109, 159, 161, 180; and Canada expeditions, 124, 145, 164, 207, 211, 234
New Jersey, 20, 48, 159; and Canada expeditions, 124, 135, 136, 211, 216; factionalism in, 135-36
New London, Connecticut, 152, 211, 258
Newport, Rhode Island, 153, 158
New York, 70, 162, 172, 204, 212; aristocracy of, 38, 48; politics of, 43, 48, 52-53, 57, 65, 130, 168; economy of, 47, 51, 135; trade in, 49, 52, 58; application of laws in, 51-52; leaders of, 52, 54, 78; epidemic in, 71; competition with Canada, 73, 100; and neutrality, 74, 76; rivalry with Massachusetts Bay,

85, 123, 153, 172; and Canada expeditions, 124, 125, 130, 131, 139, 162, 164, 211, 215, 216; and Rehoboth Congress, 159, 169
Nicholl, William, 54
Nicholson, Colonel Francis, 124, 130, 165, 175, 179, 205; as lieutenant governor of Virginia, 55; role in Canada expeditions, 111, 121, 128, 133, 155, 166, 177, 210-11, 233; rivalry with Vetch, 134, 173, 242, 256, 258, 260; and New Jersey legislature, 135, 137; suggested for New York governorship, 141, 168; influence with Indians, 153; role in Rehoboth Congress, 159, 164; role in Port Royal campaign, 173, 180, 183, 184-85, 186-87; character of, 207, 267, 276; and government of Nova Scotia, 243, 245, 249-50, 253, 255, 272-73; and survey of colonial governments, 254-55; discredited, 265, 266, 267, 274-75
Noddles Island, 214, 220
Noell, Thomas, 71
North Carolina, 217
Northey, Sir Edward, 97
Northumberland, 6
Nottingham, Earl of. *See* Finch, Daniel
Nova Scotia, vii, 101, 151, 166, 189, 244-45; trade of, 82, 102, 241; proposed Scottish settlement of, 93, 115; in peace negotiations, 161, 188, 194, 243, 244, 263; French inhabitants of, 189, 194, 195, 196-97, 241, 270-72; supply of, 235, 273; expenses of, 238, 251; settlement of, 240-41, 271, 280; governors of, 253, 269

Ogilvy, James, First Earl of Seafield, 115
Ohio Valley, 138
Oneidas. *See* Five Nations
Onondagas. *See* Five Nations
Order in Council, 98
Ordnance Board, 238
Orkney, Earl of. *See* Hamilton, George
Oudenarde, battle of, 118
Oxford, Earl of. *See* Harley, Robert

Paddon, Captain, commander of the *Edgar*, 223, 224

Palatines, 241, 257
Parliament, 16, 48, 49
Parmyter, Paroculus, 34, 52
Partridge, Colonel, leader in western Massachusetts, 85
Passamaquoddy Bay, 182
Paterson, William, 115; role in Darien Colony, 16, 17, 20, 21, 25, 26, 39
Payne, William, 59, 60
Peace negotiations, 242; colonial implications, 161, 167
Peartree, Mr., New York leader, 131
Pelham-Holles, Sir Thomas, Duke of Newcastle, 282
Penhallow, Samuel, 159
Penn, William, 55, 137
Pennicuik, Captain, of the *St. Andrew*, 22, 25, 26
Pennsylvania, ix, 124, 156, 211; refusal to join Canada expeditions, 137, 138, 216
Penobscot River, 188
Pentagoet, 188
Pentland Hills uprising, 5
Perkins, Captain of H.M.S. *Despatch*, 224
Philipps, Richard, 277, 280
Phillips, John, Jr., 84
Phillipse, Frederick, 50, 54
Phillipse family, 43, 131
Phips, Constantine, 95
Phips, Sir William, expedition of, in 1690, 145, 176, 220, 226
Pigeon, Major David, 172, 203
Pilots, 219-20, 226
Pitt, William, 208
Placentia, 228
Plymouth, Massachusetts, 83
Pontchartrain, M., 76, 81, 82, 104, 234, 253-54
Popple, William, 116, 207
Port Royal, 82, 104, 149, 159, 173, 186-87; plans for attack on, 152, 161, 163, 167, 173, 175, 179, 182; siege of, 182-86. *See also* Annapolis Royal
Portsmouth, England, 121, 210
Praying Indians, 81
Price-fixing, 145
Prince Edward Island. *See* St. John, Isle of
Pringle, Robert, 115, 141, 168, 266
Prior, Matthew, 231
Prisoner exchange, 79

Privateers, vii, 19, 170
Privy Council, 92, 95, 98, 111, 277, 280
Protestant succession, 248
Pulteney, Sir William, 279

Quakers, opposition to Canada expedition, 135-38
Quartering, debate over payments for, 146
Quary, Colonel Robert, 92, 106, 217
Quebec, vii, 62, 79; fortifications of, 104; inhabitants on news of British shipwrecks, 233-34
Quedar, Peter Schuyler's Indian name, 174
Queen Anne's War, viii, 69, 101, 150-51
Queensbury, Duke of. *See* Douglas, James

Ramillies, battle of, 118
Randolph, Edward, 49, 217
Rate of Exchange, problem of, 212
Reading, Colonel, 183, 186
Rednap, Colonel, 131, 145, 183, 204
Rehoboth Congress, 152, 158, 160-62
Reserve, H.M.S., 173
Revolution of 1688. *See* Glorious Revolution
Rhode Island, 48, 50, 250; role in Canada expedition, 124, 128, 145, 151, 162, 164, 207, 211; Assembly receives Vetch and Nicholson, 128; sends delegates to intercolonial conference, 158; role in Port Royal expedition, 161, 162, 180
Rigaud, Philippe de Marquis de Vaudreuil, 191, 210, 233; and neutrality, 77, 80, 81; and prisoner exchange, 80, 82; on illegal trade, 82, 83; knowledge of English attack plans, 143, 144-45; and fall of Port Royal, 189, 190-91, 196
Rising Sun (ship), 55
"Robinson, Mr.," pseudonym of Samuel Vetch's father, 11
Rochester, Earl of. *See* Hyde, Laurence
Roman Catholicism, extension by France in America, 72
Rouse, Captain, of H.M.S. *Saphire*, 236
Rouse, William, charged with illegal trade, 84

Rouville, Herter de, 144
Royal Regiment of Dragoons of Scotland (Second Cavalry), "Scots Greys," 12
Rye House plot, 9

Sacheverall, Dr. Henry, 174
Saffin, John, 59, 64, 70
St. Andrew (ship), 26
Saint-Castin, Baron, 188-89, 190, 191
St. Christopher Island, 64
St. George's Church, Southwark, England, 284
St. John, Henry, Viscount Bolingbroke, 211, 242; and Canada expedition, 208, 209-10, 231, 255; Tory affiliation, 209, 256, 261, 265; peace negotiations, 209, 243, 244
St. John, Isle of (Prince Edward Island), 62
St. Lawrence River, 148, 219, 220
Salem, Massachusetts, 62
Saltonstall, Gurdon, 125, 130, 153, 160, 164, 174; and Canada expeditions, 129, 131-32, 133, 211
Saphire, H.M.S., 221, 223, 228, 229-30, 236
Schuyler, Abraham, 131
Schuyler, Brant, 48
Schuyler, John, 131
Schuyler, Peter, 57, 74, 143; as leader of Indian commission, 43, 75, 110, 126, 131, 142-43, 161, 171; role in Canada expeditions, 101, 133, 172, 211
Schuyler family, 54
Scotland, imperialism of, viii; union with England, viii, 103; colonization by, 3-4, 105; illegal trade of, 50
"Scots Greys." *See* Royal Regiment of Dragoons
Scott, James, Duke of Monmouth, 8, 10
Seafield, Earl of. *See* Ogilvy, James
Sea power, 169, 208
Senecas. *See* Five Nations
Sewall, Samuel, 90, 149, 171, 214; relations with Vetch, 84, 149, 199, 236; opposition to Dudley, 90, 165; supports Canada expeditions, 104, 230; criticism of Schuyler, 172
Seymour, John, 168

Shaftesbury, Earl of. *See* Cooper, Antony
Shannon Expedition, 178
Shannon, Viscount. *See* Boyle, Henry
Sheffield, John, Duke of Buckingham, 207
Shelly, Giles, 50
Shrewsbury, Duke of. *See* Talbot, Charles
Shirreff, William, 274, 275
Shute, Samuel, 282
Sloughter, Henry, 78, 100
Smith, Captain, 163
Smith, William, 52, 57, 63
Society for the Promotion of the Gospel, 95, 266
Somers, Lord John, 116, 139
Sophia, Electress, 262
Southack, Captain Cyprian, 83, 148, 173, 219, 221, 252
South Seas Company, 209, 281
Spain, 18, 118, 139; colonies of, 140
Spanish River, 228
Spencer, Charles, Earl of Sunderland, 98, 105, 115, 122, 152, 171; party rivalry, 118, 176, 207, 265; and postponement of Canada expedition, 155, 156, 160, 174
Spotswood, Alexander, 217
Staats, Samuel, 57
Stairs, Lord. *See* Dalrymple, John
Stanhope, James, 19, 265, 269
Stantonhall, Northumberland, 7
Star Bomb (ship), 183
Steel, Mr., Vetch's agent, 259
Steinkirk, battle of, 13
Stoughton, William, 59
Stuart, James, the Catholic Pretender, vii, 256
Subercase, Daniel d'Auger de, 144, 150, 196, 243; role in seige of Port Royal, 183, 184-85, 186, 187-88
Sunderland, Earl of. *See* Spencer, Charles
Surveyor of the King's Woods, 280

Talbot, Charles, Duke of Shrewsbury, 207
Taylor, Colonel William, 145, 159, 183, 236
Territorial claims, of British in America, 113
Tory party, 121, 209, 256; colonial

policy of, viii, 207, 267; foreign policy of, 118, 140, 176; Vetch's attitude toward, 119; on sea power, 169, 208; comes to power, 207, 242
Townsend, Colonel Penn, 91, 236
Townshend, Charles, Lord, 265, 283
Trade, illegal, 50, 58, 98-99; with northern colonies, 56, 58, 72, 75, 79-80, 82-83, 126, 132, 150; effect of Queen Anne's War on, 71; fur, 72, 75, 132; Nova Scotia's with Canada, 194; role of Annapolis Royal in, 194
Treaty of Ryswick, vii, 13, 58
Treaty of Utrecht, 242, 253, 279
Tremont Street, Boston, 235
Triton's Prize, H.M.S., 221, 229
Trois Rivières, 112

Unicorn (ship), 26, 31
Union, of England and Scotland, viii, 115
Usher, John, 92
Utrecht, 11. See also Treaty of Utrecht

Van Cortlandt family, 43, 54
Van Dam, Rip, 54, 65
Vane, Charles, 229, 237; criticism of Vetch, 247-48
Van Rensselaer family, 43
Vauban, Sébastien, Le Prestre de, 192
Vaudreuil, Marquis de. *See* Rigaud, Philippe de
Vaughan, George, 109
Veitch, Ebenezer, 7
Veitch, Elizabeth, 7
Veitch, James, 7
Veitch, John, grandfather of Samuel, 4
Veitch, John, brother of Samuel, 7, 10
Veitch, Marion Fairly, 5, 11, 39, 99
Veitch, William, brother of Samuel, 5, 11, 13, 14; as Darien Councilor, 17, 35, 37
Veitch, William, father of Samuel, 4, 39, 115, 244; career of, 5-11
Vetch, Alida, 68, 250, 258, 278
Vetch, Billy, 250, 258, 278
Vetch, Margaret Livingston, 79, 148, 252, 278, 284, 250; courtship of, 41, 44, 45; description of, 42; family life, 61, 68, 236, 251, 258; and the *Mary,* 63; evades Nicholson, 258, 259; death of, 285
Vetch, Samuel, imperialistic view of, viii-ix, 70, 119-20, 169, 217, 250,

285-86; petitions for Nova Scotia lands, ix, 280; arrival in New York, 4; born, 6; life in Netherlands, 9-11, 13-14; military service under William of Orange, 11-14; illnesses of, 14, 258; and Darien venture, 15, 18, 22, 25; William Paterson on, 21, 27, 28, 39-40; on Thomas and Robert Drummond, 27, 28; welcomed by Scots in New York, 30; memorial to Nanfan, 31; rebuked by Company of Scotland, 33; aids in fitting out Thomas Drummond's sloop, 34; as trader, 34-36, 40, 47-48, 53, 79-80, 82; in New York, 35, 39, 43, 45-46, 53, 54, 85, 171-72; character of, 36, 113-14, 285-86; courtship and marriage, 44, 45; association with Winthrops, 55; and Indian relations, 55, 72, 149, 151; social position of, 55, 235; partnership with John Borland, 56; accused of illegal trade, 58-65, 68, 70, 83-93, 94-99, 198-99; and Cornbury, 68; daughter Alida born, 68; seeks military commission, 70, 242; presents accounts of Regulars, 71; plans for Canada conquest, 79, 100-3, 108-11, 166-67; and Joseph Dudley, 87, 95, 171; Samuel Sewall on, 91; goes to England, 93, 94; son William born, 99; visits Scotland, 99; spies in Canada, 104; presents "Canada Surveyed," 106; political sympathies, 116, 118-19, 178-79, 207, 261-62; commissioned colonel and adjutant general, 119; promised governorship of Canada, 119
  Canada Expedition, 1709: organization of, 121; conveys instructions to colonies, 124; and choice of commander, 133; reports successes to English government, 139; French learn of his leadership, 144; expenses of, 147; writes ministry about fleet, 148; on effect of failure, 151; on withdrawal of British support, 152, 155, 158
  Sails from England, 123; arrives in Rhode Island, 128; receives word of Lovelace's death, 128; arrives in New York, 130; and Francis Nicholson, 134, 173, 256, 258-59, 266-67; addresses New Jersey legislature, 135; impatience with New Jersey

factionalism, 137; on Quakers, 137; hopes for rewards, 140; receives present from Massachusetts legislature, 146-47; submits expenses to British government, 147; defends prisoner exchange, 150; and Rehoboth Congress, 152, 153, 154, 162; rebukes Ingoldesby, 153; desire for colonial governorship, 153, 167, 265; feeling against, in New York, 162; opposed by Sir Henry Ashurst, 165; and Shannon Expedition, 177
Port Royal Expedition: designated commander of, 173; attitude toward, 179-81; commands north flank of attack, 183; problems in governing Annapolis Royal, 187; evaluates condition of Annapolis Royal, 191-92; treatment of French inhabitants, 195-97; returns to Boston, 197-98; and Robert Livingston's victualing offer, 201; returns to Annapolis Royal, 202; seeks to strengthen Annapolis Royal, 204; requests English aid, 205; requests instructions, 238; goes to Annapolis Royal in 1712, 244; on non-support of Annapolis Royal garrison, 245; gains credit for Annapolis Royal garrison, 250; sends supplies to Annapolis Royal, 276
Canada Expedition, 1711: designated commander of New England troops, 205-6; ordered to Boston, 211; Sir Hovenden Walker on, 213; chain of command under, 221-22; distrusts French pilot, 222; distrusts Walker's course, 223-24; learns of losses, 225-26; protests decision to abandon, 226-27; opposes attack on Newfoundland, 229
Purchases house in Boston, 235; role in European peace negotiations, 243, 262-63, 270; Vane's criticism of, 247; replaced as governor of Nova Scotia, 253; dismissed as governor of Nova Scotia, 255; sails for England, 259; reports to Board of Trade on Nova Scotia, 264, 279, 283-84; claims for preferment, 265; defense against Hobby, 268; commissioned governor of Nova Scotia, 269; and application for Massachusetts governorship, 281; **British** supporters of, 283; death, 284

Vetch children, 259
Vice-Admiralty Court, of Boston, 60; of New York, 63, 64
Virginia, 168, 216

Wake, William, Archbishop of Canterbury, 283
Walker, Sir Hovenden, 210, 211; Canada expedition, 210, 213, 219, 230, 232; character of, 210, 220, 227-28; and Vetch, 213, 222, 226-27; entertains Five Nations representatives, 214-15; role in St. Lawrence catastrophe, 223-28; dismissed from Navy, 231
Walley, John, 145
Walpole, Robert, 265, 283
Walters, Robert, 57
Walton, Colonel Shadrach, 183, 221; testifies against attack on Newfoundland, 229
Wanton, Colonel William, 145, 159
War of League of Augsbury, vii, viii, 12
War of the Spanish Succession, viii, 69
Weaver, Thomas, 57, 63, 64
Wenham, Thomas, 34, 40, 50, 65, 131
Wessels, Peter, 37
West Indies, 58, 169, 208, 243
Wharton, William, 96
Whetham, Brigadier Thomas, 150, 156
Whig party, and Vetch's plan for conquest of Canada, 102; gains power, 104, 265; Sunderland as member of, 115; favorable toward Canada expedition, 116-18; attitude toward Governor Dudley, 165-66; trial of Sacheverell, 174; popular opinion opposes, 176; foreign policy of, 177-78, 261-62; split in, 282
Whiting, Colonel, 183, 204
Willett, Colonel Thomas, 54
Willey, Edward, 235
William III, 11-12, 16, 19, 69
Windsor, H.M.S., 224
Winthrop, Fitzjohn, 55, 59
Winthrop, Mrs. Fitzjohn, 238
Winthrop, John, 83
Winthrop, Wait Still, 55-56, 58-60, 63
Winthrop family, 58
Wood Creek, New York, as base for Canada expedition, 126, 135, 148, 153-54; in Vetch's plans, 152; forts at, 161, 162, 171; forces withdrawn from, 233

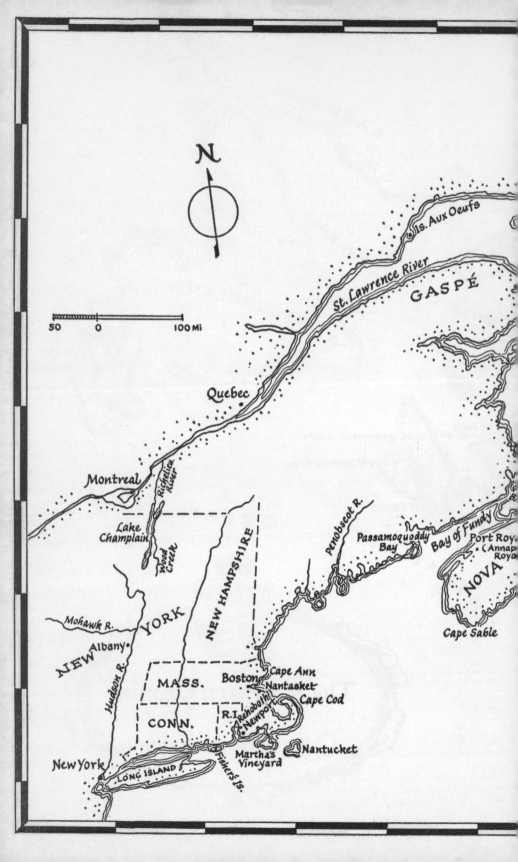